STUDY GUIDE

STUDY GUIDE

RICHARD O. STRAUB

University of Michigan, Dearborn

to accompany

Invitation to the Life Span

KATHLEEN STASSEN BERGER

WORTH PUBLISHERS

Study Guide
by Richard O. Straub
to accompany
Berger: **Invitation to the Life Span**

Printed in the United States of America

ISBN 10: 1-4292-1902-5
ISBN 13: 978-1-4292-1902-0

First printing 2010

Worth Publishers
41 Madison Avenue
New York, NY 10010
www.worthpublishers.com

Contents

Preface

This Study Guide is designed for use with *Invitation to the Life Span* by Kathleen Stassen Berger. It is intended to help you to evaluate your understanding of that material, and then to review any problem areas. "How to Manage Your Time Efficiently, Study More Effectively, and Think Critically" provides detailed instructions on how to use the textbook and this Study Guide for maximum benefit. It also offers additional study suggestions based on principles of time management, effective note-taking, evaluation of exam performance, and an effective program for improving your comprehension while studying from textbooks.

Each chapter of the Study Guide includes a Chapter Overview, a Chapter Review section to be completed after you have read the text chapter, and two review tests. Most sections of the Chapter Review also include several Application questions that evaluate your understanding of the text chapter's broader conceptual material and its application to real-world situations. Many sections also include one or more Study Tips and Think About It questions designed to engage your critical thinking skills and promote deeper reasoning about the material. For the two review tests, the correct answers are given, followed by textbook page references (so you can easily go back and reread the material), and complete explanations not only of why the answer is correct but also of why the other choices are incorrect.

I would like to thank Betty and Don Probert of The Special Projects Group for their exceptional work in all phases of this project. My thanks also to Sharon Prevost, Danielle Storm, Jenny Chiu, and Stacey Alexander for their skillful assistance in the preparation of this Study Guide. We hope that our work will help you to achieve your highest level of academic performance in this course and to acquire a keen appreciation of human development.

Richard O. Straub
January 2010

How to Manage Your Time Efficiently, Study More Effectively, and Think Critically

How effectively do you study? Good study habits make the job of being a college student much easier. Many students, who *could* succeed in college, fail or drop out because they have never learned to manage their time efficiently. Even the best students can usually benefit from an in-depth evaluation of their current study habits.

There are many ways to achieve academic success, of course, but your approach may not be the most effective or efficient. Are you sacrificing your social life or your physical or mental health in order to get A's on your exams? Good study habits result in better grades *and* more time for other activities.

Evaluate Your Current Study Habits

To improve your study habits, you must first have an accurate picture of how you currently spend your time. Begin by putting together a profile of your present living and studying habits. Answer the following questions by writing *yes* or *no* on each line.

_______ **1.** Do you usually set up a schedule to budget your time for studying, recreation, and other activities?

_______ **2.** Do you often put off studying until time pressures force you to cram?

_______ **3.** Do other students seem to study less than you do, but get better grades?

_______ **4.** Do you usually spend hours at a time studying one subject, rather than dividing that time between several subjects?

_______ **5.** Do you often have trouble remembering what you have just read in a textbook?

_______ **6.** Before reading a chapter in a textbook, do you skim through it and read the section headings?

_______ **7.** Do you try to predict exam questions from your lecture notes and reading?

_______ **8.** Do you usually attempt to paraphrase or summarize what you have just finished reading?

_______ **9.** Do you find it difficult to concentrate very long when you study?

_______ **10.** Do you often feel that you studied the wrong material for an exam?

Thousands of college students have participated in similar surveys. Students who are fully realizing their academic potential usually respond as follows: (1) yes, (2) no, (3) no, (4) no, (5) no, (6) yes, (7) yes, (8) yes, (9) no, (10) no.

Compare your responses to those of successful students. The greater the discrepancy, the more you could benefit from a program to improve your study habits. The questions are designed to identify areas of weakness. Once you have identified your weaknesses, you will be able to set specific goals for improvement and implement a program for reaching them.

Manage Your Time

Do you often feel frustrated because there isn't enough time to do all the things you must and want to do? Take heart. Even the most productive and successful people feel this way at times. But they establish priorities for their activities and they learn to budget time for each of them. There's much in the saying "If you want something done, ask a busy person to do it." A busy person knows how to get things done.

If you don't now have a system for budgeting your time, develop one. Not only will your academic accomplishments increase, but you will actually find more time in your schedule for other activities. And you won't have to feel guilty about "taking time off," because all your obligations will be covered.

Establish a Baseline

As a first step in preparing to budget your time, keep a diary for a few days to establish a summary, or baseline, of the time you spend in studying, socializing, working, and so on. If you are like many students, much of your "study" time is nonproductive; you may sit at your desk and leaf through a book, but the time is actually wasted. Or you may procrastinate. You are always getting ready to study, but you rarely do.

Besides revealing where you waste time, your time-management diary will give you a realistic picture of how much time you need to allot for meals, commuting, and other fixed activities. In addition, careful records should indicate the times of the day when you are consistently most productive. Table 1 shows a sample time-management diary.

Table 1 Sample Time-Management Diary

Monday		
Activity	Time Completed	Duration Hours: Minutes
Sleep	7:00	7:30
Dressing	7:25	:25
Breakfast	7:45	:20
Commute	8:20	:35
Coffee	9:00	:40
French	10:00	1:00
Socialize	10:15	:15
Videogame	10:35	:20
Coffee	11:00	:25
Psychology	12:00	1:00
Lunch	12:25	:25
Study Lab	1:00	:35
Psych. Lab	4:00	3:00
Work	5:30	1:30
Commute	6:10	:40
Dinner	6:45	:35
TV	7:30	:45
Study Psych.	10:00	2:30
Socialize	11:30	1:30
Sleep		

Prepare a similar chart for each day of the week. When you finish an activity, note it on the chart and write down the time it was completed. Then determine its duration by subtracting the time the previous activity was finished from the newly entered time.

Plan the Term

Having established and evaluated your baseline, you are ready to devise a more efficient schedule. Buy a calendar that covers the entire school term and has ample space for each day. Using the course outlines provided by your instructors, enter the dates of all exams, term paper deadlines, and other important academic obligations. If you have any long-range personal plans (concerts, weekend trips, etc.), enter the dates on the calendar as well. Keep your calendar up to date and refer to it often. I recommend carrying it with you at all times.

Develop a Weekly Calendar

Now that you have a general picture of the school term, develop a weekly schedule that includes all of your activities. Aim for a schedule that you can live with for the entire school term. A sample weekly schedule, incorporating the following guidelines, is shown in Table 2.

1. Enter your class times, work hours, and any other fixed obligations first. *Be thorough.* Using information from your time-management diary, allow plenty of time for such things as commuting, meals, laundry, and the like.

2. Set up a study schedule for each of your courses. The study habits survey and your time-management diary will direct you. The following guidelines should also be useful.

(a) Establish regular study times for each course. The 4 hours needed to study one subject, for example, are most profitable when divided into shorter periods spaced over several days. If you cram your studying into one 4-hour block, what you attempt to learn in the third or fourth hour will interfere with what you studied in the first 2 hours. Newly acquired knowledge is like wet cement. It needs some time to "harden" to become memory.

(b) Alternate subjects. The type of interference just mentioned is greatest between similar topics. Set up a schedule in which you spend time on several *different* courses during each study session. Besides reducing the potential for interference, alternating subjects will help to prevent mental fatigue with one topic.

(c) Set weekly goals to determine the amount of study time you need to do well in each course. This will

Table 2 Sample Weekly Schedule

Time	Mon.	Tues.	Wed.	Thurs.	Fri.	Sat.
7–8	Dress Eat	Dress Eat	Dress Eat	Dress Eat	Dress Eat	
8–9	Psych.	Study Psych.	Psych.	Study Psych.	Psych.	Dress Eat
9–10	Eng.	Study Eng.	Eng.	Study Eng.	Eng.	Study Eng.
10–11	Study French	Free	Study French	Open Study	Study French	Study Stats.
11–12	French	Study Psych. Lab	French	Open Study	French	Study Stats.
12–1	Lunch	Lunch	Lunch	Lunch	Lunch	Lunch
1–2	Stats.	Psych. Lab	Stats.	Study or Free	Stats.	Free
2–3	Bio.	Psych. Lab	Bio.	Free	Bio.	Free
3–4	Free	Psych.	Free	Free	Free	Free
4–5	Job	Job	Job	Job	Job	Free
5–6	Job	Job	Job	Job	Job	Free
6–7	Dinner	Dinner	Dinner	Dinner	Dinner	Dinner
7–8	Study Bio.	Study Bio.	Study Bio.	Study Bio.	Free	Free
8–9	Study Eng.	Study Stats.	Study Psych.	Open Study	Open Study	Free
9–10	Open Study	Open Study	Open Study	Open Study	Free	Free

This is a sample schedule for a student with a 16-credit load and a 10-hour-per-week part-time job. Using this chart as an illustration, make up a weekly schedule, following the guidelines outlined here.

depend on, among other things, the difficulty of your courses and the effectiveness of your methods. Many professors recommend studying at least 1 to 2 hours for each hour in class. If your time-management diary indicates that you presently study less time than that, do not plan to jump immediately to a much higher level. Increase study time from your baseline by setting weekly goals [see (4)] that will gradually bring you up to the desired level. As an initial schedule, for example, you might set aside an amount of study time for each course that matches class time.

(d) Schedule for maximum effectiveness. Tailor your schedule to meet the demands of each course. For the course that emphasizes lecture notes, schedule time for a daily review soon after the class. This will give you a chance to revise your notes and clean up any hard-to-decipher shorthand while the material is still fresh in your mind. If you are evaluated for class participation (for example, in a language course), allow time for a review just before the class meets. Schedule study time for your most difficult (or least motivating) courses during hours when you are the most alert and distractions are fewest.

(e) Schedule open study time. Emergencies, additional obligations, and the like could throw off your schedule. And you may simply need some extra time periodically for a project or for review in one of your courses. Schedule several hours each week for such purposes.

3. After you have budgeted time for studying, fill in slots for recreation, hobbies, relaxation, household errands, and the like.

4. Set specific goals. Before each study session, make a list of specific goals. The simple note "7–8 PM: study psychology" is too broad to ensure the most effective use of the time. Formulate your daily goals according to what you know you must accomplish during the term. If you have course outlines with advance assignments, set systematic daily goals that will allow you, for example, to cover fifteen chapters before the exam. And be realistic: Can you actually expect to cover a 78-page chapter in one session? Divide large tasks into smaller units; stop at the most logical resting points. When you complete a specific goal, take a 5- or 10-minute break before tackling the next goal.

5. Evaluate how successful or unsuccessful your studying has been on a daily or weekly basis. Did you reach most of your goals? If so, reward yourself immediately. You might even make a list of five to ten rewards to choose from. If you have trouble studying regularly, you may be able to motivate yourself by making such rewards contingent on completing specific goals.

6. Finally, until you have lived with your schedule for several weeks, don't hesitate to revise it. You may need to allow more time for chemistry, for example, and less for some other course. If you are trying to study regularly for the first time and are feeling burned out, you probably have set your initial goals too high. Don't let failure cause you to despair and abandon the program. Accept your limitations and revise your schedule so that you are studying only 15 to 20 minutes more each evening than you are used to. The point is to identify a regular schedule with which you can achieve some success. Time management, like any skill, must be practiced to become effective.

Techniques for Effective Study

Knowing how to put study time to best use is, of course, as important as finding a place for it in your schedule. Here are some suggestions that should enable you to increase your reading comprehension and improve your note-taking. A few study tips are included as well.

Using SQ3R to Increase Reading Comprehension

How do you study from a textbook? If you are like many students, you simply read and reread in a *passive* manner. Studies have shown, however, that most students who simply read a textbook cannot remember more than half the material ten minutes after they have finished. Often, what is retained is the unessential material rather than the important points upon which exam questions will be based.

This *Study Guide* employs a program known as SQ3R (Survey, Question, Read, Recite, and Review) to facilitate, and allow you to assess, your comprehension of the important facts and concepts in *Invitation to the Life Span* by Kathleen Stassen Berger.

Research has shown that students using SQ3R achieve significantly greater comprehension of textbooks than students reading in the more traditional passive manner. Once you have learned this program, you can improve your comprehension of any textbook.

Survey Before reading a chapter, determine whether the text or the study guide has an outline or list of objectives. Read this material and the summary at the end of the chapter. Next, read the textbook chapter fairly quickly, paying special attention to the major headings and subheadings. This survey will give you an idea of the chapter's contents and organization. You will then be able to divide the chapter into logical sections in order to formulate specific goals for a more careful reading of the chapter.

In this Study Guide, the *Chapter Overview* summarizes the major topics of the textbook chapter. This section also provides a few suggestions for approaching topics you may find difficult.

Question You will retain material longer when you have a use for it. If you look up a word's definition in order to solve a crossword puzzle, for example, you will remember it longer than if you merely fill in the letters as a result of putting other words in. Surveying the chapter will allow you to generate important questions that the chapter will proceed to answer. These question correspond to "mental files" into which knowledge will be sorted for easy access.

As you survey, jot down several questions for each chapter section. One simple technique is to generate questions by rephrasing a section heading. For example, the "Preoperational Thought" head could be turned into "What is preoperational thought?" Good questions will allow you to focus on the important points in the text. Examples of good questions are those that begin as follows: "List two examples of . . .." "What is the function of . . .?" "What is the significance of . . .?" Such questions give a purpose to your reading. Similarly, you can formulate questions based on the chapter outline.

Read When you have established "files" for each section of the chapter, review your first question, begin reading, and continue until you have discovered its answer. If you come to material that seems to answer an important question you don't have a file for, stop and write down the question.

Using this Study Guide, read the chapter one section at a time. First, preview the section by skimming it, noting headings and boldface items. Next, as you read the chapter section, search for the answer to each of your questions.

Be sure to read everything. Don't skip photo or art captions, graphs, marginal notes. In some cases, what may seem vague in reading will be made clear by a simple graph. Keep in mind that test questions are sometimes drawn from illustrations and charts.

Recite When you have found the answer to a question, close your eyes and mentally recite the question and its answer. Then *write* the answer next to the question. It is important that you recite an answer in your own words rather than the author's. Don't rely on your short-term memory to repeat the author's words verbatim.

Recitation is an extremely effective study technique, recommended by many learning experts. In addition to increasing reading comprehension, it is useful for review. Trying to explain something in your own words clarifies your knowledge, often by revealing aspects of your answer that are vague or incomplete. If you repeatedly rely upon "I know" in recitation, you really may not know.

Recitation has the additional advantage of simulating an exam, especially an essay exam; the same skills are required in both cases. Too often students study without ever putting the book and notes aside, which makes it easy for them to develop false confidence in their knowledge. When the material is in front of you, you may be able to recognize an answer, but will you be able to recall it later, when you take an exam that does not provide these retrieval cues?

After you have recited and written your answer, continue with your next question. Read, recite, and so on.

Review When you have answered the last question on the material you have designated as a study goal, go back and review. Read over each question and your written answer to it. Your review might also include a brief written summary that integrates all of your questions and answers. This review need not take longer than a few minutes, but it is important. It will help you retain the material longer and will greatly facilitate a final review of each chapter before the exam.

In this Study Guide, the *Chapter Review* section contains fill-in and one- or two-sentence essay questions for you to complete after you have finished reading the text and have written answers to your questions. The correct answers are given at the end of the chapter. Generally, your answer to a fill-in question should match exactly (as in the case of important terms, theories, or people). In some cases, the answer is not a term or name, so a word close in meaning will suffice. You should go through the Chapter Review several times before taking an exam, so it is a good idea to mentally fill in the answers until you are ready for a final pretest review. Textbook page references are provided with each section title, in case you need to reread any of the material.

At the end of most Chapter Review sections and sometimes within longer sections you will find one or more Applications, Think About It questions, and Study Tips. Application questions evaluate your ability to apply text material to real-life situations. Many students find questions of this type difficult on exams, and you should make certain you understand the correct answers to any questions you miss. Think About It questions are intended to promote deeper thinking about the material by making meaningful connections between it and your own life experiences. Although questions of this type often do not have a single "correct" answer, they promote critical thinking skills and the kind of deep processing of material that many instructors prefer to evaluate on exams. Finally, the Study Tips focus on practical suggestions for facilitating your mastery of the material.

Also provided to facilitate your review are two *Progress Tests* that include multiple-choice questions and, where appropriate, matching or true–false questions. These tests are not to be taken until you have read the chapter, written answers to your questions, and completed the *Chapter Review.* Correct answers, along with explanations of why each alternative is correct or incorrect, are provided at the end of the chapter. The relevant text page numbers for each question are also given. If you miss a question, read these explanations and, if necessary, review the text pages to further understand why. The *Progress Tests* do not test every aspect of a concept, so you should treat an incorrect answer as an indication that you need to review the concept.

The chapter concludes with *Key Terms.* It is important that the answers be written from memory, and in list form, in your own words. The *Answers* section at the end of the chapter gives a definition of each term, sometimes along with an example of its usage and/or a tip to help you remember its meaning.

One final suggestion: Incorporate SQ3R into your time-management calendar. Set specific goals for completing SQ3R with each assigned chapter. Keep a record of chapters completed, and reward yourself for being conscientious. Initially, it takes more time and effort to "read" using SQ3R, but with practice, the steps will become automatic. More importantly, you will comprehend significantly more material and retain what you have learned longer than passive readers do.

Taking Lecture Notes

Are your class notes as useful as they might be? One way to determine their worth is to compare them with those taken by other good students. Are yours as thorough? Do they provide you with a comprehensible outline of each lecture? If not, then the following suggestions might increase the effectiveness of your note-taking.

1. Keep a separate notebook for each course. Use standard notebook pages. Consider using a ring binder, which would allow you to revise and insert notes while still preserving lecture order.

2. Take notes in the format of a lecture outline. Use roman numerals for major points, letters for supporting arguments, and so on. Some instructors will make this easy by delivering organized lectures and, in some cases, by outlining their lectures on the board. If a lecture is disorganized, you will probably want to reorganize your notes soon after the class.

3. As you take notes in class, leave a wide margin on one side of each page. After the lecture, expand or clarify any shorthand notes while the material is fresh in your mind. Use this time to write important questions in the margin next to notes that answer them. This will facilitate later review and will allow you to anticipate similar exam questions.

Evaluate Your Exam Performance

How often have you received a grade on an exam that did not do justice to the effort you spent preparing for the exam? This is a common experience that can leave one feeling bewildered and abused. "What do I have to do to get an A?" "The test was unfair!" "I studied the wrong material!"

The chances of this happening are greatly reduced if you have an effective time-management schedule and use the study techniques described here. But it can happen to the best-prepared student and is most likely to occur on your first exam with a new professor.

Remember that there are two main reasons for studying. One is to learn for your own general academic development. Many people believe that such knowledge is all that really matters. Of course, it is possible, though unlikely, to be an expert on a topic without achieving commensurate grades, just as one can, occasionally, earn an excellent grade without truly mastering the course material. During a job interview or in the workplace, however, your A in Cobol won't mean much if you can't actually program a computer. In order to keep career options open after you graduate, you must know the material and maintain competitive grades. In the short run, this means performing well on exams, which is the second main objective in studying.

Probably the single best piece of advice to keep in mind when studying for exams is to *try to predict exam questions.* This means ignoring the trivia and focusing on the important questions and their answers (with your instructor's emphasis in mind).

A second point is obvious. How well you do on exams is determined by your mastery of both lecture and textbook material. Many students (partly because of poor time management) concentrate too much on one at the expense of the other.

To evaluate how well you are learning lecture and textbook material, analyze the questions you missed on the first exam. If your instructor does not review exams during class, you can easily do it yourself. Divide the questions into two categories: those drawn primarily from lectures and those drawn primarily from the textbook. Determine the percentage of questions you missed in each category. If your errors are evenly distributed and you are satisfied with your grade, you have no problem. If you are weaker in one area, you will need to set future goals for increasing and/or improving your study of that area.

Similarly, note the percentage of test questions drawn from each category. Although exams in most courses cover both lecture notes and the textbook, the relative emphasis of each may vary from instructor to instructor. While your instructors may not be entirely consistent in making up future exams, you may be able to tailor your studying for each course by placing additional emphasis on the appropriate area.

Exam evaluation will also point out the types of questions your instructor prefers. Does the exam consist primarily of multiple-choice, true–false, or essay questions? You may also discover that an instructor is fond of wording questions in certain ways. For example, an instructor may rely heavily on questions that require you to draw an analogy between a theory or concept and a real-world example. Evaluate both your instructor's style and how well you do with each format. Use this information to guide your future exam preparation.

Important aids, not only in studying for exams but also in determining how well prepared you are, are the Progress and Thinking Critically Tests provided in this Study Guide. If these tests don't include all of the types of questions your instructor typically writes, make up your own practice exam questions.

Spend extra time testing yourself with question formats that are most difficult for you. There is no better way to evaluate your preparation for an upcoming exam than by testing yourself under the conditions most likely to be in effect during the actual test.

A Few Practical Tips

Even the best intentions for studying sometimes fail. Some of these failures occur because students attempt to work under conditions that are simply not conducive to concentrated study. To help ensure the success of your time-management program, here are a few suggestions that should assist you in reducing the possibility of procrastination or distraction.

1. If you have set up a schedule for studying, make your roommate, family, and friends aware of this commitment, and ask them to honor your quiet study time. Close your door and post a "Do Not Disturb" sign.

2. Set up a place to study that minimizes potential distractions. Use a desk or table, not your bed or an extremely comfortable chair. Keep your desk and the walls around it free from clutter. If you need a place other than your room, find one that meets as many of the above requirements as possible—for example, in the library stacks.

3. Do nothing but study in this place. It should become associated with studying so that it "triggers" this activity, just as a mouth-watering aroma elicits an appetite.

4. Never study with the television on or with other distracting noises present. If you must have music in the background in order to mask outside noise, for example, play soft instrumental music. Don't pick vocal selections; your mind will be drawn to the lyrics.

5. Study by yourself. Other students can be distracting or can break the pace at which your learning is most efficient. In addition, there is always the possibility that group studying will become a social gathering. Reserve that for its own place in your schedule.

If you continue to have difficulty concentrating for very long, try the following suggestions.

6. Study your most difficult or most challenging subjects first, when you are most alert.

7. Start with relatively short periods of concentrated study, with breaks in between. If your attention starts to wander, get up immediately and take a break. It is better to study effectively for 15 minutes and then take a break than to fritter away 45 minutes out of an hour. Gradually increase the length of study periods, using your attention span as an indicator of successful pacing.

Critical Thinking

Having discussed a number of specific techniques for managing your time efficiently and studying effectively, let us now turn to a much broader topic: What exactly should you expect to learn as a student of developmental psychology?

Most developmental psychology courses have two major goals: (1) to help you acquire a basic understanding of the discipline's knowledge base, and (2) to help you learn to think like a psychologist. Many students devote all of their efforts to the first of these goals, concentrating on memorizing as much of the course's material as possible.

The second goal—learning to think like a psychologist—has to do with critical thinking. Critical thinking has many meanings. On one level, it refers to an attitude of healthy skepticism that should guide your study of psychology. As a critical thinker, you learn not to accept any explanation or conclusion about behavior as true until you have evaluated the evidence. On another level, critical thinking refers to a systematic process for examining the conclusions and arguments presented by others. In this regard, many of the features of the SQ3R technique for improving reading comprehension can be incorporated into an effective critical thinking system.

To learn to think critically, you must first recognize that psychological information is transmitted through the construction of persuasive arguments. An argument consists of three parts: an assertion, evidence, and an explanation (Mayer and Goodchild, 1990).

An assertion is a statement of relationship between some aspect of behavior, such as intelligence, and another factor, such as age. Learn to identify and evaluate the assertions about behavior and mental processes that you encounter as you read your textbook, listen to lectures, and engage in discussions with classmates. A good test of your understanding of an assertion is to try to restate it in your own words. As you do so, pay close attention to how important terms and concepts are defined. When a researcher asserts that "intelligence declines with age," for example, what does he or she mean by "intelligence"? Assertions such as this one may be true when a critical term ("intelligence") is defined one way (for example, "speed of thinking"), but not when defined in another way (for example, "general knowledge"). One of the strengths of psychology is the use of *operational* definitions that specify how key terms and concepts are measured, thus eliminating any ambiguity about their meaning. "Intelligence," for example, is often operationally defined as performance on a test measuring various cognitive skills. Whenever you encounter an assertion that is ambiguous, be skeptical of its accuracy.

When you have a clear understanding of an argument's assertion, evaluate its supporting evidence, the second component of an argument. Is it *empirical*? Does it, in fact, support the assertion? Psychologists accept only *empirical (observable) evidence* that is based on direct measurement of behavior. Hearsay, intuition, and personal experiences are not acceptable evidence. Chapter 1 discusses the various research methods used by developmental psychologists to gather empirical evidence. Some examples include surveys, observations of behavior in natural settings, and experiments.

As you study developmental psychology, you will become aware of another important issue in evaluating evidence—determining whether or not the research on which it is based is faulty. Research can be faulty for many reasons, including the use of an unrepresentative sample of subjects, experimenter bias, and inadequate control of unanticipated factors that might influence results. Evidence based on faulty research should be discounted.

The third component of an argument is the explanation provided for an assertion, which is based on the evidence that has been presented. While the argument's assertion merely *describes* how two things (such as intelligence and age) are related, the explanation tells *why*, often by proposing some theoretical mechanism that causes the relationship. Empirical evidence that thinking speed slows with age (the assertion), for example, may be explained as being caused by age-related changes in the activity of brain cells (a physiological explanation).

Be cautious in accepting explanations. In order to think critically about an argument's explanation, ask yourself three questions: (1) Can I restate the explanation in my own words?; (2) Does the explanation make sense based on the stated evidence?; and (3) Are there alternative explanations that adequately explain the assertion? Consider this last point in relation to our sample assertion: It is possible that the slower thinking speed of older adults is due to their having less recent experience than younger people with tasks that require quick thinking (a disuse explanation).

Because psychology is a relatively young science, its theoretical explanations are still emerging, and often change. For this reason, not all psychological arguments will offer explanations. Many arguments will only raise additional questions for further research to address.

Some Suggestions for Becoming a Critical Thinker

1. Adopt an attitude of healthy skepticism in evaluating psychological arguments.

2. Insist on unambiguous operational definitions of an argument's important concepts and terms.

3. Be cautious in accepting supporting evidence for an argument's assertion.

4. Refuse to accept evidence for an argument if it is based on faulty research.

5. Ask yourself if the theoretical explanation provided for an argument "makes sense" based on the empirical evidence.

6. Determine whether there are alternative explanations that adequately explain an assertion.

7. Use critical thinking to construct your own effective arguments when writing term papers, answering essay questions, and speaking.

8. Polish your critical-thinking skills by applying them to each of your college courses, and to other areas of life as well. Learn to think critically about advertising, political speeches, and the material presented in popular periodicals.

Some Closing Thoughts

I hope that these suggestions help make you more successful academically, and that they enhance the quality of your college life in general. Having the necessary skills makes any job a lot easier and more pleasant. Let me repeat my warning not to attempt to make too drastic a change in your life-style immediately. Good habits require time and self-discipline to develop. Once established they can last a lifetime.

1

chapter

THE SCIENCE OF Development

Chapter Overview

The first chapter introduces the study of human development. The first section defines development, briefly describing the how, why, and who of this definition. The second section explains the life-span perspective, which identifies five characteristics of the scientific study of human development.

The chapter then describes four broad theories—psychoanalytic theory, behaviorism, cognitive theory, and systems theory—that will be used throughout the book to present information and to provide a framework for interpreting events and issues in human development. Each theory has developed a unique vocabulary with which to describe and explain events as well as to organize ideas into a cohesive system of thought.

The next section discusses the strategies developmentalists use in their research, beginning with the scientific method and including scientific observation, experiments, and surveys. To study people over time, developmentalists have created several research designs: cross-sectional, longitudinal, and cross-sequential.

The final section discusses several common hazards in interpreting research, including confusing correlation with causation and ignoring the ethics of research with humans. In addition to ensuring confidentiality and safety, developmentalists who study children are especially concerned that the benefits of research outweigh the risks.

NOTE: Answer guidelines for all Chapter 1 questions begin on page 14.

Chapter Review

When you have finished reading the chapter, work through the material that follows to review it. Complete the sentences and answer the questions. In some cases, Study Tips explain how best to learn a difficult concept, while Think About It and Applications help you to know how well you understand the material. Check your understanding of the material by consulting the answers beginning on page 14. Do not continue with the next section until you understand each answer. If you need to, review or reread the appropriate section in the textbook before continuing.

Defining Development (pp. 4–7)

1. The scientific study of human development can be defined as the science that seeks to understand how & why people of all ages & circumstances Δ or remain the same all time

2. In order, the basic steps of the scientific method are

   a. personal observation (Pose a question)

   b. Develop a hypothesis

   c. Test hypothesis

   d. Draw conclusion

   e. report result

3. A specific, testable prediction that forms the basis of a research project is called a hypothesis.

4. To repeat an experimental test procedure and obtain the same results is to replicate the test of the hypothesis.

5. The question of how much of any characteristic is the result of genes and how much is the result of experience is the _____ - _____ debate. In this debate, _____ refers to environmental influences and _____ refers to the influence of genes that people inherit.

6. Genes and environment _____ (affect/do not affect) every aspect of development.

7. A time when certain things must occur for normal development is a _____. At certain points during early childhood, there may also be a _____, when a particular development occurs most easily. An example of this is _____.

8. Deviations from development _____ (indicate/do not necessarily indicate) a problem. To assume so is to commit the _____ - _____ - _____ error. Following the methods of _____ helps prevent this mistake in reasoning.

9. The third crucial element in the definition of developmental science is the issue of whether individuals _____ or _____ _____ _____ over time.

10. To make their study easier, developmentalists segment life into separate _____ of growth and three domains of development: _____, _____, and _____. Even with such divisions, developmentalists realize that there is a _____ connection between age-focused specialties and that all domains occur _____.

STUDY TIP: The ***nature–nurture issue***—the controversy over the relative contributions of genes and experience to the development of psychological traits and behavior—is developmental science's biggest and most enduring debate. Developmental psychologists explore the issue by asking, for example, how differences in intelligence, personality, and psychological disorders are influenced by heredity and by environment. As a simple way to think about current views regarding this issue, remember this brief statement: *Nurture works on what nature endows.* Our species is biologically endowed with an enormous capacity to learn and to adapt. Moreover, every psychological event is simultaneously a biological event.

APPLICATIONS:

11. Professor Cohen predicts that because "baby boomers" grew up in an era that promoted independence and assertiveness, people in their forties and fifties will respond differently to a political survey than will people in their twenties and thirties. The professor's prediction regarding political attitudes is an example of a _____.

12. Professor Stefik warns her students to be skeptical of the results of a controversial study because it has not been replicated. By this, she means that
    a. the researcher did not predict the results.
    b. the researcher did not specify whether nature or nurture would be the primary influence.
    c. the study has not yet been repeated by other researchers in order to verify the original findings.
    d. the results are statistically insignificant.

The Life-Span Perspective (pp. 7–17)

13. The approach that takes into account all phases of life is the _____ - _____ perspective. This perspective notes that development is _____, _____, _____, _____, and _____.

14. An important insight emerging from the fact that development is multidirectional is that human development does not always follow a straight, _____ growth pattern. One way to express this variability is to note that some characteristics are stable over time, called _____, and other characteristics are not stable over time, called _____.

15. A group of people born within a few years of each other is called a _____. These people tend to be affected by history in _____ (the same way/different ways).

16. A contextual influence that is determined by a person's income, wealth, education, place of resi-

dence, and occupation is called ______________ ______________, which is often abbreviated ______________.

17. The "patterns of behavior that are passed from one generation to the next" constitute a ______________.

18. A collection of people who share certain attributes, such as ancestry, national origin, religion, culture, and language, is called a(n) ______________ ______________.

19. A group of people who are regarded by themselves or by others as distinct on the basis of physical appearance constitute a ______________.

20. Although race was once thought to be a ______________ category, it is actually an idea created by ______________. Thus, it is a ______________ ______________.

21. The idea that genes alone do not determine development led to an ______________ approach. This understanding of human development can be seen in research on the origins of ______________ in young people. This perspective focuses on the effects of ______________ forces on the expression of ______________ inheritance. One study found that mistreated boys were more likely to be overly ______________ if they had a particular variation in the ______________ gene. However, even if they inherited the ______________ (high/low) variation of this gene, boys who had *not* been mistreated tended to become peaceable adults.

22. (A View From Science) Another example of the value of a multidisciplinary approach can be seen in research on ______________ ______________ —brain cells that respond to ______________ ______________.

23. One of the most encouraging aspects of the science of development is that development is characterized by ______________, or the ability to change throughout life. For instance, although depression is partly ______________, it need not destroy a life. Many depressed adults have been helped by a combination of ______________ and ______________ therapy.

APPLICATIONS:

24. Professor Jorgenson believes development is plastic. By this she means that

- **a.** change in development occurs in every direction, not always in a straight line.
- **b.** human lives are embedded in many different contexts.
- **c.** many cultures influence development.
- **d.** every individual, and every trait within each individual, can be altered at any point in the life span.

25. Summarizing her presentation on race and biology, Trisha notes that

- **a.** a racial group is a collection of people who share ancestral heritage.
- **b.** race is a biological construction defined by the genetic traits of a group of people.
- **c.** social scientists recognize that all racial categories are imprecise.
- **d.** all of these statements are true.

26. Maya explains to her friend that experts today view race as a social construction. By this, she means that race is

- **a.** a valid biological category.
- **b.** a meaningless concept.
- **c.** an idea created by society.
- **d.** none of these answers.

27. Son Yi's mother is puzzled by the many differences between the developmental psychology textbook she used in 1976 and her daughter's contemporary text. Son Yi explains that the differences are the result of ______________ ______________.

Theories of Human Development (pp. 17–25)

STUDY TIP: As you study this section, consider what each of the theories has to say about your own development, as well as that of friends and relatives in other age groups. It is also a good idea to keep the following questions in mind as you study each theory: Which of the theory's principles are generally accepted by contemporary developmentalists? How has the theory been criticized? In what ways does this theory agree with the other theories? In what ways does it disagree?

28. Whereas ______________ make specific, testable predictions about human growth, a ______________ ______________ provides a general framework for explaining development.

29. Psychoanalytic theory interprets human development in terms of inner ______________ and ______________, many of which are ______________ (conscious/unconscious).

30. According to Freud's ______________ theory, children experience sexual pleasures and desires during the first six years as they pass through three stages. From infancy to early childhood to the preschool years, these stages are the ______________ stage, the ______________ stage, and the ______________ stage.

31. One of Freud's most influential ideas was that each stage includes its own potential ______________.

Specify the focus of sexual pleasure and the major developmental need associated with each of Freud's stages.

oral ____

____

anal ____

____

phallic ____

____

genital ____

____

32. Erik Erikson's theory of development, which focuses on social and cultural influences, describes ______________ (number) developmental stages, each characterized by a particular developmental ______________ related to the person's relationship to the social environment.

33. Unlike Freud, Erikson proposed stages of development that ______________ (span/do not span) a person's lifetime.

Complete the following chart regarding Erikson's stages of psychosocial development.

Age Period	Stage
Birth to 1 yr.	trust vs. ______________
1–3 yrs.	autonomy vs. ______________
3–6 yrs.	initiative vs. ______________
6–11 yrs.	______________ vs. inferiority
Adolescence	identity vs. ______________
Young adulthood	______________ vs. isolation
Middle adulthood	______________ vs. stagnation
Older adulthood	______________ vs. despair

34. A major theory in American psychology, which directly opposed psychoanalytic theory, was ______________. This theory, which emerged early in the twentieth century under the influence of ______________, is also called ______________ theory because of its emphasis on learning behavior, step by step.

35. Behaviorists have formulated laws of behavior that are believed to apply ______________ (only at certain ages/at all ages).

36. The learning process, which is called ______________, takes two forms: ______________ ______________ and ______________ ______________.

37. In classical conditioning, which was discovered by the Russian scientist ______________ and is also called ______________ conditioning, a person or an animal learns to associate a(n) ______________ stimulus with a meaningful one.

38. According to ______________, the learning of more complex responses is the result of ______________ conditioning, in which a person learns that a particular behavior produces a particular ______________, such as a reward. This type of learning is also called ______________ conditioning.

39. The process of repeating a consequence to make it more likely that the behavior in question will recur is called ______________.

STUDY TIP: The best way to differentiate between classical conditioning and operant conditioning is to ask yourself two questions: (1) Is the behavior voluntary (operant conditioning) or involuntary (classical conditioning)? (2) Does the learning involve an association between two stimuli (classical conditioning) or between a response and an outcome (operant conditioning)? Test your understanding on the following examples.

40. a. After receiving a mild shock from the "invisible fence" surrounding his yard, a dog no longer crosses the boundary.

____

b. You flinch when someone yells, "Duck!"

____

c. You ask more questions in class after the professor praises you for a good question.

____

d. The pupil of your eye dilates (opens wider) after you enter a darkened theater.

____

---

41. A major extension of behaviorism that emphasizes the ways that people learn new behaviors by observing others is called _______________ _______________ theory. The process whereby a child patterns his or her behavior after a parent or teacher, for example, is called _______________ .

42. This type of learning is connected to the individual's _______________ and _______________ . Human social learning is also related to _______________ , _______________ , and _______________ .

43. The structure and development of thought processes and the way those thought processes shape our attitudes, beliefs, and behaviors are the focus of _______________ theory. An important pioneer of cognitive theory is _______________ , who realized that babies are curious and thoughtful, creating their own _______________ of their world.

44. In Piaget's first stage of development, the _______________ stage, children experience the world through their senses and motor abilities. This stage occurs between birth and age _______________ .

45. According to Piaget, during the preschool years (up to age _______________), children are in the _______________ stage. A hallmark of this stage is that imagination flourishes and _______________ becomes a significant means of self-expression.

46. Piaget believed that children begin to think logically in a consistent way at about _______________ years of age. At this time, they enter the _______________ _______________ stage.

47. In Piaget's final stage, the _______________ _______________ stage, reasoning expands from the purely concrete to encompass _______________ thinking. Piaget believed most children enter this stage by age _______________ .

48. According to Piaget, cognitive development is guided by the need to maintain a state of mental balance, called _______________ _______________ .

49. When new experiences challenge existing understanding, creating a kind of imbalance, the individual experiences _______________ _______________ , which eventually leads to cognitive growth.

50. According to Piaget, people adapt to new experiences either by reinterpreting them to fit into, or _______________ with, old ideas. Some new experiences force people to revamp old ideas so that they can _______________ new experiences.

51. Proponents of another influential cognitive theory, called _______________ _______________ , think some of Piaget's conclusions were wrong.

52. The approach that emphasizes the influence of the systems that support the developing person is called the _______________ - _______________ approach. This approach was emphasized by _______________ .

53. According to this model, the family, the peer group, and other aspects of the immediate social setting constitute the _______________ .

54. Community institutions such as school and church make up the _______________ .

55. Cultural values, political philosophies, economic patterns, and social systems make up the _______________ .

56. The system that emphasizes the importance of historical conditions on development is the _______________ .

57. Systems that link one system to another constitute the ____________________ .

58. As a reflection of the impact of biology on development, this systems approach was renamed ____________________ theory.

59. The related approach to development which stresses fluctuations and transitions is ____________________-____________________ theory.

STUDY TIP: According to Urie Bronfenbrenner, each person is significantly affected by interactions among several overlapping systems. These include the *microsystems* that immediately shape development, surrounding *exosystems* in the community and environment, the cultural and political *macrosystem*, the historical *chronosystem*, and the *mesosystems* by which the various systems interact. To reinforce your understanding of Bronfenbrenner's ecological model, complete the following table by filling in specific examples of the overlapping systems that provide the context of *your* development today (general descriptions and examples of the system are provided to get you started). Remember that although these are presented in linear form, they are overlapping and interacting.

System	Description	Examples
Microsystems	Immediate influences	your parents
Exosystems	Microsystem support	your school
Mesosystems	Interactions among systems	your parents working with your teachers
Macrosystem	Influences micro-, meso-, and exosystems	
Chronosystem	Historical time	

APPLICATIONS:

60. A pigeon is rewarded for producing a particular response, and so learns to produce that response to obtain rewards. Psychologists describe this chain of events as ____________________ ____________________ .

61. Professor Swenson believes that much of our learning involves associating neutral stimuli with meaningful stimuli. He would most likely agree with the writings of ____________________ .

62. Dr. Thomas strongly endorses the views of Erik Erikson. She would most likely disagree with Freud regarding the importance of
   a. unconscious forces in development.
   b. irrational forces in personality formation.
   c. early childhood experiences.
   d. sexual urges in development.

63. After watching several older children climbing around a new jungle gym, 5-year-old Jennie decides to try it herself. Which of the following best accounts for her behavior?
   a. modeling
   b. plasticity
   c. cohort effect
   d. classical conditioning

64. I am 8 years old. Although I understand some logical principles, I have trouble thinking about hypothetical concepts. According to Piaget, I am in the ________________ ________________ stage of development.

65. Two-year-old Jamail has a simple understanding for "Dad." Each time he encounters a man with a child, he calls him "Dad." When he learns that these other men are not "Dad," Jamail experiences ________________ .

66. Four-year-old Bjorn takes great pride in successfully undertaking new activities. Erikson would probably say that Bjorn is capably meeting the psychosocial challenge of

____

67. Dr. Bazzi believes that development is a lifelong process of gradual and continuous growth. Based on this information, with which of the following theories would Dr. Bazzi most likely agree?
   a. Piaget's cognitive theory
   b. Erikson's psychosocial theory
   c. Freud's psychoanalytic theory
   d. behaviorism

68. Dr. Ahmed is conducting research that takes into consideration the relationship between the individual and the environment. Evidently, Dr. Ahmed is using the ________________-________________ approach.

69. Jahmal is writing a paper on the role of the social context in development. He would do well to consult the writings of ________________ .

Using the Scientific Method (pp. 26–33)

70. When researchers observe and record, in a systematic and objective manner, what research participants do, they are using ________________ ________________ .

71. In the science of human development, people may be observed in a ________________ setting or in a ________________ .

72. A chief limitation of observation is that it does not indicate the ________________ of the behavior being observed.

73. The method that allows a scientist to determine cause and effect is the ________________ . In this method, researchers manipulate a(n) ________________ variable to determine its effect on a(n) ________________ variable.

74. In an experiment, the participants who receive a particular treatment constitute the ________________ ________________ ; the participants who do not receive the treatment constitute the ________________ ________________ .

STUDY TIP: To distinguish between independent variables and dependent variables, remember that independent variables are manipulated (controlled) directly by the researcher to determine how they affect dependent variables. Dependent variables are the behaviors and mental processes that psychologists are striving to understand. In a sense, dependent variables *depend* on the actions of independent variables. When you are struggling to distinguish two variables, try the following exercise. Ask yourself, "Which of these two variables can affect the other?" Consider, for example, a researcher investigating caffeine and reaction time. After randomly assigning students either to a group that drinks a highly caffeinated drink or to a group that drinks a weakly caffeinated drink, she measures each student's speed in pushing a button in response to a signal light. Which variable is the independent variable, and which is the dependent variable? If the answer is not obvious, try the test question, "Which variable can affect the other?" Clearly, reaction time cannot affect caffeine. So, in this example, the dose of caffeine is the independent variable and reaction time is the dependent variable.

75. In a(n) ________________, scientists collect information from a large group of people by personal interview, written questionnaire, or some other means.

76. Research that involves the comparison of people of different ages is called a ________________-________________ research design.

77. With cross-sectional research, it is very difficult to ensure that the various groups differ only in their ________________. In addition, every cross-sectional study will, to some degree, reflect ________________ differences in addition to age effects.

78. Research that follows the same people over a relatively long period of time is called a ________________ research design.

State three drawbacks of this type of research design.

79. The research method that combines the longitudinal and cross-sectional methods is the ________________-________________ research method.

APPLICATIONS:

80. To study the effects of temperature on mood, Dr. Sanchez had students fill out questionnaires in very warm or very cool rooms. In this study, the independent variable consisted of
   a. the number of students assigned to each group.
   b. the students' responses to the questionnaire.
   c. the room temperature.
   d. the subject matter of the questions.

81. Esteban believes that high doses of caffeine slow a person's reaction time. To test his belief, he has five friends each drink three 8-ounce cups of coffee and then measures their reaction time on a learning task. What is wrong with Esteban's research strategy?
   a. No independent variable is specified.
   b. No dependent variable is specified.
   c. There is no comparison condition.
   d. There is no provision for replication of the findings.

82. In an experiment testing the effects of group size on individual effort in a tug-of-war task, the amount of individual effort is the ________________ variable.

83. An example of longitudinal research would be an investigator comparing the performance of
   a. several different age groups on a memory test.
   b. the same group of people, at different ages, on a test of memory.
   c. an experimental group and a comparison group on a test of memory.
   d. several different age groups on a test of memory as each group is tested repeatedly over a period of years.

84. Dr. Weston is comparing research findings for a group of 30-year-olds with findings for the same individuals at age 20, as well as with findings for groups who were 30 in 1990. Which research method is she using? ________________

85. To find out whether people's attitudes regarding an issue vary with their ages, Karen distributes the same survey to groups of people in their twenties, thirties, forties, fifties, and sixties. Karen is evidently conducting ________________-________________ research.

Cautions from Science (pp. 34–38)

86. A number that indicates the degree of relationship between two variables is a ________________. To say that two variables are related in this way ________________ (does/does not) necessarily imply that one caused the other. A correlation is ________________ if both variables tend to ________________ together; a correlation is ________________ if one variable tends to ________________ when the other ________________; a correlation is ________________ if there is no evident connection between the two variables.

STUDY TIP: A common mistake in understanding correlation is the belief that a negative correlation indicates a weak or absent relationship between two variables. Remember that correlation does *not* prove causation; it indicates only the degree to which you can predict changes in one variable from another.

The strength of a correlation, indicated by the numerical value of the correlation coefficient, is independent of the *direction* (positive or negative) of the relationship. A negative correlation simply means that two variables change in opposite directions, such as when sales of hot chocolate decrease as the average daily temperature increases.

87. Because numbers can be easily summarized, compared, charted, and replicated, scientists often rely on data produced by ________________ research. This method may lose some nuances and individual distinctions, and so many developmental researchers use ________________ research that asks ________________-________________ questions. This method reflects ________________ and ________________ diversity and complexity. But it is also more vulnerable to bias and harder to ________________.

88. Developmental researchers work from a set of moral principles that constitute their ________________ ________________ ________________. Researchers who study humans must obtain ________________ ________________, which refers to written permission, and ensure that their participants are not ________________ and that they are allowed to stop at any time.

89. To ensure that research is not unintentionally slanting, scientific ________________, ________________, and replication are crucial.

APPLICATIONS:

90. If height and body weight are correlated, which of the following is true?

a. There is a cause-and-effect relationship between height and weight.
b. Knowing a person's height, we can predict his or her weight.
c. All people of the same height will weigh the same amount.
d. None of these facts is true.

91. For her developmental psychology research project, Lakia decides she wants to focus primarily on qualitative data. Which research method should she use? ________________

Progress Test 1

Multiple-Choice Questions

Circle your answers to the following questions and check them against the answers beginning on page 16. If your answer is incorrect, read the explanation for why it is incorrect and then consult the appropriate pages of the text (in parentheses following the correct answer).

1. The *science of human development* is defined as the study of

a. how and why people change or remain the same over time.
b. psychosocial influences on aging.
c. individual differences in learning over the life span.
d. all of these factors.

2. The research method that involves the use of open-ended questions and obtains answers that are not easily translated into categories is

a. the survey.
b. qualitative research.
c. cross-sectional study.
d. quantitative research.

3. Nature is to nurture as

a. environment is to genes.
b. genes are to environment.
c. continuity is to discontinuity.
d. discontinuity is to continuity.

4. The dynamic-systems theory emphasizes the idea(s) that

a. human development is always changing and that change in one area affects all others.
b. developmental science should emphasize quantitative data.
c. a person's position in society is determined primarily by social factors such as income and education.
d. concepts such as race are based on social perceptions.

5. The ecological-systems approach to developmental psychology focuses on the

a. biochemistry of the body systems.
b. macrosystems only.
c. internal thinking processes.
d. overall environment of development.

6. The science of development focuses on
   a. the sources of continuity from the beginning of life to the end.
   b. the sources of discontinuity throughout life.
   c. the "nonlinear" character of human development.
   d. all of this information.

7. Brain cells that respond to actions performed by another person are called
   a. cohort neurons.
   b. mirror neurons.
   c. butterfly cells.
   d. premotor cells.

8. A hypothesis is a
   a. conclusion.
   b. prediction to be tested.
   c. statistical test.
   d. correlation.

9. A developmentalist who is interested in studying the influences of a person's immediate environment on his or her behavior is focusing on which system?
   a. mesosystem
   b. macrosystem
   c. microsystem
   d. exosystem

10. Socioeconomic status is determined by a combination of variables, including
    a. age, education, and income.
    b. income, ethnicity, and occupation.
    c. income, education, and occupation.
    d. age, ethnicity, and occupation.

11. In an experiment that tests the effects of group size on individual effort in a tug-of-war task, the number of people in each group is the
    a. hypothesis.
    b. independent variable.
    c. dependent variable.
    d. level of significance.

12. Which research method would be most appropriate for investigating the relationship between parents' religious beliefs and their attitudes toward middle-school sex education?
    a. experimentation
    b. longitudinal research
    c. naturalistic observation
    d. the survey

13. To establish cause, which type of research study would an investigator conduct?
    a. an experiment
    b. a survey
    c. scientific observation
    d. correlational

14. Developmentalists who carefully observe the behavior of schoolchildren during recess are using a research method known as
    a. the case study.
    b. cross-sectional research.
    c. scientific observation.
    d. cross-sequential research.

15. Which developmental theory emphasizes the influence of unconscious drives and motives on behavior?
    a. psychoanalytic
    b. behaviorism
    c. cognitive
    d. sociocultural

16. Which of the following is the correct order of the psychosexual stages proposed by Freud?
    a. oral stage; anal stage; phallic stage; latency; genital stage
    b. anal stage; oral stage; phallic stage; latency; genital stage
    c. oral stage; anal stage; genital stage; latency; phallic stage
    d. anal stage; oral stage; genital stage; latency; phallic stage

17. Erikson's psychosocial theory of human development describes
    a. eight crises all people are thought to face.
    b. four psychosocial stages and a latency period.
    c. the same number of stages as Freud's, but with different names.
    d. a stage theory that is not psychoanalytic.

18. An American psychologist who explained complex human behaviors in terms of operant conditioning was
    a. Urie Bronfenbrenner.
    b. Ivan Pavlov.
    c. B. F. Skinner.
    d. Jean Piaget.

19. Pavlov's dogs learned to salivate at the sound of a tone because they associated the tone with food. Pavlov's experiment with dogs was an early demonstration of
    a. classical conditioning.
    b. operant conditioning.
    c. positive reinforcement.
    d. social learning.

20. A child who calls all furry animals "doggie" will experience cognitive ____________ when she encounters a hairless breed for the first time. This may cause her to revamp her concept of "dog" in order to ____________ the new experience.
    a. disequilibrium; accommodate
    b. disequilibrium; assimilate
    c. equilibrium; accommodate
    d. equilibrium; assimilate

21. Which is the correct sequence of stages in Piaget's theory of cognitive development?
    a. sensorimotor, preoperational, concrete operational, formal operational
    b. sensorimotor, preoperational, formal operational, concrete operational
    c. preoperational, sensorimotor, concrete operational, formal operational
    d. preoperational, sensorimotor, formal operational, concrete operational

22. You teach your dog to "speak" by giving her a treat each time she does so. This is an example of
    a. classical conditioning.
    b. respondent conditioning.
    c. reinforcement.
    d. modeling.

True or False Items

Write T (*true*) or F (*false*) on the line in front of each statement.

________ 1. Scientists rarely repeat an experiment.

________ 2. The case study of David clearly demonstrates that for some children only nature (or heredity) is important.

________ 3. Observation usually indicates a clear relationship between cause and effect.

________ 4. Each social context influences development independently.

________ 5. Cohort differences are an example of the impact of the social context on development.

________ 6. Every trait of an individual can be molded into different forms and shapes.

________ 7. Because of its limitations, qualitative research is rarely used in developmental research.

________ 8. The influences between and within Bronfenbrenner's systems are unidirectional and independent.

________ 9. People of different ethnic groups can all share one culture.

________ 10. Longitudinal research is particularly useful in studying development over a long age span.

________ 11. The concepts of critical periods and sensitive periods do not apply to human development.

________ 12. Behaviorists study what people actually do, not what they might be thinking.

________ 13. Erikson's eight developmental stages are centered not on a body part but on each person's relationship to the social environment.

________ 14. According to Piaget, a state of cognitive equilibrium must be attained before cognitive growth can occur.

________ 15. In part, cognitive theory examines how an individual's understandings and expectations affect his or her behavior.

________ 16. According to Piaget, children begin to think only when they reach preschool age.

Progress Test 2

Progress Test 2 should be completed during a final chapter review. Answer the following questions after you thoroughly understand the correct answers for the Chapter Review and Progress Test 1.

Multiple-Choice Questions

1. An individual's personal sphere of development refers to his or her
    a. microsystem and mesosystem.
    b. exosystem.
    c. macrosystem.
    d. microsystem, mesosystem, exosystem, macrosystem, and chronosystem.

2. Developmental psychologists explore three domains of development:
    a. physical, cognitive, psychosocial.
    b. physical, biosocial, cognitive.
    c. biosocial, cognitive, psychosocial.
    d. biosocial, cognitive, emotional.

3. The most important principle of the developmental research code of ethics is
    a. never physically or psychologically harm those who are involved in research.
    b. maintain confidentiality at all costs.
    c. obtain informed consent from all participants.
    d. ensure that participants do not understand the true purpose of their research study.

4. The difference-equals-deficit error occurs when a person falsely believes that
   a. genes exert a stronger influence on developmental abnormalities than the environment.
   b. the environment exerts a stronger influence on developmental abnormalities than genes.
   c. nature and nurture contribute equally to deviations from average development.
   d. deviations from average development are necessarily inferior.

5. According to the ecological-systems approach, the macrosystem would include
   a. the peer group.
   b. the community.
   c. cultural values.
   d. the family.

6. An idea that is built more on shared perceptions than on objective reality is a
   a. cohort effect.
   b. difference-equals-deficit error.
   c. social construction.
   d. hypothesis.

7. In an experiment, the treatment of interest is given to the ______ group; the no-treatment group is the ______ group.
   a. experimental; comparison
   b. comparison; experimental
   c. dependent; independent
   d. independent; dependent

8. A cohort is defined as a group of people
   a. of similar national origin.
   b. who share a common language.
   c. born within a few years of each other.
   d. who share the same religion.

9. In a test of the effects of noise, groups of students performed a proofreading task in a noisy or a quiet room. To what group were students in the noisy room assigned?
   a. experimental
   b. comparison
   c. randomly assigned
   d. dependent

10. In differentiating ethnicity and culture, we note that
    a. ethnicity is an exclusively biological phenomenon.
    b. an ethnic group is a group of people who were born within a few years of each other.
    c. people of many ethnic groups can share one culture, yet maintain their ethnic identities.
    d. racial identity is always an element of culture.

11. If developmentalists discovered that poor people are happier than wealthy people, this would indicate that wealth and happiness are
    a. unrelated.
    b. correlated.
    c. examples of nature and nurture, respectively.
    d. causally related.

12. The plasticity of development refers to the fact that
    a. development is not always linear.
    b. each human life must be understood as embedded in many contexts.
    c. there are many reciprocal connections between childhood and adulthood.
    d. human characteristics can be molded into different forms and shapes.

13. In an experiment that tests the effects of noise level on mood, mood is the
    a. hypothesis.
    b. independent variable.
    c. dependent variable.
    d. scientific observation.

14. Research on mirror neurons has revealed that
    a. when experts in dance watch a performance, their brains are activated as if they themselves were performing.
    b. the action of mirror neurons in part explains why children learn so quickly.
    c. neural activity mirrors the intentions and emotions of people around us.
    d. all of these answers are correct.

15. Which of the following statements concerning ethnicity and culture is NOT true?
    a. Ethnicity is determined genetically.
    b. Race is a social construction.
    c. Racial identity is an element of ethnicity.
    d. Ethnic identity provides people with shared values and beliefs.

16. Of the following terms, the one that does NOT describe a stage of Freud's theory of childhood sexuality is
    a. phallic.
    b. oral.
    c. anal.
    d. sensorimotor.

17. According to Erikson, an adult who has difficulty establishing a secure, mutual relationship with a life partner might never have resolved the crisis of
   a. initiative versus guilt.
   b. autonomy versus shame and doubt.
   c. intimacy versus isolation.
   d. identity versus role confusion.

18. Who would be most likely to agree with the statement, "anything can be learned"?
   a. Jean Piaget
   b. Paul Baltes
   c. John B. Watson
   d. Erik Erikson

19. Classical conditioning is to ________________ as operant conditioning is to ________________.
   a. Skinner; Pavlov
   b. Watson; Piaget
   c. Pavlov; Skinner
   d. Piaget; Watson

20. According to Piaget, an infant first comes to know the world through
   a. senses and motor abilities.
   b. naming and counting.
   c. preoperational thought.
   d. instruction from parents.

21. According to Piaget, the stage of cognitive development that generally characterizes preschool children (2 to 6 years old) is the
   a. preoperational stage.
   b. sensorimotor stage.
   c. oral stage.
   d. psychosocial stage.

22. In Piaget's theory, cognitive equilibrium refers to
   a. a state of mental balance.
   b. a kind of imbalance that leads to cognitive growth.
   c. the ultimate stage of cognitive development.
   d. the first stage in the processing of information.

23. A child who must modify an old idea in order to incorporate a new experience is using the process of
   a. assimilation.
   b. accommodation.
   c. cognitive equilibrium.
   d. information processing.

Matching Items

Match each definition or description with its corresponding term.

Terms

________ 1. independent variable
________ 2. dependent variable
________ 3. culture
________ 4. replicate
________ 5. chronosystem
________ 6. exosystem
________ 7. mesosystem
________ 8. socioeconomic status
________ 9. cohort
________ 10. ethnic group
________ 11. cross-sectional research
________ 12. longitudinal research
________ 13. continuity
________ 14. discontinuity

Definitions or Descriptions

a. group of people born within a few years of each other
b. determined by a person's income, education, occupation, and so on
c. research study comparing people of different ages at the same time
d. the historical conditions that affect development
e. collection of people who share certain attributes, such as national origin
f. shared values, patterns of behavior, and customs maintained by people in a specific setting
g. local institutions such as schools
h. the variable manipulated in an experiment
i. connections between microsystems
j. to repeat a study and obtain the same findings
k. the variable measured in an experiment
l. research study retesting one group of people at several different times
m. stability in development
n. lack of stability in development

Key Terms

Using your own words, write a brief definition or explanation of each of the following terms on a separate piece of paper.

1. science of human development
2. scientific method
3. replication
4. nature
5. nurture
6. critical period
7. sensitive period
8. difference-equals-deficit error
9. life-span perspective
10. cohort
11. socioeconomic status (SES)
12. ethnic group
13. social construction
14. epigenetic
15. mirror neurons
16. developmental theory
17. psychoanalytic theory
18. behaviorism
19. conditioning
20. classical conditioning
21. operant conditioning
22. reinforcement
23. social learning theory
24. cognitive theory
25. ecological-systems approach
26. dynamic-systems theory
27. scientific observation
28. experiment
29. independent variable
30. dependent variable
31. survey
32. cross-sectional research
33. longitudinal research
34. cross-sequential research
35. correlation
36. quantitative research
37. qualitative research

Answers

CHAPTER REVIEW

1. how and why people—all people, everywhere, of every age—change or remain the same over time
2. **a.** ask a question
   b. develop a hypothesis
   c. test the hypothesis
   d. draw conclusions
   e. report the results
3. hypothesis
4. replicate
5. nature–nurture; nurture; nature
6. affect
7. critical period; sensitive period; language
8. do not necessarily indicate; difference-equals-deficit; science
9. change; remain the same
10. stages; biosocial; cognitive; psychosocial; reciprocal; simultaneously
11. hypothesis
12. **c.** is the answer. Although any of the other points may be true, none has anything to do with replication.
13. life-span; multidirectional; multicontextual; multicultural; multidisciplinary; plastic
14. linear; continuity; discontinuity
15. cohort; the same way
16. socioeconomic status; SES
17. culture
18. ethnic group
19. race
20. biological; society; social construction
21. epigenetic; violence; social; genetic; aggressive; MAOA; low
22. mirror neurons; actions performed by someone else
23. plasticity; genetic; drugs; cognitive
24. **d.** is the answer. a. describes the multidirectional nature of development. b. describes the multicontextual nature of development. c. describes the multicultural nature of development.
25. **c.** is the answer. This is because developmentalists believe that race is a social construction.
26. **c.** is the answer.
27. changing social conditions and cohort effects
28. hypotheses; developmental theory

29. motives; drives; unconscious
30. psychoanalytic; oral; anal; phallic
31. conflicts

Oral stage: The mouth is the focus of pleasurable sensations, and sucking and feeding are the most stimulating activities.

Anal stage: The anus is the focus of pleasurable sensations, and toilet training is the most important activity.

Phallic stage: Pleasure is derived from genital stimulation.

Genital stage: Mature sexual interests that last throughout adulthood emerge.

32. eight; crisis
33. span

Age Period	Stage
Birth to 1 yr.	trust vs. mistrust
1–3 yrs.	autonomy vs. shame and doubt
3–6 yrs.	initiative vs. guilt
6–11 yrs.	industry vs. inferiority
Adolescence	identity vs. role confusion
Young adulthood	intimacy vs. isolation
Middle adulthood	generativity vs. stagnation
Older adulthood	integrity vs. despair

34. behaviorism; John B. Watson; learning
35. at all ages
36. conditioning; classical conditioning; operant conditioning
37. Ivan Pavlov; respondent; neutral
38. B. F. Skinner; operant; consequence; instrumental
39. reinforcement
40. The examples in a. and c. are operant conditioning because a response's recurrence is determined by its consequences. The answers to b. and d. are classical conditioning because two stimuli are associated.
41. social learning; modeling
42. perceptions; interpretations; self-understanding; social reflection; self-efficacy
43. cognitive; Jean Piaget; schemas
44. sensorimotor; 2
45. 6; preoperational; language
46. 6; concrete operational
47. formal operational; abstract (hypothetical); 12
48. cognitive equilibrium
49. cognitive disequilibrium
50. assimilate; accommodate
51. information processing
52. ecological-systems; Urie Bronfenbrenner
53. microsystem
54. exosystem
55. macrosystem
56. chronosystem
57. mesosystem
58. bioecological
59. dynamic-systems
60. operant conditioning. This is an example of operant conditioning because a response recurs due to its consequences.
61. Pavlov. In classical conditioning, developed by Pavlov, an organism comes to associate a neutral stimulus with a meaningful one and then responds to the former stimulus as if it were the latter.
62. **d.** is the answer. Unlike Freud, who emphasized sexual urges in development, Erikson put more emphasis on family and culture.
63. modeling
64. concrete operational. During Piaget's concrete operational stage children can understand and apply logical operations, but only to what they personally see, hear, touch, and experience.
65. disequilibrium. When Jamail experiences something that conflicts with his existing understanding, he experiences disequilibrium. Piaget believed that this could lead to cognitive growth.
66. initiative vs. guilt. Children at this stage either feel adventurous or guilty.
67. **d.** is the answer. Each of the other theories emphasizes that development is a discontinuous process that occurs in stages.
68. ecological-systems. Bronfenbrenner, who recommended this approach, argued that developmentalists need to examine all the systems that surround the development of each person.
69. Bronfenbrenner. He advocated an ecological-systems approach.
70. scientific observation
71. natural; laboratory
72. cause
73. experiment; independent; dependent
74. experimental group; comparison group (control group)
75. survey
76. cross-sectional
77. ages; cohort

78. longitudinal

Over time, some participants may leave the study. Some people may "improve" simply because they are familiar with the goals of the study. The biggest problem is the changing historical context.

79. cross-sequential

80. **c.** is the answer. Room temperature is the variable being manipulated.

81. **c.** is the answer. In order to determine the effects of caffeine on reaction time, Esteban needs to measure reaction time (the dependent variable) in a comparison group that does not receive caffeine (the independent variable).

82. dependent. The group size would be the independent variable. A hypothesis for this experiment might be that the larger the group, the less effort each person exerts.

83. **b.** is the answer. a. is an example of cross-sectional research. c. is an experiment. d. is an example of cross-sequential research.

84. cross-sequential research. Dr. Weston's research combines the features of cross-sectional research (comparing people of different ages who share certain characteristics) and longitudinal research (comparing the same group of people over time).

85. cross-sectional. Karen is surveying people of different ages about a particular issue.

86. correlation; does not; positive; increase (or decrease); negative; increase; decreases; zero

87. quantitative; qualitative; open-ended; cultural; contextual; replicate

88. code of ethics; informed consent; harmed

89. training; collaboration

90. **b.** is the answer. Correlation does not imply causation but it does allow prediction.

91. a case study. Methods such as scientific observation, the survey, and the experiment yield *quantitative,* rather than *qualitative,* data.

PROGRESS TEST 1

Multiple-Choice Questions

1. **a.** is the answer. (p. 4)

   b. & c. The study of development is concerned with a broader range of phenomena, including physical aspects of development, than these answers specify.

2. **b.** is the answer. (p. 36)

   a. In this research method, a large number of people are questioned either through written questionnaires or in person.

   c. In this research method, groups of people who differ in age are compared.

   d. This type of research provides data that can be expressed with numbers.

3. **b.** is the answer. (p. 5)

4. **a.** is the answer. (pp. 24–25)

5. **d.** is the answer. This approach sees development as occurring within five interacting levels, or environments. (p. 24)

6. **d.** is the answer. (pp. 4–5)

7. **b.** is the answer. (p. 14)

8. **b.** is the answer. (p. 4)

9. **c.** is the answer. (p. 24)

   a. This refers to systems that link one system to another.

   b. This refers to cultural values, political philosophies, economic patterns, and social conditions.

   d. This includes the community structures that affect the functioning of smaller systems.

10. **c.** is the answer. (p. 10)

11. **b.** is the answer. (p. 28)

    a. A possible hypothesis for this experiment would be that the larger the group, the less hard a given individual will pull.

    c. The dependent variable is the measure of individual effort.

    d. Significance level refers to the numerical value specifying the possibility that the results of an experiment could have occurred by chance.

12. **d.** is the answer. (p. 29)

    a. Experimentation is appropriate when one is seeking to uncover cause-and-effect relationships; in this example, the researcher is only interested in determining whether the parents' beliefs *predict* their attitudes.

    b. Longitudinal research would be appropriate if the researcher sought to examine the development of these attitudes over a long period of time.

    c. Mere observation would not allow the researcher to determine the attitudes of the participants.

13. **a.** is the answer. (p. 28)

    b., c., & d. These research methods do not indicate what causes people to do what they do.

14. **c.** is the answer. (p. 26)

a. In this method, *one* person is studied over a period of time.

b. & d. In these research methods, two or more *groups* of participants are studied and compared.

15. **a.** is the answer. (p. 17)

b. Behaviorism emphasizes the influence of the immediate environment on behavior.

c. Cognitive theory emphasizes the impact of conscious thought processes on behavior.

d. Sociocultural theory emphasizes the influence on development of social interaction in a specific cultural context.

16. **a.** is the answer. (pp. 18, 19)

17. **a.** is the answer. (p. 18)

b. & c. Whereas Freud identified four stages of psychosexual development, Erikson proposed eight psychosocial stages.

d. Although his theory places greater emphasis on social and cultural forces than Freud's did, Erikson's theory is nevertheless classified as a psychoanalytic theory.

18. **c.** is the answer. (p. 20)

19. **a.** is the answer. In classical conditioning, a neutral stimulus—in this case, the bell—is associated with a meaningful stimulus—in this case, food. (p. 20)

b. In operant conditioning, the consequences of a voluntary response determine the likelihood of its being repeated. Salivation is an involuntary response.

c. & d. Positive reinforcement and social learning pertain to voluntary, or operant, responses.

20. **a.** is the answer. (p. 23)

b. Because the dog is not furry, the child's concept of dog cannot incorporate (assimilate) the discrepant experience without being revamped.

c. & d. Equilibrium exists when ideas (such as what a dog is) and experiences (such as seeing a hairless dog) do not clash.

21. **a.** is the answer. (p. 23)

22. **c.** is the answer. (p. 21)

a. & b. Teaching your dog in this way is an example of operant, rather than classical (respondent), conditioning.

d. Modeling involves learning by imitating others.

True or False Items

1. F Just the opposite. Scientists always try to replicate their or other people's work. (p. 4)

2. F The case study of David shows that both nature and nurture are important in affecting outcome. (pp. 3–4)

3. F A disadvantage of observation is that the variables are numerous and uncontrolled, and therefore cause-and-effect relationships are difficult to pinpoint. (p. 28)

4. F Each social context affects the way a person develops, and each is affected by the other contexts. (p. 9)

5. T (p. 9)

6. T (p. 15)

7. F Qualitative research often reveals information that would be lost if an observation were expressed in numbers. (p. 36)

8. F Quite the reverse is true. (p. 24)

9. T (p. 11)

10. T (p. 32)

11. F These terms apply to all animals, including humans. (p. 5)

12. T (p. 19)

13. T (p. 18)

14. F On the contrary, disequilibrium often fosters greater growth. (p. 23)

15. T (p. 22)

16. F The hallmark of Piaget's theory is that, at every age, individuals think about the world in unique ways. (pp. 22–23)

PROGRESS TEST 2

Multiple-Choice Questions

1. **d.** is the answer. (p. 24)

2. **c.** is the answer. (p. 7)

3. **a.** is the answer. (p. 36)

b. & c. Although these are important aspects of the code of ethics, protecting participants from harm is the most important.

4. **d.** is the answer. (p. 6)

5. **c.** is the answer. (p. 24)

a. & d. These are part of the microsystem.

b. This is part of the exosystem.

6. **c.** is the answer. (p. 12)

7. **a.** is the answer. (p. 28)

   c. & d. Independent and dependent refer to treatments and behaviors, respectively.

8. **c.** is the answer. (p. 9)

   a., b., & d. These are attributes of an ethnic group.

9. **a.** is the answer. The experimental group is the one in which the variable or treatment—in this case, noise—is present. (p. 28)

   b. Students in the quiet room would be in the comparison condition.

   c. Presumably, all students in both groups were randomly assigned to their groups.

   d. The word *dependent* refers to a kind of variable in experiments; groups are either experimental or control.

10. **c.** is the answer. (p. 11)

    a. & d. Ethnicity refers to shared attributes, such as ancestry, national origin, religion, and language.

    b. This describes a cohort.

11. **b.** is the answer. (p. 34)

    a. Wealth and happiness clearly *are* related.

    c. For one thing, poverty is clearly an example of nurture, not nature.

    d. Correlation does not imply causation.

12. **d.** is the answer. (p. 15)

13. **c.** is the answer. (p. 28)

    a. Hypotheses make *specific,* testable predictions.

    b. Noise level is the independent variable.

    d. Scientific observation is a research method in which participants are watched, while their behavior is recorded unobtrusively.

14. **d.** is the answer. (p. 14)

15. **a.** is the answer. Ethnic identity is a product of the social environment and the individual's consciousness. (pp. 11–12)

16. **d.** is the answer. This is one of Piaget's stages of cognitive development. (pp. 18, 19)

17. **d.** is the answer. (p. 19)

18. **c.** is the answer. (p. 19)

    a. Piaget formulated a cognitive theory of development.

    b. Baltes originated the life-span perspective.

    d. Erikson formulated a psychoanalytic theory of development.

19. **c.** is the answer. (p. 20)

20. **a.** is the answer. These behaviors are typical of infants in the sensorimotor stage. (pp. 22, 23)

    b., c., & d. These are typical of older children.

21. **a.** is the answer. (p. 23)

    b. The sensorimotor stage describes development from birth until 2 years of age.

    c. This is a psychoanalytic stage described by Freud.

    d. This is not the name of a stage; "psychosocial" refers to Erikson's stage theory.

22. **a.** is the answer. (p. 23)

    b. This describes disequilibrium.

    c. This is formal operational thinking.

    d. Piaget's theory does not propose stages of information processing.

23. **b.** is the answer. (p. 23)

    a. Assimilation occurs when new experiences do not clash with existing ideas.

    c. Cognitive equilibrium is mental balance, which occurs when ideas and experiences do not clash.

    d. Information processing refers to an approach to cognition that disagreed with many of Piaget's concepts.

Matching Items

1. h (p. 28)	**6.** g (p. 24)	**11.** c (p. 30)
2. k (p. 28)	**7.** i (p. 24)	**12.** l (p. 32)
3. f (p. 10)	**8.** b (p. 10)	**13.** m (p. 8)
4. j (p. 4)	**9.** a (p. 9)	**14.** n (p. 8)
5. d (p. 24)	**10.** e (p. 11)	

KEY TERMS

1. The **science of human development** seeks to understand how and why all people, everywhere, change or remain the same over time. (p. 4)

2. The **scientific method** is a way to answer questions that requires empirical research and data-based conclusions. The five basic steps of the scientific method are (1) pose a research question; (2) develop a hypothesis; (3) test the hypothesis; (4) draw conclusions; and (5) report the results, which allows for replication. (p. 4)

3. **Replication** means to repeat a test of a research hypothesis and to try to obtain the same results using different participants. (p. 4)

4. **Nature** refers to all the traits that a person inherits from his or her parents. (p. 5)

5. **Nurture** refers to all the environmental influences that affect development. (p. 5)

6. A **critical period** is a time when a particular type of development must occur. (p. 5)

7. A **sensitive period** is a time when a particular type of development happens most easily. (p. 5)

8. The **difference-equals-deficit error** is the false belief that deviations from average development are always inferior. (p. 6)

9. The **life-span perspective** approaches human development by taking into account all phases of life, not just childhood or adulthood. (p. 7)

10. A **cohort** is a group of people who, because they were born within a few years of each other, experience many of the same historical changes. (p. 9)

11. An individual's **socioeconomic status (SES)** is determined by his or her income, wealth, education, place of residence, and occupation. (p. 10)

12. An **ethnic group** is a collection of people whose ancestors were born in the same region, often sharing a language, culture, and religion. (p. 11)

13. A **social construction** is an idea that is based on shared perceptions, not on objective reality. (p. 12)

14. **Epigenetic** refers to the effects of environmental forces on how genes are expressed. (p. 12)

15. **Mirror neurons** are cells in a person's brain that respond to the observed actions of others in the same way they would if the observer had done that action. (p. 14)

16. A **developmental theory** is a systematic statement of principles and generalizations that provides a framework for understanding how and why people change as they grow older. (p. 17)

17. **Psychoanalytic theory** interprets human development in terms of inner drives and motives, many of which are irrational and unconscious. (p. 17)

18. **Behaviorism** studies observable behavior; it is also called learning theory because it describes the laws and processes by which behavior is learned. (p. 19)

19. **Conditioning** is the learning process that occurs either through the association of two stimuli (classical conditioning) or through the use of positive or negative reinforcement or punishment (operant conditioning). (p. 20)

20. **Classical conditioning** is the learning process by which a neutral stimulus becomes associated with a meaningful one so that both are responded to in the same way. (p. 20)

21. **Operant conditioning** is the process by which a response is gradually learned through reinforcement or punishment. (p. 21)

22. **Reinforcement** is the process by which a particular action is followed by something desired, which makes the person or animal more likely to repeat the action. (p. 21)

23. An extension of behaviorism, **social learning theory** emphasizes that people often learn new behaviors through observation and imitation of other people. (p. 22)

24. **Cognitive theory** emphasizes that the way people think and understand the world shapes their attitudes, beliefs, and behaviors. (p. 22)

25. The **ecological-systems approach** to developmental research takes into consideration the interrelationship between the individual and the environment. (p. 24)

26. The **dynamic-systems theory** views human development as in a constant state of flux (dynamic) and as the product of the interaction between systems within the person and the environment. (p. 24)

27. **Scientific observation** is the unobtrusive watching and recording of participants' behavior in a systematic and objective manner, either in the laboratory or in a natural setting. (p. 26)

28. The **experiment** is the research method designed to untangle cause from effect by manipulating one variable to observe the effect on another variable. (p. 28)

29. The **independent variable** is the variable that is manipulated in an experiment to observe what effect it has on the dependent variable. (p. 28)

30. The **dependent variable** is the variable that may change as a result of whatever new condition or situation is added in an experiment. (p. 28)

    Example: In the study of the effects of a new drug on memory, the participants' memory is the dependent variable.

31. The **survey** is the research method in which information is collected from a large number of people, either through written questionnaires, personal interviews, or some other means. (p. 29)

32. In **cross-sectional research,** groups of people who differ in age but share other important characteristics are compared with regard to the variable under investigation. (p. 30)

33. In **longitudinal research,** the same group of individuals is followed over time, and their development is repeatedly assessed. (p. 32)

34. **Cross-sequential research** follows a group of people of different ages over time, thus combining the strengths of the cross-sectional and longitudinal methods. (p. 33)

35. **Correlation** is a number indicating the degree of relationship between two variables, such that one is likely (or unlikely) to occur when the other occurs or one is likely to increase (or decrease) when the other increases (or decreases). (p. 34)

36. **Quantitative research** collects data that are expressed with numbers. (p. 36)

37. **Qualitative research** collects non-numerical descriptions of participants' characteristic behaviors and ideas. (p. 36)

chapter 2

GENES AND PRENATAL Development

Chapter Overview

Conception occurs when the male and female reproductive cells—the sperm and ovum, respectively—come together to create a new, one-celled zygote with its own unique combination of genetic material. The genetic material furnishes the instructions for development—not only for obvious physical characteristics, such as sex, coloring, and body shape but also for certain psychological characteristics, such as bashfulness, moodiness, and vocational aptitude.

Every year, scientists make new discoveries and reach new understandings about genes and their effects on the development of individuals. This chapter presents some of their findings, including that most human characteristics are polygenic and multifactorial—the result of the interaction of many genetic and environmental influences. Perhaps the most important findings have come from research into the causes of genetic and chromosomal abnormalities. The chapter discusses the most common of these abnormalities and includes a section on genetic counseling.

Prenatal development is the most dramatic and extensive transformation of the entire life span. During prenatal development, the individual changes from a one-celled zygote to a complex human baby. This development is outlined in Chapter 2.

For the developing person, birth marks the most radical transition of the entire life span. No longer sheltered from the outside world, the fetus becomes a separate human being who begins life almost completely dependent upon his or her caregivers. Chapter 2 also examines the birth process and its possible variations and problems, including the importance of the parent–infant bond.

The chapter concludes with a discussion of how nature and nurture interact to affect development, focusing on alcoholism, nearsightedness, and certain birth defects, often caused by exposure to teratogens.

NOTE: Answer guidelines for all Chapter 2 questions begin on page 33.

Chapter Review

When you have finished reading the chapter, work through the material that follows to review it. Complete the sentences and answer the questions. In some cases, Study Tips explain how best to learn a difficult concept, while Think About It and Applications help you to know how well you understand the material. As you proceed, evaluate your performance for each section by consulting the answers beginning on page 41. Do not continue with the next section until you understand each answer. If you need to, review or reread the appropriate section in the textbook before continuing.

STUDY TIP: This chapter contains a lot of technical material that you might find difficult to master. Not only are there many terms for you to remember, but you must also understand the basic principles of how genes interact with environmental influences to affect development. Learning this material will require a great deal of rehearsal. Working the chapter review several times, making flash cards, and mentally reciting terms are all useful techniques for rehearsing this type of material.

The Beginning of Life (pp. 43–49)

1. The work of body cells is done under the direction of instructions stored in molecules of _______________. Each molecule is called a _______________.

2. With one exception, human cells have _______________ chromosomes, arranged in _______________ pairs.

STUDY TIP: It is easy to confuse the various elements of heredity (chromosomes, genes, and DNA). You might find it helpful to think of a metaphor. If chromosomes are the "books" of heredity, the genes that make each of us a distinctive human being are the "words," and DNA molecules are the "letters." You can also keep the relationship among genes, DNA, and chromosomes straight by thinking visually. Chromosomes are the largest of the units. They are made up of genes, which are in turn made up of DNA.

3. The human reproductive cells, which are called ________________, include the male's ________________ and the female's ________________. Each of these cells has only ________________ chromosomes.

4. When the gametes combine, a living cell called a ________________ is formed.

5. This new cell receives ________________ chromosomes from the father and ________________ from the mother. The genetic instructions in chromosomes are organized into units called ________________. These instructions are transmitted to cells via four chemicals that are abbreviated ________________, ________________, ________________ and ________________.

6. An organism's entire genetic inheritance is called its ________________. The actual appearance and manifest behavior of the person is called the ________________.

7. Genes with codes that vary from other versions of that gene are called ________________. The sum total of these genetic instructions for a given species is called its ________________.

8. Identical, or monozygotic, twins, who develop from one ________________, ________________ (are/are not) genetically identical. This occurs about once in every ________________ (how many?) conceptions.

9. Twins who begin life as two separate zygotes created by the fertilization of two ova are called ________________, or ________________, twins. Such twins have approximately ________________ percent of their genes in common.

10. The incidence of dizygotic births varies by the mother's ________________ and ________________.

11. The 44 chromosomes that are independent of the sex chromosomes are called ________________.

12. The developing person's sex is determined by the ________________ pair of chromosomes. In the female, this pair is composed of two ________________-shaped chromosomes and is designated ________________. In the male, this pair includes one ________________ and one ________________ chromosome and is therefore designated ________________.

13. The critical factor in the determination of a zygote's sex is which ________________ (sperm/ovum) reaches the other gamete first. The natural sex ratio at birth is about ________________. In a stressful pregnancy, ________________ (XX/XY) embryos are more likely to be miscarried, or ________________.

14. Most human characteristics are affected by many genes, and so they are ________________, and by many factors, and so they are ________________. To differentiate humans from other animals, ________________ genes, which control the interaction of other genes, are crucial.

15. A phenotype that reflects the sum of the contributions of all the genes involved in its determination illustrates the ________________ pattern of genetic interaction. Examples include genes that affect ________________ and ________________.

16. Less often, genes interact in a ________________ fashion. In one example of this pattern, some genes are more influential than others; this is called the ________________–________________ pattern. In this pattern, the more influential allele is called the ________________ gene, and the weaker one is called the ________________ gene.

17. A person who has a gene in his or her genotype that is not expressed in the phenotype but that can be passed on to the person's offspring is said to be a ________________ of that gene.

18. The percentage of the variation in a trait within a particular population, in a particular context and era, that can be traced to genes is called its ________________.

STUDY TIP: A common mistake in trying to understand the concept of heritability is to apply this statistic to the traits of an individual person. You need to remember that heritability refers to the variation in a trait that occurs within a large *group* of individuals that can be traced to genetic influences, not to the traits of an individual person. As an example, although research studies may demonstrate that the heritability of a particular trait is 60 percent, it is incorrect to conclude that there is a 60 percent probability that an individual who manifests that trait in his or her phenotype will inherit the trait. Remember that heritability is a general statistic that applies only to *populations*, not individuals.

19. If your mother is much taller than your father, it is most likely that your height will be
- **a.** about the same as your mother's because the X chromosome determines height.
- **b.** about the same as your father's because the Y chromosome determines height.
- **c.** somewhere between your mother's and father's heights because the genes for height are additive.
- **d.** greater than both your mother's and father's because of your grandfather's dominant gene.

20. Some men are color-blind because they inherit a particular recessive gene from their mothers. That recessive gene is carried on the ________________ chromosome.

21. Winona inherited a gene from her mother that, regardless of her father's contribution to her genotype, will be expressed in her phenotype. Evidently, the gene Winona received from her mother is a ________________ gene.

Genetic Problems (pp. 50–57)

22. Many fetuses with chromosomal abnormalities are ________________ ________________. Nevertheless, about 1 in every ________________ newborns has one chromosome too few or one too many, leading to a cluster of characteristics called a ________________.

23. The most common extra-chromosome syndrome is ________________ ________________, which is also called ________________-________________. Most individuals with this syndrome have special ________________ characteristics, and all are slow to develop ________________. People with this syndrome age ________________ (faster/more slowly) than other adults.

List several of the physical and psychological characteristics associated with Down syndrome.

24. About 1 in every 500 infants is either missing a ________________ chromosome or has two or more such chromosomes. One resulting syndrome is ________________ ________________, in which a girl inherits only one ________________ chromosome; another is ________________ ________________, in which a boy inherits the________________ chromosome pattern.

25. Most of the known single-gene disorders are ________________ (dominant/recessive). Genetic disorders usually ________________ (are/are not) seriously disabling. Severe dominant disorders are ________________ (common/rare) because people with these disorders usually ________________ (do/do not) have children.

26. One exception is the disorder that causes its victims to exhibit uncontrollable tics and explosive outbursts, called ________________ ________________.

27. Three common recessive disorders that are not sex-linked are ________________ ________________, ________________, and ________________-________________ ________________.

28. In some individuals, part of the X chromosome is attached by such a thin string of molecules that it seems about to break off; this abnormality is called ________________ ________________ syndrome. Another sex-linked condition is ________________, in which the blood does not ________________ normally. The most common X-linked condition is ________________ ________________.

THINK ABOUT IT: About 1 baby in 30 is born with a serious genetic problem. If this is so, you will have encountered many people who have such problems. Indeed, in any population of 30 people you might expect to encounter 1 person who has a serious genetic problem. Remember, however, that "serious" does not mean "disabling." Think back to your elementary school days. About how many children were in your fifth- or sixth-grade class? Were you aware that any of these children had a serious genetic problem?

APPLICATIONS:

29. Randy's son was born with an XXY chromosomal pattern. It is likely that his son's condition will
  - **a.** go undetected until puberty.
  - **b.** benefit from hormone supplements.
  - **c.** develop some female sex characteristics at puberty.
  - **d.** have all of these characteristics.

30. Which of the following is an inherited abnormality that quite possibly could develop into a recognizable syndrome?
  - **a.** Just before dividing to form a sperm or ovum, corresponding gene segments of a chromosome pair break off and are exchanged.
  - **b.** Just before conception, a chromosome pair splits imprecisely, resulting in a mixture of cells.
  - **c.** A person inherits an X chromosome in which part of the chromosome is attached to the rest of it by a very slim string of molecules.
  - **d.** A person inherits a recessive gene on his Y chromosome.

31. Jason has an inherited, dominant disorder that causes him to exhibit uncontrollable tics and explosive outbursts. Jason most likely would be diagnosed with ________________ ________________.

32. Sixteen-year-old Joey experiences some mental slowness and hearing and heart problems, yet he is able to care for himself and is unusually sweet-tempered. Joey probably has ________________ ________________.

33. Through ________________ ________________, couples today can learn more about their genes and about their chances of conceiving a child with chromosomal or other genetic abnormalities. Methods of postconception testing include ________________ ________________, tests for pregnancy-associated plasma protein, ________________-________________ assay, ________________, ________________ ________________ ________________ (CVS), and ________________.

34. In the United States and many other nations, every newborn is tested for ________________, a recessive condition that will result in severe retardation if the common food substance ________________ is consumed.

THINK ABOUT IT: Genetic testing and counseling have made wondrous strides in recent years. At the same time, these advances have created potential new dilemmas that earlier cohorts of parents-to-be were less likely to face. Consider, for example, the following question: If your unborn child was fated to develop a life-threatening chronic illness, would you want him or her to know? Would you want to know? Why or why not?

From Zygote to Newborn (pp. 57–63)

35. Prenatal development is divided into ________________ main periods. The first two weeks of development are called the ________________ period; from the ________________ week through the ________________ week is known as the ________________ period; and from this point until birth is the ________________ period.

36. Within hours after conception, the zygote begins to ________________ and ________________. At about the eight-cell stage, the cells start to ________________, with various cells beginning to specialize and reproduce at different rates. As a result of these processes, cells change from being ________________ ________________ that are able to produce any type of cell to becoming specialized cells.

37. One consequence of this process is that cells on the outer side of the developing mass become the ________________. About 10 days after conception, the zygote begins to burrow into the lining of the uterus, a process called ________________. This process ________________ (is/is not) automatic.

38. At the beginning of the period of the embryo, a thin line down the middle of the developing individual forms a structure that will become the ________________ ________________, which becomes the ________________ ________________ and eventually will develop into the ________________ ________________ ________________.

Briefly describe the major features of development during the second month.

39. From the start of the ninth week after conception until birth, the organism is called the ________________.

40. The genital organs are fully formed by week ________________. If the fetus is a male, the ________________ gene commands development of the male ________________ ________________. Without that gene, the fetus begins to develop female organs.

41. By the end of the ________________ month, the fetus is fully formed. Development proceeds from the head to tail, a pattern called ________________ growth, with the body's extremities developing last, a pattern called ________________ growth. These developmental patterns may be visible on an ultrasound, or ________________.

42. The age at which a fetus has at least some chance of surviving outside the uterus is called the ________________ ________________ ________________, which occurs about ________________ weeks after conception. This barrier ________________ (has/has not) been reduced by advances in neonatal care, probably because maintaining life depends on some ________________ response.

THINK ABOUT IT: Compared with the gestation periods of other mammals, the nine-month gestation period in humans is relatively long. Compared with the slow human development in other aspects of the life span, however, nine months seems a little on the short side. In fact, some evolutionary biologists have suggested that humans ought to be *in utero* 15 or 16 months! What sorts of evolutionary pressures might have contributed to this "compromise" in the time allotted for prenatal development?

43. Karen and Brad report to their neighbors that, 6 weeks after conception, a sonogram of their child-to-be revealed female sex organs. The neighbors are skeptical of their statement because
   a. sonograms are never administered before the ninth week.
   b. sonograms only reveal the presence or absence of male sex organs.
   c. the fetus does not begin to develop female sex organs until about the eighth week.
   d. it is impossible to determine that a woman is pregnant until seven weeks after conception.

Birth (pp. 63–71)

44. About ________________ (how many?) weeks after conception, the fetal brain signals the release of certain ________________ into the mother's bloodstream, which trigger her ________________ ________________ to contract and relax. The normal birth process begins when these contractions become regular. The average length of labor is ________________ hours for first births and usually quicker for subsequent births.

45. Some babies are born in the ________________ position, with buttocks or, rarely, feet first. Such babies are generally delivered surgically in order to prevent the state of oxygen deprivation called ________________.

46. The newborn is usually rated on the ________________ ________________, which assigns a score of 0, 1, or 2 to each of the following five characteristics: ________________ ________________. This rating is made twice, at ________________ minute(s) after birth and again at ________________ minutes. If the second score is ________________ or better, all is well.

47. A growing number of North American mothers today use a professional birth coach, or ________________, to assist them.

48. In about 31 percent of U.S. births, a surgical procedure called a ________________ ________________ is performed.

49. Newborns who weigh less than ________________ are classified as ________________-________________ babies. Below 3 pounds, 5 ounces, they are called ________________-________________-________________ babies; at less than 2 pounds, 3 ounces, they are ________________-________________-________________ babies. Worldwide, rates of this condition ________________ (vary/do not vary) from nation to nation.

50. Babies who are born 3 or more weeks before the standard 38 weeks have elapsed are called ________________.

51. Infants who weigh substantially less than they should, given how much time has passed since conception, are called ________________ ________________ ________________ ________________.

52. Causes of SGA are many and varied, including ________________ and ________________, ________________, ________________, and ________________. However, maternal ________________ use is a more common reason.

53. Another other common reason for low birthweight is ________________ births.

54. The incidence of birth complications can be reduced by a ________________ father-to-be and other family members.

55. LBW babies are more likely to become adults who are ________________ and have health problems, such as ________________ and disorders affecting the ________________.

56. For vulnerable infants, parents are encouraged to help with early caregiving in the hospital. This ________________ stress in both infant and parents. One example of early caregiving is ________________ ________________, in which mothers of low-birthweight infants spend at least an hour a day holding their infants between their breasts.

57. Parents can also help their newborn by administering ________________ therapy.

58. Some new mothers experience a profound feeling of sadness called ________________ ________________.

59. The term used to describe the close relationship that begins within the first hours after birth is the ________________-________________ ________________. Research on monkeys using the strategy of ________________-________________ suggests that bonding need not occur immediately.

STUDY TIP: "Going metric" will help you remember the differences among low-birthweight (LBW), very-low-birthweight (VLBW), and extremely-low-birthweight (ELBW) babies. Remember two numbers: 2,500 (grams) and 500 (grams). The LBW threshold is a weight below 2,500 grams. Two decreases of 500 grams each are the criteria for VLBW (2,500 grams minus [2 × 500] equals 1,500 grams). For ELBW, it's three decreases of 500 grams each (2,500 grams minus (3 × 500 grams) equals 1,000 grams). To remember the criterion for a preterm birth, think of "3 (weeks)," which rhymes with "pre." Thus, a preterm birth is one that occurs 3 or more weeks early. Small for gestational age (SGA) is self-defining. A SGA baby is one who gained weight too slowly during gestation (pregnancy).

THINK ABOUT IT: Thanks to recent medical breakthroughs, even extremely-low-birthweight infants have a decent chance of surviving. As a result, ethical and social dilemmas often arise regarding the rights of the fetus as a separate individual. For example, judges have ordered pregnant women who were close to term to have blood transfusions and surgical births, even when those procedures were unwanted by the women. How do you feel about this? Who should have the authority to decide in such cases?

APPLICATIONS:

60. Three-year-old Kenny was born underweight and premature. Today, he is small for his age. What would be the most likely reason for Kenny's small size? ________________

61. Your sister and brother-in-law, who are about to adopt a 6-month-old, are worried that the child will never bond with them. What advice should you offer?

a. Tell them that, unfortunately, this is true; they would be better off waiting for a younger child who has not yet bonded.
b. Tell them that, although the first year is a biologically determined critical period for attachment, there is a 50/50 chance that the child will bond with them.
c. Tell them that bonding is a long-term process between parent and child that is determined by the nature of interaction throughout infancy, childhood, and beyond.
d. Tell them that if the child is female, there is a good chance that she will bond with them, even at this late stage.

62. Which of the following newborns would be most likely to have problems in body structure and functioning?
a. Anton, whose Apgar score is 6
b. Debora, whose Apgar score is 7
c. Sheila, whose Apgar score is 3
d. Simon, whose Apgar score is 9

63. At birth, Clarence was classified as small for gestational age. It is likely that Clarence
a. was born in a rural hospital.
b. suffered several months of prenatal malnutrition.
c. was born in a large city hospital.
d. comes from a family with a history of such births.

64. Of the following, who is most likely to give birth to a low-birthweight child?
a. 21-year-old Janice, who was herself a low-birthweight baby
b. 25-year-old May Ling, who gained 25 pounds during her pregnancy
c. 16-year-old Donna, who diets frequently despite being underweight
d. 30-year-old Maria, who has already given birth to four children

65. An infant is born 38 weeks after conception, weighing 4 pounds. How would that infant be classified in terms of weight and timing?

____

66. An infant who was born at 35 weeks, weighing 6 pounds, would be called a ______________ infant.

67. One minute and five minutes after he was born, Malcolm was tested using the Apgar scale. The characteristics of a newborn tested by the scale are ______________________________

______________________________.

Nature, Nurture, and the Phenotype (pp. 71–78)

68. State four general principles of genetic influences on development that virtually all developmentalists accept.

a. ______________________________

____

b. ______________________________

____

____

c. ______________________________

____

d. ______________________________

____

69. The increase in the rate of the vision problem of ______________, or ______________, among children in East Asia has been attributed to the increasing amount of time spent by children in the ______________ ______________. In other parts of the world, this problem may be caused by genes or by poor ______________, especially lack of ______________ ______________.

70. Certain ______________ traits encourage drinking and drug taking. These traits include ______________________________.

Women are advised to ______________ (completely abstain from/drink only moderate amounts of) alcohol during pregnancy because high doses of alcohol may cause ______________ ______________ ______________.

71. Harmful agents and conditions that can result in birth defects, called ______________, include ______________________________.

72. Substances that impair the child's action and intellect by harming the brain are called ______________ ______________.

73. The time when a particular part of the body is most susceptible to teratogenic damage is called its ______________ ______________. This is followed by a ______________ ______________ during which exposure can interfere with recent growth. For physical structure and form, this is the ______________ ______________. However,

_______________ _______________ are harmful to the brain at any time.

74. Some teratogens have a _______________ effect—that is, the substances are harmless until exposure reaches a certain level.

STUDY TIP: To emphasize the variety of teratogens to which pregnant women may be exposed every day, imagine that you have decided to become a parent. If you are a male, some teratogens to which you are exposed may affect your unborn child. Make a list of all the teratogens you have experienced recently that you would want to avoid to ensure that your body is teratogen-free for the year during which fertilization and gestation occur. If you are stumped, check the Internet for ideas.

APPLICATIONS:

75. Genetically, Claude's potential height is 6'0. Because he did not eat a balanced diet, however, he grew to only 5'9". Claude's actual height is an example of a _______________ .

76. A person's skin turns yellow-orange as a result of a carrot-juice diet regimen. This is an example of
    a. an environmental influence.
    b. an alteration in genotype.
    c. polygenic inheritance.
    d. incomplete dominance.

77. Laurie and Brad, who both have a history of alcoholism in their families, are concerned that the child they hope to have will inherit a genetic predisposition to alcoholism. Based on information presented in the text, what advice should you offer them?
    a. "Stop worrying, alcoholism is only weakly genetic."
    b. "It is almost certain that your child will become alcoholic."
    c. "Social influences, such as the family and peer environment, play a critical role in determining whether alcoholism is expressed."
    d. "Wait to have children until you are both middle aged, in order to see if the two of you become alcoholic."

Progress Test 1

Multiple-Choice Questions

Circle your answers to the following questions and check them against the answers beginning on page 35. If your answer is incorrect, read the explanation for why it is incorrect and then consult the appropriate pages of the text (in parentheses following the correct answer).

1. When a sperm and an ovum merge, a one-celled _______________ is formed.
    a. zygote c. gamete
    b. reproductive cell d. monozygote

2. Genes are separate units that provide the chemical instructions that each cell needs to become
    a. a zygote.
    b. a chromosome.
    c. a specific part of a functioning human body.
    d. deoxyribonucleic acid (DNA).

3. In the male, the 23rd pair of chromosomes is designated _______________ ; in the female, this pair is designated _______________.
    a. XX; XY c. XO; XXY
    b. XY; XX d. XXY; XO

4. Because the 23rd pair of chromosomes in females is XX, each ovum carries an:
    a. XX zygote. c. XY zygote.
    b. X zygote. d. X chromosome.

5. When a zygote splits, the two identical, independent clusters that develop become
    a. dizygotic twins. c. fraternal twins.
    b. monozygotic twins. d. trizygotic twins.

6. Most of the known single-gene disorders are
    a. dominant. c. seriously disabling.
    b. recessive. d. sex-linked.

7. When we say that a characteristic is multifactorial, we mean that:
    a. many genes are involved.
    b. many environmental factors are involved.
    c. many genetic and environmental factors are involved.
    d. the characteristic is polygenic.

8. Genes are segments of molecules of:
    a. genotype.
    b. deoxyribonucleic acid (DNA).
    c. karyotype.
    d. phenotype.

9. In the United States, newborns are tested for the recessive genetic disorder
    a. phenylketonuria.
    b. Alzheimer's disease.
    c. Down syndrome.
    d. fragile X syndrome.

10. A chromosomal abnormality that affects males only involves a(n)
   a. XO chromosomal pattern.
   b. XXX chromosomal pattern.
   c. YY chromosomal pattern.
   d. XXY chromosomal pattern.

11. Some developmentalists believe that the epidemic increase in nearsightedness among children in Hong Kong, Singapore, and Taiwan is partly the result of
   a. the recent epidemic of rubella.
   b. vitamin A deficiency.
   c. the increasing amount of time spent by children in close study.
   d. mutations in the Pax6 gene.

12. Babies born with trisomy-21 (Down syndrome) are often
   a. born to older parents.
   b. unusually aggressive.
   c. abnormally tall by adolescence.
   d. blind.

13. To say that a trait is polygenic means that
   a. many genes make it more likely that the individual will inherit the trait.
   b. several genes must be present in order for the individual to inherit the trait.
   c. the trait is multifactorial.
   d. most people carry genes for the trait.

14. Some genetic diseases are recessive, so the child cannot inherit the condition unless both parents
   a. have Klinefelter syndrome.
   b. carry the same recessive gene.
   c. have XO chromosomes.
   d. have the disease.

15. The third through the eighth week after conception is called the
   a. embryonic period.
   b. ovum period.
   c. fetal period.
   d. germinal period.

16. The primitive streak develops into the
   a. respiratory system.
   b. umbilical cord.
   c. brain and spinal column.
   d. circulatory system.

17. To say that a teratogen has a "threshold effect" means that it is
   a. virtually harmless until exposure reaches a certain level.
   b. harmful only to low-birthweight infants.
   c. harmful to certain developing organs during periods when these organs are developing most rapidly.
   d. harmful only if the pregnant woman's weight does not increase by a certain minimum amount during her pregnancy.

18. The most critical factor in attaining the age of viability is development of the
   a. placenta.
   b. eyes.
   c. brain.
   d. skeleton.

19. An embryo begins to develop male sex organs if __________, and female sex organs if __________.
   a. genes on the *Y* chromosome send a signal; no signal is sent from an *X* chromosome
   b. genes on the *Y* chromosome send a signal; genes on the *X* chromosome send a signal
   c. genes on the *X* chromosome send a signal; no signal is sent from an *X* chromosome
   d. genes on the *X* chromosome send a signal; genes on the *Y* chromosome send a signal

20. A teratogen
   a. cannot cross the placenta during the period of the embryo.
   b. is usually inherited from the mother.
   c. can be counteracted by good nutrition most of the time.
   d. may be a virus, a drug, a chemical, or environmental pollutants.

21. The birth process begins
   a. when the fetus moves into the right position.
   b. when the uterus begins to contract at regular intervals to push the fetus out.
   c. about eight hours (for firstborns) after the uterus begins to contract at regular intervals.
   d. when the baby's head appears at the opening of the vagina.

22. The Apgar scale is administered
   a. only if the newborn is in obvious distress.
   b. once, just after birth.
   c. twice, one minute and five minutes after birth.
   d. repeatedly during the newborn's first hours.

23. Low-birthweight babies born near the due date but weighing substantially less than they should
   a. are classified as preterm.
   b. are called small for gestational age.
   c. usually have no sex organs.
   d. show many signs of immaturity.

Matching Items

Match each term with its corresponding description or definition.

Terms

_______ 1. gametes
_______ 2. chromosome
_______ 3. genotype
_______ 4. phenotype
_______ 5. monozygotic
_______ 6. dizygotic
_______ 7. additive
_______ 8. fragile X syndrome
_______ 9. carrier
_______ 10. zygote
_______ 11. alleles
_______ 12. XX
_______ 13. XY

Descriptions or Definitions

a. chromosome pair inherited by genetic females
b. identical twins
c. sperm and ovum
d. the first cell of the developing person
e. a person who has a recessive gene in his or her genotype that is not expressed in the phenotype
f. fraternal twins
g. a pattern in which each gene in question makes an active contribution to the final outcome
h. a DNA molecule
i. the behavioral or physical expression of genetic potential
j. a chromosomal abnormality
k. alternate versions of a gene
l. chromosome pair inherited by genetic males
m. a person's entire genetic inheritance

Progress Test 2

Progress Test 2 should be completed during a final chapter review. Answer the following questions after you thoroughly understand the correct answers for the Chapter Review and Progress Test 1.

Multiple-Choice Questions

1. Which of the following provides the best broad description of the relationship between heredity and environment?
a. Heredity is the primary influence, with environment affecting development only in severe situations.
b. Heredity and environment contribute equally to development.
c. Environment is the major influence on physical characteristics.
d. Heredity directs the individual's potential, and environment determines whether and to what degree the individual reaches that potential.

2. If a man carries the recessive gene for cystic fibrosis and his wife does not, the chances of their having a child with cystic fibrosis
a. is one in four.
b. is 50/50.
c. is zero.
d. depends on the wife's ethnic background.

3. With the exception of sperm and egg cells, each human cell contains:
a. 23 genes.
b. 23 chromosomes.
c. 46 genes.
d. 46 chromosomes.

4. The disorder in which a genetic female inherits only one X chromosome is called
a. trisomy-21.
b. Down syndrome.
c. Turner syndrome.
d. Klinefelter syndrome.

5. Dizygotic twins result when
a. a single egg is fertilized by a sperm and then splits.
b. a single egg is fertilized by two different sperm.
c. two eggs are fertilized by two different sperm.
d. either a single egg is fertilized by one sperm or two eggs are fertilized by two different sperm.

6. Molecules of DNA that in humans are organized into 23 complementary pairs are called
a. zygotes.
b. genes.
c. chromosomes.
d. ova.

7. Shortly after the zygote is formed, it begins the processes of duplication and division. Each resulting new cell has
   a. the same number of chromosomes as was contained in the zygote.
   b. half the number of chromosomes as was contained in the zygote.
   c. twice, then four times, then eight times the number of chromosomes as was contained in the zygote.
   d. all the chromosomes except those that determine sex.

8. If an ovum is fertilized by a sperm bearing a Y chromosome
   a. a female will develop.
   b. cell division will result.
   c. a male will develop.
   d. spontaneous abortion will occur.

9. When the male cells in the testes and the female cells in the ovaries divide to produce gametes, the process differs from that in the production of all other cells. As a result of the different process, the gametes have
   a. one rather than both members of each chromosome pair.
   b. 23 chromosome pairs.
   c. X but not Y chromosomes.
   d. chromosomes from both parents.

10. Most human traits are
   a. polygenic and multifactorial.
   b. determined by a single gene.
   c. determined by dominant–recessive patterns.
   d. unaffected by environmental factors.

11. Genotype is to phenotype as ______________ is to ________________ .
   a. genetic potential; physical expression
   b. physical expression; genetic potential
   c. sperm; ovum
   d. gamete; zygote

12. The genes that influence height and skin color interact according to the ________________ pattern.
   a. dominant–recessive
   b. X-linked
   c. additive
   d. nonadditive

13. X-linked recessive genes explain why some traits seem to be passed from
   a. father to son.
   b. father to daughter.
   c. mother to daughter.
   d. mother to son.

14. In order, the correct sequence of prenatal stages of development is
   a. embryo; germinal; fetus
   b. germinal; fetus; embryo
   c. germinal; embryo; fetus
   d. ovum; fetus; embryo

15. Monika is preparing for the birth of her first child. If all proceeds normally, she can expect that her labor will last about
   a. 7 hours.
   b. 8 hours.
   c. 10 hours.
   d. 12 hours.

16. Kangaroo care refers to
   a. the rigid attachment formed between mothers and offspring in the animal kingdom
   b. the fragmented care that the children of single parents often receive.
   c. a program of increased involvement by mothers of low-birthweight infants.
   d. none of these.

17. Among the characteristics rated on the Apgar scale are
   a. shape of the newborn's head and nose.
   b. presence of body hair.
   c. interactive behaviors.
   d. muscle tone and color.

18. A newborn is classified as low birthweight if he or she weighs less than
   a. 7 pounds.
   b. 6 pounds.
   c. $5^1/_2$ pounds.
   d. 4 pounds.

19. Which of the following is NOT true regarding alcohol use and pregnancy?
   a. Alcohol in high doses is a proven teratogen.
   b. Not every pregnant woman who drinks heavily has a newborn with fetal alcohol syndrome.
   c. Most doctors in the United States advise pregnant women to use alcohol in moderation during pregnancy.
   d. Only after a fetus is born does fetal alcohol syndrome become apparent.

20. Which Apgar score indicates that a newborn is in normal health?
   a. 4
   b. 5
   c. 6
   d. 7

21. The critical period for preventing physical defects appears to be the
    a. zygote period.
    b. embryonic period.
    c. fetal period.
    d. entire pregnancy.

22. By the eighth week after conception, the embryo has almost all the basic organs EXCEPT the
    a. skeleton.
    b. elbows and knees.
    c. male and female sex organs.
    d. fingers and toes.

23. A newborn is classified as preterm if he or she is born
    a. one or more weeks early.
    b. two or more weeks early
    c. three or more weeks early.
    d. four or more weeks early.

Matching Items

Match each definition or description with its corresponding term.

Terms

_______ 1. embryonic period
_______ 2. fetal period
_______ 3. placenta
_______ 4. preterm
_______ 5. teratogens
_______ 6. anoxia
_______ 7. doula
_______ 8. critical period
_______ 9. primitive streak
_______ 10. fetal alcohol syndrome
_______ 11. germinal period

Definitions or Descriptions

a. term for the period during which a developing baby's body parts are most susceptible to damage
b. agents and conditions that can damage the developing organism
c. the time when viability is attained
d. the precursor of the central nervous system
e. lack of oxygen, which, if prolonged during the birth process, may lead to brain damage
f. characterized by abnormal facial characteristics, slowed growth, behavior problems, and mental retardation
g. a woman who helps with the birth process
h. the life-giving organ that nourishes the embryo and fetus
i. when implantation occurs
j. the prenatal period when all major body structures begin to form
k. a baby born 3 or more weeks early

True or False Items

Write T (*true*) or F (*false*) on the line in front of each statement.

_______ 1. Most human characteristics are multifactorial, caused by the interaction of genetic and environmental factors.
_______ 2. Most dominant disorders are sex-linked.
_______ 3. Research suggests that susceptibility to alcoholism is at least partly the result of genetic inheritance.
_______ 4. The human reproductive cells (ova and sperm) are called gametes.
_______ 5. Only a very few human traits are polygenic.
_______ 6. The zygote contains all the biologically inherited information—the genes and chromosomes—that a person will have during his or her life.
_______ 7. Many genetic conditions are recessive; thus, a child will have the condition even if only the mother carries the gene.
_______ 8. Two people who have the same phenotype may have a different genotype for a trait such as eye color.
_______ 9. When cells divide to produce reproductive cells (gametes), each sperm or ovum receives only 23 chromosomes, half as many as the original cell.

_______ 10. Eight weeks after conception, the embryo has formed almost all the basic organs.

_______ 11. In general, behavioral teratogens have the greatest effect during the embryonic period.

_______ 12. The effects of cigarette smoking during pregnancy remain highly controversial.

_______ 13. The Apgar scale is used to measure vital signs such as heart rate, breathing, and reflexes.

_______ 14. Research has shown that immediate mother–infant contact at birth is necessary for the normal emotional development of the child.

_______ 15. Low birthweight is often correlated with maternal malnutrition.

_______ 16. Cesarean sections are rarely performed in the United States today because of the resulting danger to the fetus.

Key Terms

Using your own words, write on a separate piece of paper a brief definition or explanation of each of the following terms.

1. deoxyribonucleic acid (DNA)
2. chromosome
3. gamete
4. zygote
5. gene
6. genotype
7. phenotype
8. allele
9. genome
10. monozygotic (MZ) twins
11. dizygotic (DZ) twins
12. XX
13. XY
14. polygenic
15. multifactorial
16. regulator gene
17. additive gene
18. dominant–recessive pattern
19. carrier
20. heritability
21. Down syndrome
22. fragile X syndrome
23. genetic counseling
24. phenylketonuria (PKU)
25. germinal period
26. embryonic period
27. fetal period
28. placenta
29. implantation
30. embryo
31. fetus
32. sonogram
33. age of viability
34. Apgar scale
35. doula
36. cesarean section
37. low birthweight (LBW)
38. very low birthweight (VLBW)
39. extremely low birthweight (ELBW)
40. preterm birth
41. small for gestational age (SGA)
42. kangaroo care
43. postpartum depression
44. parent–infant bond
45. fetal alcohol syndrome (FAS)
46. teratogens
47. threshold effect

Answers

CHAPTER REVIEW

1. DNA; chromosome
2. 46; 23
3. gametes; sperm; ovum; 23
4. zygote
5. 23; 23; genes; A, T, C, G
6. genotype; phenotype
7. alleles; genome
8. zygote; are; 250
9. dizygotic; fraternal; 50
10. ethnicity; age
11. autosomes
12. 23rd; X; XX; X; Y; XY
13. sperm; 50/50; XY; spontaneously aborted

14. polygenic; multifactorial; regulator
15. additive; height; skin color (or hair curliness)
16. nonadditive; dominant–recessive; dominant; recessive
17. carrier
18. heritability
19. **c.** is the answer. It is unlikely that the other factors account for height differences from one generation to the next.
20. X. Color blindness is X-linked. Since the Y chromosome is much smaller than the X, an X-linked recessive gene almost never has a dominant counterpart on the Y. Thus, color blindness most often occurs in males.
21. dominant. The dominant gene is always expressed in the person's phenotype. For a recessive gene to be expressed, the individual must inherit a recessive gene from both parents.
22. spontaneously aborted; 200; syndrome
23. Down syndrome; trisomy-21; facial; language; faster

Most people with Down syndrome have certain facial characteristics—a thick tongue, round face, slanted eyes—as well as distinctive hands, feet, and fingerprints. Many also have hearing problems, heart abnormalities, muscle weakness, and short stature. Almost all experience some mental slowness, especially in language.

24. sex; Turner syndrome; X; Klinefelter syndrome; XXY
25. dominant; are not; rare; do not
26. Tourette syndrome
27. cystic fibrosis, thalassemia, sickle-cell anemia
28. fragile X; hemophilia; clot; color blindness
29. **d.** is the answer. This is referred to as Klinefelter's syndrome. A boy with an extra X chromosome will be somewhat slow in elementary school, but not until age 12 or so will it be clear that something is wrong.
30. **c.** is the answer. This describes the fragile X syndrome. The phenomenon described in a. merely contributes to genetic diversity; b. is an example of a particular nonadditive gene interaction pattern. Regarding d., for a recessive gene to be expressed, both parents must pass it on to the child.
31. Tourette syndrome
32. Down syndrome
33. genetic counseling; preimplantation testing; alpha-fetoprotein; sonogram; chronic villi sampling; amniocentesis
34. phenylketonuria (PKU); phenylalanine
35. three; germinal; third; eighth; embryonic; fetal
36. duplicate; divide; differentiate; stem cells
37. placenta; implantation; is not
38. primitive streak; neural tube; central nervous system

The head begins to take shape as eyes, ears, nose, and mouth form. A tiny blood vessel that will become the heart begins to pulsate. The upper arms, then the forearms, hands, palms, and webbed fingers appear. Legs, feet, and webbed toes follow. At eight weeks, the embryo has all the basic organs and body parts, including a sexual-reproductive system that is the same in both sexes.

39. fetus
40. 12; SRY; sex organs
41. third; cephalocaudal; proximodistal; sonogram
42. age of viability; 22; has not; brain
43. **c.** is the answer. Before that time, the embryo's sex organs are the same in both males and females.
44. 38; hormones; uterine muscles; 12
45. breech; anoxia
46. Apgar scale; heart rate, breathing, muscle tone, color, and reflexes; one; five; 7
47. doula
48. cesarean section
49. 2,500 grams (5 1/2 pounds); low-birthweight; very-low-birthweight; extremely-low-birthweight; vary
50. preterm
51. small for gestational age
52. genetics; illness; infection; exhaustion; malnutrition; drug
53. multiple
54. supportive
55. overweight; diabetes; heart
56. reduces; kangaroo care
57. massage
58. postpartum depression
59. parent–infant bond; cross-fostering
60. Kenny's mother smoked heavily during her pregnancy. Although every psychoactive drug slows prenatal growth, tobacco is the most prevalent cause of SGA.
61. **c.** is the answer.

62. **c.** is the answer. If a newborn's Apgar score is below 7, the infant may have a problem. The lower the score, the more likely that a problem exists.
63. **b.** is the answer. Where a baby is born generally will not affect its size at birth. And certainly size is not hereditary.
64. **c.** is the answer. Donna's risk factor for having an LBW baby is her weight (teens tend not to eat well and can be undernourished).
65. low-birthweight; small-for-gestational age. Thirty-eight weeks is full term, so a baby at 4 pounds would be small-for-gestational age and, of course, low birthweight.
66. preterm. Any birth before 38 weeks is preterm.
67. reflexes, breathing, muscle tone, heart rate, and color
68. **a.** Genes affect every aspect of human behavior.

    b. Most environmental influences on children raised in the same household are not shared.

    c. Nongenetic influences begin at conception and continue lifelong, sometimes altering genetic instructions.

    d. People of all ages choose friends and environments, in a process called niche-picking, that are compatible with their genes.
69. nearsightedness; myopia; close study of books and papers; nutrition; vitamin A
70. genetic; a quick temper, sensation seeking, and high anxiety; completely abstain from; fetal alcohol syndrome
71. teratogens; viruses, drugs, chemicals, pollutants, extreme stress, and malnutrition
72. behavioral teratogens
73. critical period; sensitive period; first two months; psychoactive drugs
74. threshold
75. phenotype. The phenotype is the observable characteristics of a person. Genotype is the individual's entire genetic inheritance, or genetic potential.
76. **a.** is the answer. Genotype is a person's genetic potential, established at conception. Polygenic inheritance refers to the influence of many genes on a particular trait. Incomplete dominance refers to the phenotype being influenced primarily, but not exclusively, by the dominant gene.
77. **c.** is the answer. Despite a strong genetic influence on alcoholism, the environment also plays a critical role.

PROGRESS TEST 1

Multiple-Choice Questions

1. **a.** is the answer. (p. 44)

    b. & c. The reproductive cells (sperm and ova), which are also called gametes, are individual entities.

    d. Monozygote refers to one member of a pair of identical twins.
2. **c.** is the answer. (p. 44)

    a. The zygote is the first cell of the developing person.

    b. Chromosomes are molecules of DNA that *carry* genes.

    d. DNA molecules contain genetic information.
3. **b.** is the answer. (p. 47)
4. **d.** is the answer. When the gametes are formed, one member of each chromosome pair splits off; because in females both are X chromosomes, each ovum must carry an X chromosome. (p. 47)

    a., b., & c. The zygote refers to the merged sperm and ovum that is the first new cell of the developing individual.
5. **b.** is the answer. *Mono* means "one." Thus, monozygotic twins develop from one zygote. (p. 46)

    a. & c. Dizygotic, or fraternal, twins develop from two (*di*) zygotes.

    d. A trizygotic birth would result in triplets (*tri*), rather than twins.
6. **a.** is the answer. (p. 51)

    c. & d. Most dominant disorders are neither seriously disabling nor sex-linked.
7. **c.** is the answer. (p. 48)

    a., b., & d. *Polygenic* means "many genes"; *multifactorial* means "many factors," which are not limited to either genetic or environmental factors.
8. **b.** is the answer. (p. 44)

    a. Genotype is a person's genetic potential.

    c. A karyotype is a picture of a person's chromosomes.

    d. Phenotype is the actual expression of a genotype.
9. **a.** is the answer. (p. 55)
10. **d.** is the answer. (pp. 50–51)

    a. & b. These chromosomal abnormalities affect females.

    c. There is no such abnormality.

11. **c.** is the answer. (p. 72)

a. Rubella has not been mentioned as a major reason for the recent increase in nearsightedness in these countries.

b. Vitamin A deficiencies may be a factor in the vision problems of children among certain African ethnic groups.

d. The rapid changes in the prevalence of nearsightedness suggest that an environmental factor is the culprit.

12. **a.** is the answer. (p. 50)

13. **b.** is the answer. (p. 48)

14. **b.** is the answer. (p. 51)

a. & c. These abnormalities involve the sex chromosomes, not genes.

d. For an offspring to inherit a recessive condition, the parents need only be carriers of the recessive gene in their genotypes; they need not actually have the disease.

15. **a.** is the answer. (p. 57)

b. This term, which refers to the germinal period, is not used in the text.

c. The fetal period is from the ninth week until birth.

d. The germinal period covers the first two weeks.

16. **c.** is the answer. (p. 60)

17. **a.** is the answer. (p. 76)

b., c., & d. Although low birthweight (b.), critical periods of organ development (c.), and maternal malnutrition (d.) are all hazardous to the developing person during prenatal development, none is an example of a threshold effect.

18. **c.** is the answer. (p. 61)

19. **d.** is the answer. (p. 47)

20. **d.** is the answer. (p. 73)

a. In general, teratogens can cross the placenta at any time.

b. Teratogens are agents in the environment, not heritable genes (although *susceptibility* to individual teratogens has a genetic component).

c. Although nutrition is an important factor in healthy prenatal development, the text does not suggest that nutrition alone can usually counteract the harmful effects of teratogens.

21. **b.** is the answer. (p. 63)

22. **c.** is the answer. (p. 63)

23. **b.** is the answer. (p. 68)

Matching Items

1. c (p. 43)	**6.** f (p. 47)	**11.** k (pp. 44–45)
2. h (p. 43)	**7.** g (p. 48)	**12.** a (p. 47)
3. m (p. 44)	**8.** j (p. 51)	**13.** l (p. 47)
4. i (p. 44)	**9.** e (p. 49)	
5. b (p. 46)	**10.** d (p. 44)	

PROGRESS TEST 2

Multiple-Choice Questions

1. **d.** is the answer. (p. 71)

2. **c.** is the answer. Cystic fibrosis is a recessive-gene disorder; therefore, for a child to inherit this disease, he or she must receive the recessive gene from both parents. (p. 51)

3. **d.** is the answer. (pp. 43–44)

a. & c. Human cells contain thousands of genes.

4. **c.** is the answer. (p. 50)

a. & b. This syndrome involves inheriting an *extra* chromosome.

d. This syndrome involves inheriting three sex chromosomes in an XXY pattern.

5. **c.** is the answer. (p. 47)

a. This would result in monozygotic twins.

b. Only one sperm can fertilize an ovum.

d. A single egg fertilized by one sperm would produce a single offspring or monozygotic twins.

6. **c.** is the answer. (p. 43)

a. Zygotes are fertilized ova.

b. Genes are the smaller units of heredity that are organized into sequences on chromosomes.

d. Ova are female reproductive cells.

7. **a.** is the answer. (p. 44)

8. **c.** is the answer. The ovum will contain an X chromosome; with the sperm's Y chromosome, it will produce the male XY pattern. (p. 47)

a. Only if the ovum is fertilized by an X chromosome from the sperm will a female develop.

b. Cell division will occur regardless of whether the sperm contributes an X or a Y chromosome.

d. Spontaneous abortions are likely to occur when there are chromosomal or genetic abnormalities; the situation described is perfectly normal.

9. **a.** is the answer. (p. 43)

   b. & d. These are true of all body cells *except* the gametes.

   c. Gametes have either X or Y chromosomes.

10. **a.** is the answer. (p. 48)
11. **a.** is the answer. Genotype refers to the sum total of all the genes a person inherits; phenotype refers to the actual expression of the individual's characteristics. (p. 44)
12. **c.** is the answer. (p. 48)
13. **d.** is the answer. X-linked genes are located only on the X chromosome. Because males inherit only one X chromosome, they are more likely than females to have these characteristics in their phenotype. (pp. 51–52)
14. **c.** is the answer. (p. 57)
15. **d.** is the answer. (p. 63)

    a. The average length of labor for subsequent births is 7 hours.

16. **c.** is the answer. (p. 69)
17. **d.** is the answer. (p. 63)
18. **c.** is the answer. (p. 67)
19. **c.** is the answer. Most doctors in the United States advise pregnant women to abstain completely from alcohol. (pp. 72–73)
20. **d.** is the answer. (p. 63)
21. **b.** is the answer. (p. 76) **ANS. B, RIGHT?**
22. **c.** is the answer. The sex organs do not begin to take shape until the fetal period. (p. 60)
23. **c.** is the answer. (p. 68)

Matching Items

1. j (p. 57)	**5.** b (p. 73)	**9.** d (p. 60)
2. c (p. 57)	**6.** e (p. 63)	**10.** f (p. 73)
3. h (p. 59)	**7.** g (p. 65)	**11.** i (p. 57)
4. k (p. 68)	**8.** a (p. 75)	

True or False Items

1. T (p. 48)
2. F Since these disorders appear in the phenotype, they would have to occur only in males to be sex-linked. (p. 51)
3. T (p. 72)
4. T (p. 43)
5. F Most traits are polygenic. (p. 48)
6. T (p. 44)
7. F A trait from a recessive gene will be part of the phenotype only when the person has two recessive genes for that trait. (p. 51)
8. T (pp. 44–45)
9. T (p. 43)
10. T (p. 60)
11. F Behavioral teratogens can affect the fetus at any time during the prenatal period. (pp. 75–76)
12. F There is no controversy about the damaging effects of smoking during pregnancy. (p. 76)
13. T (p. 63)
14. F Though highly desirable, mother–infant contact at birth is not necessary for the child's normal development or for a good parent–child relationship. Many opportunities for bonding occur throughout childhood. (p. 70)
15. T (p. 68)
16. F One-third of the births in the United States are now cesarean. (p. 65)

KEY TERMS

1. **DNA (deoxyribonucleic acid)** is the molecule that contains the chemical instructions for cells to manufacture various proteins. (p. 43)
2. **Chromosomes** are molecules of DNA that contain the genes organized in precise sequences. Each cell contains 46 chromosomes (23 pairs). (p. 43)
3. **Gametes** are the human reproductive cells. (p. 43)
4. The **zygote** is the single cell formed during conception by the fusing of two gametes, a sperm and an ovum. (p. 44)
5. **Genes** are segments of a chromosome, which is a DNA molecule; they are the basic units for the transmission of hereditary instructions. (p. 44)
6. The total of all the genes a person inherits—his or her genetic potential—is called the **genotype.** (p. 44)
7. The actual physical or behavioral expression of a genotype, the result of the interaction of the genes with each other and with the environment, is called the **phenotype.** (p. 44)
8. An **allele** is one of the normal versions of a gene that has several possible sequences of base pairs. (pp. 44–45)

9. The **genome** is the full set of genes that are the instructions to make an individual member of a certain species. (p. 45)
10. **Monozygotic (MZ) twins** develop from one zygote that splits apart, producing genetically identical zygotes; also called *identical twins.* (p. 46)

    Memory aid: Mono means "one"; **monozygotic twins** develop from one fertilized ovum.
11. **Dizygotic (DZ) twins** develop from two separate ova fertilized by different sperm at roughly the same time, and therefore are no more genetically similar than ordinary siblings; also called fraternal twins (p. 47)

    Memory aid: A fraternity is a group of two (di) or more nonidentical individuals.
12. **XX** is the 23rd chromosome pair that, in humans, determines that the developing fetus will be female. (p. 47)
13. **XY** is the 23rd chromosome pair that, in humans, determines that the developing fetus will be male. (p. 47)
14. Most human traits are **polygenic;** that is, they are affected by many genes. (p. 48)
15. Most human traits are also **multifactorial**—that is, influenced by many factors, including genetic and environmental factors. (p. 48)
16. A **regulator gene** controls the interactions of other genes, including their expression, duplication, and transcription. (p. 48)
17. When a trait is determined by **additive genes,** the phenotype reflects the sum of the contributions of all the alleles involved. The alleles affecting height, for example, interact in this fashion. (p. 48)
18. The **dominant–recessive pattern** is the interaction of a pair of alleles in such a way that the phenotype reveals the influence of the dominant gene more than that of the recessive gene. (p. 48)
19. A person who has a recessive gene that is not expressed in his or her phenotype but that can be passed on to the person's offspring is called a **carrier** of that gene. (p. 49)
20. **Heritability** is a statistic that refers to the percentage of variation in a particular trait within a particular population, in a particular context and era, that can be traced to genes. (p. 49)
21. **Down syndrome** (*trisomy-21*) is the most common extra-chromosome condition. People with Down syndrome age faster than others, often have unusual facial features and heart abnormalities, and invariably develop Alzheimer's disease. (p. 50)
22. The **fragile X syndrome** is a single-gene disorder in which part of the X chromosome is attached by such a thin string of molecules that it seems about to break off. Although the characteristics associated with this syndrome are quite varied, some mental deficiency is relatively common. (p. 51)
23. **Genetic counseling** involves consultations and tests through which couples can learn more about their genes, and can thus make informed decisions about their childbearing and child-rearing future. (p. 53)
24. **Phenylketonuria (PKU)** is a genetic disorder in which the body cannot metabolize the amino acid phenylalanine, which is found in many foods. (p. 55)
25. The first two weeks of development after conception, characterized by rapid cell division and the beginning of cell differentiation, are called the **germinal period.** (p. 57)

    Memory aid: A *germ cell* is one from which a new organism can develop. The ***germ*inal period** is the first stage in the development of the new organism.
26. The **embryonic period** is approximately the third through the eighth week of prenatal development, when the basic forms of all body structures develop. (p. 57)
27. From the ninth week after conception until birth is the **fetal period,** when the organs grow in size and mature in functioning. (p. 57)
28. The **placenta** is the organ that develops in the uterus to protect and nourish the developing person. (p. 59)
29. **Implantation** is the process by which the developing organism burrows into the placenta that lines the uterus, where it can be nourished and protected during growth. (p. 59)
30. **Embryo** is the name given to the developing human organism from about the third through the eighth week after conception. (p. 60)
31. **Fetus** is the name for the developing human organism from the start of the ninth week after conception until birth. (p. 60)
32. A **sonogram** is an image of an unborn fetus produced with high-frequency sound waves. (p. 61)
33. About 22 weeks after conception, the fetus attains the **age of viability,** at which point it may survive outside the uterus if specialized medical care is available. (p. 61)

34. Newborns are rated at one and then at five minutes after birth according to the **Apgar scale.** This scale assigns a score of 0, 1, or 2 to each of five characteristics: heart rate, breathing, muscle tone, color, and reflexes. A score of 7 or better indicates that all is well. (p. 63)
35. A **doula** is a woman who works alongside medical staff to assist a woman through labor and delivery. (p. 65)
36. In a **cesarean section (c-section),** the fetus is removed from the mother surgically. (p. 65)
37. A birthweight of less than $5^{1}/_{2}$ pounds (2,500 grams) is called **low birthweight (LBW).** Low-birthweight infants are at risk for many immediate and long-term problems. (p. 67)
38. A birthweight of less than 3 pounds, 5 ounces (1,500 grams) is called **very low birthweight (VLBW).** (p. 67)
39. A birthweight of less than 2 pounds, 3 ounces (1,000 grams) is called **extremely low birthweight (ELBW).** (p. 67)
40. When an infant is born 3 or more weeks before the due date, it is said to be a **preterm birth.** (p. 68)
41. Infants who weigh substantially less than they should, given how much time has passed since conception, are called **small for gestational age (SGA),** or small-for-dates. (p. 68)
42. **Kangaroo care** occurs when the mother of a low-birthweight infant spends at least one hour a day holding her infant between her breasts. (p. 69)
43. **Postpartum depression** is a new mother's feeling of sadness and inadequacy in the days and weeks after giving birth. (p. 70)
44. The term **parent–infant bond** describes the strong feelings of attachment between parent and child as parents hold, examine, and feed their newborn. (p. 70)
45. Prenatal alcohol exposure may cause **fetal alcohol syndrome (FAS),** a cluster of birth defects that includes abnormal facial characteristics, slow physical growth, behavior problems, and retarded mental development. (p. 73)
46. **Teratogens** are agents and conditions, such as viruses, drugs, chemicals, extreme stress, and malnutrition, that can impair prenatal development and lead to birth defects or even death. (p. 73)
47. A **threshold effect** is the harmful effect of a substance that occurs when exposure to it reaches a certain level. (p. 76)

THE FIRST TWO YEARS

Body and Brain

3 chapter

Chapter Overview

Chapter 3 is the first of a two-chapter unit that describes the developing person from birth to age 2 in terms of biosocial, cognitive, and psychosocial development.

The chapter begins with observations on the overall growth of infants, including information on brain growth and infant sleep patterns. The chapter then turns to a discussion of sensory, perceptual, and motor abilities and the ages at which the average infant acquires them. Preventive medicine, the importance of immunizations during the first two years, the possible causes of sudden infant death syndrome (SIDS), and the importance of nutrition during the first two years are discussed next.

Chapter 3 also explores the ways in which the infant comes to learn about, think about, and adapt to his or her surroundings. It focuses on the various ways in which infant intelligence is revealed: through sensorimotor intelligence, perception, memory, and language development. The discussion includes a description of Jean Piaget's theory of sensorimotor intelligence, which maintains that infants think exclusively with their senses and motor skills. Piaget's six stages of sensorimotor intelligence are examined, as is information-processing theory, which compares cognition to the ways in which computers analyze data.

Finally, the chapter turns to the most remarkable cognitive achievement of the first two years: the acquisition of language. Beginning with a description of the infant's first attempts at language, the chapter follows the sequence of events that leads to the child's ability to utter two-word sentences. The chapter concludes with an examination of three classic hypotheses on how children learn language and a fourth, hybrid perspective, which combines aspects of each.

NOTE: Answer guidelines for all Chapter 3 questions begin on page 55.

Chapter Review

When you have finished reading the chapter, work through the material that follows to review it. Complete the sentences and answer the questions. In some cases, Study Tips explain how best to learn a difficult concept, while Think About It and Applications help you to know how well you understand the material. As you proceed, evaluate your performance for each section by consulting the answers beginning on page 55. Do not continue with the next section until you understand each answer. If you need to, review or reread the appropriate section in the textbook before continuing.

STUDY TIP: As you can see from the list of Key Terms, this chapter introduces many important new words for you to remember. You will need to spend extra time committing these terms to memory. Many students find flash cards and quizzing a study partner helpful for learning new terminology. To help remember the key parts of a neuron, you might find it useful to practice drawing and labeling dendrites, axons, myelin, and synapses.

Body Changes (pp. 86–93)

1. At birth, the average infant measures ________________ and weighs about ________________ .
2. By age 2, body weight has ________________ (doubled/tripled/quadrupled). The typical 2-year-old is almost ____________ percent of his or her adult height.
3. A standard, or average, measurement that is calculated for a specific group or population is a ________________ .
4. When nutrition is temporarily inadequate, the body stops growing but the brain does not. This is called ________________-________________ .

THINK ABOUT IT: Growth in early infancy is astoundingly rapid. You can begin to appreciate just how rapid this growth is by projecting the growth patterns of the infant onto an adult, such as yourself. If you were gaining weight at the rate of an infant, your weight would be tripled one year from today. How much would you weigh? If you were growing at the rate of an infant during the first year, you would add an inch each month. What would your height be a year from today?

5. The brain's communication system consists primarily of nerve cells called ________________, which are connected by intricate networks of nerve fibers, called ________________ and ________________. About ________________ percent of these cells are in the brain's outer layer called the ________________.

6. Each neuron has many ________________ but only a single ________________.

7. Neurons communicate with one another at intersections called ________________. While traveling down the length of the ________________, the electrical impulses become chemicals called ________________ that carry information across the ________________ ________________ to the ________________ of a "receiving" neuron. The transmission of neural impulses is speeded up in axons covered by ________________.

8. During the first months of life, brain development is most noticeable in the ________________. The growth of ________________ is the major reason that brain weight triples in the first two years.

9. Before birth, neurons and synapses increase rapidly, or ________________. Following this growth, some neurons wither in the process called ________________. This process ________________ (is/is not) lifelong, but most intense before age ________________.

10. The last part of the brain to mature is the ________________ ________________, which is the area for ________________, ________________, and ________________ ________________.

THINK ABOUT IT: The text cites several lines of research evidence that environmental events after birth can shape the development of a child's brain and affect overall cognitive functioning in the years beyond infancy. In the face of this evidence, many parents wonder how far they should go in providing their babies with enriched environmental experiences. Based on your reading of this section of the text chapter, what practical advice would you offer to prospective parents?

11. A life-threatening condition that occurs when an infant is held by the shoulders and quickly shaken back and forth is ________________ ________________ ________________. Crying stops because of ruptured ________________ ________________ in the brain, which results in broken ________________ connections.

12. Newborns typically sleep about ________________ (how many?) hours a day, primarily in________________ (active/quiet) sleep.

13. Over the first months of life, the relative amount of time spent in the different ________________ of sleep changes. The stage of sleep characterized by flickering eyes behind closed lids and ________________ is called ________________ ________________. During this stage of sleep, brain waves are fairly ________________ (slow/rapid). This stage of sleep ________________ (increases/decreases) over the first months, as does the dozing stage called ________________ ________________. Slow-wave sleep, also called ________________ ________________, increases markedly at about ________________ months of age.

APPLICATIONS:

14. The Farbers, who are first-time parents, are wondering whether they should be concerned because their 12-month-old daughter, who weighed 8 pounds at birth and measured 21 inches, now weighs only 20 pounds and measures 30 inches. You should tell them that
    a. this slow weight gain is a cause for immediate concern.
    b. their daughter's weight and height are well below average for her age.
    c. growth patterns for a first child are often erratic.
    d. although their daughter's weight has not tripled, it is still within range of the norm.

15. Concluding her presentation on sleep, Lakshmi notes each of the following EXCEPT
   a. dreaming occurs during REM sleep.
   b. quiet sleep increases markedly at about 3 or 4 months.
   c. the dreaming brain is characterized by slow brain waves.
   d. regular and ample sleep is an important factor in a child's emotional regulation.

16. I am a chemical that carries information between nerve cells in the brain. What am I?

____

17. Sharetta's pediatrician informs her parents that Sharetta's 1-year-old brain is exhibiting proliferation. In response to this news, Sharetta's parents
   a. smile, because they know their daughter's brain is developing new neural connections.
   b. worry, because this may indicate increased vulnerability to a later learning disability.
   c. know that this process, in which axons become coated, is normal.
   d. are alarmed, because this news indicates that the frontal area of Sharetta's cortex is immature.

18. Trying to impress his professor, Erik explains that we know humans have a critical period for learning certain skills because the brain cannot form new synapses after age 13. Should the professor be impressed with Erik's knowledge of biosocial development?
   a. Yes, although each neuron may have already formed as many as 15,000 connections with other neurons.
   b. Yes, although the branching of dendrites and axons does continue through young adulthood.
   c. No. Although Erik is correct about neural development, the brain attains adult size by about age 7.
   d. No. Synapses form throughout life.

Moving and Perceiving (pp. 93–100)

19. An unlearned, involuntary response to a stimulus is called a _______________. These are assessed in newborns by the _______________ _______________ _______________ _______________ Scale.

20. The involuntary response that causes the newborn to take the first breath even before the umbilical cord is cut is called the _______________ _______________.

21. Shivering, crying, and tucking the legs close to the body are examples of reflexes that help to maintain _______________ _______________ _______________.

22. A third set of reflexes manages _______________. One of these is the tendency of the newborn to suck anything that touches the lips; this is the _______________ reflex. Another is the tendency of newborns to turn their heads and start to suck when something brushes against their cheek; this is the _______________ reflex. Other important reflexes that facilitate this behavior are _______________, _______________, and _______________ _______________.

STUDY TIP: Infants have a number of reflexes that are critical for survival and others that indicate normal body and brain functioning. Filling in the missing information in the table below will provide you with a handy summary of those reflexes. In some cases, the description is provided; in other cases, the reflex name is given. First, try to complete the table from memory; then check text psge 95.

23. Reflex(es)	Description
a.	breathing, hiccupping, sneezing, and thrashing
b. Maintaining constant body temperature	
c.	Sucking, rooting, swallowing
d. Babinski reflex	

Reflex(es)	Description
e.	Infants move their legs as if to walk when they are held upright and their feet touch a flat surface
f. Swimming	
g.	Infants grip things that touch their palms
h. Moro reflex	

24. Large movements such as walking and running are called ________________ ________________ skills.

25. Most infants are able to crawl on all fours (sometimes called creeping) between ________________ and ________________ months of age. For crawling to develop, infants must first gain enough ________________ ________________ to support themselves. Another important factor in motor-skill development is ________________ .

List the major hallmarks in children's mastery of walking.

26. Abilities that require more precise, small movements, such as picking up a coin, are called ________________ ________________ skills. By ________________ months of age, most babies can reach for and grab almost any object of the right size.

27. Although the ________________ in which motor skills are mastered is the same in all healthy infants, the ________________ of acquisition of skills varies greatly.

28. Motor skill norms vary from one ________________ group to another.

29. Motor skill acquisition in monozygotic twins ________________ (is/is not) more similar than in dizygotic twins, suggesting that genes ________________ (do/do not) play an important role. Another influential factor is the ________________ ________________ of infant care.

30. The response of the visual, auditory, and other sensory systems when they detect stimuli is called ________________ ; ________________ occurs when the brain tries to make sense out of a stimulus so that the individual becomes aware of it.

31. Generally speaking, newborns' hearing ________________ (is/is not) very acute at birth. Newborns ________________ (can/cannot) perceive differences in voices, rhythms, and cadences long before they achieve comprehension of ________________ . Infants also become accustomed to the rules of their ________________ .

32. The least mature of the senses at birth is ________________ . Newborns' visual focusing is best for objects between ________________ and ________________ inches away.

33. Experience and increasing brain maturation accounts for improvements in other visual abilities, such as the infant's ability to see ________________ and then notice ________________ . By 3 months, they look more intently at a human ________________ . The ability to use both eyes in a coordinated manner to focus on one object, which is called ________________ ________________ , appears at about ________________ of age.

34. Taste, smell, and touch ________________ (function/do not function) at birth. The ability to be comforted by human ________________ is a skill tested in the ________________ Neonatal Assessment Scale.

35. The infant's early sensory abilities seem organized for two goals: ________________ ________________ and ________________.

APPLICATIONS:

36. Sensation is to perception as __________ is to __________.
   a. hearing; seeing
   b. detecting a stimulus; making sense of a stimulus
   c. making sense of a stimulus; detecting a stimulus
   d. tasting; smelling

37. Like all newborns, Serena is able to:
   a. differentiate one sound from another.
   b. see objects more than 30 inches from her face quite clearly.
   c. use her mouth to recognize objects by taste and touch.
   d. do all of these things.

38. Three-week-old Nathan should have the least difficulty focusing on the sight of:
   a. stuffed animals on a bookshelf across the room from his crib.
   b. his mother's face as she holds him in her arms.
   c. the checkerboard pattern in the wallpaper covering the ceiling of his room.
   d. the family dog as it dashes into the nursery.

Surviving in Good Health (pp. 100–105)

39. Globally, today most children ________________ (do/do not) live to adulthood. A key factor in reducing the childhood death rate was the development of ________________—a process that stimulates the body's ________________ system to defend against contagious diseases. Other reasons for a decrease in infant mortality are ________________.

40. Yet another reason for lower infant mortality worldwide is a decrease in ________________ ________________ ________________ ________________, in which seemingly healthy infants die unexpectedly in their ________________.

State several risk factors for SIDS.

41. In most North American and European cultures, children ________________ (do/do not) sleep with their parents. In contrast, parents in ________________, ________________, and ________________ ________________ traditionally practice ________________ with their infants. This practice ________________ (does/does not) seem to be harmful unless the adult is ________________. However, this practice correlates with ________________, ________________ ________________, and maternal ________________ ________________.

42. The ideal infant food is ________________ ________________, beginning with the thick, high-calorie fluid called ________________. The only situations in which formula may be healthier for the infant than breast milk are when ________________ ________________.

State several advantages of breast milk over cow's milk for the developing infant.

43. Most doctors recommend exclusive breast-feeding for the first ________________ (how many?) months.

APPLICATIONS:

44. To promote optimal nutrition for her new baby, Emma's pediatrician recommends exclusive breast-feeding for the first ________________ (how many months?) because breast milk provides the newborn with a thick, high-calorie fluid, called ________________.

45. Before she became pregnant, Nell had a bout of the measles. After the baby was born, her pediatrician recommended breast-feeding because ________________ ________________.

Infant Cognition (pp. 105–111)

46. The first major theorist to realize that infants are active learners was ________________ .

47. When infants begin to explore the environment through sensory and motor skills, they are displaying what Piaget called ________________ intelligence. In number, Piaget described ________________ stages of development of this type of intelligence.

48. (text and Table 3.5) The first two stages of sensorimotor intelligence are examples of ________________ ________________ ________________ . Stage one begins with newborns' awareness of reflexes, such as ________________ and ________________ , and ________________ . It lasts from birth to ________________ of age.

49. Stage two begins when newborns show signs of ________________ of their ________________ and senses to the specifics of the environment. This process involves ________________ and ________________ .

Describe the development of the sucking reflex during stages one and two.

50. (text and Table 3.5) In stages three and four, development switches to ________________ ________________ ________________ , involving the baby with an object or with another person. During stage three, which occurs between ________________ and ________________ months of age, infants repeat a specific action that has just elicited a pleasing response.

Describe a typical stage-three behavior.

51. In stage four, which lasts from ________________ to ________________ months of age, infants can better ________________ events. At this stage, babies also engage in purposeful actions, or ________________-directed behavior.

52. A major cognitive accomplishment of infancy is the ability to understand that objects exist even when they are ________________ . This awareness is called ________________ ________________ . To test for this awareness, Piaget devised a procedure to observe whether an infant will ________________ for a hidden object. Using this test, Piaget concluded that this awareness does not develop until about ________________ of age. More recent research studies have shown that this ability actually begins to emerge at ________________ months.

53. (text and Table 3.5) During stage five, which lasts from ________________ to ________________ months, infants begin experimenting in thought and deed. They do so through ________________ ________________ ________________ , which involve taking in experiences and trying to make sense of them.

Explain what Piaget meant when he described the stage-five infant as a "little scientist."

54. Stage six, which lasts from ________________ to ________________ months, is the stage of anticipating and solving simple problems by using ________________ ________________ . One sign that children have reached stage six is ________________ ________________ , which is their emerging ability to imitate behaviors they noticed earlier.

STUDY TIP: Jean Piaget was the first major theorist to realize that each stage of life has its own characteristic way of thinking. To deepen your understanding of Piaget's stages of sensorimotor development, fill in the missing information in the chart on the next page. See how much you can fill in without reviewing the textbook. To get you started, the first stage has been completed.

55. Typical Age Range	Stage	Behavior Indicating a Child Is in This Stage
0–1 month	reflexes	reflexive cries
a. 1–4 months		
b. 4–8 months		
c. 8–12 months		
d. 12–18 months		
e. 18–24 months		

APPLICATIONS:

56. A 9-month-old repeatedly reaches for his sister's doll, even though he has been told "no" many times. This is an example of ________________ ________________.

57. Before putting her dolly to bed, 18-month-old Jessica sings her a song. According to Piaget, Jessica's behavior is an example of the use of

a. new means through active experimentation.
b. mental combinations.
c. new adaptation and anticipation.
d. first acquired adaptations.

58. Nine-month-old Akshay, who looks out of his crib for a toy that has fallen, is clearly demonstrating an understanding of ________________ ________________.

59. A 20-month-old girl who is able to try out various actions mentally without actually having to perform them is learning to solve simple problems by using ________________ ________________.

60. Seven-month-old Francisca is attempting to interact with her smiling mother. She is demonstrating an ability that typically occurs in stage ____________ of sensorimotor development.

61. Angelo realizes that sucking a pacifier is different from sucking a nipple. Angelo is in stage ________________ of cognitive development.

62. A perspective on human cognition that is modeled on how computers analyze data is the ________________-________________ theory.

63. A firm surface that appears to dropoff is called a ________________ ________________.

Although perception of this dropoff was once linked to ________________ maturity, later research found that infants as young as ________________ are able to perceive the dropoff, as evidenced by changes in their ________________ ________________ and their wide open eyes.

64. According to classic developmental theory, infants ________________ (store/do not store) memories in the first year (Freud called this phenomenon ________________ ________________) and do not remember things that occurred a day or two earlier until about ________________ years of age (Piaget called this ability ________________ ________________).

65. Research has shown, however, that babies can show that they remember when three conditions are met:

a. ________________________________
b. ________________________________
c. ________________________________

66. When these conditions are met, infants as young as ________________ months "remembered" events from two weeks earlier if they experienced a ________________ ________________ prior to retesting.

67. By about ________________ months, infants become capable of retaining information for longer periods of time, with less training or reminding.

APPLICATION:

68. Professor Norman frequently uses examples of how computers analyze data to help the class understand how human memory works. Professor Norman evidently is a fan of
   a. Jean Piaget.
   b. Carolyn Rovee-Collier.
   c. information-processing theory.
   d. dynamic perception theory.

Language Learning (pp. 111–119)

69. Newborns show a preference for hearing ________________ over other sounds, including the high-pitched, simplified adult speech called ________________-________________ speech, which is sometimes called ________________ ________________.

70. Between ________________ and ________________ months of age, babies begin to repeat certain syllables, a phenomenon referred to as ________________.

71. Although deaf babies babble at first, they stop because they can't hear responses. Deaf babies may also use ________________ ________________ to babble.

72. The average baby speaks a few words at about ________________ of age. They understand ________________ (more/fewer) words than they speak.

73. When vocabulary reaches approximately 50 expressed words, it suddenly begins to build rapidly, at a rate of ________________ words a month. This language spurt is called the ________________ ________________ because toddlers learn a disproportionate number of ________________.

74. Another characteristic of infant language development is the use of the ________________, in which a single word expresses a complete thought. The first words take on nuances of tone, loudness, and cadence that are precursors of the first ________________.

75. Language acquisition may be shaped by our ________________, as revealed by the fact that English-speaking infants learn more ________________ than Chinese or Korean infants, who learn more ________________. Alternatively, the entire ________________ ________________ may determine language acquisition.

76. Children begin to produce their first two-word sentences at about ________________ months, showing a clearly emerging understanding of ________________, which refers to all the methods that languages use to communicate meaning, apart from the words themselves. A child's grammar correlates with the size of his or her ________________.

77. Reinforcement and association account for language development, according to the learning theory of ________________. One study that followed mother–infant pairs over time found that the frequency of early ________________ ________________ predicted the child's rate of language acquisition many months later.

78. The theorist who stressed that language is too complex to be mastered so early and easily through conditioning is ________________. Because all young children ________________ (master/do not master) basic grammar at about the same age, there is, in a sense, a ________________ ________________. This theorist also maintained that all children are born with a LAD, or ________________ ________________ ________________, that enables children to quickly derive the rules of grammar from the speech they hear.

Summarize the research support for hypothesis two.

79. A third, ________________-________________, hypothesis proposes that the starting point for language is its social reason for existing: ________________.

80. A new ________________ perspective combines aspects of several hypotheses. A fundamental aspect of this perspective is that ________________ ________________.

STUDY TIP: To review the sequences of sensorimotor and language development, and to deepen your understanding of their interrelationship, see if you can fill in the missing information in the chart below. For each listed age (column 1), write down the corresponding sensorimotor stage (column 2) and hallmarks or milestones of language development (column 3).

81. Age	Sensorimotor Stage	Language Milestones
a. 0–1 month		
b. 1–4 months		
c. 4–8 months		
d. 8–12 months		
e. 12–18 months		
f. 18–24 months		

APPLICATIONS:

82. At about 21 months, Darrell, who is typical of his age group, will
   a. have a vocabulary of between 250 and 350 words.
   b. begin to speak in holophrases.
   c. put words together to form rudimentary sentences.
   d. be characterized by all of these abilities.

83. As an advocate of the social-pragmatic theory, Professor Caruso believes that
   a. infants communicate in every way they can because they are social beings.
   b. biological maturation is a dominant force in language development.
   c. infants' language abilities mirror those of their primary caregivers.
   d. language develops in many ways for many reasons.

84. As soon as her babysitter arrives, 21-month-old Christine holds on to her mother's legs and, in a questioning manner, says "bye-bye." Because Christine clearly is "asking" her mother not to leave, her utterance can be classified as a ________________.

85. Six-month-old Lars continually repeats a variety of sound combinations such as "ba-ba-ba." This form of language is called ________________.

86. Monica firmly believes that her infant daughter "taught" herself language because of the seemingly effortless manner in which she has mastered new words and phrases. Monica is evidently a proponent of the hypothesis proposed by ______________________ .

87. Like most Korean toddlers, Noriko has acquired a greater number of ______________ (nouns/verbs) in her vocabulary than her North American counterparts, who tend to acquire more ______________ (nouns/verbs).

Progress Test 1

Multiple-Choice Questions

Circle your answers to the following questions and check them with the answers beginning on page 57. If your answer is incorrect, read the explanation for why it is incorrect and then consult the appropriate pages of the text (in parentheses following the correct answer).

1. The average North American newborn
   a. weighs approximately 6 pounds.
   b. weighs approximately 7½ pounds.
   c. is "overweight" because of the diet of the mother.
   d. weighs 10 percent less than what is desirable.

2. The major motor skill most likely to be mastered by an infant by 4 months is
   a. sitting without support.
   b. sitting with head steady.
   c. turning the head in search of a nipple.
   d. grabbing an object with thumb and forefinger.

3. Head-sparing is the phenomenon in which
   a. the brain continues to grow even though the body stops growing as a result of malnutrition.
   b. the infant's body grows more rapidly during the second year.
   c. axons develop more rapidly than dendrites.
   d. dendrites develop more rapidly than axons.

4. Dreaming is characteristic of
   a. slow-wave sleep. c. REM sleep.
   b. transitional sleep. d. quiet sleep.

5. (A View from Science) Research studies of the more than 100,000 Romanian children orphaned and severely deprived in infancy reported all of the following EXCEPT
   a. all of the children were overburdened with stress.
   b. after adoption, the children gained weight quickly.
   c. during early childhood, many still showed signs of emotional damage.
   d. most of the children placed in healthy adoptive homes eventually recovered.

6. Compared with formula-fed infants, breast-fed infants tend to have
   a. greater weight gain.
   b. fewer allergies and stomach upsets.
   c. less frequent feedings during the first few months.
   d. more social approval.

7. The infant's first "motor skills" are
   a. fine motor skills. c. reflexes.
   b. gross motor skills. d. unpredictable.

8. Which of the following is said to have had the greatest impact on human mortality reduction and population growth?
   a. improvements in infant nutrition
   b. oral rehydration therapy
   c. medical advances in newborn care
   d. childhood immunization

9. Which of the following is true of motor-skill development in healthy infants?
   a. It follows the same basic sequence the world over.
   b. It occurs at different rates from individual to individual.
   c. It follows norms that vary from one ethnic group to another.
   d. All of these statements are true.

10. According to Piaget, when a baby repeats an action that has just triggered a pleasing response from his or her caregiver, a stage ______ behavior has occurred.
    a. one c. three
    b. two d. six

11. Sensorimotor intelligence begins with a baby's first
    a. attempt to crawl.
    b. reflexes.
    c. auditory perception.
    d. adaptation of a reflex.

12. Toward the end of the first year, infants usually learn how to
    a. accomplish simple goals.
    b. manipulate various symbols.
    c. solve complex problems.
    d. pretend.

13. An 18-month-old toddler puts a collar on a stuffed dog, then pretends to take it for a walk. The infant's behavior is an example of
    a. new adaptation and anticipation.
    b. making interesting sights last.
    c. new means through active experimentation.
    d. mental combinations.

14. When an infant begins to understand that objects exist even when they are out of sight, she or he has begun to understand the concept of object
    a. displacement.
    b. importance.
    c. permanence.
    d. location.

15. Today, most cognitive psychologists view language acquisition as
    a. primarily the result of imitation of adult speech.
    b. a behavior that is determined primarily by biological maturation.
    c. a behavior determined entirely by learning.
    d. determined by both biological maturation and learning.

16. The average baby speaks a few words at about
    a. 6 months.
    b. 9 months.
    c. 12 months.
    d. 24 months.

17. A single word used by toddlers to express a complete thought is
    a. a holophrase.
    b. child-directed speech.
    c. babbling.
    d. an assimilation.

18. A distinctive form of language, with a particular pitch, structure, etc., that adults use in talking to infants is called
    a. a holophrase.
    b. the LAD.
    c. child-directed speech.
    d. conversation.

19. A toddler who taps on the computer's keyboard after observing her mother sending e-mail the day before is demonstrating
    a. assimilation.
    b. accommodation.
    c. deferred imitation.
    d. dynamic perception.

20. In Piaget's theory of sensorimotor intelligence, reflexes that involve the infant's own body are examples of
    a. primary circular reactions.
    b. secondary circular reactions.
    c. tertiary circular reactions.
    d. none of these reactions.

21. The purposeful actions that begin to develop in sensorimotor stage four are called
    a. reflexes.
    b. accommodations.
    c. goal-directed behaviors.
    d. mental combinations.

Matching Items

Match each definition or description with its corresponding term.

Terms

_______ 1. neurons
_______ 2. dendrites
_______ 3. object permanence
_______ 4. Noam Chomsky
_______ 5. gross motor skill
_______ 6. fine motor skill
_______ 7. reflex
_______ 8. B. F. Skinner
_______ 9. holophrase
_______ 10. prefrontal cortex
_______ 11. sensorimotor intelligence

Definitions or Descriptions

a. theorist who believed that verbal behavior is conditioned
b. picking up an object
c. a single word used to express a complete thought
d. theorist who believed that language ability is innate
e. communication networks among nerve cells
f. walking or running
g. an unlearned, involuntary response
h. thinking through the senses and motor skills
i. nerve cells
j. the brain area that specializes in anticipation, planning, and impulse control
k. the realization that something that is out of sight continues to exist

Progress Test 2

Progress Test 2 should be completed during a final chapter review. Answer the following questions after you thoroughly understand the correct answers for the Chapter Review and Progress Test 1.

Multiple-Choice Questions

1. Dendrite is to axon as neural _______________ is to neural _______________.
   a. input; output
   b. output; input
   c. myelin; synapse
   d. synapse; myelin

2. A reflex is best defined as a(n)
   a. fine motor skill.
   b. motor ability mastered at a specific age.
   c. involuntary response to a given stimulus.
   d. gross motor skill.

3. A norm is
   a. a standard, or average, that is derived for a specific group or population.
   b. a point on a ranking scale of 0 to 100.
   c. a milestone of development that all children reach at the same age.
   d. all of the above.

4. Regarding the brain's cortex, which of the following is NOT true?
   a. The cortex houses about 70 percent of the brain's neurons.
   b. The cortex is the brain's outer layer.
   c. The cortex is the location of most thinking, feeling, and sensing.
   d. Only primates have a cortex.

5. During the first weeks of life, babies seem to focus reasonably well on
   a. little in their environment.
   b. objects at a distance of 4 to 30 inches.
   c. objects at a distance of 1 to 3 inches.
   d. objects several feet away.

6. Which sleep stage increases markedly at about 3 or 4 months?
   a. REM
   b. transitional
   c. fast-wave
   d. slow-wave

7. An advantage of breast milk over formula is that it
   a. is always sterile and at body temperature.
   b. contains traces of medications ingested by the mother.
   c. can be given without involving the father.
   d. contains more protein and vitamin D than does formula.

8. Synapses are
   a. nerve fibers that receive electrochemical impulses from other neurons.
   b. nerve fibers that transmit electrochemical impulses to other neurons.
   c. intersections between the axon of one neuron and the dendrites of other neurons.
   d. chemical signals that transmit information from one neuron to another.

9. Neural proliferation and pruning demonstrate that
   a. the pace of acquisition of motor skills varies markedly from child to child.
   b. Newborns sleep more than older children because their immature nervous systems cannot handle the higher, waking level of sensory stimulation.
   c. The specifics of brain structure and growth depend partly on the infant's experience.
   d. Good nutrition is essential to healthy biosocial development.

10. Jumping is to using a crayon as _______ is to _______.
    a. fine motor skill; gross motor skill
    b. gross motor skill; fine motor skill
    c. reflex; fine motor skill
    d. reflex; gross motor skill

11. Some infant reflexes are critical for survival. Hiccups and sneezes help the infant maintain _________, and leg tucking maintains _________.
    a. feeding; oxygen supply
    b. feeding; a constant body temperature
    c. oxygen supply; feeding
    d. oxygen supply; a constant body temperature

12. (A View from Science) Compared with the brains of laboratory rats that were raised in barren cages, those of rats raised in stimulating, toy-filled cages
    a. were better developed and had more dendrites.
    b. had fewer synaptic connections.
    c. showed less transient exuberance.
    d. displayed all of these characteristics.

13. Infant sensory and perceptual abilities appear to be especially organized for
    a. obtaining adequate nutrition and comfort.
    b. comfort and social interaction.

c. looking.
d. touching and smelling.

14. Stage five (12 to 18 months) of sensorimotor intelligence is best described as
a. first acquired adaptations.
b. the period of the "little scientist."
c. procedures for making interesting sights last.
d. new means through symbolization.

15. Research suggests that the concept of object permanence
a. fades after a few months.
b. is a skill some children never acquire.
c. may occur earlier and more gradually than Piaget recognized.
d. involves pretending as well as mental combinations.

16. Which of the following is an example of a stage three behavior?
a. 1-month-old infant stares at a mobile suspended over her crib
b. a 2-month-old infant sucks a pacifier
c. realizing that rattles make noise, a 4-month-old infant laughs with delight when his mother puts a rattle in his hand
d. a 12-month-old toddler licks a bar of soap to learn what it tastes like

17. According to Piaget, the use of deferred imitation is an example of stage ________ behavior.
a. three
b. four
c. five
d. six

18. For Noam Chomsky, the language acquisition device refers to
a. the human predisposition to acquire language.
b. the portion of the human brain that processes speech.
c. the vocabulary of the language to which the child is exposed.
d. all of these.

19. The first stage of sensorimotor intelligence lasts until
a. infants can anticipate events that will fulfill their needs.
b. infants begin to adapt their reflexes to the environment.
c. infants interact with objects to produce exciting experiences.
d. infants are capable of thinking about past and future events.

20. What is the correct sequence of stages of language development?
a. crying, babbling, cooing, first word
b. crying, cooing, babbling, first word
c. crying, babbling, first word, cooing
d. crying, cooing, first word, babbling

21. Compared with hearing babies, deaf babies
a. are less likely to babble.
b. are more likely to babble.
c. typically never babble.
d. are more likely to babble using hand signals.

22. According to Skinner, children acquire language
a. as a result of an inborn ability to use the basic structure of language.
b. through reinforcement and other aspects of conditioning.
c. mostly because of biological maturation.
d. in a fixed sequence of predictable stages.

23. A fundamental idea of the hybrid model of language acquisition is that
a. all humans are born with an innate language acquisition device.
b. learning some aspects of language is best explained by one hypothesis at one age, by other hypotheses at another age.
c. language development occurs too rapidly and easily to be entirely the product of conditioning.
d. imitation and reinforcement are crucial to the development of language.

True or False Items

Write T (*true*) or F (*false*) on the line in front of each statement.

_______ 1. Newborns sleep is primarily quiet sleep, as opposed to active sleep.
_______ 2. Putting babies to sleep on their stomachs increases the risk of SIDS.
_______ 3. Reflexive hiccups, sneezes, and thrashing are signs that the infant's reflexes are not functioning properly.
_______ 4. Infants of all ethnic backgrounds develop the same motor skills at approximately the same age.
_______ 5. The typical 2-year-old is almost one-fifth its adult weight and one-half its adult height.
_______ 6. Vision is better developed than hearing in most newborns.
_______ 7. Today, most infants in industrialized nations are breast-fed up to 6 months.

_______ 8. Telling an infant to stop crying and go to sleep is pointless because such self-control requires brain capacity that is not yet present.

_______ 9. Dendrite growth is the major reason that brain weight increases so dramatically in the first two years.

_______ 10. The only motor skills apparent at birth are reflexes.

_______ 11. The prefrontal cortex is one of the first brain areas to mature.

Matching Items

Match each definition or description with its corresponding term.

Terms

_______ 1. goal-directed behavior
_______ 2. visual cliff
_______ 3. primary circular reaction
_______ 4. child-directed speech
_______ 5. new adaptation and anticipation
_______ 6. "little scientist"
_______ 7. mental combinations
_______ 8. secondary circular reaction
_______ 9. tertiary circular reaction
_______ 10. LAD

Definitions or Descriptions

a. a device for studying depth perception
b. understanding how to reach a goal
c. able to put two ideas together
d. the first two of Piaget's sensorimotor stages involving the infant's own body
e. Piaget'sensorimotor stages three and four involving people and objects
f. a hypothetical device that facilitates language development
g. also called baby talk or motherese
h. Piaget's term for the stage-five toddler
i. purposeful actions
j. the last of Piaget's sensorimotor stages involving active exploration and experimentation

Key Terms

Using your own words, write a brief definition or explanation of each of the following terms on a separate piece of paper.

1. norm
2. head-sparing
3. neuron
4. cortex
5. axon
6. dendrite
7. synapse
8. neurotransmitter
9. prefrontal cortex
10. shaken baby syndrome
11. REM sleep
12. reflex
13. gross motor skills
14. fine motor skills
15. sensation
16. perception
17. binocular vision
18. immunization
19. sudden infant death syndrome (SIDS)
20. co-sleeping
21. sensorimotor intelligence
22. assimilation
23. accommodation
24. object permanence
25. "little scientist"
26. information-processing theory
27. visual cliff
28. reminder session
29. child-directed speech
30. babbling
31. naming explosion

32. holophrase
33. language acquisition device (LAD)

Answers

CHAPTER REVIEW

1. 20 inches (51 centimeters); 7 1/2 pounds (3.4 kilograms)
2. quadrupled; 50
3. norm
4. head-sparing
5. neurons; axons; dendrites; 70; cortex
6. dendrites; axon
7. synapses; axon; neurotransmitters; synaptic gap; dendrite; myelin
8. cortex; dendrites
9. proliferate; pruning; is; 2
10. prefrontal cortex; anticipation; planning; impulse control
11. shaken baby syndrome; blood vessels; neural
12. 17; active
13. stages; dreaming; REM sleep; rapid; decreases; transitional sleep; quiet sleep; 3 or 4
14. **d.** is the answer. Although slowdowns in growth during infancy are often a cause for concern, their daughter's weight and height are within the range of most 1-year-old babies.
15. **c.** is the answer. The dreaming brain is characterized by rapid brain waves.
16. neurotransmitter
17. **a.** is the answer. Proliferation results in an increase of neural connections during infancy, some of which will disappear because they are not used; that is, they are not needed to process information.
18. **d.** is the answer. Although synapses do form more rapidly in infancy than at any other time, they do not stop forming after infancy.
19. reflex; Brazelton Neonatal Behavioral Assessment
20. breathing reflex
21. constant body temperature
22. feeding; sucking; rooting; swallowing; crying; spitting up
23. **a.** reflexes that maintain oxygen supply
    b. crying, shivering, tucking in their legs, pushing blankets away
    c. reflexes that facilitate feeding
    d. infants' toes fan upward when their feet are stroked
    e. stepping reflex
    f. infants stretch out their arms and legs when they are held on their stomachs
    g. Palmar grasping reflex
    h. infants fling their arms outward and then clutch them against their chests in response to a loud noise
24. gross motor
25. 8; 10; muscle strength; practice

On average, a child can walk while holding a hand at 9 months, can stand alone momentarily at 10 months, and can walk well, unassisted, at 12 months.

26. fine motor; 6
27. sequence; age
28. ethnic
29. is; do; cultural pattern
30. sensation; perception
31. is; can; meaning; language
32. vision; 4; 30 (10 and 75 centimeters)
33. shapes; details; face; binocular vision; 3 months
34. function; touch; Brazelton
35. social interaction; comfort
36. **b.** is the answer. Answers a. and d. are incorrect because sensation and perception operate in all of these sensory modalities.
37. **a.** is the answer. Objects more than 30 inches away are out of focus for newborns. The ability to recognize objects by taste or touch does not emerge until about one month of age.
38. **b.** is the answer. This is true because, at birth, focusing is best for objects between 4 and 30 inches away.
39. do; immunization; immune; better nutrition, access to clean water, oral rehydration, and treated sleeping nets in malarial areas
40. sudden infant death syndrome (SIDS); sleep

The risk factors for SIDS include low birthweight, heavy clothing, soft bedding, teenage parenthood, and maternal smoking.

41. do not; Asia; Africa; Latin America; co-sleeping; does not; drugged or drunk; poverty; preterm birth; cigarette smoking
42. breast milk; colostrum; the mother is HIV-positive or using toxic or addictive drugs

Breast milk is always sterile and at body temperature; it contains more iron, vitamins, and other nutrients; it provides all the immunity against disease that the mother has; it is more digestible than any formula; and it decreases the risk of allergies, asthma, obesity, and heart disease.

43. four to six

44. four to six months; colostrum

45. Having had measles, Nell has developed an immunity to the disease. With breast milk, she will pass the resulting antibodies onto her newborn.

46. Piaget

47. sensorimotor; six

48. primary circular reactions; sucking; grasping; sensations; 1 month

49. adaptation; reflexes; assimilation; accommodation

Stage-one infants suck everything that touches their lips. By about 1 month, they start to adapt their reflexive sucking. After several months, they have organized the world into objects to be sucked to soothe hunger, objects to be sucked for comfort, and objects not to be sucked at all.

50. secondary circular reactions; 4; 8

A stage-three infant may squeeze a duck, hear a quack, and squeeze the duck again.

51. 8; 12; anticipate; goal

52. no longer in sight; object permanence; search; 8 months; 4 1/2

53. 12; 18; tertiary circular reactions

The stage-five "little scientist" uses trial and error in creative and active exploration.

54. 18; 24; mental combinations; deferred imitation

55. 0–1 month: reflexes (Stage 1); reflexive cries
 a. 1–4 months: first acquired adaptations (Stage 2); sucking a thumb for comfort but not sucking a whole hand
 b. 4–8 months: making interesting sights last (Stage 3); shaking a doll that says "Mama"
 c. 8–12 months: new adaptation and anticipation (Stage 4); pointing at a toy to get Dad to bring it to him or her
 d. 12–18 months: new means through active experimentation (Stage 5); pushing all the buttons on the remote control
 e. 18–24 months: new means through mental combinations (Stage 6); learning that the furry little teddy bear isn't real but can be used for cuddling and security

56. goal-directed behavior

57. **b.** is the answer. Jessica realizes the doll isn't real, but she also knows she can do "real things" with the doll.

58. object permanence. Akshay knows that out of sight doesn't mean the object ceases to exist.

59. mental combinations. The child is able to think about something before actually doing anything, a major advance in cognitive development.

60. four. This is the stage of new adaptation and anticipation. The infant becomes more deliberate and purposeful in responding to people and objects.

61. two. This is the stage of first acquired adaptations, when the infant accommodates and coordinates reflexes.

62. information-processing

63. visual cliff; visual; 3 months; heart rate

64. do not store; infantile amnesia; 1 1/2; deferred imitation

65. (a) experimental conditions are similar to real life; (b) motivation is high; (c) retrieval is strengthened by reminders and repetition

66. 3; reminder session

67. 10

68. **c.** is the answer. Information-processing theory compares human thinking processes, by analogy, to computer analysis of data.

69. speech; child-directed; baby talk (or motherese)

70. 6; 9; babbling

71. hand gestures

72. 1 year; more

73. 50 to 100; naming explosion; nouns

74. holophrase; grammar

75. culture; nouns; verbs; social context

76. 21; grammar; vocabulary

77. B. F. Skinner; maternal responsiveness

78. Noam Chomsky; master; universal grammar; language acquisition device

Support for this hypothesis comes from the fact that all babies babble ma-ma and da-da sounds at about 6 to 9 months. No reinforcement is needed. Infants merely need dendrites to grow, mouth muscles to strengthen, neurons to connect, and speech to be heard.

79. social-pragmatic; communication

80. hybrid; some learning of language is best explained by one hypothesis at one age and other aspects by another perspective at another age

81. **a.** 0–1 month: reflexes (Stage 1); crying, facial expressions
   b. 1–4 months: first acquired adaptations (Stage 2); cooing, laughing, squealing, growling, crooning, vowel sounds
   c. 4–8 months: making interesting sights last (Stage 3); babbling at 6 months
   d. 8–12 months: new adaptation and anticipation (Stage 4); at 10 months, comprehension of simple words; speechlike intonations
   e. 12–18 months: new means through active experimentation (Stage 5); first spoken words at 12 months; vocabulary growth up to about 50 words
   f. 18–24 months: new means through mental combinations (Stage 6); three or more words learned per day, first two-word sentence at 21 months, multiword sentences at 24 months

82. **c.** is the answer. The first two-word sentence is uttered at about 21 months.

83. **a.** is the answer. b. is more consistent with Noam Chomsky's hypothesis, c. would be based on B. F. Skinner's hypothesis, and d. is consistent with the hybrid perspective.

84. holophrase. These are one-word utterances that express a complete, meaningful thought.

85. babbling. This form of speech, which begins between 6 and 9 months of age, is characterized by the extended repetition of certain syllables (such as "ma-ma").

86. Noam Chomsky. Chomsky and his followers believe that language is too complex to be learned through reinforcement alone.

87. verbs; nouns. Korean is considered a verb-friendly language, because verbs appear at the beginning of sentences. North Americans use nouns first in their sentences.

PROGRESS TEST 1

Multiple-Choice Questions

1. **b.** is the answer. (p. 86)

2. **b.** is the answer. (pp. 95, 96)

   a. The age norm for this skill is 6–7 months.

   c. This is a reflex, not an acquired motor skill.

   d. This skill is acquired between 9 and 14 months.

3. **a.** is the answer. (p. 87)

4. **c.** is the answer. (p. 93)

5. **c.** is the answer. (p. 92)

6. **b.** is the answer. This is because breast milk is more digestible than cow's milk or formula. (p. 104)

   a., c., & d. Breast- and bottle-fed babies do not differ in these attributes.

7. **c.** is the answer. (p. 94)

   a. & b. These motor skills do not emerge until somewhat later; reflexes are present at birth.

   d. On the contrary, reflexes are quite predictable.

8. **d.** is the answer. (p. 100)

9. **d.** is the answer. (pp. 96–97)

10. **c.** is the answer. (p. 107)

11. **b.** is the answer. This was Piaget's most basic contribution to the study of infant cognition—that intelligence is revealed in behavior at every age. (p. 106)

12. **a.** is the answer. (p. 107)

    b. & c. These abilities are not acquired until children are much older.

    d. Pretending is associated with stage six (18 to 24 months).

13. **d.** is the answer. (p. 108)

14. **c.** is the answer. (p. 107)

15. **d.** is the answer. (pp. 118–119)

16. **c.** is the answer. (p. 113)

17. **a.** is the answer. (p. 114)

    b. Child-directed speech is the speech adults use with infants.

    c. Babbling refers to the first syllables a baby utters.

    d. An assimilation involves interpreting new experiences to fit into old ideas.

18. **c.** is the answer. (p. 112)

    a. A holophrase is a single word uttered by a toddler to express a complete thought.

    b. According to Noam Chomsky, the LAD, or language acquisition device, is an innate ability in humans to acquire language.

    d. These characteristic differences in pitch and structure are precisely what distinguish child-directed speech from regular conversation.

19. **c.** is the answer (p. 108)

    a. & b. In Piaget's theory, these refer to processes by which mental concepts incorporate new experiences (assimilation) or are modified in response to new experiences (accommodation).

d. Dynamic perception is perception that is primed to focus on movement and change.

20. **a.** is the answer. (p. 106)

b. Secondary circular reactions involve the baby with an object or with another person.

c. Tertiary circular reactions involve active exploration and experimentation, rather than mere reflexive action.

21. **c.** is the answer. (p. 107)

a. Reflexes are involuntary (and therefore unintentional) responses.

b. Accommodations involve restructuring old ideas to include new experiences.

d. Mental combinations are actions that are carried out mentally, rather than behaviorally. Moreover, mental combinations do not develop until a later age, during sensorimotor stage six.

Matching Items

1. i (p. 88)	**6.** b (p. 96)	**11.** h (p. 105)
2. e (p. 88)	**7.** g (p. 94)	
3. k (p. 107)	**8.** a (p. 116)	
4. d (p. 117)	**9.** c (p. 114)	
5. f (p. 95)	**10.** j (p. 90)	

PROGRESS TEST 2

Multiple-Choice Questions

1. **a.** is the answer. (p. 88)

2. **c.** is the answer. (p. 94)

a., b., & d. Each of these refers to voluntary responses that are acquired only after a certain amount of practice; reflexes are involuntary responses that are present at birth and require no practice.

3. **a.** is the answer. (p. 86)

b. This defines percentile, which is not discussed in the text.

4. **d.** is the answer. All mammals have a cortex. (p. 88)

5. **b.** is the answer. (p. 98)

a. Although focusing ability seems to be limited to a certain range, babies do focus on many objects in this range.

c. This is not within the range at which babies *can* focus.

d. Babies have very poor distance vision.

6. **d.** is the answer. (p. 93)

7. **a.** is the answer. (p. 104)

b. If anything, this is a potential *disadvantage* of breast milk over formula.

c. So can formula.

d. Breast milk contains more iron, certain vitamins, and other nutrients than cow's milk; it does not contain more protein and vitamin D, however.

8. **c.** is the answer. (p. 88)

a. These are dendrites.

b. These are axons.

d. These are neurotransmitters.

9. **c.** is the answer. (p. 90)

10. **b.** is the answer. (pp. 95, 96)

c. & d. Reflexes are involuntary responses; climbing and using a crayon are both voluntary responses.

11. **d.** is the answer. (p. 94)

12. **a.** is the answer. (p. 92)

13. **d.** is the answer. (p. 99)

14. **b.** is the answer. (p. 108)

a. & c. These are stages two and three.

d. This is not one of Piaget's stages of sensorimotor intelligence.

15. **c.** is the answer. (p. 108)

16. **c.** is the answer. (p. 107)

a. & b. These are examples of stages one and two behaviors.

d. This is an example of a stage five behavior.

17. **d.** is the answer. (p. 108)

18. **a.** is the answer. Chomsky believed that this device is innate. (p. 117)

19. **b.** is the answer. (p. 106)

a. & c. Both of these occur later than stage one.

d. This is a hallmark of stage six.

20. **b.** is the answer. (p. 112)

21. **d.** is the answer. (p. 113)

a. & b. Hearing and deaf babies do not differ in the overall likelihood that they will babble.

c. Deaf babies definitely babble.

22. **b.** is the answer. (pp. 115–116)

a., c., & d. These views on language acquisition describe the theory offered by Noam Chomsky.

23. **b.** is the answer. (p. 118)

a. & c. These ideas are consistent with Noam Chomsky's hypothesis.

d. This is the central idea of B. F. Skinner's hypothesis.

True or False Items

1. F In fact, just the opposite is true. (p. 93)
2. T (p. 102)
3. F Hiccups, sneezes, and thrashing are common during the first few days, and they are entirely normal reflexes. (p. 94)
4. F Although all healthy infants develop the same motor skills in the same sequence, the age at which these skills are acquired can vary greatly from infant to infant. (pp. 96–97)
5. T (pp. 86–87)
6. F Vision is relatively poorly developed at birth, whereas hearing is well developed. (p. 98)
7. F Only one-third of all babies are breast-fed up to 6 months. (p. 105)
8. T (p. 90)
9. T (p. 88)
10. T (p. 94)
11. F In fact, the prefrontal cortex is probably the last area of the brain to attain maturity. (p. 90)

Matching Items

1. i (p. 107)	**5.** b (p. 107)	**9.** j (p. 106)
2. a (p. 109)	**6.** h (p. 108)	**10.** f (p. 117)
3. d (p. 106)	**7.** c (p. 108)	
4. g (p. 112)	**8.** e (p. 108)	

KEY TERMS

1. A **norm** is an average, or standard, measurement calculated for a specific population. (p. 86)
2. **Head-sparing** is a biological mechanism in which the brain continues to grow even though the body stops growing in a malnourished child. (p. 87)
3. A **neuron,** or nerve cell, is the main component of the central nervous system, especially the brain. (p. 88)
4. The **cortex** is the outer layers of the brain that is involved in most thinking, feeling, and sensing. (p. 88)

   Memory aid: Cortex in Latin means "bark." As bark covers a tree, the cortex is the "bark of the brain."
5. An **axon** is the nerve fiber that sends electrochemical impulses from one neuron to the dendrites of other neurons. (p. 88)
6. A **dendrite** is a nerve fiber that receives the electrochemical impulses transmitted from other neurons via their axons. (p. 88)
7. A **synapse** is the intersection between the axon of a sending neuron and the dendrites of a receiving neuron. (p. 88)
8. **Neurotransmitters** are chemicals in the brain that carry messages from the axon of a sending neuron to the dendrite of a receiving neuron. (p. 88)
9. The **prefrontal cortex** is the area in the front of the brain that specializes in anticipation, planning, and impulse control. (p. 90)
10. **Shaken baby syndrome** is a life-threatening condition in which blood vessels in an infant's brain have been ruptured and neural connections have been broken because the infant has been forcefully shaken back and forth. (p. 91)
11. **REM (rapid eye movement) sleep** is a stage of sleep characterized by flickering eyes behind closed eyelids, dreaming, and rapid brain waves. (p. 93)
12. A **reflex** is an unlearned, involuntary action or movement emitted in response to a specific stimulus. (p. 94)
13. **Gross motor skills** are physical abilities that demand large body movements, such as walking, jumping, and running. (p. 95)
14. **Fine motor skills** are physical abilities that require precise, small movements, such as picking up a coin. (p. 96)
15. **Sensation** is the response of a sensory system when it detects a stimulus. (p. 97)
16. **Perception** is the mental processing of sensory information when the brain interprets it. (p. 97)
17. **Binocular vision** is the ability to focus both eyes in a coordinated fashion in order to see one image. (p. 98)

    Memory aid: Bi- indicates "two"; ocular means something pertaining to the eye. Binocular vision is vision for "two eyes."
18. **Immunization** is the process through which the body's immune system is stimulated (as by a vaccine) to defend against attack by a particular contagious disease. (p. 100)
19. **Sudden infant death syndrome (SIDS)** is a situation in which a seemingly healthy infant, at least 2 months of age, suddenly stops breathing and dies unexpectedly in his or her sleep. (p. 102)

20. **Co-sleeping** is the custom in which parents and their infants sleep together. (Also called *bed-sharing.*) (p. 103)
21. Piaget's stages of **sensorimotor intelligence** (from birth to about 2 years old) are based on his cognitive development theory that infants think exclusively with their senses and motor skills. (p. 105)
22. In Piaget's theory, **assimilation** refers to a type of adaptation in which new experiences are interpreted to fit into existing ideas. (p. 106)
23. In Piaget's theory, **accommodation** refers to a type of adaptation in which existing ideas are modified to include new experiences. (p. 106)
24. **Object permanence** is the understanding that objects continue to exist even when they cannot be seen, touched, or heard. (p. 107)
25. **"Little scientist"** is Piaget's term for the stage-five toddler who learns about the properties of objects in his or her world through active experimentation. (p. 108)
26. **Information-processing theory** is a perspective that compares thinking to the ways in which a computer analyzes data, through the processes of sensory input, connections, stored memories, and output. (p. 108)
27. A **visual cliff** is an experimental apparatus that provides the illusion of a sudden dropoff between one horizontal surface and another. (p. 109)
28. A **reminder session** is any perceptual experience that helps people recollect an idea, a thing, or an experience. (p. 110)
29. **Child-directed speech** is a form of speech used by adults when talking to infants. It is simplified, it has a higher pitch, and it is repetitive; it is also called *baby talk* or *motherese.* (p. 112)
30. **Babbling,** which begins between 6 and 9 months of age, is characterized by the extended repetition of certain syllables (such as "ma-ma"). (p. 113)
31. The **naming explosion** refers to the dramatic increase in the infant's vocabulary, especially in the number of nouns, that begins at about 18 months of age. (p. 113)
32. Another characteristic of infant speech is the use of the **holophrase,** in which a single word is used to convey a complete, meaningful thought. (p. 114)
33. According to Chomsky, children possess an innate **language acquisition device (LAD),** which is a hypothesized mental structure that enables them to acquire language, including the basic aspects of grammar, vocabulary, and intonation. (p. 117)

4

chapter

THE FIRST TWO YEARS

Psychosocial Development

Chapter Overview

Chapter 4 describes the emotional and social life of the developing person during infancy. It begins with a description of the infant's emerging emotions and how they reflect social awareness. Two emotions, pleasure and pain, are apparent at birth and are soon joined by joy, anger, sadness, and fear. As self-awareness develops, many new emotions emerge, including embarrassment, shame, guilt, and pride.

The second section explores theories of infant psychosocial development. These include the psychoanalytic theories of Freud and Erikson along with behaviorist, cognitive, and systems theories, which help us understand how the infant's emotional and behavioral responses begin to take on the various patterns that form personality. Temperament, which affects later personality and is primarily inborn, is influenced by the individual's interactions with the environment.

The third section explores the social context in which emotions develop. Emotions and relationships are then examined from the perspective of parent–infant interaction. Videotaped studies of parents and infants, combined with laboratory studies of attachment, have greatly expanded our understanding of psychosocial development. By referencing their caregivers' signals, infants learn when and how to express their emotions. This section concludes by exploring the impact of day care on infants.

NOTE: Answer guidelines for all Chapter 4 questions begin on page 71.

Chapter Review

When you have finished reading the chapter, work through the material that follows to review it. Complete the sentences and answer the questions. In some cases, Study Tips explain how best to learn a difficult concept, while Think About It and Applications help you to know how well you understand the material. As you proceed, evaluate your performance for each section by consulting the answers beginning on page 71 . Do not continue with the next section until you understand each answer. If you need to, review or reread the appropriate section in the textbook before continuing.

Introduction **and** ***Emotional Development***
(pp. 123–129)

1. Psychosocial development includes _______________ development and _______________ development.
2. The first emotions that can be reliably discerned in infants are _______________ and _______________ . Other early infant emotions include _______________ and _______________ . Infants' pleasure in seeing faces is first expressed by the _______________ _______________ , which appears at about _______________ weeks.
3. Anger becomes evident by about _______________ months. During infancy, anger _______________ (is/is not) a healthy response, and usually occurs in response to _______________ . In contrast, sadness indicates _______________ and is accompanied by an increase in the stress hormone _______________ .

4. Fully formed fear emerges at about _______________ months. One expression of this new emotion is _______________ _______________; another is _______________ _______________, or fear of abandonment, which is normal at age _______________ year(s) and intensifies by age _______________ year(s). During the second year, anger and fear typically _______________ (increase/decrease) and become more _______________ toward specific things.

5. Toward the end of the second year, the new emotions of _______________, _______________, _______________, and _______________ become apparent. These emotions require an awareness of _______________ _______________.

6. An important foundation for emotional growth is _______________; very young infants have no sense of _______________. This emerging sense of "me"and "mine" leads to a new _______________ of others. This sense usually emerges at the same time as advances in _______________ and using _______________-_______________ pronouns. This occurs at about _______________ months.

7. Pride is linked with the infant's maturing _______________. Telling toddlers that they are strong or smart may _______________ (help/hinder) their self-awareness, making it seem as if pride comes from _______________ _______________ _______________.

8. Emotional development depends partly on maturation of the developing _______________, along with having varied _______________ and good _______________. Infants' understanding of themselves is related to maturation of the brain's left _______________ _______________. Emotional development is directly tied to brain development in _______________ awareness and reactions to _______________.

9. The stimulation of one sensory stimulus to the brain by another is called _______________. This type of experience is partly _______________ and less common among _______________ (infants/older children) than it is among _______________ (infants/older children). The ability to link experiences in one sense with those in another is called _______________-_______________ perception.

10. The maturation of the cortical area called the _______________ _______________ _______________ is directly connected to emotional self-regulation. As emotional development proceeds, specific emotions come to be aroused by particular _______________. This indicates that infant emotional reactions depend partly on _______________.

11. Chronic early stress, such as occurs with _______________, can impair the brain's _______________, which regulates various bodily functions and hormone production. Helpful behaviors such as _______________ _______________ demonstrate the crucial role fathers can play in helping new mothers.

STUDY TIP/APPLICATION: Most students (in fact, most people) find it difficult to understand how young children cannot be self-aware. To enhance your understanding of this limitation in young children, first briefly describe the nature and findings of the classic rouge-and-mirror experiment on self-awareness in infants. Then, try it out with young children of different ages.

APPLICATIONS:

12. Chella and David are planning a night out for the first time since their infant was born nine months ago. As they prepare to leave, baby Lili begins to cry, indicating _______________ _______________. Then, when the unfamiliar babysitter approaches her, she cries and clings tightly to her mother, a sign of _______________ _______________.

Theories of Infant Psychosocial Development (pp. 129–138)

13. In Freud's theory, development begins with the ________________ stage, so named because the ________________ is the infant's prime source of gratification and pleasure.

14. According to Freud, in the second year, the prime focus of gratification comes from stimulation and control of the bowels. Freud referred to this period as the ________________ stage.

15. Freud believed that the potential conflicts of these stages had ________________ (short-term/long-term) consequences. If the conflicts are not resolved, the child may become an adult stuck in the first stage, with an ________________ ________________.

16. (A View from Science) To avoid conflict and the development of an "anal personality," ________________ theory advised parents to delay toilet training until the child was ready. This theory has been undermined by ________________ research that has found that toilet training occurs in a diversity of ways. Another approach based on principles of ________________ claims that toilet training can occur in as short a period as one day. The influential theorist ________________ believes that toilet training should begin around age ________________, when children are "ready" based on their ________________, ________________, and ________________ maturity.

17. The theorist who believed that development occurs through a series of psychosocial crises is ________________. According to his theory, the crisis of infancy is one of ________________ ________________, whereas the crisis of toddlerhood is one of ________________.

18. According to the perspective of ________________, personality is molded through the processes of ________________ and ________________ of the child's spontaneous behaviors. A strong proponent of this position was ________________.

19. Later theorists incorporated the role of ________________ learning, that is, infants' tendencies to observe and ________________ the personality traits of their parents. The theorist most closely associated with this type of learning is ________________.

20. Both psychoanalytic and behaviorist theories emphasize the role of ________________, especially the ________________. In retrospect, this focus is too ________________ (narrow/broad).

21. According to cognitive theory, a person's ________________ and ________________ determine his or her perspective on the world. Early experiences are important because ________________, ________________, and ________________ make them so. Infants use their early relationships to build a ________________ ________________ that becomes a frame of reference for organizing perceptions and experiences. Following this view, the child's ________________ of early experiences is crucial.

22. Cognitive theory also takes into account the social ________________, or cultural beliefs, of the entire community. Such ideas make up an ________________, a theory of child rearing that underlies the values and practices of a particular culture or ethnic group.

23. According to ________________ theory, every inherited trait affects the social context, and vice versa. Each infant is born with a ________________ predisposition to develop certain emotional traits. Among these are the traits of ________________. Unlike personality traits—that is, traits that are ________________, temperament traits originate in the ________________.

24. The classic long-term study of children's temperament is the ________________ ________________ ________________ ________________. The study found that by 3 months, infants can be clustered into one of four types: ________________, ________________, ________________, and ________________.

25. Other researchers studied adult personality traits and came up with the Big Five. These include ________________, ________________, ________________, ________________, and ________________. Researchers found both ________________ and ________________ in these traits, with each trait affecting the others and maturation affecting them all.

26. Physically close, ________________ parenting predicts toddlers who later are less ________________ and more ________________, in comparison to physically far, ________________ parenting, which produces children with the opposite traits.

STUDY TIP: Several theories of development have provided different explanations for how infants' emotions and temperaments develop. To help you remember the theories, complete the chart below and use it as a study aid. Some elements are filled in to give you a headstart.

27. Theory	**Stages or Continuous**	**Important Concepts**	**Effects on Emotional Development**
Psychoanalytic Theory Freud	stages	Oral and anal stages sexual impulses and unconscious conflicts	If conflicts not resolved, fixation may occur.
Erikson			
Behaviorism	continuous		
Cognitive Theory			
Systems Theory			
Sociocultural Theory			

APPLICATIONS:

28. Professor Kipketer believes that infants' emotions are molded as their parents reinforce or punish their behaviors. Professor Kipketer evidently is a proponent of ____________________ .

29. Mashiyat, who advocates systems theory in explaining the origins of personality, points to research evidence that
   a. infants are born with definite and distinct temperaments that can change.
   b. early temperamental traits almost never change.
   c. an infant's temperament does not begin to clearly emerge until 2 years of age.
   d. temperament appears to be almost completely unaffected by the social context.

30. Dr. Hidalgo believes that infants use their early relationships to develop a set of assumptions that become a frame of reference for later experiences. Dr. Hidalgo evidently is a proponent of ____________ ______________ .

31. Felix has an unusually strong need to regulate all aspects of his life. Freud would probably say that Felix is
   a. demonstrating the temperament he developed during infancy.
   b. fixated at the anal stage.
   c. fixated in the oral stage.
   d. experiencing the crisis of trust versus mistrust.

The Development of Social Bonds (pp. 138–150)

32. An important factor in healthy psychosocial development is ______________ ______________ ______________ between the developing child and the caregiving context. Children who are high in the Big Five trait of ______________ are more affected by their parents' responsiveness than are ______________ children. Ineffective or harsh parenting combined with a child's ______________ temperament is likely to create an antisocial, destructive child.

33. The coordinated interaction of response between infant and caregiver is called ______________ . Partly through this interaction, infants learn to ______________________________ and to develop some of the basic skills of ______________ ______________ . Synchrony usually begins with ______________ (infants/parents) imitating ______________ (infants/parents).

34. To study the importance of synchrony in development, researchers use an experimental device, called the ______________-______________ technique, in which the caregiver ______________ (does/does not) show any facial expression.

35. The emotional bond that develops between slightly older infants and their caregivers is called ______________ .

36. Approaching and following the caregiver are signs of ______________-______________ behaviors, while snuggling, touching, and holding are signs of ______________-______________ behaviors.

37. An infant who derives comfort and confidence from the secure base provided by the caregiver is displaying ______________ ______________ (type B). In this type of relationship, the caregiver acts as a ______________ ______________ ______________ from which the child is willing to venture forth.

38. By contrast, ______________ ______________ is characterized by an infant's fear, anger, or indifference. Two extremes of this type of relationship are ______________-______________ ______________ (type A) and ______________-______________/ ______________ ______________ (type C).

(text and Table 4.4) Briefly describe the two types of insecure attachment as well as disorganized attachment.

39. The procedure developed by Mary Ainsworth to measure attachment is called the ________________ ________________. Approximately ________________ (what proportion?) of all normal infants tested with this procedure demonstrate secure attachment. When infant–caregiver interactions are inconsistent, infants are classified as ________________.

40. The most troubled infants may be those who are type ________________. Attachment status ________________ (can/cannot) change.

41. The search for information about another person's feelings is called ________________ ________________.

42. In ________________ (most/some/a few) nations and ethnic groups, fathers spend much less time with infants than mothers do.

43. The social information from fathers tends to be more ________________ than that from mothers, who are more ________________ and ________________.

44. Infant day care outside the home by strangers is common in countries such as ________________ ________________, where it is subsidized by the ________________, but scarce in countries such as ________________ ________________, where it is not subsidized. Infant day care programs include ________________ day care, in which children of various ages are cared for in a paid caregiver's home, and ________________ day care, in which several paid providers care for children in a designated place.

45. Early day care may be detrimental when the mother is ________________ and the infant spends more than ________________ (how many?) hours each week in a poor-quality program. Research suggests that boys are affected ________________ (more than/less than/the same as) girls are. Out-of-home day care is better than in-home care if an infant's family does not provide adequate ________________ and ________________.

46. (Table 4.6) Researchers have identified five factors that are essential to high-quality day care:

a. ________________

b. ________________

c. ________________

d. ________________

e. ________________

STUDY TIP: Most students find it easier to remember the characteristics associated with secure and insecure attachment and their consequences if they are neatly summarized in a table. Complete the table below as a way of organizing the information.

47. Attachment Style	Characteristic Behavior of Infant	Characteristics of Parents
Secure (Type B)	Infant plays happily and comfortably, sometimes glancing at Mom for reassurance.	Parent is sensitive and responsive to infant's needs; synchrony is high; parents are not stressed; parents have a working model from their own parents.
Insecure-avoidant (Type A)		
Insecure-resistant/ambivalent (Type C)		
Disorganized		

APPLICATIONS:

48. One-year-old Kirsten and her Mom are participating in a laboratory test of attachment. When Mom returns to the playroom after a short absence, Kirsten, who is securely attached, is most likely to

a. cry and protest her Mom's return.
b. climb into her Mom's arms, then leave to resume play.
c. climb into her Mom's arms and stay there.
d. continue playing without acknowledging her Mom.

49. After a scary fall, 18-month-old Miguel looks to his mother to see if he should cry or laugh. Miguel's behavior is an example of

_______________ _______________ .

50. Which of the following is a clear sign of Isabel's attachment to her grandmother, her full-time caregiver?

a. She turns to her grandmother when distressed.
b. She protests when Grandma leaves a room.
c. She may cry when strangers appear.
d. These are all signs of infant attachment.

51. Concluding her report on the impact of day care on young children, Deborah notes that infants are likely to become insecurely attached if

a. their own mothers are insensitive caregivers.
b. the quality of day care is poor.
c. more than 20 hours per week are spent in day care.
d. all of these conditions exist.

52. Kalil's mother left him alone in the room for a few minutes. When she returned, Kalil seemed indifferent to her presence. According to Mary Ainsworth's research with children in the Strange Situation, Kalil is probably

a. a normal, independent infant.
b. an abused child.
c. insecurely attached.
d. securely attached.

53. Two-year-old Anita and her mother spend many hours together in well-coordinated mutual responding: When Anita smiles, her mother smiles. When Anita pouts, her mother shows distress. Their behavior illustrates

_______________ .

Conclusions in Theory and Practice (pp. 150–152)

54. Although the first two years are important, early _______________ and _______________ development is influenced by the _______________ behavior, the quality of _______________ _______________, patterns within the child's _______________, and traits that are _______________ .

Progress Test 1

Multiple-Choice Questions

Circle your answers to the following questions and check them with the answers beginning on page 72. If your answer is incorrect, read the explanation for why it is incorrect and then consult the appropriate pages of the text (in parentheses following the correct answer).

1. Newborns have two identifiable emotions

a. shame and distress.
b. pleasure and pain.
c. anger and joy.
d. pride and guilt.

2. Parenting that results in children who are self-aware but less obedient is called

a. proximal parenting.
b. distal parenting.
c. synchrony.
d. scaffolding.

3. An infant's fear of being left by the mother or other caregiver, called _______, is most obvious at about _______ .

a. separation anxiety; 2 to 4 months
b. stranger wariness; 2 to 4 months
c. separation anxiety; 9 to 14 months
d. stranger wariness; 9 to 14 months

4. Social referencing refers to

a. parenting skills that change over time.
b. changes in community values regarding, for example, the acceptability of using physical punishment with small children.
c. the support network for new parents provided by extended family members.
d. the infant response of looking to trusted adults for emotional cues in uncertain situations.

5. A key difference between temperament and personality is that

a. temperamental traits are learned.
b. personality includes traits that are primarily learned.
c. personality is more stable than temperament.
d. personality does not begin to form until much later, when self-awareness emerges.

6. The concept of a working model is most consistent with
   a. psychoanalytic theory.
   b. behaviorism.
   c. cognitive theory.
   d. sociocultural theory.

7. Freud's oral stage corresponds to Erikson's crisis of
   a. orality versus anality.
   b. trust versus mistrust.
   c. autonomy versus shame and doubt.
   d. secure versus insecure attachment.

8. Erikson believed that the development of a sense of trust in early infancy depends on
   a. the quality of the infant's food.
   b. the child's genetic inheritance.
   c. consistency, continuity, and sameness of experience.
   d. the introduction of toilet training.

9. Keisha is concerned that her 15-month-old daughter, who no longer seems to enjoy face-to-face play, is showing signs of insecure attachment. You tell her
   a. not to worry; face-to-face play almost disappears toward the end of the first year.
   b. she may be right to worry, because face-to-face play typically increases throughout infancy.
   c. not to worry; attachment behaviors are unreliable until toddlerhood.
   d. that her child is typical of children who spend more than 20 hours in day care each week.

10. "Easy," "slow to warm up," and "difficult" are descriptions of different
    a. forms of attachment.
    b. types of temperament.
    c. types of parenting.
    d. toddler responses to the Strange Situation.

11. The more physical play of fathers has been described as __________ parenting.
    a. proximal
    b. distal
    c. disorganized
    d. insecure

12. *Synchrony* is a term that describes
    a. the carefully coordinated interaction between caregiver and infant.
    b. a mismatch of the temperaments of caregiver and infant.
    c. a research technique involving videotapes.
    d. the concurrent evolution of different species.

13. The emotional tie that develops between an infant and his or her primary caregiver is called
    a. self-awareness.
    b. synchrony.
    c. affiliation.
    d. attachment.

14. Research studies using the still-face technique have demonstrated that
    a. a parent's responsiveness to an infant aids development.
    b. babies become more upset when a parent leaves the room than when the parent's facial expression is not synchonized with the infant's.
    c. beginning at about 2 months, babies become very upset by a still-faced caregiver.
    d. beginning at about 10 months, babies become very upset by a still-faced caregiver.

15. Interest in people, as evidenced by the social smile, appears for the first time when an infant is __________ weeks old.
    a. 3
    b. 6
    c. 9
    d. 12

True or False Items

Write T (*true*) or F (*false*) on the line in front of each statement.

_______ 1. The major developmental theories all agree that maternal care is better for children than nonmaternal care.

_______ 2. Approximately 25 percent of infants display secure attachment.

_______ 3. A baby at 11 months is likely to display both stranger wariness and separation anxiety.

_______ 4. Emotional development is affected by maturation of conscious awareness.

_______ 5. A securely attached toddler is most likely to stay close to his or her mother even in a familiar environment.

_______ 6. Current research shows that the majority of infants in day care are slow to develop cognitive skills.

_______ 7. Infants use their fathers for social referencing when they look for encouragement.

_______ 8. Temperament is genetically determined and is unaffected by environmental factors.

_______ 9. Self-awareness enables toddlers to feel pride as well as guilt.

_______ 10. Synesthesia (one sense triggering another) is a normal brain process.

Progress Test 2

Progress Test 2 should be completed during a final chapter review. Answer the following questions after you thoroughly understand the correct answers for the Chapter Review and Progress Test 1.

Multiple-Choice Questions

1. Infant–caregiver interactions that are marked by inconsistency are usually classified as
   a. disorganized.
   b. insecure-avoidant.
   c. insecure-resistant.
   d. insecure-ambivalent.

2. Freud's anal stage corresponds to Erikson's crisis of
   a. autonomy versus shame and doubt.
   b. trust versus mistrust.
   c. orality versus anality.
   d. identity versus role confusion.

3. Not until the sense of self begins to emerge do babies realize that they are seeing their own faces in the mirror. This realization usually occurs
   a. shortly before 3 months.
   b. at about 6 months.
   c. between 15 and 24 months.
   d. after 24 months.

4. When there is goodness of fit, the parents of a slow-to-warm-up boy will
   a. give him extra time to adjust to new situations.
   b. encourage independence in their son by frequently leaving him for short periods of time.
   c. put their son in regular day care so other children's temperaments will "rub off" on him.
   d. do all of these things.

5. Emotions such as shame, guilt, embarrassment, and pride emerge at the same time that
   a. the social smile appears.
   b. aspects of the infant's temperament can first be discerned.
   c. self-awareness begins to emerge.
   d. parents initiate toilet training.

6. Research by the NYLS on temperamental characteristics indicates that
   a. temperament is probably innate.
   b. the interaction of parent and child determines later personality.
   c. parents pass their temperaments on to their children through modeling.
   d. self-awareness contributes to the development of temperament.

7. In the second six months, stranger wariness is a
   a. result of insecure attachment.
   b. result of social isolation.
   c. normal emotional response.
   d. setback in emotional development.

8. The caregiving environment can affect a child's temperament through
   a. the development of brain areas related to emotional regulation.
   b. the child's working model of relationships.
   c. parental expectations.
   d. all of these factors.

9. While observing mothers playing with their infants in a playroom, you notice one mother who often teases her son, ignores him when he falls down, and tells him to "hush" when he cries. Mothers who display these behaviors usually have infants who exhibit which type of attachment?
   a. secure
   b. insecure-avoidant
   c. insecure-resistant
   d. disorganized

10. The later consequences of secure attachment and insecure attachment for children are
    a. balanced by the child's current rearing circumstances.
    b. irreversible, regardless of the child's current rearing circumstances.
    c. more significant in girls than in boys.
    d. more significant in boys than in girls.

11. The attachment pattern marked by anxiety and uncertainty is
    a. insecure-avoidant.
    b. insecure-resistant/ambivalent.
    c. disorganized.
    d. type B.

12. Compared with mothers, fathers are more likely to
    a. engage in more imaginative, exciting play.
    b. encourage intellectual development in their children.
    c. encourage social development in their children.
    d. read to their toddlers.

13. Like Freud, Erikson believed that:
 a. problems arising in early infancy last a lifetime.
 b. inability to resolve a conflict in infancy may result in later fixation.
 c. human development can be viewed in terms of psychosexual stages.
 d. all of these are true.

14. Which of the following is an example of social learning?
 a. Sue discovers that a playmate will share a favorite toy if she asks politely.
 b. Jon learns that other children are afraid of him when he raises his voice.
 c. Zach develops a hot temper after seeing his father regularly display anger and, in turn, receive respect from others.
 d. All of these are examples of social learning.

15. Which of the following is NOT true regarding synchrony?
 a. There are wide variations in the frequency of synchrony from baby to baby.
 b. Synchrony appears to be uninfluenced by cultural differences.
 c. The frequency of mother–infant synchrony has varied over historical time.
 d. Parents and infants spend about one hour a day in face-to-face play.

Matching Items

Match each theorist, term, or concept with its corresponding description or definition.

Theorists, Terms, or Concepts

_______ **1.** temperament
_______ **2.** Erikson
_______ **3.** Strange Situation
_______ **4.** synchrony
_______ **5.** trust versus mistrust
_______ **6.** Freud
_______ **7.** social referencing
_______ **8.** autonomy versus shame and doubt
_______ **9.** self-awareness
_______ **10.** Ainsworth
_______ **11.** proximity-seeking behaviors
_______ **12.** contact-maintaining behaviors

Descriptions or Definitions

a. looking to caregivers for emotional cues
b. the crisis of infancy
c. the crisis of toddlerhood
d. approaching and following
e. theorist who described psychosexual stages of development
f. researcher who devised a laboratory procedure for studying attachment
g. laboratory procedure for studying attachment
h. a person's relatively consistent inborn traits
i. touching, snuggling, and holding
j. coordinated interaction between parent and infant
k. theorist who described psychosocial stages of development
l. a person's sense of being distinct from others

Key Terms

Using your own words, write a brief definition or explanation of each of the following terms on a separate piece of paper.

1. social smile
2. stranger wariness
3. separation anxiety
4. self-awareness
5. trust versus mistrust
6. autonomy versus shame and doubt
7. social learning
8. working model
9. ethnotheory
10. temperament
11. Big Five
12. proximal parenting
13. distal parenting
14. goodness of fit
15. synchrony
16. still-face technique
17. attachment
18. secure attachment

19. insecure-avoidant attachment
20. insecure-resistant/ambivalent attachment
21. disorganized attachment
22. Strange Situation
23. social referencing
24. family day care
25. center day care

Answers

CHAPTER REVIEW

1. emotional; social
2. pleasure; pain; curiosity; happiness; social smile; 6
3. 6; is; frustration; withdrawal; cortisol
4. 9; stranger wariness; separation anxiety; 1; 2; decrease; targeted (focused)
5. pride; shame; embarrassment; guilt; other people
6. self-awareness; self; consciousness; pretending; first-person; 18
7. self-concept; hinder; pleasing other people
8. brain; experiences; nutrition; temporoparietal junction; social; stress
9. synesthesia; genetic; older children; infants; cross-modal
10. anterior cingulate gyrus; people; memory
11. abuse; hypothalamus; kangaroo care

Study Tip: In the classic self-awareness experiment, babies look in a mirror after a dot of rouge is put on their nose. If the babies react to the mirror image by touching their noses, it is clear they know they are seeing their own faces. Most babies demonstrate this self-awareness between 15 and 24 months of age.

12. separation anxiety; stranger wariness
13. oral; mouth
14. anal
15. long-term; oral fixation
16. psychoanalytic; cross-cultural; behaviorism; T. Berry Brazelton; 2; cognitive; emotional; biological
17. Erik Erikson; trust versus mistrust; autonomy versus shame and doubt
18. behaviorism; reinforcement; punishment; John Watson
19. social; imitate; Albert Bandura
20. parents; mother; narrow
21. values; thoughts; beliefs; perceptions; memories; working model; interpretation
22. constructions; ethnotheory
23. systems; genetic; temperament; learned; genes
24. New York Longitudinal Study (NYLS); easy; difficult; slow to warm up; hard to classify
25. openness; conscientiousness; extroversion; agreeableness; neuroticism; change; continuity
26. proximal; self-aware; compliant; distal
27. Only Freud and Erikson proposed stage theories. Other theories see development as continuous throughout the lifespan.

    Erikson emphasized psychosocial conflicts at each stage. If the conflicts are not resolved, the effects could last a lifetime, for example, creating a suspicious and pessimistic adult (mistrusting).

    Behaviorism emphasizes that emotions and personality are molded as parents reinforce or punish a child's spontaneous behavior. The result can last a lifetime if no other reinforcement or punishment changes the behavior.

    Cognitive theory believes that infants develop a working model that serves as a frame of reference later in life. They use this model to organize their perceptions and experiences.

    Systems theory holds that each person is born with a unique temperament that affects and is affected by life's experiences.

    Sociocultural theory contends that social and cultural factors have a significant influence on development and continue throughout the life span.
28. behaviorism. Behaviorists focus on learning through reinforcement or punishment and by observing others.
29. **a.** is the answer. Systems theory is an epigenetic approach, holding that every inherited trait affects the social context, and vice versa.
30. cognitive theory. Cognitive theory holds that thoughts and values determine a person's perspective.
31. **b.** is the answer. According to Freud, if the conflict at a particular stage is not resolved, the person becomes fixated at that stage. So, being fixated at the anal stage, Felix has a strong need for self-control.
32. goodness of fit; neuroticism; easygoing; negative
33. synchrony; read other people's emotions; social interaction; parents; infants

34. still-face; does not

35. attachment

36. proximity-seeking; contact-maintaining

37. secure attachment; base for exploration

38. insecure attachment; insecure-avoidant attachment; insecure-resistant/ambivalent attachment

Some infants are avoidant: They engage in little interaction with their mothers before and after her departure. Others are anxious and resistant: They cling nervously to their mothers, are unwilling to explore, become very upset when she leaves, and refuse to be comforted when she returns. Others are disorganized: They show an inconsistent mixture of behaviors toward their mothers.

39. Strange Situation; two-thirds; disorganized

40. D; can

41. social referencing

42. most

43. encouraging; cautious; protective

44. France, Israel, and Sweden; government; India, Ethiopia, and most Latin American nations; family; center

45. insensitive; 20; more than; stimulation; attention

46. (a) adequate attention to each infant; (b) encouragement of sensorimotor and language development; (c) attention to health and safety; (d) well-trained and professional caregivers; (e) warm and responsive caregivers

47. Insecure-avoidant: They have less confidence and play independently without maintaining contact with the parent. Parents are neglectful, stressed, intrusive, and controlling, and the father is an active alcoholic.

Insecure-resistant/ambivalent: This child is unwilling to leave the parent's lap. Parent is abusive and depressed.

Disorganized: This type has elements of the other types; the infant shifts between hitting and kissing the parent, from staring to crying. The most troubled children are classified as type D. The parent is abusive, paranoid, and stressed. The mother is an active alcoholic.

48. **b.** is the answer. Securely attached infants use their caregiver as a secure base. Kirsten returns to her mother for reassurance, and then resumes play.

49. social referencing. Miguel is asking his mother how he should react by looking at her after the fall.

50. **d.** is the answer.

51. **d.** is the answer.

52. **c.** is the answer. Insecure-resistant/ambivalent infants usually become upset when the caregiver leaves but may resist or seek contact when she returns.

53. synchrony. Synchrony is a coordinated and smooth exchange of responses between a caregiver and an infant. Usually, it begins with the caregiver imitating the infant's behavior.

54. emotional; social; parents'; day care; culture; inborn

PROGRESS TEST 1

Multiple-Choice Questions

1. **b.** is the answer. (p. 124)

a., c., & d. These emotions emerge later in infancy, at about the same time as self-awareness emerges.

2. **b.** is the answer. (p. 136)

3. **c.** is the answer. (p. 125)

4. **d.** is the answer. (p. 145)

5. **b.** is the answer. (p. 134)

6. **c.** is the answer. (p. 132)

7. **b.** is the answer. (pp. 129, 131)

a. Orality and anality refer to personality traits that result from fixation in the oral and anal stages, respectively.

c. According to Erikson, this is the crisis of toddlerhood, which corresponds to Freud's anal stage.

d. This is not a developmental crisis in Erikson's theory.

8. **c.** is the answer. (p. 131)

9. **a.** is the answer. (p. 141)

c. Attachment behaviors are reliably found during infancy.

d. There is no indication that the child attends day care.

10. **b.** is the answer. Another type is "hard to classify." (pp. 134–135)

a. "Secure" and "insecure" are different forms of attachment.

c. The chapter does not describe different types of parenting.

d. The Strange Situation is a test of attachment rather than of temperament.

11. **a.** is the answer. (p. 146)

c. & d. These terms were not used to describe parenting styles.

12. **a.** is the answer. (p. 140)

13. **d.** is the answer. (p. 141)

a. Self-awareness refers to the infant's developing sense of "me and mine."

b. Synchrony describes the coordinated interaction between infant and caregiver.

c. Affiliation describes the tendency of people at any age to seek the companionship of others.

14. **a.** is the answer. (p. 141)

b. In fact, just the opposite is true.

c. & d. Not usually at 2 months, but clearly at 6 months, babies become very upset by a still-faced caregiver.

15. **b.** is the answer. (p. 124)

True or False Items

1. F Systems theorists contend that the entire social context can have an impact on the infant's development. (p. 134) **OK?**
2. F About two-thirds of infants display secure attachment. (p. 143)
3. T (p. 125)
4. T (p. 126)
5. F A securely attached toddler is most likely to explore the environment, with the mother's presence being enough to give him or her the courage to do so. (p. 142)
6. F Researchers believe that high-quality day care is not likely to harm the child. In fact, it is thought to be beneficial to the development of cognitive and social skills. (pp. 148–149)
7. T (p. 146)
8. F Temperament is a product of both genes and experience. (p. 134)
9. T (p. 126)
10. T (p. 127)

PROGRESS TEST 2

Multiple-Choice Questions

1. **a.** is the answer. (p. 143)
2. **a.** is the answer. (pp. 129, 131)
3. **c.** is the answer. (p. 126)
4. **a.** is the answer. (p. 139)
5. **c.** is the answer. (p. 125)

a. & b. The social smile, as well as temperamental characteristics, emerge well before the first signs of self-awareness.

d. Contemporary developmentalists link these emotions to self-consciousness, rather than any specific environmental event such as toilet training.

6. **a.** is the answer. (pp. 134–135)

b. & c. Although environment, especially parents, affects temperamental tendencies, the study noted that temperament was established within 3 months of birth.

d. Self-awareness is not a temperamental characteristic.

7. **c.** is the answer. (p. 125)
8. **d.** is the answer. (pp. 134–135)
9. **d.** is the answer. (p. 143)
10. **a.** is the answer. (pp. 144–145)

c. & d. The text does not suggest that the consequences of secure and insecure attachment differ in boys and girls.

11. **b.** is the answer. (p. 143)

a. Insecure-avoidant attachment is marked by behaviors that indicate an infant is uninterested in a caregiver's presence or departure.

c. Disorganized attachment is marked only by the inconsistency of infant–caregiver behaviors.

d. Type B, or secure attachment, is marked by behaviors that indicate an infant is using a caregiver as a base from which to explore the environment.

12. **a.** is the answer. (p. 146)
13. **a.** is the answer. (p. 131)

b. & c. Freud alone would have agreed with these statements.

14. **c.** is the answer. (p. 132)

a. & b. Social learning involves learning by observing others. In these examples, the children are learning directly from the consequences of their own behavior.

15. **b.** is the answer. (p. 140)

Matching Items

1. h (p. 134)	**5.** b (p. 131)	**9.** l (p. 126)
2. k (p. 131)	**6.** e (p. 129)	**10.** f (pp. 142–143)
3. g (p. 143)	**7.** a (p. 145)	**11.** d (p. 141)
4. j (p. 140)	**8.** c (p. 131)	**12.** i (p. 141)

KEY TERMS

1. A **social smile** occurs when an infant smiles in response to a human face; evident in infants about 6 weeks after birth. (p. 124)
2. A common early fear in response to some person, thing, or situation, **stranger wariness** is first noticeable at about 9 months. (p. 125)
3. **Separation anxiety**, which is the infant's fear of being left by a familiar caregiver, is usually strongest at 9 to 14 months. (p. 125)
4. **Self-awareness** refers to a person's realization that he or she is a distinct individual, whose body, mind, and actions are separate from other people. Self-awareness makes possible many new self-conscious emotions, including shame, embarrassment, and pride. (p. 126)
5. In Erikson's theory, the psychosocial crisis of infancy is one of **trust versus mistrust,** in which the infant learns whether the world is essentially a secure place in which basic needs will be met. (p. 131)
6. In Erikson's theory, the psychosocial crisis of toddlerhood is one of **autonomy versus shame and doubt,** in which toddlers strive to rule their own actions and bodies. (p. 131)
7. **Social learning** is learning by observing others. (p. 132)
8. According to cognitive theory, infants use early social relationships to develop a set of assumptions called a **working model** that organizes their perceptions and experiences. (p. 132)
9. An **ethnotheory** is a theory of child rearing that underlies the values and practices of an ethnic group or culture. It is usually not apparent to the people within the culture. (p. 133)
10. **Temperament** refers to the "constitutionally based individual differences" in emotions, activity, and self-regulation. (p. 134)
11. The **Big Five** are stable, basic clusters of personality traits that include openness, conscientiousness, extroversion, agreeableness, and neuroticism. (p. 135)
12. **Proximal parenting** practices involve close physical contact between child and caregiver. (p. 136)
13. **Distal parenting** practices involve remaining distant from a baby. (p. 136)
14. **Goodness of fit** is a similarity of temperament and values that produces a smooth interaction between the individual and the social context. (p. 139)
15. **Synchrony** refers to a coordinated, rapid, and smooth interaction between caregiver and infant that helps infants learn to express and read emotions. (p. 140)
16. The **still-face technique** is an experimental device in which an adult keeps his or her face unmoving and expressionless in face-to-face interaction with an infant. (p. 141)
17. According to Mary Ainsworth, **attachment** is the enduring emotional bond that a person forms with another. (p. 141)
18. A **secure attachment** is one in which the infant obtains comfort and confidence from the base of exploration provided by a caregiver. (p. 142)
19. **Insecure-avoidant attachment** is the pattern of attachment in which the infant seems uninterested in the caregiver's presence, departure, or return. (p. 143)
20. **Insecure-resistant/ambivalent attachment** is the pattern of attachment in which an infant resists active exploration, becomes very upset when the caregiver leaves, and both resists and seeks contact when the caregiver returns. (p. 143)
21. **Disorganized attachment** is the pattern of attachment that is neither secure nor insecure and is marked by inconsistent infant–caregiver interactions. (p. 143)
22. The **Strange Situation** is a laboratory procedure developed by Mary Ainsworth for assessing attachment. Infants are observed in a playroom, in several successive episodes, while the caregiver and a stranger move in and out of the room. (p. 143)
23. When infants engage in **social referencing,** they are looking to trusted adults for emotional cues on how to react to unfamiliar or ambiguous objects or events. (p. 145)
24. **Family day care** is regular care provided for several children in a paid nonrelative's home. (p. 147)
25. **Center day care** is regular care provided for children by several paid adults in a place designed for that purpose. (p. 147)

5 chapter

EARLY CHILDHOOD

Body and Mind

Chapter Overview

Chapter 5 introduces the developing person between the ages of 2 and 6. The chapter begins by outlining growth rates and the changes in shape that occur from ages 2 through 6, as well as the toddler's eating habits. A description of the acquisition of gross and fine motor skills follows, noting the environmental hazards that interfere with the development of these skills. The discussion of brain growth and development focuses on the brain's role in physical and cognitive development. The developing limbic system is also described, along with its role in the expression and regulation of emotions during early childhood.

In countless everyday instances, as well as in the findings of numerous research studies, young children reveal themselves to be remarkably thoughtful, insightful, and perceptive thinkers whose grasp of the causes of everyday events, memory of the past, and mastery of language are sometimes astonishing. The third section begins with Piaget's and Vygotsky's views of cognitive development at this age. According to Piaget, young children's thought is prelogical: Between the ages of about 2 and 6, they are capable of symbolic thought but unable to perform many logical operations and are limited by irreversible, centered, and static thinking. Lev Vygotsky, a contemporary of Piaget's, saw learning as a social activity more than as a matter of individual discovery. Vygotsky focused on the child's zone of proximal development and the relationship between language and thought.

The next section focuses on what young children can do, including their emerging abilities to theorize about the world. This leads into a section on language development during early childhood. Although young children demonstrate rapid improvement in vocabulary and grammar, they have difficulty with comparisons and certain rules of grammar. A discussion of whether bilingualism in young children is useful concludes the section on language. This is followed by a discussion of preschool education, and an evaluation of its impact on children.

The final section begins with a discussion of the important issues of injury control and accidents, the major cause of childhood death. This section concludes with an in-depth exploration of child maltreatment, including its prevalence, contributing factors, consequences for future development, treatment, and prevention.

NOTE: Answer guidelines for all Chapter 5 questions begin on page 89.

Chapter Review

When you have finished reading the chapter, work through the material that follows to review it. Complete the sentences and answer the questions. In some cases, Study Tips explain how best to learn a difficult concept, while Think About It and Applications help you to know how well you understand the material. As you proceed, evaluate your performance for each section by consulting the answers beginning on page 89. Do not continue with the next section until you understand each answer. If you need to, review or reread the appropriate section in the textbook before continuing.

Body Changes (pp. 160–165)

1. In early childhood, from age ____2____ to ____6____, children add almost (3 inch) 7 Cm in height and gain about 2 1/2 pds (2 Kg) in weight per year. By age 6, the average child in a developed nation weighs about 46 lbs (21 Kgs) and measures ____117 cm____ in height. At age 5, the child's ratio of height to weight, called the ____Boda____ ____max____ ____index____, is lower than at any other age in the life span.

2. In multiethnic countries, children of African descent tend to be tallest, followed by Eropeen, then Asian, and then Latino.

3. Size and shape differences within (between/within) groups are greater than the average differences between (between/within) groups.

4. Household income also affects physical growth. In Brazil, for instance, whereas low income once correlated with malnutrition today, a more frequent problem is obesity.

5. Overfeeding in childhood increases later risk of two chronic illnesses: heart disease and diabetes. During early childhood, children need fewer (fewer/more) calories per pound than they did as infants.

6. An additional problem for American children is that they consume too many sweetened cereals & drinks. One result of too much sugar is tooth decay, the most common disease of young children in developed nations.

7. Young children generally insist that a particular experience occur in an exact sequence and manner, a phenomenon called just right.

8. Young children spend the majority of time in play, which is an important factor in developing their motor skill. Muscle growth, brain maturation, and guided practice advance their development of gross motor skills.

9. Skills that involve small body movements, such as pouring liquids and cutting food, are called fine motor skills. Most 2-year-olds have greater difficulty with these skills primarily because they have not developed the muscular control, patience, or judgement needed.

10. Environmental hazards such as lead in the water and air, pesticide in the soil, BPA in plastic, and secondhand cigarette smoke impair children's development.

Brain Development (pp. 166–170)

11. By age 2, most pruning of the brain's dendrites has occurred, and the brain weighs 75 percent of its adult weight. By age 6, the brain has attained about 90 percent of its adult weight.

12. Some of the brain's increase in size during childhood is due to the continued proliferation of ________ pathways, but most of it occurs because of the ongoing process of ________.

13. The long, thick band of nerve fibers that connects the right and left sides of the brain, called the ________ ________, grows and ________ rapidly during early childhood. This helps children better coordinate functions that involve ________ ________.

14. The two sides of the body and brain ________ (are/are not) identical. The specialization of the two sides of the body and brain is called ________.

15. Adults who are ________ (right-/left-) handed tend to have a thicker corpus callosum, probably because as children they had a greater need to ________ both sides of the body in a right-handed world.

16. The left hemisphere of the brain controls the ________ side of the body and contains areas dedicated to ________, detailed ________, and ________.

The right hemisphere controls the ________________ side of the body and contains brain areas dedicated to ________________ and ________________ impulses. As a rule, though, every cognitive skill requires ________________ (the right/the left/ both) side(s) of the brain.

17. The part of the brain that enables children to focus attention is the ________________ ________________. This area is sometimes called the ________________ because all other areas of the brain are ruled by its decisions.

18. Two signs of an undeveloped prefrontal cortex are ________________ and ________________, which is the tendency to stick to a thought or action for a long time.

19. The part of the brain that plays a crucial role in the expression and regulation of emotions is the ________________ ________________. Within this system is the ________________, which registers emotions, particularly ________________ and ________________. Next to this area is the ________________, which is a central processor of ________________, especially of ________________. Another structure in this brain region is the ________________, which responds to signals from the other limbic system parts to produce ________________ that activate other parts of the brain and body.

THINK ABOUT IT: Students, and people in general, often have difficulty understanding the limitations of the young child's thinking and emotional impulsiveness. To increase your understanding, make a list of behaviors that demonstrate the child's immaturity, then observe and compare 2- or 3-year-olds with 6-year-olds.

STUDY TIP: Learning (and remembering) developmental changes in height, weight, brain maturation, and other aspects of biological development requires a lot of rote memorization. A good way to facilitate your learning is to design and complete a simple organizational chart. Your chart might look something like the one below.

20. Physical Changes in Early Childhood (2–6 years)

	Changes	Description
Height (in inches)	3 inches per year	The child is taller and thinner and, on average, 46 inches by 6 years of age.
Weight (in pounds)		
Brain functions General		
Prefrontal cortex		
Limbic system		
Motor skills Gross		
Fine		

APPLICATIONS:

21. Three-year-old Kyle's parents are concerned because Kyle, who generally seems healthy, doesn't seem to have the hefty appetite he had as an infant. Should they be worried?

- **a.** Yes, because appetite normally increases throughout early childhood.
- **b.** Yes, because appetite remains as good during early childhood as it was earlier.
- **c.** No, because caloric need is less during early childhood than during infancy.
- **d.** There is not enough information to determine whether Kyle is developing normally.

22. Rodesia is a left-handed adult. It is most likely that she

- **a.** has a thinner corpus callosum.
- **b.** has a thicker corpus callosum.
- **c.** experienced delayed maturation of her prefrontal cortex.
- **d.** experienced accelerated maturation of her prefrontal cortex.

23. Following an automobile accident, Amira developed severe problems with her speech. Her doctor believes that the accident injured the ___left half___ of her brain.

24. Yolanda, who is 5 years old, has improved dramatically in her ability to throw and catch a baseball. Which aspect of her brain development contributed most to enable these abilities by enhancing communication among the brain's various specialized areas?

- **a.** increasing brain weight
- **b.** proliferation of dendrite networks
- **c.** myelination
- **d.** increasing specialization of brain areas

25. Two-year-old Ali is quite clumsy, falls down frequently, and often bumps into stationary objects. Ali most likely

- **a.** has a neuromuscular disorder.
- **b.** has an underdeveloped right hemisphere of the brain.
- **c.** is suffering from an iron deficiency.
- **d.** is a normal 2-year-old whose gross motor skills will improve dramatically during early childhood.

26. Climbing a fence is an example of a ___gross motor skill___

27. Which of the following activities would probably be the most difficult for a 5-year-old child?

- **a.** climbing a ladder
- **b.** catching a ball
- **c.** throwing a ball
- **d.** pouring juice from a pitcher without spilling it

Thinking During Childhood (pp. 171–178)

28. Piaget referred to cognitive development between the ages of 2 and 6 as ______________ intelligence. The child's verbal ability at this age enables ___critical___ thinking.

29. Young children's tendency to contemplate the world exclusively from their personal perspective is referred to as ___egocentric___. This tendency ___is___ (is/is not) equated with selfishness. Their tendency to think about one aspect of a situation at a time is called ___centration___. Children also tend to focus on ______________ to the exclusion of other attributes of objects and people.

30. Young children's understanding of the world tends to focus on ___static___ (static/dynamic) reasoning, which means that they tend to think of their world as ___unchanging___. Another characteristic of preoperational thinking is ___irreversibility___—the inability to recognize that reversing a process will restore the original conditions from which the process began. The idea that amount is unaffected by changes in appearance is called ______________.

31. Yet another characteristic of preoperational thought is ______________, or the belief that natural objects and phenomena are alive. Research demonstrates that many children simultaneously hold ideas that are both ______________ and ______________.

32. Much of the research on the social side of early cognition is inspired by the Russian psychologist ______________. According to this perspective, a child is an ______________ ______________, whose intellectual growth is stimulated by older and more skilled members of society.

33. Vygotsky believed that adults can most effectively help a child solve a problem by presenting ______________, by offering ______________, by providing ______________, and by encouraging ______________. This emphasizes that children's intellectual growth is stimulated by their ______________ ______________ in ______________ experiences and explorations.

34. Vygotsky suggested that for each developing individual there is a ________________ ________________ ________________, a range of skills that the person can exercise with assistance but is not yet able to perform independently.

35. How and when new skills are developed depends, in part, on the willingness of tutors to ________________ the child's participation in the learning process.

36. Vygotsky believed that language is essential to the advancement of thinking in two crucial ways. The first is through the internal dialogue in which a person talks to himself or herself, called ________________ ________________. In young children, this dialogue is likely to be ________________ (expressed silently/uttered aloud).

37. According to Vygotsky, another way language advances thinking is through ________________ ________________.

STUDY TIP: When many students first read Piaget's description of the limits of preoperational thought, they have the same reaction many developmentalists did—they don't believe it. To bring to life the fact that the preoperational child sees the world from his or her own perspective (egocentrism) and has not yet mastered the principle of conservation (the idea that properties such as mass, volume, and number remain the same despite changes in appearance), you might try one of Piaget's classic tests with a younger sibling, relative, or friend—for example, cut two hot dogs into different numbers of pieces or pour milk from a tall, thin glass into a short, fat glass, and ask the child which hot dog is bigger or which glass has more milk in it.

APPLICATIONS:

38. An experimenter first shows a child two rows of checkers that each have the same number of checkers. Then, with the child watching, the experimenter elongates one row and asks the child if each of the two rows still has an equal number of checkers. This experiment tests the child's understanding of ________________.

39. Five-year-old Dani believes that a "party" is the one and only attribute of a birthday. She says that Daddy doesn't have a birthday because he never has a party. This thinking demonstrates the tendency Piaget called ________________.

40. Darrell understands that 6 + 3 = 9 means that 9 - 6 = 3. He has mastered the concept of ________________.

41. Which of the following terms does NOT belong with the others?

a. focus on appearances
b. static reasoning
c. reversibility
d. centration

42. In describing the limited logical reasoning of young children, a developmentalist is LEAST likely to emphasize

a. irreversibility. **c.** its action-bound nature.
b. centration. **d.** its static nature.

43. A young child fails to put together a difficult puzzle on her own, so her mother encourages her to try again, this time guiding her by asking questions such as, "For this space, do we need a big piece or a little piece?" With Mom's help, the child successfully completes the puzzle. Lev Vygotsky would attribute the child's success to

a. additional practice with the puzzle pieces.
b. imitation of her mother's behavior.
c. the social interaction with her mother that restructured the task to make its solution more attainable.
d. modeling and reinforcement.

44. Comparing the views of Piaget with those of Vygotsky, active learning is to guided participation as egocentrism is to

a. apprenticeship. **c.** scaffold.
b. structure. **d.** fast-mapping.

45. The term ________________-________________ highlights the idea that children attempt to construct theories to explain everything they see and hear.

46. At about ________________ years, young children acquire an understanding of others' thinking, or a ________________ ________________ ________________.

Describe the theory of mind of children between the ages of 3 and 6.

47. Most 3-year-olds ________________ (have/do not have) difficulty realizing that a belief can be false.

48. Research studies reveal that theory-of-mind development depends partly on ________________ maturation, particularly of the brain's ________________ ________________. General ________________ ability is also important in strengthening young children's theory of mind. A third helpful factor is having at least one ________________ ________________. Finally, the ________________ ________________ may be a factor.

THINK ABOUT IT: One theory of how people acquire a theory of mind is that it is inborn. However, there are many reasons to suppose that as children grow into different cultures, their theories of mind emerge. Cultural variations in theories of mind are often revealed through language. For example, children in Samoa typically do not try to get out of trouble by saying, "I did not do it on purpose," as they often do in European American cultures; instead, they deny having done the deed at all.

APPLICATIONS:

49. A 4-year-old tells the teacher that a clown should not be allowed to visit the class because "Pat is 'fraid of clowns." The 4-year-old thus shows that he can anticipate how another will feel. This is evidence of the beginnings of ________________.

50. Five-year-old Rhoda has a 7-year-old sister and a 9-year-old brother. Her same-age friend, Veronica, has a 3-year-old brother. Which of the following is most likely to be true?
   a. Rhoda will develop a theory of mind sooner than Veronica will.
   b. Veronica will develop a theory of mind sooner than Rhoda will.
   c. They will develop a theory of mind at about the same time.
   d. Neither will develop a theory of mind until about age 7.

Language (pp. 179–182)

51. Two aspects of development that make ages 2 to 6 the prime time for learning language are ________________ and ________________ in the language areas of the brain. Another is the characteristic ________________ interaction of early childhood.

52. Although early childhood does not appear to be a ________________ period for language development, it does seem to be a ________________ period for the learning of vocabulary, grammar, and pronunciation.

53. During early childhood, a dramatic increase in language occurs, with ________________ increasing rapidly.

54. Through the process called ________________-________________, young children often learn words after only one or two hearings.

55. Because young children do not understand that word meaning depends on context, they have difficulty with words that express ________________. They also have trouble with words expressing relationships of ________________ and ________________.

56. The structures, techniques, and rules that a language uses to communicate meaning define its ________________.

57. Young children's tendency to apply rules of grammar when they should not is called ________________.

Give an example of this tendency.

58. (A View Form Science) Most developmentalists agree that bilingualism _______________ (is/is not necessarily) an asset to children in today's world. Even so, language-minority children are at a(n) _______________ (advantage/disadvantage) in most ways. Bilingual children typically process the two languages in _______________ (the same/different) areas of their brains. The best solution is for children to become _______________ _______________, who are fluent in both languages.

STUDY TIP: To better understand the cognitive and linguistic processes of young children, you might examine several well-loved children's books. Many characteristics of preoperational thinking and language are reflected in such books. For example, much of the fun in the *Amelia Bedelia* books is based entirely on the main character's literal interpretation of her instructions.

APPLICATIONS:

59. Six-year-old Stefano produces sentences that follow such rules of word order as "the initiator of an action precedes the verb, the receiver of an action follows it." This demonstrates that he has a knowledge of _______________ .

60. Two-year-old Amelia says, "We goed to the store." She is making a grammatical _______________ .

61. Dr. Jones, who believes that children's language growth greatly contributes to their cognitive growth, evidently is a proponent of the ideas of
   a. Piaget.
   b. Chomsky.
   c. Flavell.
   d. Vygotsky.

Early-Childhood Education (pp. 182–188)

62. Compared with a hundred years ago, when children didn't start school until _______________ _______________, today most _______________- to _______________-year-olds in developed nations are in school.

63. Many new programs use an educational model inspired by _______________ that allows children to _______________. Many programs are also influenced by _______________, who believed that children learn from other _______________ under the watchful guidance of adults.

64. One type of preschool was opened by _______________ for poor children in Rome. This _______________-_______________ school was based on the belief that children needed structured, individualized projects in order to give them a sense of _______________ .

65. Another new early-childhood curriculum called _______________ _______________ encourages children to master skills not usually seen in American schools until about age _______________ .

66. Other preschool programs are more _______________-directed. These programs explicitly teach basic skills, including _______________, _______________, and _______________, typically using _______________ _______________ by a teacher.

67. In 1965, _______________ _______________ _______________ was inaugurated to give low-income children some form of compensatory education during early childhood.

68. Longitudinal research found that graduates of similar but more intensive, well-evaluated programs scored _______________ (higher/no higher) on math and reading achievement tests and were more likely to attend college and less likely to go to jail.

STUDY TIP: To help you understand why an early-education program does not succeed, refer back to Chapter 4, which discussed the pros and cons of infant day care. Similar factors most likely apply to education during early childhood. List several characteristics of high-quality early childhood education.

APPLICATION:

69. Noreen, a nursery school teacher, is given the job of selecting holiday entertainment for a group of young children. If Noreen agrees with the ideas of Vygotsky, she is most likely to select
   a. a simple TV show that every child can understand.
   b. a hands-on experience that requires little adult supervision.
   c. brief, action-oriented play activities that the children and teachers will perform together.
   d. holiday puzzles for children to work on individually.

Injuries and Maltreatment (pp. 188–193)

70. The leading cause of childhood death is ________________ .
71. Not until age ________________ does any disease become a greater cause of mortality.
72. Instead of "accident prevention," many experts speak of ________________ ________________ (or ________________ ________________), an approach based on the belief that most accidents ________________ (are/are not) preventable.
73. Preventive community actions that reduce everyone's chance of injury are called ________________ ________________ . Preventive actions that avert harm in a high-risk situation constitute ________________ ________________ . Actions aimed at minimizing the impact of an adverse event that has already occurred constitute ________________ ________________ .
74. Until about 1960, the concept of child maltreatment was mostly limited to rare and ________________ outbursts of a disturbed stranger. Today, it is known that most perpetrators of maltreatment are the child's ________________ ________________ .
75. Intentional harm to or avoidable endangerment of someone under age 18 defines child ________________ . Actions that are deliberately harmful to a child's well-being are classified as ________________ . A failure to act appropriately to meet a child's basic needs is classified as ________________ .
76. The number of cases of ________________ ________________, in which authorities have been officially notified, is much ________________ (higher/lower) than the number of unverified cases.
77. Often the first sign of maltreatment is ________________ ________________, such as slow growth or lack of curiosity.
78. Severely maltreated children suffer ________________, ________________, and ________________ handicaps.

Describe other deficits of children who have been maltreated.

79. Public policy measures and other efforts designed to prevent maltreatment from ever occurring are called ________________ ________________ . An approach that focuses on spotting and treating the first symptoms of maltreatment is called ________________ ________________ . Last-ditch measures, such as removing a child from an abusive home, jailing the perpetrator, and so forth, constitute ________________ ________________ .
80. Once maltreatment has been substantiated, the first priority is ________________ ________________ for the child's long-term care.
81. Some children are officially removed from their biological parents and placed in a ________________ ________________ arrangement with another adult or family who is paid to nurture them.
82. In another type of foster care, called ________________ ________________, a relative of the maltreated child becomes the approved caregiver. A final option is ________________ .

APPLICATIONS:

83. To prevent accidental death in childhood, some experts urge forethought and planning for safety and measures to limit the damage of such accidents when they do occur. This approach is called ______________ ______________ .

84. After his daughter scraped her knee, Ben gently cleansed the wound and bandaged it. Ben's behavior is an example of ______________ prevention.

85. Helga comes to school with large black-and-blue marks on her arm. Her teacher suspects
   a. ongoing abuse and neglect by Helga's own parents.
   b. a rare outburst from a unfamiliar perpetrator.
   c. abuse by a neighbor or friend of Helga's family.
   d. abuse by a mentally ill perpetrator.

86. A mayoral candidate is calling for sweeping policy changes to help ensure the well-being of children by promoting home ownership, high-quality community centers, and more stable neighborhoods. If these measures are effective in reducing child maltreatment, they would be classified as ______________ prevention.

Progress Test 1

Multiple-Choice Questions

Circle your answers to the following questions and check them with the answers beginning on page 91. If your answer is incorrect, read the explanation for why it is incorrect and then consult the appropriate pages of the text (in parentheses following the correct answer).

1. During early childhood, the most common disease of young children in developed nations is
   a. undernutrition.
   b. malnutrition.
   c. tooth decay.
   d. diabetes.

2. The brain center for language is usually located in the
   a. right hemisphere.
   b. left hemisphere.
   c. corpus callosum.
   d. space just below the right ear.

3. Which of the following is an example of tertiary prevention of child maltreatment?
   a. removing a child from an abusive home
   b. home visitation of families with infants by a social worker
   c. new laws establishing stiff penalties for child maltreatment
   d. public policy measures aimed at creating stable neighborhoods

4. The brain area that registers emotions is the
   a. hippocampus.
   b. hypothalamus.
   c. amygdala.
   d. prefrontal cortex.

5. Children's problems with tooth decay result primarily from their having too much ______ in their diet.
   a. iron
   b. sugar
   c. fat
   d. carbohydrates

6. The brain's ongoing myelination during childhood helps children
   a. control their actions more precisely.
   b. react more quickly to stimuli.
   c. control their emotions.
   d. do all of these things.

7. The leading cause of death in childhood is
   a. accidents.
   b. untreated diabetes.
   c. malnutrition.
   d. cancer.

8. Regarding lateralization, which of the following is NOT true?
   a. Some cognitive skills require only one side of the brain.
   b. Brain centers for generalized emotional impulses can be found in the right hemisphere.
   c. The left hemisphere contains brain areas dedicated to logical reasoning.
   d. The right side of the brain controls the left side of the body.

9. In young children, perseveration is a sign of
   a. immature brain functions.
   b. maltreatment.
   c. abuse.
   d. amygdala.

10. The area of the brain that directs and controls the other areas is the

a. corpus callosum.
b. myelin sheath.
c. prefrontal cortex.
d. amygdala.

11. Which of the following is true of the corpus callosum?

a. It enables short-term memory.
b. It connects the two halves of the brain.
c. It must be fully myelinated before gross motor skills can be acquired.
d. All of these statements are correct.

12. By about 5 years of age, children are better able to catch and then throw a ball, in part, because

a. the brain areas associated with this ability become more fully myelinated.
b. the corpus callosum begins to function.
c. fine motor skills have matured by age 2.
d. gross motor skills have matured by age 2.

13. During early childhood, inadequate lateralization of the brain and immaturity of the prefrontal cortex may contribute to deficiencies in

a. cognition.
b. peer relationships.
c. emotional control.
d. all of these abilities.

14. Piaget believed that children are in the preoperational stage from ages

a. 6 months to 1 year. **c.** 2 to 6 years.
b. 1 to 3 years. **d.** 5 to 11 years.

15. Which of the following is NOT a characteristic of preoperational thinking?

a. focus on appearance
b. static reasoning
c. abstract thinking
d. centration

16. Which of the following provides evidence that early childhood is a sensitive period, rather than a critical period, for language learning?

a. People can and do master their native language after early childhood.
b. Vocabulary, grammar, and pronunciation are acquired especially easily during early childhood.
c. Neurological characteristics of the young child's developing brain facilitate language acquisition.
d. All of these abilities provide evidence.

17. According to Vygotsky, children learn because adults do all of the following EXCEPT

a. present challenges.
b. offer assistance.
c. encourage motivation.
d. provide reinforcement.

18. Reggio Emilia is

a. the educator who first opened nursery schools for poor children in Rome.
b. the early-childhood curriculum that allows children to discover ideas at their own pace.
c. a form of early-childhood education that encourages children to master skills not usually seen until age 7 or so.
d. the Canadian system for promoting bilingualism in young children.

19. Young children sometimes apply the rules of grammar even when they shouldn't. This tendency is called

a. overregularization. **c.** practical usage.
b. literal language. **d.** single-mindedness.

20. The Russian psychologist Vygotsky emphasized that

a. language helps children form ideas.
b. children form concepts first, then find words to express them.
c. language and other cognitive developments are unrelated at this stage.
d. preschoolers learn language only for egocentric purposes.

21. Private speech can be described as

a. a way of formulating ideas to oneself.
b. fantasy.
c. an early learning difficulty.
d. the beginnings of deception.

22. The child who has not yet grasped the principle of conservation is likely to

a. insist that a tall, narrow glass contains more liquid than a short, wide glass, even though both glasses actually contain the same amount.
b. be incapable of egocentric thought.
c. be unable to reverse an event.
d. do all of these things.

23. In later life, High/Scope graduates showed

a. better report cards, but more behavioral problems.
b. significantly higher IQ scores.
c. higher scores on math and reading achievement tests.

d. alienation from their original neighborhoods and families.

24. A quality preschool program is generally one that
   a. involves behavioral control.
   b. has teachers who know how to respond to the needs of children.
   c. focuses on instruction in conservation and other logical principles.
   d. has professionals demonstrate toys to the children.

25. Many preschool programs that are inspired by Piaget stress _______, in contrast to alternative programs that stress _________.
   a. academics; school readiness
   b. readiness; academics
   c. child development; school readiness
   d. academics; child development

26. Through the process called fast-mapping, children
   a. immediately assimilate new words by connecting them through their assumed meaning to categories of words they have already mastered.
   b. acquire the concept of conservation at an earlier age than Piaget believed.
   c. are able to move beyond egocentric thinking.
   d. become skilled in the practical use of language.

True or False Items

Write T (*true*) or F (*false*) on the line in front of each statement.

_______ 1. Growth between ages 2 and 6 results in body proportions more similar to those of an adult.
_______ 2. For most people, the brain center for language is located in the left hemisphere.
_______ 3. At age 5, the body mass index is lower than at any other age.
_______ 4. Fine motor skills are usually easier for preschoolers to master than are gross motor skills.
_______ 5. Most serious childhood injuries truly are "accidents."
_______ 6. Children often fare as well in kinship care as they do in conventional foster care.
_______ 7. Myelination is essential for basic communication between neurons.
_______ 8. In conservation problems, many young children are unable to understand the transformation because they focus exclusively on appearances.
_______ 9. Young children use private speech more selectively than older children.
_______ 10. Children typically develop a theory of mind at about age 7.
_______ 11. Preoperational children tend to focus on one aspect of a situation to the exclusion of all others.
_______ 12. With the beginning of preoperational thought, most young children can understand words that express comparison.
_______ 13. A young child who says "You comed up and hurted me" is demonstrating a lack of understanding of English grammar.
_______ 14. Vygotsky believed that cognitive growth is largely a social activity.
_______ 15. *Theory-theory* refers to the tendency of young children to see the world as an unchanging reflection of their current construction of reality.

Progress Test 2

Progress Test 2 should be completed during a final chapter review. Answer the following questions after you thoroughly understand the correct answers for the Chapter Review and Progress Test 1.

Multiple-Choice Questions

1. Each year from ages 2 to 6, the average child gains and grows, respectively,
   a. 2 pounds and 1 inch.
   b. 3 pounds and 2 inches.
   c. 4½ pounds and 3 inches.
   d. 6 pounds and 6 inches.

2. The center for appreciation of music, art, and poetry is usually located in the brain's
   a. right hemisphere.
   b. left hemisphere.
   c. right or left hemisphere.
   d. corpus callosum.

3. Seeing her toddler reach for a brightly glowing burner on the stove, Sheila grabs his hand and says, "No, that's very hot." Sheila's behavior is an example of
   a. primary prevention.
   b. secondary prevention.
   c. tertiary prevention.
   d. none of these types of prevention.

4. When parents or caregivers do not meet a child's basic physical, educational, or emotional needs, it is referred to as:
   a. abuse.
   b. neglect.
   c. endangering.
   d. maltreatment.

5. Which of the following is true of a developed nation in which many ethnic groups live together?
   a. Ethnic variations in height and weight disappear.
   b. Ethnic variations in stature persist, but are substantially smaller.
   c. Children of African descent tend to be tallest, followed by Europeans, Asians, and Latinos.
   d. Cultural patterns exert a stronger-than-normal impact on growth patterns.

6. Which of the following is an example of perseveration?
   a. 2-year-old Jason sings the same song over and over
   b. 3-year-old Kwame falls down when attempting to kick a soccer ball
   c. 4-year-old Kara pours water very slowly from a pitcher into a glass
   d. None of these is an example.

7. Which of the following is an example of a fine motor skill?
   a. kicking a ball
   b. running
   c. drawing with a pencil
   d. jumping

8. Children who have been maltreated often
   a. regard other children and adults as hostile and exploitative.
   b. are fearful and aggressive.
   c. are lonelier than other children.
   d. have all of these characteristics.

9. The left half of the brain contains areas dedicated to all of the following EXCEPT
   a. language.
   b. logic.
   c. analysis.
   d. creative impulses.

10. Most gross motor skills can be learned by healthy children by about age
   a. 2.
   b. 3.
   c. 6.
   d. 7.

11. Andrea is concerned because her 3-year-old daughter has been having nightmares. Her pediatrician tells her
   a. not to worry, because nightmares are often caused by increased activity in the amygdala, which is normal during early childhood.
   b. nightmares are a possible sign of an overdeveloped prefrontal cortex.
   c. to monitor her daughter's diet, because nightmares are often caused by too much sugar.
   d. to consult a neurologist, because nightmares are never a sign of healthy development.

12. The brain area that is a central processor for memory is the
   a. hippocampus.
   b. amygdala.
   c. hypothalamus.
   d. prefrontal cortex.

13. The appetites of young children seem __________ they were in the first two years of life.
   a. larger than
   b. smaller than
   c. about the same as
   d. erratic, sometimes smaller and sometimes larger than

14. Piaget believed that preoperational children fail conservation of liquid tests because of their tendency to
   a. focus on appearance.
   b. fast-map.
   c. overregularize.
   d. exhibit all of these behaviors.

15. A young child who focuses his or her attention on only one feature of a situation is demonstrating a characteristic of preoperational thought called
   a. centration.
   b. overregularization.
   c. reversibility.
   d. egocentrism.

16. One characteristic of preoperational thought is
   a. the ability to categorize objects.
   b. the ability to count in multiples of 5.
   c. the inability to perform logical operations.
   d. difficulty adjusting to changes in routine.

17. The zone of proximal development represents the
   a. skills or knowledge that are within the potential of the learner but are not yet mastered.
   b. influence of a child's peers on cognitive development.
   c. explosive period of language development during the play years.
   d. normal variations in children's language proficiency.

18. According to Vygotsky, language advances thinking through private speech and by
   a. helping children to privately review what they know.
   b. helping children explain events to themselves.
   c. serving as a mediator of the social interaction that is a vital part of learning.
   d. facilitating the process of fast-mapping.

19. Irreversibility refers to the
   a. inability to understand that other people view the world from a different perspective than one's own.
   b. inability to think about more than one idea at a time.
   c. failure to understand that changing the arrangement of a group of objects doesn't change their number.
   d. failure to understand that undoing a process will restore the original conditions.

20. Scaffolding of a child's cognitive skills can be provided by
   a. a mentor.
   b. the objects or experiences of a culture.
   c. the child's past learning.
   d. all of these answers.

21. Which theorist would be most likely to agree with the statement, "Adults should focus on helping children learn rather than on what they cannot do"?
   a. Piaget
   b. Vygotsky
   c. Montessori
   d. Emilia

22. Seeing his cousin Jack for the first time in several months, 3-year-old Zach notices how long Jack's hair has become. "You're turning into a girl," he exclaims. Zach's comment reflects the preoperational child's
   a. egocentrism.
   b. tendency to focus on appearance.
   c. static reasoning.
   d. irreversibility.

23. Most 5-year-olds have difficulty understanding comparisons because
   a. they have not yet begun to develop grammar.
   b. they don't understand that meaning depends on context.
   c. of their limited vocabulary.
   d. of their tendency to overregularize.

24. Overregularization indicates that a child
   a. is clearly applying rules of grammar.
   b. persists in egocentric thinking.
   c. has not yet mastered the principle of conservation.
   d. does not yet have a theory of mind.

25. Regarding the value of preschool education, most developmentalists believe that
   a. most disadvantaged children will not benefit from an early preschool education.
   b. most disadvantaged children will benefit from an early preschool education.
   c. the early benefits of preschool education are likely to disappear by grade 3.
   d. the relatively small benefits of antipoverty measures such as Head Start do not justify their huge costs.

Matching Items

Match each term or concept with its corresponding description or definition.

Terms or Concepts

_______ 1. corpus callosum
_______ 2. kinship care
_______ 3. foster care
_______ 4. injury control
_______ 5. child abuse
_______ 6. child neglect
_______ 7. primary prevention
_______ 8. secondary prevention
_______ 9. tertiary prevention
_______ 10. scaffold
_______ 11. theory of mind
_______ 12. zone of proximal development
_______ 13. fast-mapping
_______ 14. conservation
_______ 15. private speech
_______ 16. guided participation

Descriptions or Definitions

a. the idea that amount is unaffected by changes in shape or placement
b. the cognitive distance between a child's actual and potential levels of development
c. the process whereby the child learns through social interaction with a mentor
d. our understanding of mental processes in ourselves and others
e. the process by which words are learned after only one hearing
f. the internal use of language to form ideas
g. to structure a child's participation in learning encounters
h. legal placement of a child in the care of someone other than his or her biological parents
i. a form of care in which a relative of a maltreated child takes over from the biological parents
j. procedures to prevent unwanted events or circumstances from ever occurring
k. actions that are deliberately harmful to a child's well-being
l. actions for averting harm in the immediate situation
m. failure to appropriately meet a child's basic needs
n. an approach emphasizing accident prevention
o. actions aimed at reducing the harm that has occurred
p. band of nerve fibers connecting the right and left hemispheres of the brain

Key Terms

Using your own words, write a brief definition or explanation of each of the following terms on a separate piece of paper.

1. myelination
2. corpus callosum
3. lateralization
4. perseveration
5. amygdala
6. hippocampus
7. hypothalamus
8. preoperational intelligence
9. centration
10. egocentrism
11. focus on appearance
12. static reasoning
13. irreversibility
14. conservation
15. animism
16. apprentice in thinking
17. zone of proximal development
18. scaffolding
19. private speech
20. social mediation
21. theory-theory
22. theory of mind
23. fast-mapping
24. overregularization
25. balanced bilingual
26. Reggio Emilia approach

27. Project Head Start
28. injury control/harm reduction
29. primary prevention
30. secondary prevention
31. tertiary prevention
32. child maltreatment
33. child abuse
34. child neglect
35. substantiated maltreatment
36. permanency planning
37. foster care
38. kinship care

Answers

CHAPTER REVIEW

1. 2; 6; 3 inches (about 7 centimeters); 4½ pounds (2 kilograms); 46 pounds (21 kilograms); 46 inches (117 centimeters); body mass index
2. African; Europeans; Asians; Latinos
3. within; between
4. income; malnutrition; obesity
5. heart; diabetes; fewer
6. sweetened cereals and drinks; tooth decay
7. just right
8. play; motor skills; gross motor
9. fine motor; muscular; judgment
10. lead; pesticides; BPA; cigarette smoke
11. dendrites; 75; 90
12. communication; myelination
13. corpus callosum; myelinates; both sides of the brain or body
14. are not; lateralization
15. left-; coordinate
16. right; logic; analysis; language; left; emotional; creative; both
17. prefrontal cortex; executive
18. impulsiveness; perseveration
19. limbic system; amygdala; fear; anxiety; hippocampus; memory; locations; hypothalamus; hormones
20. Weight: Children gain 4½ pounds each year. Because they are also growing rapidly, they are actually thinner than in earlier years.

    General brain functions: Increased myelination allows for greater speed of thought and greater motor abilities, such as catching and throwing a ball.

    Prefrontal cortex: Said to be the executive of the brain, the prefrontal cortex is responsible for planning and analyzing. It continues to mature through childhood and adolescence, which enables more regular sleep, more nuanced emotions, and fewer temper tantrums and uncontrollable laughter and tears.

    Limbic system: The amygdala, hippocampus, and hypothalamus in the limbic system advance during these years. The amygdala registers emotions; increased activity in this area makes the child sensitive to other people's emotions and subject to strong personal emotions, including fear.

    Gross motor skills: These large body movements improve markedly in early childhood. Children can climb a ladder, ride a tricycle, throw, catch, and kick a ball, and sometimes ski, skate, and dive.

    Fine motor skills: These small body movements are more difficult for young children because of an immature corpus callosum and prefrontal cortex and because of short, stubby fingers. The lack of fine motor skills is one reason 3-year-olds are not allowed in first grade.
21. **c.** is the answer.
22. **b.** is the answer. This is probably because left-handers have a greater need to coordinate both sides of the body.
23. left side. The left side of the brain specializes in language.
24. **c.** is the answer. The greatest myelination in early childhood occurs in the motor and sensory areas, the areas responsible for the skills that develop dramatically during this time.
25. **d.** is the answer. Because the child has better balance and coordination of both sides of the brain, motor skills improve greatly during this period.
26. gross motor skill
27. **d.** is the answer. Fine motor skills are more difficult for young children, in part because of their short, stubby fingers.
28. preoperational; symbolic
29. egocentrism; is not; centration; appearance
30. static; unchanging; irreversibility; conservation
31. animism; rational; irrational
32. Lev Vygotsky; apprentice in thinking
33. challenges; assistance; instruction; motivation; guided participation; social

34. zone of proximal development

35. scaffold

36. private speech; uttered aloud

37. social mediation

38. conservation. This is the principle that properties such as mass, volume, and number remain the same even though they appear different. In this case, the number of checkers remains the same.

39. centration. This is the tendency to focus on one aspect of a situation while ignoring everything else. Dani equates birthday with party: No party, no birthday.

40. reversibility. Young children are unable to reverse operations, so Darrell must be older than 6 years old.

41. **c.** is the answer. All of the other choices are aspects of preoperational thinking.

42. **c.** is the answer. This is typical of cognition during the first two years, when infants think exclusively with their senses and motor skills.

43. **c.** is the answer. Key to Vygotsky's theory is that children are apprentices in thinking and that they learn best by working with an older and more experienced mentor.

44. **c.** is the answer. Piaget emphasized the young child's egocentric tendency to perceive everything from his or her own perspective; Vygotsky emphasized the young child's tendency to look to others for insight and guidance.

45. theory-theory

46. 4; theory of mind

Between the ages of 3 and 6, young children realize that individuals can have thoughts and ideas that are not necessarily the same as their own thoughts.

47. have

48. neurological; prefrontal cortex; language; brother or sister; cultural exosystem

49. theory of mind

50. **a.** is the answer. In developing a theory of mind, children also understand that thoughts may not reflect reality and that individuals can believe various things.

51. maturation; myelination; social

52. critical; sensitive

53. vocabulary

54. fast-mapping

55. comparisons; time; place

56. grammar

57. overregularization

Many English-speaking children overapply the rule of adding "s" to form the plural. Thus, they are likely to say "foots" and "snows."

58. is; disadvantage; the same; balanced bilinguals

59. grammar

60. overregularization. This shows that although Amelia is applying the rules of grammar when she should not, she has a basic understanding of those rules.

61. **d.** is the answer. Vygotsky believed that children used language (private speech, in the beginning) to enhance their cognitive understanding.

62. first grade; 3; 5

63. Piaget; discover ideas at their own pace; Vygotsky; children

64. Maria Montessori; child-centered; accomplishment

65. Reggio Emilia; 7

66. teacher; reading; writing; arithmetic; direct instruction

67. Project Head Start

68. higher

Study Tip: In Chapter 4, high-quality day care was described as being characterized by (a) a low adult/child ratio, (b) a trained staff (or educated parents) who are unlikely to leave the program, (c) positive social interactions among children and adults, (d) adequate space and equipment, and (e) safety. Continuity also helps, and curriculum is important.

69. **c.** is the answer. In Vygotsky's view, learning is a social activity. Thus, social interaction that provides motivation and focuses attention facilitates learning.

70. accidents

71. 40

72. injury control; harm reduction; are

73. primary prevention; secondary prevention; tertiary prevention

74. sudden; own caregivers

75. maltreatment; abuse; neglect

76. substantiated maltreatment; lower

77. delayed development

78. physiological; academic; social

Maltreated children tend to regard other people as hostile and exploitative, and thus are fearful, aggressive, and lonelier than other children. As adolescents and adults, they often use drugs or alcohol, choose unsupportive relationships, become victims or aggressors, dissociate, experience more emotional disorders and suicide attempts.

79. primary prevention; secondary prevention; tertiary prevention
80. permanency planning
81. foster care
82. kinship care; adoption
83. injury control.
84. tertiary. Ben is applying medical treatment after the adverse event, his daughter scraping her knee.
85. **a.** is the answer. At one time, people thought child maltreatment was a rare situation, perpetrated by a mentally ill stranger. Today, they know it is more likely to be perpetrated by the child's own caregivers.
86. primary. Primary prevention refers to actions taken to prevent an adverse event from occurring to a child.

PROGRESS TEST 1

Multiple-Choice Questions

1. **c.** is the answer. (p. 162)

   a.. b., & d. All of these conditions are much more likely to occur in infancy or in adolescence than in early childhood.
2. **b.** is the answer. (p. 168)

   a. & d. The right brain is the location of areas associated with generalized emotional and creative impulses.

   c. The corpus callosum helps integrate the functioning of the two halves of the brain; it does not contain areas specialized for particular skills.
3. **a.** is the answer. (p. 193)

   b. This is an example of secondary prevention.

   c. & d. These are examples of primary prevention.
4. **c.** is the answer. (p. 169)

   a. The hippocampus is a central processor of memory.

   b. The hypothalamus produces hormones that activate other parts of the brain and body.

   c. The prefrontal cortex is responsible for regulating attention, among other things. It makes formal education more possible in children.
5. **b.** is the answer. (p. 162)
6. **d.** is the answer. (pp. 166–167)
7. **a.** is the answer. (p. 188)
8. **a.** is the answer. (p. 168)
9. **a.** is the answer. (p. 168)

   b., c., & d. Although maltreatment, whether in the form of abuse or neglect, may cause brain injury, perseveration is not necessarily a symptom of brain injury from those sources.
10. **c.** is the answer. (p. 168)

    a. The corpus callosum is the band of fibers that link the two halves of the brain.

    b. The myelin sheath is a fatty substance that surrounds the axons of some neurons in the brain.

    d. The amygdala registers emotions.
11. **b.** is the answer. (p. 167)

    a. The corpus callosum is not directly involved in memory.

    c. Myelination of the central nervous system is important to the mastery of *fine* motor skills.
12. **a.** is the answer. (p. 167)

    b. The corpus callosum begins to function long before the years between 2 and 6.

    c. & d. Neither fine nor gross motor skills have fully matured by age 2.
13. **d.** is the answer. (pp. 166–167)
14. **c.** is the answer. (p. 171)
15. **c.** is the answer. Preoperational children have great difficulty understanding abstract concepts. (pp. 171–172)
16. **d.** is the answer. (p. 179)
17. **d.** is the answer. (p. 173)
18. **c.** is the answer. (p. 184)

    a. This describes Maria Montessori.

    b. This refers to Piaget's approach.

    d. The program originated in Italy.
19. **a.** is the answer. (p. 180)

    b. & d. These terms are not identified in the text and do not apply to the use of grammar.

    c. Practical usage, which also is not discussed in the text, refers to communication between one person and another in terms of the overall context in which language is used.
20. **a.** is the answer. (p. 175)

    b. This expresses the views of Piaget.

    c. Because he believed that language facilitates thinking, Vygotsky obviously felt that language and other cognitive developments are intimately related.

    d. Vygotsky did not hold this view.
21. **a.** is the answer. (p. 175)

22. **a.** is the answer. (pp. 171–172)

    b. & c. Failure to conserve is the result of thinking that is centered on appearances. Egocentrism and irreversibility are also examples of centered thinking.

23. **c.** is the answer. (pp. 186–187)

    b. This is not discussed in the text.

    a. & d. There was no indication of greater behavioral problems or alienation in graduates of this program.

24. **b.** is the answer. (p. 187)
25. **c.** is the answer. (pp. 183, 185)
26. **a.** is the answer. (p. 179)

True or False Items

1. T (p. 160)
2. T (p. 168)
3. T (p. 160)
4. F Fine motor skills are more difficult for preschoolers to master than are gross motor skills. (p. 163)
5. F Most serious accidents involve someone's lack of forethought. (p. 188)
6. T (p. 193)
7. F Although myelination is not essential for basic communication between neurons, it is essential for fast and complex communication (pp. 166–167)
8. T (p. 172)
9. F In fact, just the opposite is true. (p. 175)
10. F Children develop a theory of mind at about age 4. (p. 177)
11. T (p. 171)
12. F Young children have difficulty understanding words of comparison such as high and low. (p. 180)
13. F In adding "ed" to form a past tense, the child has indicated an understanding of the grammatical rule for making past tenses in English, even though the construction in these two cases is incorrect. (p. 180)
14. T (p. 173)
15. F This describes static reasoning. Theory-theory is the idea that children attempt to construct a theory to explain all their experiences. (p. 176)

PROGRESS TEST 2

Multiple-Choice Questions

1. **c.** is the answer. (p. 160)
2. **a.** is the answer. (p. 168)

   b. & c. The left hemisphere of the brain contains areas associated with language development.

   d. The corpus callosum does not contain areas for specific behaviors.

3. **b.** is the answer. (p. 189)
4. **b.** is the answer. (pp. 190–191)

   a. Abuse is deliberate, harsh injury to the body.

   c. Endangerment was not discussed.

   d. Maltreatment is too broad a term.

5. **c.** is the answer. (p. 160)
6. **a.** is the answer. (p. 168)

   b. Kicking a ball is a gross motor skill.

   c. Pouring is a fine motor skill.

7. **c.** is the answer. (p. 163)

   a., b., & d. These are gross motor skills.

8. **d.** is the answer. (p. 192)
9. **d.** is the answer. Brain areas that control generalized creative and emotional impulses are found in the right hemisphere. (p. 168)
10. **c.** is the answer. (p. 163)
11. **a.** is the answer. (p. 169)

    b. Nightmares generally occur when activity in the amygdala overwhelms the slowly developing prefrontal cortex.

    c. There is no indication that nightmares are caused by diet.

    d. Increased activity in the amygdala is normal during early childhood, as are the nightmares that some children experience.

12. **a.** is the answer. (p. 169)

    b. The amygdala is responsible for registering emotions.

    c. The hypothalamus produces hormones that activate other parts of the brain and body.

    d. The prefrontal cortex is involved in planning and goal-directed behavior.

13. **b.** is the answer. (p. 160)
14. **a.** is the answer. (p. 172)

    b. & c. Fast-mapping and overregularization are characteristics of language development during early childhood; they have nothing to do with reasoning about volume.

15. **a.** is the answer. (p. 171)

b. Overregularization is the child's tendency to apply grammatical rules even when he or she shouldn't.

c. Reversibility is the concept that reversing an operation, such as addition, will restore the original conditions.

d. This term is used to refer to the young child's belief that people think as he or she does.

16. **c.** is the answer. This is why the stage is called *pre*operational. (p. 170)
17. **a.** is the answer. (p. 174)
18. **c.** is the answer. (p. 170)

a. & b. These are both advantages of private speech.

d. Fast-mapping is the process by which new words are acquired, often after only one hearing.

19. **d.** is the answer. (p. 171)

a. This describes egocentrism.

b. This is the opposite of centration.

c. This defines conservation of number.

20. **d.** is the answer. (p. 174)
21. **b.** is the answer. (pp. 173–174)

a. Piaget focused on what children cannot do.

22. **b.** is the answer. (p. 171)

a., c., & d. Egocentrism, static reasoning, and irreversibility are all characteristics of preoperational thinking, but noticing the long hair is a matter of attending to appearances.

23. **b.** is the answer. (p. 180)

a. By the time children are 3 years old, their grammar is quite impressive.

c. On the contrary, vocabulary develops so rapidly that, by age 5, children seem to be able to understand and use almost any term they hear.

d. This tendency to make language more logical by overapplying certain grammatical rules has nothing to do with understanding comparisons.

24. **a.** is the answer. (p. 180)

b., c., & d. Overregularization is a *linguistic* phenomenon rather than a characteristic type of thinking (b. and d.), or a logical principle (c.).

25. **b.** is the answer. (p. 187)

Matching Items

1. p (p. 167)	**7.** j (p. 189)	**13.** e (p. 179)
2. i (p. 193)	**8.** l (p. 189)	**14.** a (p. 172)
3. h (p. 193)	**9.** o (p. 181)	**15.** f (p. 175)
4. n (p. 188)	**10.** g (p. 174)	**16.** c (p. 173)
5. k (p. 190)	**11.** d (p. 177)	
6. m (pp. 190–191)	**12.** b (p. 174)	

KEY TERMS

1. **Myelination** is the process by which axons become coated with myelin, a fatty substance that speeds the transmission of nerve impulses between neurons. (p. 166)
2. The **corpus callosum** is a long, thick band of nerve fibers that connects the right and left hemispheres of the brain. (p. 167)
3. **Lateralization** refers to the specialization in certain functions by each side of the brain. (p. 167)
4. **Perseveration** is the tendency to stick to one thought or action for a long time. In young children, perseveration is a normal product of immature brain functions. (p. 168)

Memory Aid: To *persevere* is to continue, or persist, at something.

5. A part of the brain's limbic system, the **amygdala** registers emotions, particularly fear and anxiety. (p. 169)
6. The **hippocampus** is the part of the brain's limbic system that is a central processor of memory, especially memory for locations. (p. 169)
7. The **hypothalamus** is the brain structure that responds to the amygdala and hippocampus to produce hormones that activate other parts of the brain and body. (p. 169)
8. According to Piaget, thinking between the ages of about 2 and 6 is characterized by **preoperational intelligence,** meaning that children cannot yet perform logical operations; that is, they cannot use logical principles. This stage involves language and imagination, which require symbolic thought. (p. 171)
9. **Centration** is the tendency of preoperational children to focus only on a single aspect of a situation or object. (p. 171)
10. **Egocentrism** is Piaget's term for a type of centration in which preoperational children view the world exclusively from their own perspective. (p. 171)
11. **Focus on appearance** refers to the preoperational child's tendency to focus only on apparent attributes and ignore all others. (p. 171)
12. Preoperational thinking is characterized by **static reasoning,** in which the young child sees the world as unchanging. (p. 171)

13. **Irreversibility** is the characteristic of preoperational thought in which the young child fails to recognize that a process can be reversed to restore the original conditions of a situation. (p. 171)
14. **Conservation** is the understanding that the amount or quantity of a substance or object is unaffected by changes in its appearance. (p. 172)
15. **Animism** is the belief that natural objects and phenomena are alive. (p. 173)
16. According to Vygotsky, a young child is an **apprentice in thinking,** whose intellectual growth is stimulated and directed by older and more skilled members of society. (p. 173)
17. According to Vygotsky, each individual has a **zone of proximal development (ZPD),** which represents the skills that are within the potential of the learner but cannot be performed independently. (p. 174)
18. Tutors who utilize **scaffolding** structure children's learning experiences to foster their emerging capabilities. (p. 174)
19. **Private speech** is Vygotsky's term for the internal dialogue in which a person talks to himself or herself. Private speech, which often is uttered aloud, helps young children to think, review, decide, and explain events to themselves. (p. 175)
20. In Vygotsky's theory, **social mediation** is a human interaction that expands and advances understanding, often through words that one person uses to explain something to another. (p. 175)
21. **Theory-theory** is the idea that young children attempt to construct theories to explain everything they experience. (p. 176)
22. A **theory of mind** is an understanding of human mental processes, that is, of one's own or another's emotions, beliefs, intentions, motives, and thoughts. (p. 177)
23. **Fast-mapping** is the speedy and sometimes imprecise process by which children learn new words by tentatively connecting them to words and categories that they already understand. (p. 179)
24. **Overregularization** occurs when children apply rules of grammar when they should not. It is seen in English, for example, when children add "s" to form the plural even in irregular cases that form the plural in a different way. (p. 180)
25. A **balanced bilingual** is a person who is equally fluent in two languages. (p. 182)
26. **Reggio Emilia approach** refers to a famous program of early-childhood education that originated in the town of Reggio Emilia, Italy, and that encourages each child's creativity in a carefully designed setting. (p. 184)
27. **Project Head Start** is the most widespread, federally funded, early-childhood-education program in the United States. (p. 186)
28. **Injury control/harm reduction** is the practice of limiting the extent of injuries by anticipating, controlling, and preventing dangerous activities. (p. 188)
29. **Primary prevention** refers to actions that change overall background conditions to prevent some unwanted event or circumstance. (p. 189)
30. **Secondary prevention** involves actions that avert harm in a high-risk situation. (p. 189)
31. **Tertiary prevention** involves actions taken after an adverse event occurs, aimed at reducing the harm or preventing disability. (p. 189)
32. **Child maltreatment** is intentional harm to or avoidable endangerment of anyone under age 18. (p. 190)
33. **Child abuse** refers to deliberate actions that are harmful to a child's physical, emotional, or sexual well-being. (p. 190)
34. **Child neglect** refers to failure to appropriately meet a child's basic physical, educational, or emotional needs. (pp. 190–191)
35. Child maltreatment that has been officially reported to authorities, investigated, and verified is called **substantiated maltreatment.** (p. 191)
36. **Permanency planning** is planning for the long-term care of a child who has experienced substantiated maltreatment. (p. 193)
37. **Foster care** is a legally sanctioned, publicly supported arrangement in which children are removed from their biological parents and temporarily given to another adult to nurture. (p. 193)
38. **Kinship care** is a form of foster care in which a relative of a maltreated child becomes the child's approved caregiver. (p. 193)

6 chapter

EARLY CHILDHOOD

Psychosocial Development

Chapter Overview

Chapter 6 explores the ways in which young children begin to relate to others in an ever-widening social environment. The chapter begins where social understanding begins, with emotional development and the emergence of the sense of self. With their increasing social awareness, children are better able to regulate and control their emotions.

The next section explores how children use play to help with their emerging ability to regulate their emotions. Although play is universal, its form varies by culture and gender.

The third section discusses Baumrind's parenting patterns and their effects on the developing child. The effects of the media on parenting and family life in general are also explored.

The chapter continues with a discussion of moral development during early childhood, focusing on the origins of helpful, prosocial behaviors in young children, as well as antisocial behaviors such as the different forms of aggressive behavior. The usefulness of the different forms of discipline, including punishment, in the child's developing morality is also considered in this section.

The chapter concludes with a description of children's emerging awareness of male–female differences and gender identity. Four major theories of gender-role development are considered.

NOTE: Answer guidelines for all Chapter 6 questions begin on page 104.

Chapter Review

When you have finished reading the chapter, work through the material that follows to review it. Complete the sentences and answer the questions. In some cases, Study Tips explain how best to learn a difficult concept, while Think About It and Applications help you to know how well you understand the material. As you proceed, evaluate your performance for each section by consulting the answers beginning on page 104. Do not continue with the next section until you understand each answer. If you need to, review or reread the appropriate section in the textbook before continuing.

Emotional Development (pp. 197–204)

1. The major psychosocial accomplishment of early childhood is learning ______________________ ______________________. This ability is called ______________ ______________.

2. Between 3 and 6 years of age, according to Erikson, children are in the stage of ______________ ______________ ______________. As they acquire skills and competencies, children develop ______________, a belief in their own abilities. In the process, they develop a positive ______________ and feelings of ______________ in their accomplishments.

3. Children also develop a longer ______________ span that enables concentration, which is made possible by ______________ maturity. And they develop naive predictions, called ______________ ______________, which helps them try new things.

4. Erikson also believed that during this stage, children begin to feel ______________ when their efforts result in failure or criticism. Many people believe that ______________ is a more mature emotion than ______________, because the former emotion is ______________.

5. For the most part, children enjoy learning, playing, and practicing for their own joy; that is, they are ________________ ________________.
The importance of this type of motivation is seen when children invent and converse with ________________ ________________.

6. Motivation that comes from the outside is called ________________ ________________.
Providing reinforcement for something a person already enjoys doing ________________ (strengthens/may diminish) intrinsic motivation.

7. Emotional regulation ________________ (is/is not) valued in all cultures. Cultures and families ________________ (differ/generally do not differ) in the emotions considered most in need of control.

8. An illness or disorder that involves the mind is called ________________.

9. Neurological advances in the brain's ________________ ________________ are partly responsible for the greater capacity for self-control that occurs at about age ________________. Some children have problems with emotional control. Children who have ________________ problems and lash out at other people or things are said to be ________________ (overcontrolled/undercontrolled). Children who have ________________ problems tend to be inhibited, fearful, and withdrawn and are said to be ________________ (overcontrolled/undercontrolled).

10. Girls generally are better than boys at regulating their ________________ (internalizing/externalizing) emotions, but they are less successful with ________________ (internalizing/externalizing) ones.

11. Repeated exposure to extreme stress can kill ________________ and stop others from developing properly, making some children physiologically unable to regulate their emotions.

12. Another set of influences on emotional regulation is the child's early and current ________________ ________________. Neglect or abuse in the early years is likely to cause later ________________ or ________________ problems.

THINK ABOUT IT: To help you understand the difference between internalizing problems and externalizing problems in emotional regulation, you might list several examples of each type. Which have you engaged in?

APPLICATIONS:

13. According to Erikson, 5-year-old Samantha is incapable of feeling guilt because
 a. guilt depends on a sense of self, which is not sufficiently established in young children.
 b. she does not yet understand that she is female for life.
 c. this emotion is unlikely to have been reinforced at such an early age.
 d. guilt is associated with the resolution of the Electra complex, which occurs later in life.

14. Three-year-old Ali, who is fearful and withdrawn, is displaying signs of ________________ problems, which suggests that he is emotionally ________________.

15. Summarizing her report on neurological aspects of emotional regulation, Alycia notes that young children who have externalizing problems tend to lack neurological maturity in the brain's ________________ ________________.

Play (pp. 204–209)

16. Between ages 2 and 6, children learn how to make, and keep, ________________ as a consequence of many hours of ________________ ________________.

17. An aspect of culture that shapes play is the nature of the ________________ setting. In cities, the scarcity of undeveloped space means that play usually occurs in ________________-________________ settings.

18. Another cultural shift that has changed the nature of children's play is the increasing prevalence of ________________, which has resulted in the children displaying advanced (although confused) ________________ ________________.

19. The developmentalist who distinguished five kinds of play is ________________. These include ________________ play, in which a child plays alone; ________________ play, in which a

child watches other children play; ________________ play, in which children play together without interacting; ________________ play, in which children interact, but their play is not yet mutual and reciprocal; and ________________ play, in which children play together and take turns.

20. The type of active play that looks rough is called ____________-____________-____________ play. A distinctive feature of this form of play, which ________________ (occurs only in some cultures/is universal), is the positive facial expression that characterizes the ________________ ________________. This type of play teaches children how to enter a ________________, ________________ themselves, and respond to someone else. It may also help the ________________ ________________ to develop.

21. In ________________ play, children act out various roles and themes in stories of their own creation. This type of play helps them to explore and rehearse ________________ ________________, tests their ability to convince others of their ideas, allows them to practice ________________ their emotions, and helps them to develop a ________________ in a nonthreatening context.

STUDY TIP/APPLICATION: To help you distinguish the different types of play, complete the following table, including the basic characteristics of each type of play. Then, give an example of each type.

22.

Type of Play	Characteristics	Examples
a. Solitary play		
b. Onlooker play		
c. Parallel play		
d. Associative play		
e. Cooperative play		
f. Rough-and-tumble play		
g. Sociodramatic play		

APPLICATION:

23. Although Juvaria and Brittany are sharing drawing materials and watching each other, their play is not yet mutual or reciprocal. Mildred Parten would probably classify this type of play as ________________ play.

Challenges for Parents (pp. 209–214)

24. A significant influence on early psychosocial growth is the style of ________________ that characterizes a child's family life.

25. The early research on parenting styles, which was conducted by ________________, found that parents varied in four dimensions: their expressions of ________________, their strategies for ________________, their ________________, and their expectations for ________________.

26. Parents who adopt the ________________ style demand unquestioning obedience from their children. In this style of parenting, nurturance tends to be ________________ (low/high), maturity demands are ________________ (low/high), and parent–child communication tends to be ________________ (low/high).

27. Parents who adopt the ________________ style make few demands on their children and are lax in discipline. Such parents ________________ (are/are not very) nurturant, communicate ________________ (well/poorly), and make ________________ (few/extensive) maturity demands.

28. Parents who adopt the ________________ style set limits and enforce rules but also listen to their children. Such parents make ________________ (high/low) maturity demands, communicate ________________ (well/poorly), and ________________ (are/are not) nurturant.

29. Parents who are indifferent toward their children have adopted the ________________/ ________________ style.

30. Although this classification is generally regarded as ________________ (very useful/too simplistic), follow-up studies indicate that children raised by ________________ parents are likely to be obedient but unhappy and those raised by ________________ parents are likely to lack self-control. Those raised by ________________ parents are more likely to be articulate, successful, happy with themselves, and generous with others.

31. An important factor in the effectiveness of parenting style is the child's ________________.

STUDY TIP: Students often confuse *authoritarian* and *authoritative* when studying parenting styles. Although both words have the same root noun, *authority* ("the power or right to give commands and enforce obedience"), their suffixes have very different meanings. The suffix *-arian* denotes an occupation, and the suffix *-ative* denotes a tendency toward something. Thus, authoritative parents don't make an occupation of enforcing obedience; rather, they tend to give commands with some margin for freedom of action.

APPLICATIONS:

32. Yolanda and Tom are strict and aloof parents. Their children are most likely to be
    - a. cooperative and trusting.
    - b. obedient but unhappy.
    - c. violent.
    - d. withdrawn and anxious.

33. Which is NOT a feature of parenting used by Baumrind to differentiate authoritarian, permissive, and authoritative parents?
    - a. maturity demands for the child's conduct
    - b. efforts to control the child's actions
    - c. nurturance
    - d. adherence to stereotypical gender roles

34. Other effects on child rearing are values, climate, family ________________, and ________________.

35. Six major American organizations concerned with the well-being of children urge parents to reduce ________________ ________________.

36. Children who watch violence on television ________________ (become/do not necessarily become) more violent themselves.

37. Most young children in the United States spend more than ________________ (how many?) hours each day using some sort of media.

38. Longitudinal research demonstrates that young children who watched television violence tended to become more ________________, less ________________, and ________________-________________ teenagers.

39. Parents and children _______________ (rarely/sometimes/often) use media together.

Moral Development (pp. 214–220)

40. The ability to truly understand the emotions of another, called _______________, often leads to sharing, helping, and other examples of _______________ _______________. In contrast, dislike for others, or _______________, may lead to actions that are destructive or deliberately hurtful. Such actions are called _______________ _______________.

41. By age _______________, most children can be deliberately prosocial or antisocial. This occurs as a result of _______________ maturation, _______________ regulation, _______________ _______________ _______________, and interactions with _______________.

42. Developmentalists distinguish four types of aggression: _______________, used to obtain or retain an object or privilege; _______________, used in angry retaliation against an intentional or accidental act committed by a peer; _______________, which takes the form of insults or social rejection; and _______________, used in an unprovoked attack on a peer.

43. (text and Table 6.3) The form of aggression that often increases from age 2 to 6 is _______________ _______________. Of greater concern are _______________ _______________, because it can indicate a lack of _______________ _______________; and _______________ _______________, which is most worrisome overall.

44. State four specific recommendations for the use of punishment that are derived from developmental research findings.

a. _______________________________________

b. _______________________________________

c. _______________________________________

d. _______________________________________

45. Physical punishment _______________ (seems to increase/does not seem to increase) the possibility of long-term aggression and _______________ (temporarily increases/has no effect on) obedience.

46. (text and A View from Science) Another method of discipline, in which children's guilt and gratitude are used to control their behavior, is _______________ _______________. This method of discipline has been linked to children's decreased _______________, _______________, and _______________ acceptance.

47. The disciplinary technique most often used in North America is the _______________-_______________, in which a misbehaving child is asked to sit quietly without toys or playmates. Experts suggest a period of _______________ (how many?) minute(s) for each year of the child's age.

48. Another common practice involves the parents explaining to the child why the behavior was wrong, called _______________-_______________.

49. (A View From Science) Culture _______________ (exerts/does not exert) a strong influence on disciplinary techniques. Japanese mothers tend to use _______________________________ as disciplinary techniques more often than do North American mothers. However, discipline methods and family rules are less important than parental _______________________________. The U.S. Supreme Court has decided that teachers and parents may use _______________ _______________ to punish children. Physical punishment is _______________ (illegal in many developed nations/legal in most developed nations).

APPLICATIONS:

50. Seeking to discipline her 3-year-old son for snatching a playmate's toy, Cassandra gently says, "How would you feel if Juwan grabbed your car?" Developmentalists would probably say that Cassandra's approach

a. is too permissive and would therefore be ineffective in the long run.
b. would probably be more effective with a girl.
c. will be effective in increasing prosocial behavior because it promotes empathy.
d. will backfire and threaten her son's self-confidence.

51. When 4-year-old Seema grabs for Vincenzo's Beanie Baby, Vincenzo slaps her hand away, displaying an example of ________________ aggression.

52. Five-year-old Curtis, who is above average in height and weight, often picks on children who are smaller than he is. Curtis' behavior is an example of ________________ aggression.

53. Four-year-old Eboni shows signs of distrust toward strangers. Eboni's behavior is an example of ________________ .

Becoming Boys and Girls (pp. 221–226)

54. Social scientists distinguish between biological, or ________________ , differences between males and females, and cultural, or ________________ , differences in the ________________ and behavior of males and females.

55. By age ________________ , children can consistently apply gender labels. By age ________________ , children are convinced that certain toys are appropriate for one gender but not the other. Awareness that sex is a fixed biological characteristic does not become solid until about age ________________ .

56. Freud called the period from age 3 to 6 the ________________ ________________ . According to his view, boys in this stage develop sexual feelings about their ________________ and become jealous of their ________________ . Freud called this phenomenon the ________________ ________________ . Boys also develop, in self-defense, a powerful conscience called the ________________ .

57. During the phallic stage, little girls may experience the ________________ ________________ , in which they want to get rid of their mother and become intimate with their father.

58. In Freud's theory, children of both sexes resolve their guilt and fear through ________________ with their same-sex parent.

59. According to behaviorism, young children develop a sense of gender by being ________________ for behaviors deemed appropriate for their sex and ________________ for behaviors deemed inappropriate.

60. Behaviorists also maintain that children learn gender-appropriate behavior not only through direct reinforcement but also through ________________ ________________ .

61. Cognitive theorists focus on children's understanding of male–female differences, which is called a ________________ ________________ .

62. According to ________________ theory, gender attitudes and roles are the result of interaction between ________________ ________________ and ________________ ________________ .

63. Every culture has a system of ________________ ________________ . To break through cultural restrictiveness, some parents and teachers believe that children should be allowed to maintain a balance of male and female characteristics, or ________________ . This idea ________________ (runs counter to/supports) systems theory.

64. The current consensus is that sex differences in behavior result from an interplay among ________________ , ________________ , and ________________ mechanisms.

APPLICATIONS:

65. Bonita eventually copes with the fear and anger she feels over her hatred of her mother and love of her father by
    a. identifying with her mother.
    b. copying her brother's behavior.
    c. adopting her father's moral code.
    d. competing with her brother for her father's attention.

66. A little girl who says she wants her mother to go on vacation so that she can marry her father is voicing a fantasy consistent with the ________________ described by Freud.

67. Leonardo believes that almost all sexual patterns are learned rather than inborn. He is clearly a strong adherent of ________________ .

Progress Test 1

Multiple-Choice Questions

Circle your answers to the following questions and check them with the answers on page 106. If your answer is incorrect, read the explanation for why it is incorrect and then consult the appropriate pages of the text (in parentheses following the correct answer).

1. Young children have a clear (but not necessarily accurate) concept of self. Typically, they believe that they
   a. own all objects in sight.
   b. are great at almost everything.
   c. are much less competent than peers and older children.
   d. are more powerful than their parents.

2. According to Freud, the third stage of psychosexual development, during which the penis is the focus of psychological concern and pleasure, is the
   a. oral stage.
   b. anal stage.
   c. phallic stage.
   d. latency period.

3. Girls generally are better than boys at regulating their
   a. internalizing emotions.
   b. externalizing emotions.
   c. internalizing and externalizing emotions.
   d. prosocial behaviors.

4. The three *basic* patterns of parenting described by Diana Baumrind are
   a. hostile, loving, and harsh.
   b. authoritarian, permissive, and authoritative.
   c. positive, negative, and punishing.
   d. indulgent, neglecting, and traditional.

5. Authoritative parents are receptive and loving, but they also normally
   a. set limits and enforce rules.
   b. have difficulty communicating.
   c. withhold praise and affection.
   d. encourage aggressive behavior.

6. Children who watch a lot of violent television or play violent video games
   a. are more likely to be violent.
   b. are less creative.
   c. become lower-achieving teens.
   d. have all of these characteristics.

7. (Table 6.3) Between 2 and 6 years of age, the form of aggression that is most likely to increase is
   a. reactive.
   b. instrumental.
   c. relational.
   d. bullying.

8. During early childhood, a child's self-concept is defined largely by his or her
   a. expanding range of skills and competencies.
   b. physical appearance.
   c. gender.
   d. relationship with family members.

9. Behaviorists emphasize the importance of _____ in the development of the preschool child.
   a. identification
   b. praise and blame
   c. initiative
   d. a theory of mind

10. Children apply gender labels and have definite ideas about how boys and girls behave as early as age
    a. 2.
    b. 4.
    c. 5.
    d. 7.

11. Developmentalists agree that punishment should be
    a. avoided at all costs.
    b. immediate and harsh.
    c. delayed until emotions subside.
    d. rare and limited to behaviors the child understands and can control.

12. Externalizing problems and internalizing problems are evidence of
    a. impaired self-control.
    b. good emotional regulation.
    c. low self-esteem.
    d. an immature self-concept.

13. Three-year-old Jake, who lashes out at the family pet in anger, is displaying signs of _____ problems, which suggests that he is emotionally _____.
    a. internalizing; overcontrolled
    b. internalizing; undercontrolled
    c. externalizing; overcontrolled
    d. externalizing; undercontrolled

14. (A View from Science) Compared with North American mothers, Japanese mothers are more likely to
    a. use reasoning to control their children's social behavior.
    b. use expressions of disappointment to control their children's social behavior.
    c. express empathy for their children.
    d. use all of these techniques.

15. (Table 6.3) When her friend hurts her feelings, Maya shouts that she is a "mean old stinker!" Maya's behavior is an example of
    a. instrumental aggression.
    b. reactive aggression.
    c. bullying aggression.
    d. relational aggression.

True or False Items

Write *T (true) or F (false)* on the line in front of each statement.

_______ 1. According to Diana Baumrind, only authoritarian parents make maturity demands on their children.
_______ 2. Children of authoritative parents tend to be successful, happy with themselves, and generous with others.
_______ 3. Not until age 4 can children apply gender labels.
_______ 4. Empathy is the same as sympathy.
_______ 5. Systems theory emphasizes the interactions between social systems and biological forces.
_______ 6. Children can be truly androgynous only if their culture promotes such ideas and practices.
_______ 7. Developmentalists do not agree about how children acquire gender roles.
_______ 8. By age 4, most children have definite ideas about what toys are appropriate for each gender.
_______ 9. Identification was defined by Freud as a means of defending one's self-concept by taking on the attitudes and behaviors of another person.
_______ 10. By adolescence, undercontrolled boys may be delinquents.

Progress Test 2

Progress Test 2 should be completed during a final chapter review. Answer the following questions after you thoroughly understand the correct answers for the Chapter Review and Progress Test 1.

Multiple-Choice Questions

1. Children of permissive parents are *most* likely to lack
    a. social skills.
    b. self-control.
    c. initiative and guilt.
    d. care and concern.

2. The major psychosocial accomplishment of early childhood is
    a. learning when and how to express emotions.
    b. developing an internalized sense of initiative.
    c. developing an identity.
    d. forging positive self-esteem.

3. Which area of the brain plays an important role in the child's greater capacity for self-control that appears at age 4 or 5?
    a. temporal lobe
    b. occipital lobe
    c. prefrontal cortex
    d. hippocampus

4. Generally speaking, the motivation of young children
    a. is intrinsic.
    b. is extrinsic.
    c. is the desire to gain praise or some other reward from someone else.
    d. varies too much from country to country to be characterized.

5. Which of the following best summarizes the current view of developmentalists regarding gender differences?
    a. Developmentalists disagree on the proportion of gender differences that are biological in origin.
    b. Most gender differences are biological in origin.
    c. Nearly all gender differences are cultural in origin.
    d. There is no consensus among developmentalists regarding the origin of gender differences.

6. According to Freud, a young boy's jealousy of his father's relationship with his mother, and the guilt feelings that result, are part of the
    a. Electra complex.
    b. Oedipus complex.
    c. phallic complex.
    d. penis envy complex.

7. The style of parenting in which the parents make few demands on children, the discipline is lax, and the parents are nurturant and accepting is
   a. authoritarian.
   b. authoritative.
   c. permissive.
   d. traditional.

8. Cooperating with a playmate is to ______ as insulting a playmate is to ______ .
   a. antisocial behavior; prosocial behavior
   b. prosocial behavior; antisocial behavior
   c. emotional regulation; antisocial behavior
   d. prosocial behavior; emotional regulation

9. Antipathy refers to a person's
   a. understanding of the emotions of another person.
   b. self-understanding.
   c. feelings of anger or dislike toward another person.
   d. tendency to internalize emotions or inhibit their expression.

10. Which of the following theories advocates the development of gender identification as a means of avoiding guilt over feelings for the opposite-sex parent?
    a. behaviorism
    b. systems
    c. psychoanalytic
    d. social learning

11. A parent who wishes to use a time-out to discipline her son for behaving aggressively on the playground would be advised to:
    a. have the child sit quietly indoors for a few minutes.
    b. tell her son that he will be punished later at home.
    c. tell the child that he will not be allowed to play outdoors for the rest of the week.
    d. choose a different disciplinary technique because time-outs are ineffective.

12. The young child's readiness to learn new tasks and play activities reflects his or her
    a. emerging competency and self-awareness.
    b. theory of mind.
    c. relationship with parents.
    d. growing identification with others.

13. Emotional regulation is in part related to maturation of a specific part of the brain in the
    a. prefrontal cortex.
    b. parietal cortex.
    c. temporal lobe.
    d. occipital lobe.

14. In which style of parenting is the parents' word law and misbehavior strictly punished?
    a. permissive
    b. authoritative
    c. authoritarian
    d. traditional

15. Erikson noted that young children eagerly begin many new activities but are vulnerable to criticism and feelings of failure; they experience the crisis of
    a. identity versus role confusion.
    b. initiative versus guilt.
    c. basic trust versus mistrust.
    d. efficacy versus helplessness.

Matching Items

Match each term or concept with its corresponding description or definition.

Terms or Concepts

_______ 1. empathy
_______ 2. androgyny
_______ 3. antipathy
_______ 4. prosocial behavior
_______ 5. antisocial behavior
_______ 6. Electra complex
_______ 7. Oedipus complex
_______ 8. authoritative
_______ 9. authoritarian
_______ 10. identification
_______ 11. instrumental aggression

Descriptions or Definitions

a. forceful behavior that is intended to get or keep something that another person has
b. Freudian theory that every daughter secretly wishes to replace her mother
c. parenting style associated with high maturity demands and low parent–child communication
d. an action performed for the benefit of another person without the expectation of reward
e. Freudian theory that every son secretly wishes to replace his father
f. parenting style associated with high maturity demands and high parent–child communication
g. understanding the feelings of others
h. an action that is intended to harm someone else
i. dislike of others
j. the way children cope with their feelings of guilt during the phallic stage
k. a balance of traditional male and female characteristics in an individual

Key Terms

Using your own words, write a brief definition or explanation of each of the following terms on a separate piece of paper.

1. emotional regulation
2. initiative versus guilt
3. self-esteem
4. self-concept
5. intrinsic motivation
6. extrinsic motivation
7. psychopathology
8. externalizing problems
9. internalizing problems
10. rough-and-tumble play
11. sociodramatic play
12. authoritarian parenting
13. permissive parenting
14. authoritative parenting
15. neglectful/uninvolved parenting
16. empathy
17. antipathy
18. prosocial behavior
19. antisocial behavior
20. instrumental aggression
21. reactive aggression
22. relational aggression
23. bullying aggression
24. psychological control
25. time-out
26. sex differences
27. gender differences
28. phallic stage
29. Oedipus complex
30. superego
31. Electra complex
32. identification
33. gender schema
34. androgyny

Answers

CHAPTER REVIEW

1. when and how to express emotions; emotional regulation
2. initiative versus guilt; self-esteem; self-concept; pride
3. attention; neurological; protective optimism
4. guilt; guilt; shame; internalized
5. intrinsically motivated; imaginary friends

6. extrinsic motivation; may diminish
7. is; differ
8. psychopathology
9. prefrontal cortex; 4 or 5; externalizing; undercontrolled; internalizing; overcontrolled
10. externalizing; internalizing
11. neurons
12. care experiences; internalizing; externalizing
13. **a.** is the answer. Erikson did not equate gender constancy with the emergence of guilt (b); (c) and (d) reflect the viewpoints of learning theory and Freud, respectively.
14. internalizing; overcontrolled. Usually, with maturity, extreme fears and shyness diminish.
15. prefrontal cortex. Emotional regulation requires thinking before acting, which is the province of the prefrontal cortex. Lack of maturity there results in externalizing problems.
16. friends; social play
17. physical; child-care
18. television; sexual awareness
19. Mildred Parten; solitary; onlooker; parallel; associative; cooperative
20. rough-and-tumble; is universal; play face; relationship; assert; prefrontal cortex
21. sociodramatic; social roles; regulating; self-concept
22. No answer is right or wrong. Some examples follow.
    - **a.** Solitary play: playing alone. A girl playing with her doll in her room or a boy with his truck
    - **b.** Onlooker play: watching other children play. Sitting on a bench in the playground watching children on the see-saw.
    - **c.** Parallel play: playing with similar toys in similar ways, but not together. Two girls playing with their own dolls in different areas of a dollhouse or two boys playing with building blocks.
    - **d.** Associative play: interactive play, but not yet mutual and reciprocal. A group of children drawing with crayons.
    - **e.** Cooperative play: playing together. Playing tag.
    - **f.** Rough-and-tumble play: mimicking aggression but without intent to harm. Imitating a boxing match.
    - **g.** Sociodramatic play: acting out various roles and themes in stories they create. Pretend racing cars or playing house.
23. parallel
24. parenting
25. Diana Baumrind; warmth; discipline; communication; maturity
26. authoritarian; low; high; low
27. permissive; are; well; few
28. authoritative; high; well; are
29. neglectful/uninvolved
30. too simplistic; authoritarian; permissive; authoritative
31. temperament
32. **b.** is the answer. Authoritarian parents have behavior standards and require obedience without question. So, their children tend to be obedient but unhappy.
33. **d.** is the answer. Baumrind's categories have nothing to do with gender roles.
34. income; history
35. television watching
36. become
37. three
38. violent; creative; lower-achieving
39. rarely
40. empathy; prosocial behaviors; antipathy; antisocial behavior
41. 4 or 5; brain; emotional; theory of mind; caregivers
42. instrumental; reactive; relational; bullying
43. instrumental aggression; reactive aggression; emotional regulation; bullying aggression
44. **a.** Remember theory of mind.
    - **b.** Remember emerging self-concept.
    - **c.** Remember fast-mapping.
    - **d.** Remember that young children are not logical.
45. seems to increase; temporarily increases
46. psychological control; achievement; creativity; social
47. time-out; one
48. time-in
49. exerts; reasoning, empathy, and expressions of disappointment; warmth, support, and concern; reasonable force; illegal in many developed nations

50. **c.** is the answer.
51. instrumental. This kind of aggression involves trying to get or keep something someone else has, as Seema is doing here.
52. bullying. This kind of aggression involves repeated, unprovoked physical or verbal attacks on other people.
53. antipathy.
54. sex; gender; roles
55. 2; 4; 8
56. phallic stage; mothers; fathers; Oedipus complex; superego
57. Electra complex
58. identification
59. reinforced; punished
60. social learning
61. gender schema
62. systems; social systems; biological forces
63. gender distinctions; androgyny; runs counter to
64. biological; psychological; social
65. **a.** is the answer. According to Freud, children identify with the same-sex parents because of their guilt in hating that parent.
66. Electra complex. Resolution of this complex results in the identification noted in 65.
67. behaviorists. Behaviorists believe that children learn through rewards and punishments.

PROGRESS TEST 1

Multiple-Choice Questions

1. **b.** is the answer. (p. 199)
2. **c.** is the answer. (p. 222)

   a. & b. In Freud's theory, the oral and anal stages are associated with infant development.

   d. In Freud's theory, the latency period is associated with development during the school years.
3. **b.** is the answer. (p. 202)
4. **b.** is the answer. (p. 210)

   d. Traditional is a variation of the basic styles. Indulgent and neglecting are abusive styles and clearly harmful, unlike the styles initially identified by Baumrind.
5. **a.** is the answer. (p. 210)

   b. & c. Authoritative parents communicate very well and are quite affectionate.

   d. This is not typical of authoritative parents.
6. **d.** is the answer. (p. 213)
7. **b.** is the answer. (p. 216)
8. **a.** is the answer. (pp. 198–199)
9. **b.** is the answer. (p. 223)

   a. This is the focus of Freud's phallic stage.

   c. This is the focus of Erikson's psychosocial theory.

   d. This is the focus of cognitive theorists.
10. **a.** is the answer. (p. 221)
11. **d.** is the answer. (pp. 217–218)
12. **a.** is the answer.

    c. & d. Externalizing problems and internalizing problems are related to emotional regulation rather than self-esteem or self-concept.
13. **d.** is the answer. (p. 201)

    a. & b. Children who display internalizing problems are withdrawn and bottle up their emotions.

    c. Jake is displaying an inability to control his negative emotions.
14. **d.** is the answer. (p. 219)
15. **d.** is the answer. (p. 215)

True or False Items

1. F All parents make some maturity demands on their children; maturity demands are high in both the authoritarian and authoritative parenting styles. (p. 210)
2. T (p. 211)
3. F Children can apply gender labels by age 2. (p. 221)
4. F Sympathy is feeling sorry *for* someone; empathy is feeling sorry *with* someone. (p. 215)
5. T (p. 225)
6. T (p. 225)
7. T (pp. 222–226)
8. T (p. 221)
9. T (p. 222)
10. T (p. 202)

PROGRESS TEST 2

Multiple-Choice Questions

1. **b.** is the answer. (p. 211)
2. **a.** is the answer. (p. 197)

b. & d. Developing a sense of initiative and positive self-esteem are aspects of emotional regulation.

c. Developing a sense of identity is the task of adolescence.

3. **c.** is the answer. (p. 201)
4. **a.** is the answer. (p. 200)
5. **a.** is the answer. (p. 221)
6. **b.** is the answer. (p. 222)

   a. & d. These are Freud's versions of phallic-stage development in little girls.

   c. There is no such thing as the "phallic complex."
7. **c.** is the answer. (p. 210)

   a. & b. Both authoritarian and authoritative parents make high demands on their children.

   d. This is not one of the three parenting styles. Traditional parents could be any one of these types.
8. **b.** is the answer. (p. 215)
9. **c.** is the answer. (p. 215)

   a. This describes empathy.

   b. This describes self-concept.

   d. This describes an internalizing problem.
10. **c.** is the answer. (p. 222)

    a. & d. Behaviorism, which includes social learning, emphasizes that children learn about gender by rewards and punishments and by observing others.

    b. Systems theory focuses on the interaction of biology and environment.
11. **a.** is the answer. (p. 218)

    b. & c. Time-outs involve removing a child from a situation in which misbehavior has occurred. Moreover, threats of future punishment would likely be less effective because of the delay between the behavior and the consequence.

    d. Although developmentalists stress the need to prevent misdeeds instead of punishing them and warn that time-outs may have unintended consequences, they nevertheless can be an effective form of discipline.
12. **a.** is the answer. (pp. 198–199)

    b. This viewpoint is associated only with cognitive theory.

    c. Although parent–child relationships are important to social development, they do not determine readiness.

    d. Identification is a Freudian defensive behavior.
13. **a.** is the answer. (p. 197)
14. **c.** is the answer. (p. 210)
15. **b.** is the answer. (p. 198)

    a. & c. According to Erikson, these are the crises of adolescence and infancy, respectively.

    d. This is not a crisis described by Erikson.

Matching Items

1. g (p. 215)	**5.** h (p. 215)	**9.** c (p. 210)
2. k (p. 225)	**6.** b (p. 222)	**10.** j (p. 222)
3. i (p. 215)	**7.** e (p. 222)	**11.** a (p. 215)
4. d (p. 215)	**8.** f (p. 210)	

KEY TERMS

Writing Definitions

1. **Emotional regulation** is the ability to control when and how emotions are expressed. (p. 197)
2. According to Erikson, the crisis of early childhood is **initiative versus guilt**. In this crisis, young children eagerly take on new skills and activities and feel guilty when their efforts result in failure or criticism. (p. 198)
3. **Self-esteem** is the belief in one's own ability. (p. 198)
4. **Self-concept** refers to people's understanding of who they are. (p. 198)
5. **Intrinsic motivation** is the internal goals or drives to accomplish something for the joy of doing it. (p. 200)
6. **Extrinsic motivation** is the need for rewards from outside, such as material possessions. (p. 200)
7. **Psychopathology** is an illness or disorder of the mind. (p. 201)
8. Young children who have **externalizing problems** have trouble regulating emotions and uncontrollably lash out at other people or things. (p. 201)
9. Children who have **internalizing problems** tend to be fearful and withdrawn as a consequence of their tendencies to keep their emotions bottled up inside themselves. (p. 202)
10. **Rough-and-tumble play** is physical play that often mimics aggression but involves no intent to harm. (p. 207)
11. In **sociodramatic play,** children act out roles and themes in stories of their own creation, allowing them to rehearse social roles, practice regulating their emotions, test their ability to convince others of their ideas, and develop a self-concept in a nonthreatening context. (p. 207)

12. **Authoritarian parenting** is Baumrind's term for a style of child rearing in which the parents show little affection or nurturance for their children, maturity demands are high, and parent–child communication is low. (p. 210)

    Memory aid: Someone who is an authoritarian demands unquestioning obedience and acts in a dictatorial way.

13. **Permissive parenting** is Baumrind's term for a style of child rearing in which the parents make few demands on their children, yet are nurturant and accepting and communicate well with their children. (p. 210)

14. **Authoritative parenting** is Baumrind's term for a style of child rearing in which the parents set limits and enforce rules but are willing to listen to the child's ideas and are flexible. (p. 210)

    Memory aid: Authoritative parents act as authorities do on a subject—by discussing and explaining why certain family rules are in place.

15. **Neglectful/uninvolved parenting** is Baumrind's term for an approach to child rearing in which the parents are indifferent toward their children. (p. 210)

16. **Empathy** is a person's understanding of other people's emotions and concerns. (p. 215)

17. **Antipathy** is a person's feelings of dislike or even hatred of another person. (p. 215)

18. **Prosocial behavior** is actions that are helpful and kind but without any obvious benefit to the person doing them. (p. 215)

19. **Antisocial behavior** is actions that are deliberately hurtful or destructive to another person. (p. 215)

20. **Instrumental aggression** is hurtful behavior that is intended to get or keep something that another person has. (p. 215)

21. **Reactive aggression** is impulsive retaliation for some intentional or accidental act, verbal or physical, by another person. (p. 215)

    Memory aid: **Instrumental aggression** is behavior that is *instrumental* in allowing a child to retain a favorite toy. **Reactive aggression** is a *reaction* to another child's behavior.

22. **Relational aggression** involves insults, and other nonphysical acts, aimed at harming the social connection between the victim and other people. (p. 215)

23. An unprovoked, repeated physical or verbal attack on another person is an example of **bullying aggression**. (p. 215)

24. **Psychological control** is a form of discipline that involves threatening to withdraw love and support from a child. (p. 218)

25. A **time-out** is a form of discipline in which a child is required to stop all activity and sit quietly apart from other people for a few minutes. (p. 218)

26. **Sex differences** are biological differences between females and males. (p. 221)

27. **Gender differences** are cultural differences in the roles and behavior of males and females. (p. 221)

28. In psychoanalytic theory, the **phallic stage** is the third stage of psychosexual development, in which the penis becomes the focus of concern and pleasure. (p. 222)

29. According to Freud, boys in the phallic stage of psychosexual development develop a collection of feelings, known as the **Oedipus complex**, that center on sexual attraction to the mother and resentment of the father. (p. 222)

30. In psychoanalytic theory, the **superego** is the judgmental part of personality that internalizes the moral standards of the parents. (p. 222)

31. Girls in Freud's phallic stage may develop a collection of feelings, known as the **Electra complex**, that center on sexual attraction to the father and resentment of the mother. (p. 222)

32. In Freud's theory, **identification** is a means of defending one's self-concept by taking on the behaviors and attitudes of another person. (p. 222)

33. In cognitive theory, **gender schema** is the child's understanding of sex differences. (p. 224)

34. **Androgyny** is a balance of traditionally female and male psychological characteristics in one person. (p. 225)

7

chapter

MIDDLE CHILDHOOD

Body and Mind

Chapter Overview

This chapter introduces middle childhood, the years from 7 to 11. Changes in physical size and shape and the importance of physical activity are described, and the problems of obesity and asthma are addressed.

Next, the chapter examines the development of cognitive abilities, beginning with the views of Piaget and Vygotsky regarding the child's growing ability to use logic and reasoning (as emphasized by Piaget) and to benefit from social interactions with skilled mentors (as emphasized by Vygotsky). It also explores information-processing theory, which focuses on how brain development better enables selective attention, automization, efficient memory, and metacognition.

The next section discusses educational and environmental conditions that are conducive to learning by schoolchildren, including language learning and how reading and math are best taught.The discussion culminates in an evaluation of intelligence testing.

A final section examines how mental abilities are measured, including a critical look at the tests being used. This leads to a discussion of children with special needs, such as children with attention-deficit/hyperactivity disorder, those with learning disabilities, and children with autism, and their problems in the educational system. The causes of and treatments for these problems are discussed, with emphasis placed on insights arising from the developmental psychopathology perspective. This perspective makes it clear that the manifestations of any special childhood problem will change as the child grows older and that treatment must also consider the social context.

NOTE: Answer guidelines for all Chapter 7 questions begin on page 122.

Chapter Review

When you have finished reading the chapter, work through the material that follows to review it. Complete the sentences and answer the questions. In some cases, Study Tips explain how best to learn a difficult concept, while Think About It and Applications help you to know how well you understand the material. As you proceed, evaluate your performance for each section by consulting the answers beginning on page 122. Do not continue with the next section until you understand each answer. If you need to, review or reread the appropriate section in the textbook before continuing.

Introduction and ***A Healthy Time*** (pp. 233–239)

1. Compared with biological development during other periods of the life span, biological development during this time, known as middle childhood, smooth, is relatively (relatively smooth/often fraught with problems). For example, disease and death during these years are rare (common/rare).
2. During middle childhood, the rate of growth slow (speeds/slows) as muscle strengthen.

Describe several other features of physical development during middle childhood.

3. State three environmental factors that favor survival during middle childhood.
   a. Children have learned to be cautious
   b. Parents have instilled some health habit
   c. Society have provided immunization

4. A chronic inflammatory disorder of the airways is called asthma. This disorder is more common (more common/less common) today than in the past.

5. The causes or triggers of asthma include genes, not getting the infections and childhood diseases that would strengthen their immune systems, and exposure to allergens such as pet hair. Two other factors that correlate with asthma are poverty and air quality.

6. Some experts suggest a hygiene hypothesis for the increase in childhood allergies. According to this hypothesis, young children are over (over/under)protected from allergens; which hinders healthy development of their immune systems.

7. The use of injections and inhalers to treat asthma is an example of tertiary prevention. Less than half (how many?) of all asthmatic children in the United States benefit from this type of treatment. The best approach to treating childhood diseases is primary prevention, which in the case of asthma includes proper ventilation of homes and schools, decreased pollution, eradication of cockroaches, and safe outdoor play area.

8. The number that expresses the relationship of height to weight is the BMI 85th 95th.

   Children are said to be overweight when their body mass index is above the genetic (what number?) percentile of the growth chart for their age. Obesity is defined as having a BMI above the primary (what number?) percentile.

9. In the United States, African American girls and Mexican American boys are at particular risk for childhood obesity. However, the average child is (is/is not) heavier than his or her counterpart in 1970.

10. Overweight children are more likely to have high blood pressure. As weight increases, school achievement and self-esteem decrease (increase/decrease). In adulthood, they face increased risks of diabetes, heart disease, and stroke.

11. People who inherit a gene allele called FTO are more likely to be obese.

State several of the benefits and potential hazards of participation in structured sports activities.

better overall health, less obesity, an appreciation of cooperation and fair play.

THINK ABOUT IT: To help you differentiate and remember the various middle childhood experiences that protect against or promote adult health problems, make a list that describes your own experiences during middle childhood. For example, did your parents promote regular exercise? Excessive television watching?

APPLICATIONS:

12. Jethro plays on a Little League baseball team and enjoys casual sports with his schoolfriends. Jethro will
    a. enjoy better overall health.
    b. learn to appreciate fair play.
    c. exhibit improved problem-solving abilities.
    d. accomplish all of these things.

13. Summarizing physical development during middle childhood, Professor Wilson notes each of the following except that
   a. it is the healthiest period of the life span.
   b. mortal injuries are unusual during this time.
   c. most fatal childhood diseases occur during middle childhood.
   d. growth is slower than during early childhood.

14. Because 11-year-old Wayne is obese, he runs a greater risk of developing
   a. heart problems.
   b. diabetes.
   c. psychological problems.
   d. all of these problems.

15. Harold weighs about 20 pounds more than his friend Jay. During school recess, Jay can usually be found playing soccer with his classmates, while Harold sits on the sidelines by himself. Harold's rejection is likely due to his
   a. being physically different.
   b. being dyslexic.
   c. intimidation of his schoolmates.
   d. being hyperactive.

16. Concluding her presentation on "Asthma During Middle Childhood," Amanda mentions each of the following except that
   a. asthma is much more common today than 20 years ago.
   b. genetic vulnerability is rarely a factor in a child's susceptibility to developing asthma.
   c. the incidence of asthma continues to increase.
   d. carpeted floors, airtight windows, and less outdoor play increase the risk of asthma attacks.

Theories About Cognition (pp. 239–257)

17. According to Piaget, between ages 7 and 11, children are in the stage of __concrete__ __operational__ __though__.

18 The concept that objects can be organized into categories according to some common property is __classification__. The ability to figure out an unspoken link between two facts is called __transitive__ __inference__. This ability may be a prerequisite for __seriation__, the idea that things can be arranged in a series.

19. Although other research has found that classification and other logical abilities may appear __before__ (before/after) middle childhood, it nevertheless has supported Piaget's finding that what develops at this time is the ability to use __mental__ __categories__. This is in line with a movement away from __egocentrism__ toward a logic that is more __flexible__.

20. Unlike Piaget, Vygotsky believed that in the child's __zone__ __of__ __proximal development__ instruction by __others__ is crucial to cognitive development. In his view, formal education __is not__ (is/is not) the only context for learning. Also unlike Piaget, Vygotsky believed that __language__ was integral as a mediator for understanding and learning.

21. Vygotsky's emphasis on the __sociocultural__ context contrasts with Piaget's more __maturational__ approach.

22. At every age, having an extensive __knowlege__ __base__ in a particular area or culture makes it easier to master new knowledge in that area.

23. Educators', and psychologists', understanding of how children learn is based on the framework that was laid down by __Piaget__ and embellished by __Vigotsky__.

24. The idea that the advances in thinking that accompany middle childhood occur because of basic changes in how children take in, store, and process data is central to the __information-__ __process__ theory.

25. Advances in brain development during early childhood enables emerging __emotional__ regulation and __theory__ __of__ __mind__. Left–right coordination also emerges as the __corpus__ __callosum__ strengthens connections between the brain's two __hemispheres__. The executive functions of

the brain also begins developing, along with maturation of the prefrontal cortex.

26. Two other advances in brain function at this time include the ability to pay special heed to one source of information among many, called selective attention, and the automatization of thoughts and actions that are repeated in sequence. This advance begins with a quicker reaction time.

27. Incoming stimulus information is held for a split second in sensory memory, after which most of it is lost.

28. Meaningful material is transferred into working memory, which is also called short-term memory.

29. The part of memory that stores information for days, months, or years is long-term memory. Crucial in this component of the system is not only storage of the material but also its retrieval.

30. How readily stored material can be retrieval depends on maturation of the prefrontal cortex, which allows children to use more efficient memory strategies, and on maturation of the hypothalamus, which produces hormones that affect memory.

31. The ability to evaluate a cognitive task to determine what to do—and to monitor and adjust one's performance—is called metacognition. One aspect of this ability is metamemory, the ability to understand how memory works in order to use it well.

STUDY TIP: To help solidify your understanding of children's cognitive advances in middle childhood, try to find real-life situations. If you have a sister, brother, nephew, or niece who is about 7 years old, examine a few pages from one of their elementary school math workbooks. Look for examples of how children are tested on classification, transitive inference, seriation, and other logical constructs.

APPLICATIONS:

32. Dr. Larsen believes that the cognitive advances of middle childhood occur because of basic changes in children's selective attention, knowledge base, and memory retrieval skills. Dr. Larsen evidently is working from the information processing perspective.

33. Mei-Chin is able to sort her Legos into groups according to size. Clearly, she has an understanding of the principle of classification.

34. For the first time, 7-year-old Nathan can remember his telephone number. This is probably the result of
   a. maturation of the sensory register.
   b. increased capacity of working memory.
   c. increased capacity of long-term memory.
   d. improved speed of processing.

35. Nine-year-old Rachel has made great strides in her ability to evaluate and monitor her learning and mastery of specific tasks. In other words, Rachel has shown great improvement in her metacognition.

36. Andy, who is 7 years old, spends many hours playing with Ronny, a friend who lives down the street. Vygotsky would say that this social interaction is important to Andy's cognitive development.

Learning in School (pp. 247–257)

37. Worldwide today, most 7- to 11-year-olds attend (attend/do not attend) school. Many schools address the teaching of value during middle childhood, when children are less egocentric. In some schools this includes religious instruction, evolution, and sex education.

38. Every culture creates its own hidden curriculum, the unofficial rules and priorities that influence every aspect of school learning.

39. During middle childhood, some children learn as many as 20 new words a day. Unlike the vocabulary explosion of early childhood, this language growth is distinguished by logic and flexibility. At this time, children also become much better able to understand metaphores

40. Children are able to change from proper speech, or a formal code, to a colloquial form, or informal code, with their peers.

41. Children who speak a minority language and are learning to speak English are called English-language learner.

42. Many American children make a language shift as they replace their original language with English.

43. The approach to bilingual education in which the child's instruction occurs entirely in the second language is called immersion. In bilingual education programs, teachers instruct children in both their native language and English.

44. Any method tends to fail if children feel stupid because their cultural background is not understood.

45. (A View From Science) The cognitive advantages of bilingualism are connected to biculturalism. A common instruction pattern in North American Schools is initiation / response / evaluation: the teacher ask a question, a child responds, and the teacher stats whether or not the response is correct

46. The connection between school achievement and socioeconomic status is revealed by the fact that children from low-income families are least likely to succeed in school. Their difficulty is generally in the area of language and includes having smaller vocabulary and using simpler grammar and shorter sentences.

47. Two important factors in language learning are exposure to communication and the expectation that adults have for a child. Parents with more education tend to use more open-ended comments in communicating with their children. This type of communication encourages dialogue.

THINK ABOUT IT: Imagine that you've been given total control over the educational experiences of a group of 7-year-old children, including microsystem factors and macrosystem factors. What factors will you focus on to promote bilingualism in your group? For example, you might suggest putting English-speaking students in a class with non–English-speaking students so they could help each other out.

48. Two distinct approaches to teaching reading are the phonics approach, in which children learn the sounds of letters first, and the whole-language approach, in which children are encouraged to develop all their language skills at the same time. Most developmentalists believe that both (both approaches/neither approach/only the phonics approach/only the whole-language approach) make(s) sense.

49. In the United States, math was traditionally taught by rote. A more recent approach replaces this type of learning by making instruction more active and engaging.

50. Cross-cultural research reveals that U.S. teachers present math at a lower level with more definitions but less connections to other learning. In contrast, teachers in Japan work more collaboratively to build children's knowledge.

51. Most people assume that children learn best when class size is ___small___. Research studies demonstrate that the relationship between class size and student performance is ___complex___ (clear-cut/complex).

APPLICATIONS:

52. After moving to a new country, Arlene's parents are struck by the greater tendency of math teachers in their new homeland to work collaboratively and to emphasize social interaction in the learning process. To which country have these parents probably moved?
   - a. the United States
   - b. Germany
   - c. Japan
   - d. Australia

53. During the school board meeting, a knowledgeable parent proclaimed that the board's position on achievement testing and class size was an example of the district's "hidden curriculum." The parent was referring to
   - a. the unofficial and unstated educational priorities of the school district.
   - b. the political agendas of individual members of the school board.
   - c. the legal mandates for testing and class size established by the state board of education.
   - d. the federally sponsored measure of children's achievement in reading, math, and other subjects.

54. Four-year-old Tasha, who is learning to read by sounding out the letters of words, evidently is being taught using the ___phonics___ approach. Tabatha, on the other hand, is learning by talking and listening, reading and writing. She is being taught using the ___whole-word___ approach.

Measuring the Mind (pp. 257–267)

55. The potential to master a specific skill or to learn a certain body of knowledge is a person's ___aptitude___. The most commonly used tests to measure this potential are ___IQ___ ___tests___. In the original version of the most commonly used test of this type, a person's score was calculated as a ___quotien___ (the child's ___mental___ ___age___ divided by the child's ___chronological age___ and multiplied by 100 to determine his or her ___IQ___).

56. Tests that are designed to measure what a child has learned are called ___achievement___ tests.

57. Two highly regarded IQ tests are the ________ ________ ________ ________ ________ and the ________-________.

58. The average IQ scores of nations have ________ (increased/decreased), a phenomenon called the ________ ________.

59. To be classified as ________ ________, children must have IQs below ________ and be unusually low in ________.

60. IQ testing is controversial in part because no test can measure ________ without also measuring ________ or without reflecting the ________.

61. Many critics of IQ testing contend that we have ________ ________. Robert Sternberg believes that there are three distinct types of intelligence: ________, ________, and ________. Similarly, Howard Gardner describes ________ (how many?) distinct intelligences.

62. In the United States, the ________ ________ Act is a federal law that mandates annual standardized achievement tests for public school children.

63. The ________ is a federal project that measures achievement in reading, mathematics, and other subjects over time.

64. Two international approaches to objective assessment of children's achievement are the ________ ________

and the ______________________

______________________.

THINK ABOUT IT: The board of directors for a new private school is considering the pros and cons of using IQ testing to admit and place students. Help them out by listing the major advantages and disadvantages of IQ testing as identified by developmental psychologists.

APPLICATIONS:

65. Angela was born in 1984. In 1992, she scored 125 on an intelligence test. Using the original formula, what was Angela's mental age when she took the test? ______________

66. Concluding his presentation on the Flynn Effect, Kwame notes that the reasons for this trend include all of the following except
   a. better health.
   b. genetic variability.
   c. more schooling.
   d. smaller families.

67. Professor Allenby teaches in a public school in a large city. Following the views of Howard Gardner and Robert Sternberg , the professor is most critical of traditional aptitude and achievement tests because they
   a. inadvertently reflect certain nonacademic competencies.
   b. do not reflect knowledge of cultural ideas.
   c. measure only a limited set of abilities.
   d. underestimate the intellectual potential of disadvantaged children.

68. Children with ______________ ______________ require extra help in order to learn because of some ______________ or ______________ disability.

69. The field of study that is concerned with childhood psychological disorders is ______________ ______________. This perspective has provided several lessons that apply to all children. Three of these are that ______________ is normal, disability ______________ (changes/does not change) over time, and adolescence and adulthood may be ______________.

70. This perspective also has made diagnosticians much more aware of the ______________ ______________ of childhood problems. This awareness is reflected in the official diagnostic guide of the American Psychiatric Association, which is the ______________ ______________.

71. A condition that manifests itself in a difficulty in concentrating for more than a few moments is called ______________-______________ ______________.

72. The most common type of this disorder, which includes a need to be active, often accompanied by excitability and impulsivity, is called ______________-______________/ ______________ ______________.
Children suffering from this disorder can be ______________, ______________, and ______________.

73. Other disorders often occur together with (that is, are ______________ with) ADHD. Examples of these conditions include ______________ ______________.

74. Various possible causes of ADHD have been proposed, including neurological, such as a slow-developing ______________ ______________, which could be ______________ or the result of ______________ problems.

75. (text and A View From Science) Certain drugs that stimulate adults, such as______________ and ______________, have a reverse effect on many hyperactive children. These drugs are classified as ______________ because they affect the workings of the mind.

76. Children who have difficulty acquiring a particular skill that others acquire easily are said to have a ______________ ______________. These deficits usually ______________ (do/do not) result in lifelong impediments.

77. A disability in reading is called______________.

78. In autistic spectrum disorder, deficiencies appear in three areas: delayed ______________, impaired ______________ ______________, and unusual patterns of ______________.

79. The classic form of austistic spectrum disorder is ______________, in which the child has extremely inadequate ______________ skills,

is extremely ________________, and is unable to acquire normal ________________.

80. Children who have autistic symptoms but are very intelligent in some ways are sometimes diagnosed with ________________ ________________.

81. One possible reason for the increased incidence of autistic spectrum disorder is the greater availability of ________________ ________________, which has led to increased diagnosis.

82. Another possibility is that some new ________________ harms their developing brains. One suspected toxin was the antiseptic ________________, which is used in childhood ________________. Other possible toxins are ________________ ________________.

STUDY TIP: Complete the following chart as a way of organizing your understanding of the differences among children with special needs.

Category	Characteristics	Suggested Treatment
Attention-deficit disorder		
Attention-deficit/ hyperactivity disorder		
Learning disability		
Autism		
Autistic spectrum disorder		
Asperger syndrome		

APPLICATIONS:

83. Dr. Rutter, who believes that knowledge about normal development can be applied to the study and treatment of psychological disorders, evidently is working from the ________________ ________________ perspective.

84. Ten-year-old Clarence is quick-tempered, easily frustrated, and is often disruptive in the classroom. Clarence may be suffering from ________________.

85. In determining whether her 8-year-old student has a learning disability, the teacher looks primarily for
   a. poor performance in all subject areas.
   b. the exclusion of other explanations.
   c. a family history of the learning disability.
   d. an inability to communicate.

86. Although 9-year-old Carl has severely impaired social skills, his intelligence and speech are normal. Carl is evidently displaying symptoms of ________________ ________________.

87. Jennifer displays inadequate social skills and is extremely self-absorbed. It is likely that she suffers from ________________.

Progress Test 1

Multiple-Choice Questions

Circle your answers to the following questions and check them with the answers on page 124. If your answer is incorrect, read the explanation for why it is incorrect and then consult the appropriate pages of the text (in parentheses following the correct answer).

1. As children move into middle childhood
- **a.** the rate of accidental death increases.
- **b.** sexual urges intensify.
- **c.** the rate of weight gain increases.
- **d.** biological growth slows and steadies.

2. The ability to filter out distractions and concentrate on relevant details is called
- **a.** automatization.
- **b.** reaction time.
- **c.** selective attention.
- **d.** inclusion.

3. Dyslexia is a learning disability that affects the ability to
- **a.** do math.
- **b.** read.
- **c.** write.
- **d.** speak.

4. The developmental psychopathology perspective is characterized by its
- **a.** contextual approach.
- **b.** emphasis on the unchanging nature of developmental disorders.
- **c.** emphasis on cognitive development.
- **d.** concern with all of these considerations.

5. The time—usually measured in fractions of a second—it takes for a person to respond to a particular stimulus is called
- **a.** the interstimulus interval.
- **b.** reaction time.
- **c.** the stimulus–response interval.
- **d.** response latency.

6. The underlying problem in attention-deficit/hyperactivity disorder appears to be
- **a.** low overall intelligence.
- **b.** a neurological difficulty in paying attention.
- **c.** a learning disability in a specific academic skill.
- **d.** the existence of a conduct disorder.

7. Children who have an autistic spectrum disorder have severe deficiencies in
- **a.** social responses.
- **b.** language development.
- **c.** play patterns.
- **d.** all of these abilities.

8. Although asthma has genetic origins, several environmental factors contribute to its onset, including
- **a.** urbanization.
- **b.** airtight windows.
- **c.** dogs and cats living inside the house.
- **d.** all of these factors.

9. Tests that measure a child's potential to learn a new subject are called ________________ tests.
- **a.** aptitude
- **b.** achievement
- **c.** vocational
- **d.** intelligence

10. In the earliest aptitude tests, a child's score was calculated by dividing the child's ________ age by his or her ________ age to find the ________ quotient.
- **a.** mental; chronological; intelligence
- **b.** chronological; mental; intelligence
- **c.** intelligence; chronological; mental
- **d.** intelligence; mental; chronological

11. Selective attention refers to the ability to
- **a.** choose which of many stimuli to concentrate on.
- **b.** control emotional outbursts.
- **c.** persist at a task.
- **d.** perform a familiar action without much conscious thought.

12. Ongoing maturation of which brain area enables schoolchildren to more effectively analyze the potential consequences of their actions?
- **a.** corpus callosum
- **b.** prefrontal cortex
- **c.** brainstem
- **d.** temporal lobe

13. According to Piaget, the stage of cognitive development in which a person understands specific logical ideas and can apply them to concrete problems is called
- **a.** preoperational thought.
- **b.** operational thought.
- **c.** concrete operational thought.
- **d.** formal operational thought.

14. Japanese children outscore children in the United States in math. This difference has been attributed to which of the following?
    a. U.S. teachers present math at a lower level.
    b. Japanese teachers encourage more social interaction among groups of children.
    c. Japanese teachers are more collaborative in their teaching.
    d. Each of these practices has been offered as an explanation of national differences in math scores.

15. Information-processing theorists contend that major advances in cognitive development occur during the school years because
    a. the child's mind becomes more like a computer as he or she matures.
    b. children become better able to process and analyze information.
    c. most mental activities become automatic by the time a child is about 13 years old.
    d. the major improvements in reasoning that occur during the school years involve increased long-term memory capacity.

16. Cross-cultural research on children's cognition reveals
    a. the same patterns of development worldwide.
    b. significant variations from country to country.
    c. that children's understanding of classification is unrelated to social interaction.
    d. that children's understanding of seriation is unrelated to social interaction.

17. Some researchers believe that cognitive processing speed and capacity increase during middle childhood because of
    a. the myelination of neural axons.
    b. repetition and practice.
    c. better use of cognitive resources.
    d. all of these reasons.

18. The term for the ability to monitor and adjust one's cognitive performance—to think about thinking—is
    a. seriation.
    b. information processing.
    c. selective attention.
    d. metacognition.

19. Long-term memory is _________ permanent and _________ limited than working memory.
    a. more; less
    b. less; more
    c. more; more
    d. less; less

20. Passed in 2001, the federal law that mandates annual standardized achievement tests for public school children is the
    a. Reading First Act.
    b. National Assessment of Educational Progress.
    c. No Child Left Behind Act.
    d. Trends in Math and Science Study.

21. Which theorist believed that cultures (tools, customs, and people) teach children best?
    a. Piaget
    b. Vygotsky
    c. Wechsler
    d. Binet

22. Which aspect of memory is most likely to change during the school years?
    a. sensory memory
    b. long-term memory
    c. the efficiency of working memory
    d. All of these aspects change.

23. Which theorist emphasized the critical role of maturation in cognitive development?
    a. Piaget
    b. Vygotsky
    c. Wechsler
    d. Binet

24. Of the following, which was NOT identified as an important factor in the difference between success and failure in second-language learning?
    a. the age of the child
    b. the attitudes of the parents
    c. community values regarding second-language learning
    d. the difficulty of the language

True or False Items

Write *T (true) or F (false)* on the line in front of each statement.

_______ 1. The rate of growth in school-age children continues at a rapid pace.

_______ 2. Genes and hereditary differences in taste preferences are the most important factors in promoting childhood obesity.

_______ 3. The quick reaction time that is crucial in some sports can be readily achieved with practice.

_______ 4. The intellectual performance of children with Asperger syndrome is poor in all areas.

_______ 5. Despite the efforts of teachers and parents, most children with learning disabilities can expect their disabilities to persist and even worsen as they enter adulthood.

_______ 6. Stressful living conditions are an important consideration in diagnosing a learning disability.

_______ 7. A major objection to Piaget's theory is that he underestimated the influence of context, instruction, and culture.

_______ 8. Immersion is the best strategy for teaching English-language learners.

_______ 9. Vygotsky emphasized the child's own logical thinking.

_______ 10. Research evidence consistently demonstrates that children learn best with fewer students in each classroom.

_______ 11. Socioeconomic status does not affect bilingualism.

_______ 12. One idea for improving math education involves making each grade of elementary school math build on the previous year's instruction.

Progress Test 2

Progress Test 2 should be completed during a final chapter review. Answer the following questions after you thoroughly understand the correct answers for the Chapter Review and Progress Test 1.

Multiple-Choice Questions

1. During the years from 7 to 11, the average child
   a. develops stronger muscles.
   b. grows at a rapid rate.
   c. has decreased lung capacity.
   d. is more likely to become obese than at any other period in the life span.

2. Comorbidity refers to the presence of
   a. two or more unrelated disease conditions in the same person.
   b. abnormal neurons in the prefrontal cortex.
   c. developmental delays in physical development.
   d. any of several disorders characterized by inadequate social skills.

3. A specific learning disability that becomes apparent when a child experiences unusual difficulty in learning to read is
   a. dyslexia.
   b. Asperger syndrome.
   c. ADHD.
   d. ADD.

4. Marked delays in particular areas of learning are collectively referred to as
   a. learning disabilities.
   b. attention-deficit/hyperactivity disorder.
   c. hyperactivity.
   d. dyslexia.

5. Aptitude and achievement testing are controversial in part because
   a. most tests are unreliable with respect to the individual scores they yield.
   b. a child's intellectual potential often changes over time.
   c. they often fail to identify serious learning problems.
   d. of all of these reasons.

6. A key factor in reaction time is
   a. whether the child is male or female.
   b. brain maturation.
   c. whether the stimulus to be reacted to is an auditory or visual one.
   d. all of these conditions.

7. One of the first noticeable symptoms of autism is usually
   a. a difficulty with reading.
   b. abnormal social responsiveness.
   c. hyperactivity.
   d. unpredictable.

8. Which of the following is true of children with a diagnosed learning disability?
   a. They are not much different from other children except in one particular form of intelligence.
   b. They often have a specific physical handicap, such as hearing loss.
   c. They often lack basic educational experiences.
   d. All of these conditions are true.

9. Most important in the automatization of children's thoughts and actions is
   a. the continuing myelination of neurons.
   b. diet.
   c. activity level.
   d. all of these factors.

10. Asperger syndrome is a disorder in which
   a. body weight fluctuates dramatically over short periods of time.
   b. verbal skills seem normal, but social perceptions and skills are abnormal.
   c. an autistic child is extremely aggressive.
   d. a child of normal intelligence has difficulty mastering a specific cognitive skill.

11. Which of the following is NOT evidence of ADHD?
   a. inattentiveness
   b. poor language skills
   c. impulsivity
   d. overreactivity

12. Tests that measure what a child has already learned are called ________________ tests.
   a. aptitude
   b. vocational
   c. achievement
   d. intelligence

13. Which of the following is NOT a type of intelligence identified in Robert Sternberg's theory?
   a. academic
   b. practical
   c. achievement
   d. creative

14. The first component of the information-processing system is
   a. sensory memory.
   b. working memory.
   c. long-term memory.
   d. control process.

15. When psychologists look at the ability of children to receive, store, and organize information, they are examining cognitive development from a view based on
   a. the observations of Piaget.
   b. information processing.
   c. behaviorism.
   d. the idea that the key to thinking is the sensory register.

16. The National Assessment of Educational Progress (NAEP)
   a. measures achievement in reading, mathematics, and other subjects over time.
   b. federally mandates annual achievement testing for public school children.
   c. established a five-year cycle of international trend studies in reading ability.
   d. provides states with funding for early reading instruction.

17. Which of the following is especially helpful in making it easier to master new information in a specific subject?
   a. a large sensory register
   b. a large knowledge base
   c. unlimited long-term memory
   d. working memory

18. Language "codes" include variations in
   a. pronunciation.
   b. gestures.
   c. vocabulary.
   d. all of these aspects.

19. Increased myelination and dendrite formation in the prefrontal cortex contributes to
   a. the child's ability to selectively attend to more than one thought.
   b. the amount of information the child is able to hold in working memory.
   c. the size of the child's knowledge base.
   d. all of these things.

20. Retaining information in memory is called
   a. retrieval.
   b. storage.
   c. automatization.
   d. metacognition.

21. An example of schoolchildren's growth in metacognition is their understanding that
   a. transformed objects can be returned to their original state.
   b. rehearsal is a good strategy for memorizing, but outlining is better for understanding.
   c. objects may belong to more than one class.
   d. they can use different language styles in different situations.

22. Which of the following most accurately states the relative merits of the phonics approach and the whole-language approach to teaching reading?
   a. The phonics approach is more effective.
   b. The whole-language approach is the more effective approach.
   c. Both approaches have merit.
   d. Both approaches have been discarded in avor of newer, more interactive methods of instruction.

23. Juan attends a school that offers instruction in both English and Spanish. This strategy for teaching English-language learners is called
   a. bilingual education.
   b. immersion.
   c. heritage language instruction.
   d. ESL.

Matching Items

Match each term or concept with its corresponding description or definition.

Terms or Concepts

_______ 1. dyslexia
_______ 2. automatization
_______ 3. Asperger syndrome
_______ 4. attention-deficit/hyperactivity disorder
_______ 5. asthma
_______ 6. Flynn Effect
_______ 7. autism
_______ 8. developmental psychopathology
_______ 9. DSM-IV-TR
_______ 10. learning disability
_______ 11. working memory
_______ 12. classification
_______ 13. information processing
_______ 14. metacognition
_______ 15. concrete operational thought

Descriptions or Definitions

a. developmental perspective that conceives of cognitive development as the result of changes in the processing and analysis of information
b. Piaget's term for the ability to reason logically about direct experiences.
c. set of symptoms in which a child has impaired social skills despite having normal speech and intelligence
d. the rise in IQ score averages that has occurred in many nations
e. the diagnostic guide of the American Psychiatric Association
f. process by which thoughts and actions become routine and no longer require much thought
g. disorder characterized by self-absorption
h. chronic inflammation of the airways
i. behavior problem involving difficulty in concentrating, as well as excitability and impulsivity
j. applies insights from studies of normal development to the study of childhood disorders
k. an unexpected difficulty with one or more academic skills
l. difficulty in reading
m. area where current, conscious mental activity occurs
n. the ability to evaluate a cognitive task and to monitor one's performance on it
o. the logical principle that things can be organized into groups

Key Terms

Using your own words, write a brief definition or explanation of each of the following terms on a separate piece of paper.

1. middle childhood
2. asthma
3. body mass index (BMI)
4. overweight
5. obesity
6. concrete operational thought
7. classification
8. knowledge base
9. information-processing theory
10. selective attention
11. automatization
12. reaction time
13. sensory memory
14. working memory
15. long-term memory
16. metacognition
17. metamemory
18. hidden curriculum
19. English-language learner (ELL)
20. phonics approach
21. whole-language approach
22. aptitude

23. IQ test
24. achievement test
25. Wechsler Intelligence Scale for Children (WISC)
26. Flynn Effect
27. mental retardation
28. No Child Left Behind Act
29. National Assessment of Educational Progress (NAEP)
30. Progress in International Reading Literacy Study (PIRLS)
31. Trends in Math and Science Study (TIMSS)
32. child with special needs
33. developmental psychopathology
34. *Diagnostic and Statistical Manual of Mental Disorders* (DSM-IV-TR)
35. attention-deficit/hyperactivity disorder (ADHD)
36. comorbidity
37. learning disability
38. dyslexia
39. autistic spectrum disorder
40. autistic
41. Asperger syndrome

Answers

CHAPTER REVIEW

1. middle childhood; relatively smooth; rare
2. slows; muscles

During middle childhood, children grow taller, and they tend to be agile and neither too heavy nor too thin.

3. Three factors favor survival:

   a. Children have learned to be cautious.

   b. Parents have instilled some health habits.

   c. Societies have provided immunization.
4. asthma; more common
5. genes; immune; allergens; poverty; air quality
6. hygiene hypothesis; allergies; over; immune
7. tertiary; half; primary prevention; ventilation; pollution; play areas
8. body mass index; 85th; 95th; genetic; primary
9. African American; Mexican American; is
10. blood pressure; decrease; diabetes; heart disease; stroke
11. FTO

The benefits of sports include better overall health, less obesity, an appreciation of cooperation and fair play, improved problem-solving ability, and respect for teammates and opponents of many ethnicities and nationalities. The hazards may include loss of self-esteem as a result of criticism, injuries, reinforcement of existing prejudices, increased stress, and time taken away from learning
academic skills.

12. **d.** is the answer. Participation in sports during middle childhood helps children develop not only biologically but also cognitively and socially.
13. **c.** is the answer. Just the opposite is true.
14. **d.** is the answer.
15. **a.** is the answer. Obese children are no more likely to be dyslexic, physically intimidating, or hyperactive than other children.
16. **b.** is the answer.
17. concrete operational thought
18. classification; transitive inference; seriation
19. before; mental categories; egocentrism; flexible
20. zone of proximal development; others; is not; language
21. sociocultural; maturational
22. knowledge base
23. Piaget; Vygotsky
24. information-processing
25. emotional; theory of mind; corpus callosum; hemispheres; prefrontal cortex
26. selective attention; automatization; reaction time
27. sensory memory (the sensory register)
28. working memory; short-term memory
29. long-term memory; retrieval
30. retrieved; prefrontal cortex; hypothalamus; hormones
31. metacognition; metamemory
32. information-processing
33. classification. This is the process of organizing things into groups according to some common property.
34. **b.** is the answer. Working memory improves steadily and significantly during middle childhood.
35. metacognition. Metacognition has been referred to as "thinking about thinking."
36. social interaction. Vygotsky believed that peers, teachers, and the overall cultural context provide the bridge between the child's developmental potential and the needed skills and knowledge.
37. attend; values; religious; evolution; sex
38. hidden curriculum

39. 20; logic; flexibility; metaphors
40. formal code; informal code
41. English-language learners (ELLs)
42. language shift
43. immersion; bilingual education
44. stupid; cultural background
45. bilingualism; biculturalism; initiation/response/evaluation; asks a question; responds; states whether or not the response is correct
46. school; socioeconomic; low-income; language; vocabularies; grammar; shorter
47. exposure to communication; expectations; open-ended; dialogue
48. phonics; whole-language; both approaches
49. rote; active; engaging
50. definitions; connection; collaboratively
51. small; complex
52. **c.** is the answer.
53. **a.** is the answer.
54. phonics; whole-word
55. aptitude; IQ tests; quotient; mental age; chronological age; IQ
56. achievement
57. Wechsler Intelligence Scale for Children (WISC); Stanford-Binet
58. increased; Flynn Effect
59. mentally retarded; 70; adaptation to daily life
60. potential; achievement; culture
61. multiple intelligences; academic; creative; practical; eight
62. No Child Left Behind
63. National Assessment of Educational Progress
64. Progress in International Reading Literacy Study (PIRLS); Trends in Math and Science Study (TIMSS)

Think About It: See text pages 257–260 for a discussion of the pros and cons of IQ testing.

65. 10 years old. At the time she took the test, Angela's chronological age was 8. Knowing that her IQ was 125, we can solve the equation to yield a mental age of 10 (125 = x/8).
66. **b.** is the answer. Genetic variability has not changed in recent decades.
67. **c.** is the answer. Both Sternberg and Gardner believe that there are multiple intelligences rather than the narrowly defined abilities measured by traditional aptitude and achievement tests.
68. special needs; physical; mental
69. developmental psychopathology; abnormality; changes; better or worse
70. social context; *Diagnostic and Statistical Manual of Mental Disorders* (DSM-IV-TR)
71. attention-deficit disorder
72. attention-deficit/hyperactivity disorder; inattentive; impulsive; overactive
73. comorbid; conduct disorder, depression, anxiety, Tourette syndrome, dyslexia, bipolar disorder, autism, and schizophrenia
74. prefrontal cortex; genetic; prenatal
75. amphetamines (e.g., Adderall); methylphenidate (Ritalin); psychoactive
76. learning disability; do not
77. dyslexia
78. language; social responses; play
79. autism; social; self-absorbed; speech
80. Asperger syndrome
81. special education
82. teratogen; thimerosal; immunizations; pesticides, cleaning chemicals, and some ingredients in nail polish

Study Tip: Attention-deficit disorder: difficulty paying attention; medication plus psychotherapy

Attention-deficit/hyperactivity disorder: difficulty concentrating plus being inattentive, impulsive, and overactive; medication, psychotherapy, and special training for parents and teachers.

Learning disability, such as dyslexia: marked delay in learning a particular skill that comes easily to others; learning disabilities do not result in lifelong impediments because most people learn how to work around them.

Autism: woefully inadequate social skills, extreme self-absorption, and an inability to acquire normal speech; early training that focuses on each of the specific deficiencies. Some programs emphasize language, others focus on play, and others stress attachment. All autistic spectrum disorders involve these treatments, varying only in the degree of help needed.

Autistic spectrum disorder: inadequate social skills, impaired communication, and unusual play patterns.

Asperger syndrome, or "high-functioning" autism: extreme attention to details and deficient social understanding, but unusually intelligent in some specialized area.

83. developmental psychopathology
84. ADHD. Children with ADHD are inattentive, impulsive, and overactive.

85. **b.** is the answer.

86. Asperger syndrome. Asperger syndrome is referred to as "high-functioning" autism because the person tends to have normal or above-average intelligence, especially in a particular skill.

87. autism

PROGRESS TEST 1

Multiple-Choice Questions

1. **d.** is the answer. (p. 234)

2. **c.** (p. 243)

a. Automatization is the process in which repetition of a sequence of thoughts and actions makes the sequence routine.

b. Reaction time is the length of time it takes to respond to a stimulus.

d. Inclusion is an approach in which children with special needs are educated in regular classrooms along with all the other children.

3. **b.** is the answer. (p. 265)

a. Though not defined in the text, this is called dyscalcula.

c. & d. The text does not give labels for learning disabilities in writing or speaking.

4. **a.** is the answer. (p. 262)

b. & c. Because of its contextual approach, developmental psychopathology emphasizes *all* domains of development. Also, it points out that behaviors change over time.

5. **b.** is the answer. (p. 243)

6. **b.** is the answer. (p. 264)

7. **d.** is the answer. (p. 265)

8. **d.** is the answer. (p. 235)

9. **a.** is the answer. (p. 257)

b. Achievement tests measure what has already been learned.

c. Vocational tests, which, as their name implies, measure what a person has learned about a particular trade, are achievement tests.

d. Intelligence tests measure general aptitude, rather than aptitude for a specific subject.

10. **a.** is the answer. (p. 257)

11. **a.** is the answer. (p. 243)

b. This is emotional regulation.

d. This is automatization.

12. **b.** is the answer. (pp. 242–243)

a. Maturation of the corpus callosum contributes to left–right coordination.

c. & d. These brain areas, which were not discussed in this chapter, play important roles in regulating sleep–waking cycles (brain stem) and hearing and language abilities (temporal lobe).

13. **c.** is the answer. (p. 239)

a. Preoperational thought is "pre-logical" thinking.

b. There is no such stage in Piaget's theory.

d. Formal operational thought extends logical reasoning to abstract problems.

14. **d.** is the answer. (p. 256)

15. **b.** is the answer. (p. 242)

a. Information-processing theorists use the mind–computer metaphor at every age.

c. Although increasing automatization is an important aspect of development, the information-processing perspective does not suggest that most mental activities become automatic by age 13.

d. Most of the important changes in reasoning that occur during the school years are due to the improved processing capacity of the person's *working memory.*

16. **a.** is the answer. (pp. 241–242)

17. **d.** is the answer. (pp. 242–243)

18. **d.** is the answer. (p. 245)

a. Seriation is the idea that things can be arranged in series.

b. The information-processing perspective views the mind as being like a computer.

c. This is the ability to screen out distractions in order to focus on important information.

19. **a.** is the answer. (p. 244)

20. **c.** is the answer. (p. 260)

21. **b.** is the answer. (pp. 241–242)

a. Piaget emphasized the importance of maturation in cognitive development.

c. & d. Wechsler and Binet each developed an intelligence test.

22. **c.** is the answer. During middle childhood, selective attention and automatization improve, thus improving the efficiency of working memory. (pp. 243–244)

23. **a.** is the answer. (p. 239)

24. **d.** is the answer. (pp. 249–251)

True or False Items

1. F The rate of growth slows down during middle childhood. (p. 234)
2. F Environmental factors are more important in promoting obesity during middle childhood. (pp. 236–237)
3. F Reaction time depends on brain maturation and is not readily affected by practice. (p. 243)
4. F Children with Asperger syndrome show isolated areas of remarkable skill. (p. 266)
5. F Some children find ways to compensate for their deficiencies, and others are taught effective strategies for learning. (p. 265)
6. F Stressful living conditions must be excluded before diagnosing a learning disability. (p. 265)
7. T (p. 241)
8. F No single approach to teaching a second language is best for all children in all contexts. (pp. 250–251)
9. F This is true of Piaget. (p. 241)
10. F Research support for this popular assumption is weak. (p. 256)
11. F The likelihood of parents, school, or culture encouraging bilingualism in children depends on the family's socioeconomic status. (p. 252)
12. T (p. 256)

PROGRESS TEST 2

Multiple-Choice Questions

1. **a.** is the answer. (p. 234)

   b. & c. During this period, children's growth slows down, and they experience increased lung capacity.

   d. Although childhood obesity is a common problem, the text does not indicate that a person is more likely to become obese at this age than at any other.
2. **a.** is the answer. (p. 263)
3. **a.** is the answer. (p. 265)

   b., c. & d. These disorders do not manifest themselves in a particular academic skill but instead appear in psychological processes that affect learning in general.
4. **a.** is the answer. (p. 265)

   b. & c. ADHD is a disorder that usually does not manifest itself in specific subject areas. Hyperactivity is a facet of this disorder.

   d. Dyslexia is a learning disability in reading only.
5. **b.** is the answer. (p. 258)
6. **b.** is the answer. (p. 243)
7. **b.** is the answer. (p. 266)
8. **a.** is the answer. (p. 265)
9. **a.** is the answer. (p. 243)
10. **b.** is the answer. (p. 266)
11. **b.** is the answer. (p. 263)
12. **c.** is the answer. (p. 257)
13. **c.** is the answer. (p. 259)
14. **a.** is the answer. (p. 244)
15. **b.** is the answer. (p. 242)
16. **a.** is the answer. (p. 260)
17. **b.** is the answer. (p. 242)

    a. The sensory register briefly stores incoming sensations. Its capacity does not change with maturation.

    c. & d. Working memory and long-term memory are important in all forms of learning. Unlike a broad knowledge base in a specific area, however, these memory processes do not selectively make it easier to learn more in a specific area.
18. **d.** is the answer. (p. 249)
19. **b.** is the answer. (p. 244)
20. **b.** is the answer. (p. 244)

    a. This is the *accessing* of already learned information.

    c. Automatization is the process by which well-learned activities become routine and automatic.

    d. This is the ability to evaluate a task and to monitor and adjust one's performance on it.
21. **b.** is the answer. (p. 245)
22. **c.** is the answer. (p. 254)
23. **a.** is the answer. (pp. 250–251)

Matching Items

1. l (p. 265)	**6.** d (p. 258)	**11.** m (p. 244)
2. f (p. 243)	**7.** g (p. 266)	**12.** o (p. 239)
3. c (p. 266)	**8.** j (p. 262)	**13.** a (p. 242)
4. i(p. 263)	**9.** e (p. 263)	**14.** n (p. 245)
5. h (p. 234)	**10.** k (p. 265)	**15.** b (p. 239)

KEY TERMS

1. **Middle childhood** is the period from early childhood to adolescence, roughly ages 7 to 11. (p. 233)
2. **Asthma** is a disorder in which chronically inflamed airways make breathing difficult. (p. 234)

3. **Body mass index (BMI)** is the ratio of weight to height; it is a person's weight in kilograms divided by the square of height in meters. (p. 236)
4. A child whose body mass index (BMI) falls above the 85th percentile for children of a given age is designated as **overweight.** (p. 236)
5. **Obesity** is a body mass index (BMI) above the 95th percentile for children of a given age. (p. 236)
6. During Piaget's stage of **concrete operational thought,** lasting from ages 7 to 11, children can think logically about direct experiences and perceptions but are not able to reason abstractly. (p. 239)
7. **Classification** is the principle that things can be organized into groups according to some common property. (p. 239)
8. The **knowledge base** is a broad body of knowledge in a particular subject area that has been learned, making it easier to learn new information in that area. (p. 242)
9. **Information-processing theory** models human cognition after the computer, analyzing each component, step by step. (p. 242)
10. **Selective attention** is the ability to concentrate on some stimuli while ignoring others. (p. 243)
11. **Automatization** is the process by which thoughts and actions that are repeated often enough to become routine no longer require much conscious thought. (p. 243)
12. **Reaction time** is the length of time it takes a person to respond to a particular stimulus. (p. 243)
13. **Sensory memory** is the first component of the information-processing system that stores incoming stimuli for a split second, after which it is passed into working memory, or discarded as unimportant; also called the *sensory register.* (p. 244)
14. **Working memory** is the component of the information-processing system that handles current, conscious mental activity; also called *short-term memory.* (p. 244)
15. **Long-term memory** is the component of the information-processing system that stores unlimited amounts of information for days, months, or years. (p. 244)
16. **Metacognition** is the ability to evaluate a cognitive task to determine what to do and to monitor and adjust one's performance on that task. (p. 245)
17. An important aspect of metacognition, **metamemory** is the ability to understand how memory works in order to use it well. (p. 245)
18. The **hidden curriculum** is the unofficial, unstated, or implicit rules and priorities that influence the academic curriculum and every other aspect of school learning. (p. 248)
19. An **English-language learner (ELL)** is a child who is learning English as a second language. (p. 250)
20. The **phonics approach** is a method of teaching reading by having children learn the sounds of letters before they begin to learn words. (p. 253)
21. The **whole-language approach** is a method of teaching reading by encouraging children to develop all their language skills simultaneously. (p. 254)
22. **Aptitude** is the potential to master a specific skill or learn a certain body of knowledge. (p. 257)
23. **IQ tests** are designed to measure intellectual aptitude, or ability to learn in school; they were originally designed to yield a measure of intelligence and originally calculated as mental age divided by chronological age, multiplied by 100. (p. 257)
24. **Achievement tests** measure what a child has already learned in a particular academic subject or subjects. (p. 257)
25. The **Wechsler Intelligence Scale for Children (WISC)** is a widely used IQ test for school-age children that assesses vocabulary, general knowledge, memory, and spatial comprehension. (p. 258)
26. The **Flynn Effect** refers to the rise in average IQ scores that has occurred recently in many nations. (p. 258)
27. People are considered **mentally retarded** if their IQs fall below 70 and they are unusually low in adaptation to daily life. (p. 258)
28. The **No Child Left Behind Act** is a controversial law, enacted in 2001, that uses multiple assessments and achievement standards to try to improve public education in the United States. (p. 260)
29. The **National Assessment of Educational Progress (NAEP)** is an ongoing nationwide program of measurement of children's achievement in reading, mathematics, and other subjects. (p. 260)
30. **Progress in International Reading Literacy Study (PIRLS)** is a five-year cycle of trend studies of reading ability among fourth-graders around the world. (p. 261)

31. The **Trends in Math and Science Study (TIMSS)** is an international assessment of math and science skills of fourth- and eighth-graders. (p. 261)
32. A **child with special needs** is one who, because of physical or mental disability, requires extra help in order to learn. (p. 262)
33. **Developmental psychopathology** is a field that applies the insights into typical development to understand and remediate developmental disorders, and vice versa. (p. 262)
34. The fourth edition of the ***Diagnostic and Statistical Manual of Mental Disorders*** **(DSM-IV-TR),** developed by the American Psychiatric Association, is the leading means of diagnosing mental disorders. (p. 263)
35. **Attention-deficit/hyperactivity disorder (ADHD)** is a behavior problem in which the individual has great difficulty concentrating and is often inattentive, impulsive, and overactive. (p. 263)
36. **Comorbidity** is the presence of two or more unrelated diseases at the same time in the same person. (p. 263)
37. A **learning disability** is a difficulty in a particular area of learning that is not attributable to overall intellectual slowness, a physical disability, or an unusually stressful home environment. (p. 265)
38. **Dyslexia** is a learning disability in reading. (p. 265)
39. **Autistic spectrum disorder** is any of several disorders characterized by deficient social skills, impaired communication, and unusual patterns of play. (p. 265)
40. **Autism** is a severe disturbance of early childhood characterized by an inability to communicate with others in an ordinary way, by extreme self-absorption, and by an inability to learn normal speech. (p. 266)
41. **Asperger syndrome** is a type of autistic spectrum disorder characterized by extreme attention to details and poor social skills. (p. 266)

8 chapter

MIDDLE CHILDHOOD

Psychosocial Development

Chapter Overview

This chapter brings to a close the unit on middle childhood. We have seen that from ages 7 to 11, the child becomes stronger and more competent, mastering the biosocial and cognitive abilities that are important in his or her culture. Psychosocial accomplishments are equally impressive.

The first section explores the growing social competence of children, as described by Erikson and Freud. The section continues with a discussion of the growth of social cognition and self-understanding and closes with a discussion of the ways in which children cope with stressful situations.

The next section explores the ways in which families influence children, including the experience of living in single-parent, stepparent, and blended families. Although no particular family structure guarantees optimal child development, income, stability, and harmony are important factors in the quality of family functioning.

Children's interactions with peers and others in their ever-widening social world is the subject of the third section. Although the peer group often is a supportive, positive influence on children, some children are rejected by their peers or become the victims of bullying. Because middle childhood is also a time of expanding moral reasoning, the final section examines Kohlberg's stage theory of moral development as well as current evaluations of his theory.

NOTE: Answer guidelines for all Chapter 8 questions begin on page 138.

Chapter Review

When you have finished reading the chapter, work through the material that follows to review it. Complete the sentences and answer the questions. In some cases, Study Tips explain how best to learn a difficult concept, while Think About It and Applications help you to know how well you understand the material. As you proceed, evaluate your performance for each section by consulting the answers beginning on page 138. Do not continue with the next section until you understand each answer. If you need to, review or reread the appropriate section in the textbook before continuing.

The Nature of the Child (pp. 274–281)

Identify several signs of psychological maturation between ages 6 and 11.

1. The ability to regulate one's emotions and actions is called ______________ ______________.
2. According to Erikson, the crisis of middle childhood is ______________ ______________ ______________.
3. Freud describes middle childhood as the period of ______________, when emotional drives are ______________ and unconscious sexual conflicts are ______________.
4. As their self-understanding sharpens, children gradually become ______________ (more/less) self-critical, and their self-esteem ______________ (rises/dips). One reason is that they more often evaluate themselves through ______________ ______________. Another factor is an increase in ______________ during middle childhood.

5. Self-esteem that is unrealistically high may reduce the child's ________________ ________________, thus lowering ________________. However, the same may occur if ________________ is unrealistically low. Unrealistically high or low self-esteem also correlates with ________________. Self-esteem ________________ (is/is not) universally valued In fact, the importance of self-esteem may be a ________________ ________________, an idea held by many Americans.

6. Some children are better able to adapt within the context of adversity; that is, they seem to be more ________________. This trait is a ________________ process that represents a ________________ adaptation to stress.

7. Difficult daily ________________ as well as many ________________ ________________ may build up stress in children.

8. A key aspect of resilience is the child's own ________________ ________________ and the child's ability to develop ________________, ________________, and ________________.

9. Another element that helps children deal with problems is the ________________ ________________ they receive.

10. During middle childhood, there are typically ________________ (fewer/more) sources of social support. This can be obtained from grandparents or siblings, for example, or from ________________ and ________________. In addition, ________________ can be psychologically protective for children in difficult circumstances.

STUDY TIP: To consolidate your understanding of how stress can affect children during the school years, write a paragraph describing a hypothetical child who remains resilient despite experiencing chronic daily stress. Be sure to describe various protective factors such as social support that promote this child's resistance.

APPLICATIONS:

11. Dr. Ferris believes that skill mastery is particularly important because children develop views of themselves as either competent or incompetent in skills valued by their culture. Dr. Ferris is evidently working from the perspective of ________________________________.

12. The Australian saying that "tall poppies" are cut down underscores the fact that
    a. older children often ignore their parents and teachers.
    b. culture influences standards of social comparison.
    c. middle childhood is a time of emotional latency.
    d. personal friendships become even more important in middle childhood.

13. Concluding her presentation on resilient children, Brenda notes that
    a. children who are truly resilient are resilient in all situations.
    b. resilience is merely the absence of pathology.
    c. resilience is a stable trait that becomes apparent very early in life.
    d. resilience is a dynamic process that represents a positive adaptation to significant adversity or stress.

14. Of the following children, who is likely to have the lowest overall self-esteem?
    a. Karen, age 5
    b. David, age 7
    c. Carl, age 9
    d. Cindy, age 10

15. Ten-year-old Benjamin is less optimistic and self-confident than his 5-year-old sister. This may be explained in part by the tendency of older children to
    a. evaluate their abilities by comparing them with their own competencies a year or two earlier.
    b. evaluate their competencies by comparing them with those of others.
    c. be less realistic about their own abilities.
    d. be overly confident about their abilities.

Families and Children (pp. 282–292)

16. Research demonstrates that ________________ (shared/nonshared) influences on most traits are far greater than ________________ (shared/nonshared) influences during middle childhood. In addition, ________________ influences persist lifelong. However, recent research indicates that

parents ________________ (do/do not) have a significant influence over their children.

17. Family function refers to how well the family ____ ____.

18. A functional family nurtures school-age children by providing basic ________________, encouraging ________________, fostering the development of ________________, nurturing peer ________________, and fostering ________________ and ________________.

19. (text and Table 8.3) Family structure is defined as the ____ ____.

Identify each of the following family structures:

a. ________________________ A family that includes three or more biologically related generations, including parents and children.

b. ________________________ A family that consists of the father, the mother, and their mutual biological children.

c. ________________________ A family that consists of one parent with his or her biological children.

d. ________________________ A family consisting of two parents, at least one with biological children from previous unions and/or of the new couple.

e. ________________________ In some nations, a family that consists of one man, several wives, and their children.

f. ________________________ A family that consists of one or more nonbiological children whom adults have legally taken to raise as their own.

g. ________________________ A family that consists of one or more orphaned, neglected, abused, or delinquent children who are temporarily cared for by an adult to whom they are not biologically related.

h. ________________________ A family that consists of a parent, his or her biological children, and his or her spouse, who is not biologically related to the children.

i. ________________________ A family that consists of one or two grandparents and their grandchildren.

j. ________________________ A family that consists of a homosexual couple and the biological or adopted children of one or both partners.

Give several reasons for the benefits of the nuclear family structure.

20. Having homosexual parents ________________ (seems/does not seem) to have negative effects on children.

21. Whether children thrive in blended families depends largely on the adults' ________________ and ________________ security. Such families ________________ (are/are not necessarily) better for children than single-parent families.

22. Although the ________________ family is still the most common, more than ________________ (what percentage?) of all school-age children live in ________________-________________ households. This is the dominant family structure among ________________-________________ and in some other ethnic communities. Children in ________________ (single-mother/single-father) families are at greatest risk.

23. Extended families are more common among ________________-________________ households. The benefit is that they can share ________________ and ________________.

24. Children in polygamous families _______________ (do/do not) fare as well because income and fatherly attention per child _______________ (increases/decreases).

25. Children in every type of family structure may grow up very well or run into trouble. Thus, family _______________ seems more critical than family _______________. A family that does not support all its members is called _______________.

26. Family income _______________ (correlates/does not correlate) with optimal child development. Economic distress _______________ family functioning. According to the _______________-_______________ model, economic hardship in a family increases _______________, which often makes adults tense and _______________ toward their children. Children from low-income households have more symptoms of _______________ than those from more affluent families. Reaction to wealth may also be a problem. Children from high-income families have a disproportionate share of _______________ _______________.

27. A second factor that has a crucial impact on children is the _______________ and _______________ that characterizes family interaction. Children are particularly affected when there are multiple _______________. In any family, children's well-being declines if there is frequent _______________, and if parents abuse one another _______________ or _______________.

28. The child's _______________ _______________ of a negative family situation is crucial in determining the impact of that situation. When children feel responsible for whatever happens in their family, the problem called _______________ has occurred.

THINK ABOUT IT: Blended families are extremely common today. To review your understanding of family function, describe a hypothetical blended family that functionally is as effective as a high-functioning nuclear family.

APPLICATIONS:

29. Shen's parents have separated. Since then, his grades have dropped, he's moody, and he spends most of his time alone in his room. Research regarding the factors that contribute to problems such as Shen's found the strongest correlation between children's peace of mind and
    a. marital discord.
    b. income.
    c. illness in the family.
    d. feelings of self-blame and vulnerability.

30. Sandra's family consists of her biological mother, her stepfather, and his two daughters from a previous marriage. Sandra's family would be classified as _______________.

31. Kyle and Jessica are as different as two siblings can be, despite growing up in the same nuclear family structure. In explaining these differences, a developmentalist is likely to point to
    a. shared environmental influences.
    b. nonshared environmental influences.
    c. genetic differences and shared environmental influences.
    d. genetic differences and nonshared environmental influences.

The Peer Group (pp. 293–299)

32. Getting along with _______________ is especially important during middle childhood. Compared with younger children, school-age children are _______________ (more/less) deeply affected by others' acceptance or rejection.

33. Peers create their own _______________ _______________ _______________, which includes the particular rules and rituals that are passed down from slightly older to younger children and that _______________ (mirror/do not necessarily mirror) the values of adults.

34. _______________ (In some parts of the world/Throughout the world), the culture of children encourages _______________ from adults.

35. During the school years, gender differences persist in what children do together: girls _______________ and boys _______________.

36. Having a personal friend is ________________ (more/less) important to children than acceptance by the peer group.

37. Friendships during middle childhood become more ________________ and ________________. As a result, older children ________________ (change/do not change) friends as often and find it ________________ (easier/harder) to make new friends. They also ________________ more of their friends.

38. Middle schoolers tend to choose best friends whose ________________, ________________, and ________________ are similar to their own.

39. A research study of social acceptance among schoolchildren revealed that approximately ________________ (what proportion?) are popular, approximately ________________ are average in popularity, and approximately ________________ are unpopular.

40. The ability to understand human interactions, called ________________ ________________, begins in infancy with ________________ ________________, continues in early childhood with ________________ ________________ ________________, and by middle childhood is well established. As they improve in this area, school children also improve in ________________ ________________.

Describe how well-liked children demonstrate their newfound ability to correctly interpret social situations.

41. Children who are not really rejected but not picked as friends are ________________. Children who are actively rejected tend to be either ________________-________________ or ________________-________________.

Briefly explain why rejected children are disliked.

42. Bullying is defined as ________________ efforts to inflict harm through ________________, ________________, or ________________ attacks on a weaker person. A key aspect in the definition of bullying is that harmful attacks are ________________. The three types of bullying are ________________, ________________, and ________________.

43. Victims of bullying are often ________________-rejected children. Less often, ________________-rejected children become ________________-________________.

44. Most bullies usually ________________ (have/do not have) friends who admire them, and they are socially ________________ but without ________________.

45. Boys who are bullies are often above average in ________________, whereas girl bullies are often ________________-________________. Boys who are bullies typically use ________________ aggression, whereas girls use ________________ aggression. Both sexes use ________________ aggression.

46. The origins of bullying may lie in a ________________ ________________ or a ________________ predisposition and are then strengthened by ________________ ________________, a stressful ________________ life, ineffective ________________, hostile ________________, and other problems that intensify ________________ impulses.

47. One effective intervention in controlling bullying in Norway involved using a ________________-________________ approach to change the ________________ ________________ system.

APPLICATIONS:

48. Concluding her presentation on bullying, Olivia notes that one factor in the possible development of bullying is
   a. an inborn brain abnormality.
   b. insecure attachment.
   c. the presence of hostile siblings.
   d. any of these factors.

49. Ten-year-old Ramón, who is disliked by many of his peers because of his antagonistic, confrontational nature, would probably be labeled as ________________ .

50. In discussing friendship, 9-year-old Melissa, in contrast to a younger child, will ?
   a. deny that friends are important.
   b. state that she prefers opposite-sex playmates.
   c. stress the importance of loyalty and similar interests.
   d. be less choosy about who she calls a friend.

51. Eight-year-old Henry is unpopular because he is a very timid and anxious child. Developmentalists would classify Henry as ________________ .

52. Of the following children, who is most likely to become a bully?
   a. Karen, who is taller than average
   b. David, who is above average in verbal assertiveness
   c. Carl, who is insecure and lonely
   d. Cindy, who was insecurely attached

53. I am an 8-year-old who frequently is bullied at school. If I am like most victims of bullies, I am probably
   a. obese.
   b. unattractive.
   c. a child who speaks with an accent.
   d. anxious and insecure.

Morality in Middle Childhood (pp. 300–304)

54. Children are ________________ (more/less) likely to behave prosocially during middle childhood than earlier. Three prosocial values that are evident are ________________ ; ________________ ; and ________________ .

55. Children develop their own standards of right and wrong, guided by ________________ , ________________ , and ________________ .

56. Middle childhood may be a time of increasing ________________ in some communities because ________________ ________________ and ________________ ________________ ________________ allow children to notice differences in race and religion that they were unaware of before.

57. The theorist who has extensively studied moral development by presenting people with stories that pose ethical dilemmas is ________________ . According to his theory, the three levels of moral reasoning are ________________ , ________________ , and ________________ .

58. (Table 8.4) In preconventional reasoning, emphasis is on getting ________________ and avoiding ________________ . "Might makes right" describes Stage ________________ (One/Two), whereas "look out for number one" describes Stage ________________ (One/Two).

59. (Table 8.4) In conventional reasoning, emphasis is on ________________ ________________ , such as being a dutiful citizen, in Stage ________________ (Three/Four), or on winning approval from others, in stage ________________ (Three/Four).

60. (Table 8.4) In postconventional reasoning, emphasis is on ________________ ________________ , such as ________________ ________________ (Stage Five) and ________________ ________________ ________________ (Stage Six).

61. One criticism of Kohlberg's theory is that it does not take ________________ or ________________ differences into account.

APPLICATION:

62. During a neighborhood game of baseball, Sam insists that Bobby cannot take another swing at the bat following his third strike because, "that's the rule." Sam is evidently thinking about this issue at Kohlberg's ________________ stage of moral reasoning.

Progress Test 1

Multiple-Choice Questions

Circle your answers to the following questions and check them with the answers on page 140. If your answer is incorrect, read the explanation for why it is incorrect and then consult the appropriate pages of the text (in parentheses following the correct answer).

1. Between 9 and 11 years of age, children are likely to demonstrate moral reasoning at which of Kohlberg's stages?
   - **a.** preconventional
   - **b.** conventional
   - **c.** postconventional
   - **d.** It is impossible to predict based only on a child's age.

2. Which of the following is NOT among the highest values of middle childhood?
   - **a.** don't exclude anyone because of race
   - **b.** treat everyone equally
   - **c.** play only with children of your own sex
   - **d.** don't depend on others

3. The best strategy for helping children who are at risk of developing serious psychological problems because of multiple stresses would be to
   - **a.** obtain assistance from a psychiatrist.
   - **b.** increase the child's competencies or social supports.
   - **c.** change the household situation.
   - **d.** reduce the peer group's influence.

4. The culture of children refers to
   - **a.** the specific habits, styles, and values that reflect the rules and rituals of children.
   - **b.** a child's tendency to assess abilities by measuring them against those of peers.
   - **c.** children's ability to understand social interactions.
   - **d.** all of these factors.

5. Girls who are bullies are often above average in _______ , whereas boys who are bullies are often above average in _______ .
   - **a.** size; verbal assertiveness
   - **b.** verbal assertiveness; size
   - **c.** intelligence; aggressiveness
   - **d.** aggressiveness; intelligence

6. A family that consists of two parents, at least one with biological children from a previous union, and any children the two adults have together is called a(n) ________ family.
   - **a.** extended
   - **b.** polygamous
   - **c.** nuclear
   - **d.** blended

7. Compared with average or popular children, rejected children tend to be
   - **a.** brighter and more competitive.
   - **b.** affluent and "stuck-up."
   - **c.** economically disadvantaged.
   - **d.** socially immature.

8. School-age children advance in their awareness of classmates' opinions and accomplishments. These abilities are best described as advances in their
   - **a.** social comparison.
   - **b.** social cognition.
   - **c.** metacognition.
   - **d.** pragmatic intelligence.

9. Resilience is characterized by all but which of the following characteristics?
   - **a.** Resilience is a stable trait that a child carries throughout his or her life.
   - **b.** Resilience represents a positive adaptation to stress.
   - **c.** Resilience is more than the absence of pathology.
   - **d.** Resilience is the capacity to develop optimally despite significant adversity.

10. With their expanding social world and developing cognition, children may be stressed by a variety of disturbing problems. Which of the following is NOT a means by which children can overcome these problems?
    - **a.** school success
    - **b.** healthy diet
    - **c.** religious faith
    - **d.** after-school achievements

11. Bully-victims are typically children who would be categorized as
    - **a.** aggressive-rejected.
    - **b.** withdrawn-rejected.
    - **c.** isolated-rejected.
    - **d.** immature-rejected.

12. Bullying during middle childhood
    a. occurs only in certain cultures.
    b. is more common in rural schools than in urban schools.
    c. seems to be universal.
    d. is rarely a major problem, because other children usually intervene to prevent it from getting out of hand.

13. During the school years, children become ______ selective about their friends, and their friendship groups become ________ .
    a. less; larger
    b. less; smaller
    c. more; larger
    d. more; smaller

14. Erikson's crisis of industry versus inferiority corresponds to which of Freud's psychosexual stages?
    a. genital stage
    b. oral stage
    c. anal stage
    d. period of latency

15. Erikson's crisis of the school years is that of
    a. industry versus inferiority.
    b. acceptance versus rejection.
    c. initiative versus guilt.
    d. male versus female.

True or False Items

Write T (*true*) or F (*false*) on the line in front of each statement.

________ 1. As they evaluate themselves according to increasingly complex self-theories, school-age children typically experience a rise in self-esteem.

________ 2. During middle childhood, acceptance by the peer group is valued more than having a close friend.

________ 3. Children from low-income homes often experience more stress.

________ 4. Bullies and their victims are usually of the same gender.

________ 5. Children who are labeled "resilient" demonstrate an ability to adapt positively in all situations.

________ 6. The way a family functions seems to be a more powerful predictor of children's development than the actual structure of the family.

________ 7. Withdrawn-rejected and aggressive-rejected children both have problems regulating their emotions.

________ 8. Most aggressive-rejected children clearly interpret other people's words and behavior.

________ 9. School-age children are less able than younger children to cope with chronic stresses.

________ 10. Children's ability to cope with stress may depend as much on their appraisal of events as on the objective nature of the actual events.

________ 11. Friendship circles become wider as children grow older.

Progress Test 2

Progress Test 2 should be completed during a final chapter review. Answer the following questions after you thoroughly understand the correct answers for the Chapter Review and Progress Test 1.

Multiple-Choice Questions

1. Children who are categorized as __________ are particularly vulnerable to bullying.
    a. aggressive-rejected
    b. passive-aggressive
    c. withdrawn-rejected
    d. passive-rejected

2. Environmental influences on children's traits that result from contact with different teachers and peer groups are classified as
    a. shared influences.
    b. nonshared influences.
    c. epigenetic influences.
    d. nuclear influences.

3. Compared with parents in other family structures, married parents tend to be
    a. wealthier.
    b. better educated.
    c. healthier.
    d. all of these things.

4. More than half of all school-age children live in
    a. single-parent families.
    b. blended families.
    c. extended families.
    d. nuclear families.

5. Typically, children in middle childhood experience a decrease in self-esteem as a result of
   a. a wavering self-theory.
   b. increased awareness of personal shortcomings and failures.
   c. rejection by peers.
   d. difficulties with members of the opposite sex.

6. A 10-year-old's sense of self-esteem is most strongly influenced by his or her
   a. peers.
   b. siblings.
   c. mother.
   d. father.

7. Which of the following most accurately describes how friendships change during the school years?
   a. Friendships become more casual and less intense.
   b. Older children demand less of their friends.
   c. Older children change friends more often.
   d. Close friendships increasingly involve members of the same sex, ethnicity, and socioeconomic status.

8. Which of the following is an accurate statement about school-age bullies?
   a. They are socially perceptive but not empathic.
   b. They usually have a few admiring friends.
   c. They are adept at being aggressive.
   d. All of these statements are accurate.

9. One effective intervention to prevent bullying in the school is to
   a. change the culture through community-wide and classroom education.
   b. target one victimized child at a time.
   c. target each bully as an individual.
   d. focus on improving the academic skills of all children in the school.

10. Which of the following most accurately describes the relationship between family income and child development?
    a. Adequate family income allows children to own whatever possessions help them to feel accepted.
    b. Because parents need not argue about money, household wealth provides harmony and stability.
    c. The basic family functions are enhanced by adequate family income.
    d. Family income is not correlated with child development.

11. Two factors that most often help the child cope well with multiple stresses are social support and
    a. social comparison.
    b. religious faith.
    c. remedial education.
    d. referral to mental health professionals.

12. An 8-year-old child who measures her achievements by comparing them with those of her friends is engaging in social
    a. cognition.
    b. comparison.
    c. reinforcement.
    d. modeling.

13. In Kohlberg's theory, moral reasoning that is based on seeking rewards and avoiding punishment is called ________ reasoning.
    a. universal
    b. postconventional
    c. preconventional
    d. conventional

14. According to Freud, the period between ages 7 and 11 when a child's sexual drives are relatively quiet is the
    a. phallic stage.
    b. genital stage.
    c. period of latency.
    d. period of industry versus inferiority.

15. Children who are forced to cope with one serious ongoing stress (for example, poverty or large family size) are
    a. more likely to develop serious psychiatric problems.
    b. no more likely to develop problems.
    c. more likely to develop intense, destructive friendships.
    d. less likely to be accepted by their peer group.

Matching Items

Match each term or concept with its corresponding description or definition.

Terms or Concepts

_______ 1. relational bullying
_______ 2. nuclear family
_______ 3. social comparison
_______ 4. provocative victim
_______ 5. polygamous family
_______ 6. aggressive-rejected
_______ 7. withdrawn-rejected
_______ 8. physical bullying
_______ 9. effortful control
_______ 10. blended family
_______ 11. extended family

Descriptions or Definitions

a. another term for a bully-victim
b. adults living with their children from previous marriages as well as their own biological children
c. a father, a mother, and the biological children they have together
d. bullying involving hitting, punching, or kicking
e. children who are disliked because of their confrontational nature
f. evaluating one's abilities by measuring them against those of other children
g. three or more generations of biologically related individuals living together
h. children who are disliked because of timid, anxious behavior
i. bullying designed to destroy peer acceptance
j. a family including one man with several wives, each bearing his children
k. the ability to regulate one's emotions

Key Terms

Using your own words, write a brief definition or explanation of each of the following terms on a separate piece of paper.

1. effortful control
2. industry versus inferiority
3. social comparison
4. resilience
5. family function
6. family structure
7. nuclear family
8. blended family
9. single-parent family
10. extended family
11. polygamous family
12. culture of children
13. social cognition
14. aggressive-rejected children
15. withdrawn-rejected children
16. bullying
17. bully-victim
18. preconventional moral reasoning
19. conventional moral reasoning
20. postconventional moral reasoning

Answers

CHAPTER REVIEW

Children are more likely to have specific chores to perform, a weekly allowance, homework assignments, and responsibility for younger children and pets. They are expected to tell time and to conform to peer standards in clothing and language. They often use TV, computers, and video games without adult supervision. They are less often punished physically, and they influence decisions about their after-school care, lessons, and activities.

1. effortful control
2. industry versus inferiority
3. latency; quiet; submerged
4. more; dips; social comparison; materialism
5. effortful control; achievement; self-esteem; aggression; is not; social construction
6. resilient; dynamic; positive
7. routines; daily hassles
8. working concept; friends; skills; activities
9. social support
10. more; peers; pets; religion

11. Erik Erikson's theory of development. The question describes what is, for Erikson, the crisis of middle childhood: industry versus inferiority.
12. **b.** is the answer. This reflect the view that self-esteem is not all-important.
13. **d.** is the answer.
14. **d.** is the answer. Self-esteem decreases throughout middle childhood.
15. **b.** is the answer. Social comparison becomes important for these children as they evaluate their competencies.
16. nonshared; shared; genetic; do
17. works to meet the needs of its members
18. necessities; learning; self-respect; relationships; harmony; stability
19. genetic and legal relationships among related people living in the same household
    - **a.** extended family
    - **b.** nuclear family
    - **c.** one-parent (or single-parent) family
    - **d.** blended family
    - **e.** polygamous family
    - **f.** adoptive family
    - **g.** foster family
    - **h.** stepparent family
    - **i.** grandparents alone
    - **j.** homosexual family

Parents in a nuclear family tend to be wealthier, better educated, healthier, and less hostile than other parents. Note that nuclear families are often headed by cohabiting couples, depending on the culture. What is important for the children is the parents' commitment to each other and to them.

20. does not seem
21. emotional; economic; are not necessarily
22. nuclear; one-fourth; single-parent; African Americans; single-mother
23. low-income; expenses; responsibilities
24. do not; decreases
25. function; structure; dysfunctional
26. correlates; decreases; family-stress; stress; hostile; psychopathology; emotional disorders
27. harmony; stability; transitions; quarreling; physically; verbally
28. cognitive interpretation; parentification
29. **d.** is the answer. More important than marital discord, income, or illness is the child's interpretation of the situation. If the child blames himself or herself for the problems, psychological and academic problems are more likely to occur.
30. blended. This is a type of stepparent family. It is a particularly difficult structure for school-age children.
31. **d.** is the answer. Even within the same family, siblings experience nonshared environments.
32. peers; more
33. culture of children; do not necessarily mirror
34. Throughout the world; independence
35. talk more and share secrets; play more active games
36. more
37. intense; intimate; do not change; harder; demand
38. interests; values; backgrounds
39. one-third; one-half; one-sixth
40. social cognition; social referencing; theory of mind; effortful control

Given direct conflict with another child, well-liked children seek compromise in order to maintain the friendship. They assume that social slights are accidental and, in contrast with rejected children, do not respond with fear, self-doubt, or anger. These prosocial impulses and attitudes are a sign of social maturity.

41. neglected; aggressive-rejected; withdrawn-rejected

Aggressive-rejected children are disliked because of their antagonistic and confrontational behavior, while withdrawn-rejected children are timid, withdrawn, and anxious. Both types often misinterpret social situations, lack emotional regulation, and are likely to be mistreated at home.

42. systematic; physical, verbal; social; repeated; physical; verbal; relational
43. withdrawn; aggressive; bully-victims
44. have; perceptive; empathy
45. size; sharp-tongued; physical; verbal; relational
46. brain abnormality; genetic; insecure attachment; home; discipline; siblings; aggressive
47. dynamic-systems; whole school
48. **d.** is the answer. Parents can teach young children to restrain their aggressive impulses.
49. aggressive-rejected. Children such as Ramón tend to misread social situations and lack emotional regulation.
50. **c.** is the answer. In middle childhood, friendship becomes more selective and intimate, and

children choose each other because of similar interests, values, and backgrounds.

51. withdrawn-rejected. Withdrawn-rejected children are most likely to become bully-victims. Like aggressive-rejected children, they tend to misread social situations and lack emotional regulation.
52. **b.** is the answer. Verbal bullying is one of the three major types of bullying (physical and relational are the other two types of bullying).
53. **d.** is the answer. Surprisingly, children who are different because of obesity or looks, for example, are not necessarily singled out for bullying.
54. more; caring for family members; cooperating with others; not hurting anyone directly
55. peers; parents; culture
56. prejudice; social cognition; concrete operational thought
57. Lawrence Kohlberg; preconventional; conventional; postconventional
58. rewards; punishments; one; two
59. social rules; four; three
60. moral principles; social contracts; universal ethical principles
61. cultural; gender
62. conventional. During Stage Four, law and order, being a proper citizen means obeying the rules set down by society.

PROGRESS TEST 1

Multiple-Choice Questions

1. **b.** is the answer. (p. 302)
2. **d.** is the answer. (pp. 300–301)
3. **b.** is the answer. (pp. 279–280)
4. **a.** is the answer. (p. 293)

   b. This is social comparison.

   c. This is social cognition.
5. **b.** is the answer. (p. 297)
6. **d.** is the answer. (p. 286)

   a. In an extended family, children live with grandparents or other relatives.

   b. In a polygamous family, one man has several wives.

   c. A nuclear family has two parents and their biological children.
7. **d.** is the answer. (p. 296)
8. **b.** is the answer. (p. 295)

   a. Social comparison is the tendency to assess one's abilities by measuring them against those of others, especially those of one's peers.

   c. Metacognition, which is not discussed in this chapter, is the ability to monitor and adjust one's cognitive processes.

   d. This term was not discussed in the chapter.
9. **a.** is the answer. Resilience is a dynamic, not a stable, trait. (p. 278)
10. **b.** is the answer. (pp. 279–281)
11. **a.** is the answer. (p. 297)

    b. Withdrawn-rejected children are often the victims of bullies, but rarely are bullies themselves.

    c. & d. There are no such categories.
12. **c.** is the answer. (p. 296)

    d. In fact, children rarely intervene, unless a best friend is involved.
13. **d.** is the answer. (p. 294)
14. **d.** is the answer. (p. 275)
15. **a.** is the answer. (p. 275)

True or False Items

1. F In fact, just the opposite is true. (p. 277)
2. F In fact, just the opposite is true. (p. 294)
3. T (p. 289)
4. T (p. 297)
5. F A given child is not resilient in all situations. (p. 278)
6. T (p. 288)
7. T (p. 296)
8. F Just the opposite is true: They tend to misinterpret other people's words and behavior. (p. 296)
9. F Because of the coping strategies that many school-age children develop, they are better able than younger children to cope with stress. (p. 280)
10. T (p. 292)
11. F Friendship circles become narrower because friendships become more selective and exclusive. (p. 294)

PROGRESS TEST 2

Multiple-Choice Questions

1. **c.** is the answer. (p. 296)

   a. These are usually bullies.

   b. & d. These are not subcategories of rejected children.

2. **b.** is the answer. (p. 282)

   a. Shared influences are those that occur because children are raised by the same parents in the same home, although children raised in the same home do not necessarily share the same home environment.

   c. & d. There are no such influences.
3. **d.** is the answer. (p. 286)
4. **d.** is the answer. (p. 285)
5. **b.** is the answer. (p. 277)

   a. This tends to promote, rather than reduce, self-esteem.

   c. Only 10 percent of schoolchildren experience this.

   d. This issue becomes more important during adolescence.
6. **a.** is the answer. (p. 276–277)
7. **d.** is the answer. (p. 294)

   a., b., & c. In fact, just the opposite is true of friendship during the school years.
8. **d.** is the answer. (pp. 296–297)
9. **a.** is the answer. (pp. 298–299)
10. **c.** is the answer. (p. 289)
11. **b.** is the answer. (pp. 280–281)
12. **b.** is the answer. (p. 276)
13. **d.** is the answer. (p. 302)
14. **c.** is the answer. (p. 275)
15. **b.** is the answer. (pp. 278–279)

    c. & d. The text did not discuss how stress influences friendship or peer acceptance.

Matching Items

1. i (p. 296)	**5.** j (p. 287)	**9.** k (p. 275)
2. c (p. 285)	**6.** e (p. 296)	**10.** b (p. 286)
3. f (p. 276)	**7.** h (p. 296)	**11.** g (p. 287)
4. a (p. 297)	**8.** d (p. 296)	

KEY TERMS

1. **Effortful control** is the ability to regulate one's impulses and emotions through effort, not simply through natural inclination. (p. 275)
2. According to Erikson, the crisis of middle childhood is **industry verus inferiority,** in which children try to master many skills and develop views of themselves as either competent and industrious or incompetent and inferior. (p. 275)
3. **Social comparison** is the tendency to assess one's abilities, achievements, social status, and other attributes by measuring them against those of others, especially those of one's peers. (p. 276)
4. **Resilience** is the capacity to adapt positively despite adversity and to overcome serious stress. (p. 278)
5. **Family function** refers to the ways families work to foster the development of children by meeting their basic material needs, encouraging them to learn, helping them to develop self-respect, nurturing friendships, and fostering harmony and stability. (p. 283)
6. **Family structure** refers to the legal and genetic relationships among relatives living in the same household. (p. 284)
7. A **nuclear family** consists of two parents and their mutual biological offspring under age 18. (p. 285)
8. A **blended family** is a stepfamily that includes biological children from previous marriages plus the new couple's own children. (p. 286)
9. A **single-parent family** consists of one parent and his or her biological children under age 18. (p. 287)
10. An **extended family** consists of parents, their children, an other relatives living in one household. (p. 287)
11. A **polygamous family** consists of one man with several wives, each bearing his children. (p. 287)
12. The **culture of children** refers to the specific habits, styles, and values that reflect the rules and rituals of children. (p. 293)
13. **Social cognition** is the ability to understand social interactions. (p. 295)
14. The peer group shuns **aggressive-rejected** children because of antagonistic, confrontational behavior. (p. 296)
15. **Withdrawn-rejected** children are shunned by the peer group because of their timid, withdrawn, and anxious behavior. (p. 296)
16. **Bullying** is the repeated, systematic effort to inflict harm through physical, verbal, or social attacks on a weaker person. (p. 296)
17. A **bully-victim** is a bully who has also been a victim of bullying; also called provocative victim. (p. 297)
18. **Preconventional moral reasoning** is Kohlberg's first level of moral reasoning, emphasizing rewards and punishments. (p. 302)
19. **Conventional moral reasoning** is Kohlberg's second level of moral reasoning, emphasizing social rules. (p. 302)
20. **Postconventional moral reasoning** is Kohlberg's third level of moral reasoning, emphasizing moral principles. (p. 302)

chapter 9

ADOLESCENCE

Body and Mind

Chapter Overview

Between the ages of 11 and 18, young people cross the great divide between childhood and adulthood. This crossing encompasses all three domains of development—biosocial, cognitive, and psychosocial. Chapter 9 begins with a discussion of the dramatic changes that occur in the biosocial domain, beginning with puberty and the growth spurt. The biosocial metamorphosis of the adolescent is discussed in detail, with emphasis on factors that affect the age of puberty, sexual maturation, and changes in body rhythms.

Although adolescence is, in many ways, a healthy time of life, the text also addresses two health hazards that too often affect adolescence: sex too early and sexually transmitted illnesses.

Chapter 9 also describes the cognitive advances and limitations of adolescence. With the attainment of formal operational thought, the developing person becomes able to think in an adult way, that is, to be logical, to think in terms of possibilities, and to reason scientifically and abstractly. Neurological development is the basis of these new developments. Although brain areas dedicated to emotional arousal mature before those dedicated to emotional regulation, ongoing myelination enables faster and deeper thinking.

Even those who reach the stage of formal operational thought spend much of their time thinking at less advanced levels. The discussion of adolescent egocentrism supports this generalization in showing that adolescents have difficulty thinking rationally about themselves and their immediate experiences. Adolescent egocentrism makes them see themselves as psychologically unique and more socially significant than they really are.

The final section explores teaching and learning in middle school and high school. As adolescents enter secondary school, their grades often suffer and their level of participation decreases. The rigid behavioral demands and intensified competition of most secondary schools do not, unfortunately, provide a supportive learning environment for adolescents.

NOTE: Answer guidelines for all Chapter 9 questions begin on page 155.

Chapter Review

When you have finished reading the chapter, work through the material that follows to review it. Complete the sentences and answer the questions. In some cases, Study Tips explain how best to learn a difficult concept, while Think About It and Applications help you to know how well you understand the material. As you proceed, evaluate your performance for each section by consulting the answers beginning on page 155. Do not continue with the next section until you understand each answer. If you need to, review or reread the appropriate section in the textbook before continuing.

Puberty Begins (pp. 310–319)

1. The period of rapid physical growth and sexual maturation that ends childhood and brings the young person to adult size, shape, and sexual potential is called ________________ . The physical changes of puberty typically are complete ________________ (how long?) after puberty begins.
2. The average girl experiences her first menstrual period, called ________________ , at age ________________ .
3. The average boy experiences his first ejaculation of seminal fluid, called ________________ , at age ________________ .

4. Puberty begins when biochemical signals from the ________________ trigger hormone production in the ________________ ________________, which in turn triggers increased hormone production by the ________________ ________________. This route is called the ________________ ________________.

5. The hormone ________________ causes the gonads, the ________________ in males and the ________________ in females, to dramatically increase their production of sex hormones, especially ________________ in girls and ________________ in boys.

6. The increase in the hormone ________________ is dramatic in boys and slight in girls, whereas the increase in the hormone ________________ is marked in girls and slight in boys. Emotional extremes and sexual urges ________________ (usually do/do not usually) increase during adolescence. This is due in part to the increasingly high levels of hormones such as ________________ and ________________. Changes in these hormone levels may cause the rise in ________________ that occurs during adolescence. Conversely, human thoughts and emotions may cause ________________ levels to rise.

7. All creatures have a daily day–night cycle of biological activity called the ________________ ________________. Our daily rhythms, called ________________, cause, for instance, changes in the level of the chemical ________________, which makes people more sleepy. Adolescents typically get too ________________ (little/much) sleep. Among adolescents, ________________ (girls/boys) are particularly likely to be sleep-deprived.

8. Pubertal hormones from the ________________ cause a ________________ ________________ in sleep-wake patterns. Some people are genetically prone to ________________, which is the tendency to be more alert during the evening hours. This is especially true for ________________ (females/males).

9. Normal children begin to notice pubertal changes between the ages of ________________ and ________________. Puberty that begins before age 8 is called ________________ ________________. About two-thirds of the variation in the age of puberty is caused by ________________. This is demonstrated by the fact that ________________ ________________ reach puberty at similar ages.

10. The amount of ________________ ________________ affects the onset of puberty. Children with a relatively large proportion experience puberty ________________ (earlier/later) than their contemporaries.

11. One hormone that has been implicated in the onset of puberty is ________________, which affects appetite—more so in ________________ (females/males) than in ________________ (females/males).

12. For both sexes, fat is limited by chronic ________________, which therefore delays puberty by several years.

13. The ________________ ________________ refers to the long-term upward or downward direction of a statistical measurement. An example is the earlier growth of children over the last two centuries as ________________ and ________________ have improved. This trend ________________ (continues/has stopped) in developed nations.

14. Another influence on the age of puberty is ________________.

15. (A View from Science) Research from many nations suggests that harsh parenting may ________________ (accelerate/delay) the onset of puberty.

16. (A View from Science) Stress may cause production of the hormones that cause ________________. Support for this hypothesis comes from a study showing that early puberty in girls was associated with ________________ and ________________.

17. (A View from Science) An evolutionary explanation of the relationship between stress and puber-

ty is that ancestral females growing up in stressful environments may have increased their ______ ______ by accelerating physical maturation.

18. For girls, ______ (early/late) maturation may be especially troublesome.

Describe several common problems and developmental hazards experienced by early-maturing girls.

19. For boys, ______ (early/late/both early and late) maturation may be difficult. ______ (Early/Late) maturing boys are more ______, ______, and alcohol-abusing. It also correlates with ______ ______ and teenage ______. ______ (Early/Late) maturing boys tend to be more anxious, depressed, and afraid of sex.

STUDY TIP: To consolidate your understanding of the major physical changes that accompany puberty, list, in order, the major physical changes of puberty.

20. Girls: ______

______

Boys: ______

______

______

APPLICATIONS:

21. I am the hormone that causes the gonads to dramatically increase their production of sex hormones. I am ______.

22. Eleven-year-old Linda, who has just begun to experience the first signs of puberty, laments, "When will the agony of puberty be over?" You tell her that the major events of puberty typically end about ______ ______ after the first visible signs appear.

23. Regarding the effects of early and late maturation on boys and girls, which of the following is NOT true?
    a. Late-maturing boys are more likely to rebel against laws.
    b. Early puberty that leads to romantic relationships often leads to emotional distress.
    c. Early-maturing girls may be drawn into involvement with older boys.
    d. Late puberty is often difficult for boys.

24. Monica is 16 years old. Her parents are divorced and she lives with her mother in a city. It is most likely that she will experience puberty ______ than other teens, perhaps as a result of ______.
    a. earlier; greater stress
    b. later; greater stress
    c. earlier; poor nutrition
    d. later; poor nutrition

25. I am the sex hormone that is secreted in greater amounts by females than males. I am ______.

26. Of the following teenagers, those most likely to be distressed about their physical development are
    a. late-maturing girls.
    b. early-maturing girls.
    c. early-maturing boys.
    d. girls or boys who masturbate.

27. Most teenagers ______ (do/do not) consume the recommended daily dose of iron, calcium, zinc, and other minerals. There is a direct link between deficient diets and the availability of ______ ______ in schools.

28. Another reason for dietary deficiencies is concern about ______ ______, defined as a person's idea of how ______.

29. In an attempt to improve body image, many girls ______ ______ or take ______ ______, and many boys take ______.

30. The disorder characterized by self-starvation is ______ ______.

This disorder is suspected when a person's ________________ ________________ ________________ is ________________ (what number?) or lower, or if the person loses more than ________________ (what percent?) of body weight within a month or two.

31. Anorexia nervosa is diagnosed when four symptoms are present:
   (a) ________________
   (b) ________________
   (c) ________________
   (d) ________________

32. A more common eating disorder is ________________ ________________, which is diagnosed when three symptoms occur:
   (a) ________________
   (b) ________________
   (c) ________________

33. One family practice that seems to reduce the risk of adolescent eating disorders is ________________.

THINK ABOUT IT: To underscore the prevalence of nutritional deficiencies during adolescence, evaluate your own dietary consumption of iron, calcium, and zinc for a few days. How do your results compare with recommended minimum levels of consumption for these minerals?

APPLICATION:

34. Thirteen-year-old Kristin is more likely to
   a. drink too much milk.
   b. eat more than five servings of fruit per day.
   c. choose expensive foods over inexpensive ones.
   d. be iron deficient.

The Transformations of Puberty (pp. 319–324)

35. A major ________________ spurt occurs during puberty. Growth proceeds from the ________________ (core/extremities) to the ________________ (core/extremities).

36. Internal organs also grow during puberty. The ________________ increase in size and capacity, the ________________ doubles in size, heart rate ________________ (increases/decreases), and blood volume ________________ (increases/decreases). These changes increase the adolescent's physical ________________.

Explain why the physical demands placed on a teenager, as in athletic training, should not be the same as those for a young adult of similar height and weight.

37. During puberty, one organ system, the ________________ system, decreases in size, making teenagers ________________ (more/less) susceptible to respiratory ailments.

38. Changes in ________________ ________________ ________________ involve the sex organs that are directly involved in reproduction.

39. Sexual features other than those associated with reproduction are referred to as ________________ ________________ ________________.

Describe the major pubertal changes in the secondary sex characteristics of both sexes.

40. Sexual intimacy among teens reflects both ________________ and ________________.

Identify five reasons adolescent sexual behavior is more hazardous today than in the past.

(a) ______________________

(b) ______________________

(c) ______________________

(d) ______________________

(e) ______________________

41. A major developmental risk for sexually active adolescent girls is ______________. If this happens within a year or two of menarche, girls are at increased risk of many complications, including ______________________ ______________.

42. Worldwide, sexually active teens have higher rates of diseases caused by sexual contact, called ______________ ______________ ______________, than any other age group. One reason is that they do not have the natural ______________ ______________ that fully developed women have. Another reason is that they are unlikely to seek ______________. The most frequently reported STI is ______________. A more severe STI is ______________ ______________, which increases later risk of uterine cancer.

43. Any sexual activity between a juvenile and an older person is considered ______________ ______________ ______________.

44. Sexual abuse is more common between the ages of ______________ and ______________ than at any other time.

THINK ABOUT IT: At the beginning of puberty, many young people want to know whether they will be short or tall like one of their parents or closer in height to their grandparents. The answer is that their full adult height will probably fall somewhere in between that of their parents. One frequently used rule of thumb is to add the heights of both parents, divide by two, then add 3 inches for a boy or subtract 3 inches for a girl. The result is said to be correct within 2 inches about 95 percent of the time. How well does this formula work in your case?
____

APPLICATION:

45. Calvin, the class braggart, boasts that because his beard has begun to grow, he is more virile than his male classmates. Jacob informs him that

a. the tendency to grow facial and body hair has nothing to do with virility.
b. beard growth is determined by heredity.
c. girls also develop some facial hair and more noticeable hair on their arms and legs, so it is clearly not a sign of masculinity.
d. all of these statements are true.

Cognitive Development (pp. 324–333)

46. During adolescence, different parts of the brain grow at ______________ (the same/different) rate(s).

47. The brain's limbic system, which controls ______________ and ______________ ______________, matures ______________ (before/after) the prefrontal cortex.

48. The prefrontal cortex is more affected by ______________ and ______________.

49. Myelination and ______________ proceed from inside to the cortex and from back to front.

50. Throughout adolescence, reactions become faster because of increased ______________. Also, additional synaptic ______________ occurs, while the ______________ system becomes active.

51. The brain becomes fully mature at about age ______________.

52. The characteristic of adolescent thinking that leads young people to think only about themselves is called ______________ ______________.

53. The adolescent's belief that he or she is unique is called the ______________ ______________. An adolescent's tendency to feel that he or she is somehow immune to the consequences of dangerous or illegal behavior is expressed in the ______________ ______________.

54. Adolescents, who believe that they are under constant scrutiny from nearly everyone, create for themselves an ________________ ________________.

55. Piaget's term for the fourth stage of cognitive development is ________________ ________________ thought. Adolescent thinking ________________ (is/is not) limited by concrete experiences.

56. Piaget devised a number of famous tasks to demonstrate that formal operational adolescents imagine all possible ________________ of a problem's solution in order to draw the appropriate ________________.

Briefly describe how children reason differently about the "balance beam" problem at ages 4, 7, 10, and 14.

57. The kind of thinking in which adolescents consider unproven possibilities that are logical but not necessarily real is called ________________ thought.

58. Adolescents become more capable of ________________ reasoning—that is, they can begin with an abstract idea or ________________ and then use ________________ to draw specific ________________. This type of reasoning is a hallmark of formal operational thought.

59. This kind of reasoning contrasts with reasoning that progresses from specifics to reach a general conclusion, called ________________ reasoning.

60. The fact that adolescents can use ________________-________________ reasoning does not necessarily mean that they do use it.

61. Researchers who advocate a ________________-________________ model of cognition believe that the adult brain has two distinct processing networks, The first mode of thinking, which begins with a prior ________________, is called ________________ ________________. The second mode, Piaget's formal hypothetical-deductive reasoning, is called ________________ thought.

62. Although intuitive thinking generally is ________________ and ________________, it is also often ________________ (right/wrong).

STUDY TIP: To consolidate your understanding of how the types of thinking that are typical of the adolescent differ from one another, consider the following problem and come up with one or more examples of how an adolescent might reason about the situation using each of the different types of cognition. To get you started, the first example has been completed for you.

Problem: Returning home following spring vacation, you hear an odd noise coming from under the hood of your car. You are running late, and the noise seems to be getting louder.

63.

Type of Thinking	Examples
Egocentrism	"Why do these catastrophes always happen to me and not to someone else?" (personal fable)
Hypothetical-Deductive	
Intuitive Thought	
Analytic Thought	

APPLICATIONS:

64. An experimenter hides a ball in her hand and says, "The ball in my hand is either red or it is not red." Most preadolescent children say
a. the statement is true.
b. the statement is false.
c. they cannot tell if the statement is true or false.
d. they do not understand what the experimenter means.

65. Fourteen-year-old Monica is very idealistic and often develops crushes on people she doesn't even know. This reflects her newly developed cognitive ability to
a. deal simultaneously with two sides of an issue.
b. take another person's viewpoint.
c. imagine possible worlds and people.
d. see herself as others see her.

66. Which of the following is the BEST example of the adolescent's ability to think hypothetically?
a. Twelve-year-old Stanley feels that people are always watching him.
b. Fourteen-year-old Mindy engages in many risky behaviors, reasoning that "nothing bad will happen to me."
c. Fifteen-year-old Philip feels that no one understands his problems.
d. Thirteen-year-old Josh delights in finding logical flaws in virtually everything his teachers and parents say.

67. Frustrated because of the dating curfew her parents have set, Melinda exclaims, "You just don't know how it feels to be in love!" Melinda's thinking demonstrates
a. the invincibility fable.
b. the personal fable.
c. the imaginary audience.
d. hypothetical thinking.

68. Nathan's fear that his friends will ridicule him because of a pimple that has appeared on his nose reflects a preoccupation with

____________________ .

69. The reasoning behind the conclusion, "if it waddles like a duck and quacks like a duck, then it must be a duck," is called

____________________ .

70. Which of the following is an example of deductive reasoning?
a. Alonza is too lazy to look up an unfamiliar word he encounters while reading.
b. Brittany loves to reason from clues to figure out "whodunit" crime mysteries.
c. Morgan, who has enjoyed unscrambling anagrams for years, prefers to follow his hunches rather than systematically evaluate letter combinations.
d. When taking multiple-choice tests, Trevor carefully considers every possible answer before choosing one.

Teaching and Learning (pp. 333–343)

71. The period after primary education and before ________________ education is called ________________ education. More recently, many intermediate ________________ schools have been established to educate children in grades 6, 7, and 8.

72. During the middle school years, academic achievement often ________________ (slows down/speeds up).

State two reasons for this trend in academic achievement.

73. The digital divide that once separated ________________ from ________________ and ________________ from ________________ has been bridged. In the United States today, the greatest divide, in terms of technology use, is ________________ .

74. Potential dangers of the use of computers include sexual predators; ________________ , which occurs when one person spreads online insults and rumors about someone else; and Web sites devoted to cutting, or ________________ .

75. The first year of a new school often correlates with increased ________________ , decreased ________________ , and the onset of ____________________________ .

76. By high school, most academic subjects emphasize ________________ thinking.

77. Another feature of the high school environment is

______________-______________

testing, so called because the consequences of failing are so severe. Whenever this type of testing is a requisite for graduation, there is a potential unintended consequence of more

______________.

78. A second problem with the high school environment involves student persistence, diligence, and ______________; many adolescents express ______________ and unhappiness with school. One solution to the problem of graduates who do not go on to college is to establish

______________.

79. Adolescents are more likely to be engaged with school if the school is ______________ (small/large). Also, adolescents who are active in school ______________ and ______________ are more likely to graduate and go to college.

THINK ABOUT IT: During adolescence, formal operational thought—including scientific reasoning, logical construction of arguments, and critical thinking—becomes possible. Consider the kinds of multiple-choice and essay questions you have been given as a student. Which kind of question typically gives you the most trouble? Does this type of question require thinking at the formal operational level?

APPLICATIONS:

80. Summarizing her presentation on the mismatch between the needs of adolescents and the traditional structure of their schools, Megan notes that
   a. most high schools feature intensified competition.
   b. the curriculum of most high schools emphasizes formal operational thinking.
   c. the academic standards of most schools do not reflect adolescents' needs.
   d. all of these statements are true.

81. Malcolm, a middle schooler who lately is very sensitive to the criticism of others, feels significantly less motivated and capable than when he was in elementary school. Malcolm probably
   a. is experiencing a sense of vulnerability that is common in adolescents.
   b. is a lower-track student.
   c. is a student in a school that emphasizes rigid routines.
   d. has all of these characteristics.

82. The dangers of adolescents' increasing use of technology include
   a. cyberbullying.
   b. self-mutilation Web sites.
   c. the potential to push them toward violent sex.
   d. all of these dangers.

Progress Test 1

Multiple-Choice Questions

Circle your answers to the following questions and check them with the answers beginning on page 157. If your answer is incorrect, read the explanation for why it is incorrect and then consult the appropriate pages of the text (in parentheses following the correct answer).

1. Which of the following most accurately describes the sequence of pubertal development in girls?
   a. breasts and pubic hair, height spurt, first menstrual period, final pubic hair growth, full breast development
   b. height spurt, breasts and pubic hair, first menstrual period, full breast development
   c. first menstrual period, breasts and pubic hair, height spurt, full breast development
   d. breasts and pubic hair, height spurt, full breast development, first menstrual period

2. Although both sexes grow rapidly during adolescence, boys typically gain more than girls in their
   a. height.
   b. body fat.
   c. internal organ growth.
   d. lymphoid system.

3. For girls, the first readily observable sign of the onset of puberty is
   a. the onset of breast growth.
   b. the appearance of facial, body, and pubic hair.
   c. a change in the shape of the eyes.
   d. a lengthening of the torso.

4. More than any other group in the population, adolescent girls are likely to have
   a. asthma.
   b. acne.
   c. anemia.
   d. testosterone deficiency.

5. The HPA axis is the
   a. route followed by many hormones to regulate stress, growth, sleep, and appetite.
   b. pair of sex glands in humans.
   c. cascade of sex hormones in females and males.
   d. area of the brain that regulates the pituitary gland.

6. The secondary sex characteristic that is most noticeable in boys is
   a. breast enlargement.
   b. the appearance of facial hair.
   c. growth of the testes.
   d. a lower voice.

7. For girls, the specific event that is taken to indicate fertility is _______ ; for boys, it is _______ .
   a. the growth of breast buds; voice deepening
   b. menarche; spermarche
   c. hip widening; the testosterone surge
   d. the growth spurt; pubic hair

8. The most significant hormonal changes of puberty include an increase of _______ in _______ and an increase of _______ in _______ .
   a. estrogen; boys; estradiol; girls
   b. estradiol; boys; testosterone; girls
   c. androgen; girls; estradiol; boys
   d. estradiol; girls; testosterone; boys

9. A child who is chronically malnourished will likely
   a. begin puberty at a younger-than-average age.
   b. begin puberty later than the normal age range.
   c. never experience menarche.
   d. never experience spermarche.

10. Dr. Ramirez suspects Jennifer may be suffering from anorexia nervosa because her BMI is
    a. lower than 18.
    b. lower than 25.
    c. higher than 25.
    d. higher than 30.

11. Early physical growth and sexual maturation
    a. tend to be equally difficult for girls and boys.
    b. tend to be more difficult for boys than for girls.
    c. tend to be more difficult for girls than for boys.
    d. are easier for both girls and boys than late maturation.

12. Pubertal changes in growth and maturation typically are complete how long after puberty begins?
    a. one to two years
    b. two to three years
    c. four years
    d. The variation is too great to generalize.

13. The hypothalamus–pituitary–adrenal axis triggers
    a. puberty.
    b. the growth spurt.
    c. the development of sexual characteristics.
    d. all of these events.

14. One reason adolescents like intensity, excitement, and risk taking is that
    a. the limbic system matures faster than the prefrontal cortex.
    b. the prefrontal cortex matures faster than the limbic system.
    c. brain maturation is synchronous.
    d. puberty is occurring at a younger age today than in the past.

15. Many psychologists consider the distinguishing feature of adolescent thought to be the ability to think in terms of
    a. moral issues.
    b. concrete operations.
    c. possibility, not just reality.
    d. logical principles.

16. Piaget's last stage of cognitive development is
    a. formal operational thought.
    b. concrete operational thought.
    c. universal ethical principles.
    d. symbolic thought.

17. The adolescent who takes risks and feels immune to the laws of mortality is showing evidence of the
    a. invincibility fable.
    b. personal fable.
    c. imaginary audience.
    d. death instinct.

18. Imaginary audiences and invincibility fables are expressions of adolescent
    a. morality.
    b. thinking games.
    c. decision making.
    d. egocentrism.

19. The typical adolescent
    a. is tough-minded.
    b. is indifferent to public opinion.
    c. is self-absorbed and hypersensitive to criticism.
    d. has all of these characteristics.

20. When adolescents enter middle school, many
    a. experience a drop in their academic performance.
    b. show increased behavioral problems.
    c. lose connections to teachers.
    d. experience all of these things.

21. The psychologist who first described adolescent egocentrism is
    a. Jean Piaget.
    b. David Elkind.
    c. Lev Vygotsky.
    d. Noam Chomsky.

22. Thinking that begins with a general premise and then draws logical conclusions from it is called
    a. inductive reasoning.
    b. deductive reasoning.
    c. intuitive thinking.
    d. hypothetical reasoning.

23. Serious reflection on important issues is a wrenching process for many adolescents because of their newfound ability to reason
    a. inductively.
    b. deductively.
    c. hypothetically.
    d. symbolically.

24. Many adolescents seem to believe that *their* lovemaking will not lead to pregnancy. This belief is an expression of the
    a. digital divide.
    b. invincibility fable.
    c. imaginary audience.
    d. theory of mind.

25. Adolescents' improving ability to plan, reflect, and analyze is partly the result of maturation of the
    a. hippocampus.
    b. amygdala.
    c. limbic system.
    d. prefrontal cortex.

True or False Items

Write T (*true*) or F (*false*) on the line in front of each statement.

_______ 1. The secular trend is as strong today as ever.
_______ 2. During puberty, hormonal bursts lead to quick emotional extremes.
_______ 3. The first indicator of reproductive potential in males is menarche.
_______ 4. Lung capacity, heart size, and total volume of blood increase significantly during adolescence.
_______ 5. Puberty generally begins sometime between ages 8 and 14.
_______ 6. Girls are about two years ahead of boys in height as well as sexually and hormonally.
_______ 7. Only adolescent girls suffer from anemia.
_______ 8. Early-maturing girls tend to have lower self-esteem.
_______ 9. The appropriateness of the typical high school's high-stakes testing environment has been questioned.
_______ 10. Adolescents' egos sometimes seem to overwhelm logic.
_______ 11. When high-stakes tests are a requisite for graduation, there is a potential consequence of more high school dropouts.
_______ 12. Adolescents often create an imaginary audience as they envision how others will react to their appearance and behavior.
_______ 13. Thinking reaches heightened self-consciousness at puberty.
_______ 14. Inductive reasoning is a hallmark of formal operational thought.
_______ 15. Academic achievement often slows down during the middle school years.
_______ 16. The brain has two distinct processing networks.

Progress Test 2

Progress Test 2 should be completed during a final chapter review. Answer the following questions after you thoroughly understand the correct answers for the Chapter Review and Progress Test 1.

Multiple-Choice Questions

1. Which of the following is the correct sequence of pubertal events in boys?
    a. first pubic hairs, height spurt, first ejaculation of seminal fluid, growth of testes, enlargement of penis, final pubic-hair growth
    b. growth of testes, first pubic hairs, enlargement of penis, first ejaculation of seminal fluid, height spurt, final pubic-hair growth
    c. height spurt, first pubic hairs, first ejaculation of seminal fluid, enlargement of penis, final pubic-hair growth, growth of testes
    d. first ejaculation of seminal fluid, enlargement of penis, growth of testes, first pubic hairs, height spurt, final pubic-hair growth

2. Which of the following statements about adolescent physical development is NOT true?
   a. Hands and feet generally lengthen before arms and legs.
   b. Facial features usually grow before the head itself reaches adult size and shape.
   c. Oil, sweat, and odor glands become more active.
   d. The lymphoid system increases slightly in size, and the heart increases by nearly half.

3. In puberty, a hormone that increases markedly in girls (and only somewhat in boys) is
   a. estradiol.
   b. testosterone.
   c. androgen.
   d. menarche.

4. Nutritional deficiencies in adolescence are frequently the result of
   a. eating red meat.
   b. poor eating habits.
   c. menstruation.
   d. excessive exercise.

5. In females, puberty is typically marked by a(n)
   a. significant widening of the shoulders.
   b. significant widening of the hips.
   c. enlargement of the torso and upper chest.
   d. decrease in the size of the eyes and nose.

6. Nonreproductive sexual characteristics, such as the deepening of the voice and the development of breasts, are called
   a. gender-typed traits.
   b. primary sex characteristics.
   c. secondary sex characteristics.
   d. pubertal prototypes.

7. Puberty is initiated when hormones are released from the ________, then from the ________ gland, and then from the adrenal glands and the ________.
   a. hypothalamus; pituitary; gonads
   b. pituitary; gonads; hypothalamus
   c. gonads; pituitary; hypothalamus
   d. pituitary; hypothalamus; gonads

8. If a young girl becomes pregnant, she is at greater risk for
   a. a low-birthweight baby.
   b. high blood pressure.
   c. stillbirth.
   d. all of these conditions.

9. The number of substantiated victims of sexual abuse is greatest among children ages
   a. 12 to 15.
   b. 4 to 7.
   c. 16 to 18.
   d. 8 to 11.

10. An example of the secular trend is the
    a. complex link between pubertal hormones and emotions.
    b. effect of chronic stress on pubertal hormones.
    c. earlier growth of children due to improved nutrition and medical care.
    d. effect of chronic malnutrition on the onset of puberty.

11 Puberty is *most accurately* defined as the period
    a. of rapid physical growth that occurs during adolescence.
    b. during which sexual maturation is attained.
    c. of rapid physical growth and sexual maturation that ends childhood.
    d. during which adolescents establish identities separate from their parents.

12. Which of the following does NOT typically occur during puberty?
    a. The lungs increase in size and capacity.
    b. The heart's size and rate of beating increase.
    c. Blood volume increases.
    d. The lymphoid system decreases in size.

13. Teenagers' susceptibility to respiratory ailments typically ________ during adolescence, due to a(n) ________ in the size of the lymphoid system.
    a. increases; increase
    b. increases; decrease
    c. decreases; increase
    d. decreases; decrease

14. Adolescents who fall prey to the invincibility fable may be more likely to
    a. engage in risky behaviors.
    b. suffer from depression.
    c. have low self-esteem.
    d. drop out of school.

15. Thinking that extrapolates from a specific experience to form a general premise is called
    a. inductive reasoning.
    b. deductive reasoning.
    c. intuitive thinking.
    d. hypothetical reasoning.

16. Education during grades 7 through 12 is generally called
    a. primary education
    b. secondary education
    c. tertiary education.
    d. analytical education.

17. When young people overestimate their significance to others, they are displaying
    a. concrete operational thought.
    b. adolescent egocentrism.
    c. a lack of cognitive growth.
    d. immoral development.

18. The imaginary audience refers to adolescents imagining that:
    a. they are immune to the dangers of risky behaviors.
    b. they are always being scrutinized by others.
    c. their own lives are unique, heroic, or even legendary.
    d. the world revolves around their actions.

19. The brain area that predominates in quick, emotional reactions is the
    a. prefrontal cortex.
    b. amygdala.
    c. dendrite.
    d. axon.

20. Analytic thinking is to ______ thinking as emotional force is to ________ thinking.
    a. intuitive; egocentric
    b. egocentric; intuitive
    c. formal; intuitive
    d. intuitive; formal

21. One of the hallmarks of formal operational thought is
    a. egocentrism.
    b. deductive reasoning.
    c. symbolic thinking.
    d. all of these types of thinking

22. The pathways that form the brain's dual-processing networks involve the
    a. hypothalamus and the amygdala.
    b. cerebellum and the corpus callosum.
    c. prefrontal cortex and the limbic system.
    d. left and right cerebral hemispheres.

23. In the United States, the greatest divide between Internet users and nonusers is now
    a. gender.
    b. age.
    c. ethnicity.
    d. income.

Matching Items 1

Match each term or concept with its corresponding description or definition.

Terms or Concepts

________ 1. puberty
________ 2. gonadotropin-releasing hormone (GnRH)
________ 3. testosterone
________ 4. estradiol
________ 5. growth spurt
________ 6. primary sex characteristics
________ 7. menarche
________ 8. spermarche
________ 9. secondary sex characteristics
________ 10. body image
________ 11. anorexia nervosa
________ 12. bulimia nervosa

Descriptions or Definitions

a. onset of menstruation
b. period of rapid physical growth and sexual maturation that ends childhood
c. an affliction characterized by self-starvation
d. hormone that causes the gonads to enlarge and increase their production of sex hormones
e. hormone that increases dramatically in girls during puberty
f. first sign is increased bone length
g. attitude toward one's physical appearance
h. an affliction characterized by binge-purge eating
i. the sex organs involved in reproduction
j. first ejaculation containing sperm
k. hormone that increases dramatically in boys during puberty
l. physical characteristics not involved in reproduction

Matching Items 2

Match each term or concept with its corresponding description or definition.

Terms or Concepts

_______ 1. invincibility fable
_______ 2. imaginary audience
_______ 3. high-stakes test
_______ 4. hypothetical thought
_______ 5. deductive reasoning
_______ 6. inductive reasoning
_______ 7. formal operational thought
_______ 8. dual-process model
_______ 9. adolescent egocentrism

Descriptions or Definitions

a. the tendency of adolescents to focus on themselves to the exclusion of others
b. adolescents feel immune to the consequences of dangerous behavior
c. the idea held by many adolescents that others are intensely interested in them, especially in their appearance and behavior
d. the idea that there are two thinking networks in the brain
e. reasoning about propositions that may or may not reflect reality
f. the last stage of cognitive development, according to Piaget
g. thinking that moves from premise to conclusion
h. thinking that moves from a specific experience to a general premise
i. an evaluation that is critical in determining success or failure

Key Terms

Using your own words, write a brief definition or explanation of each of the following terms on a separate piece of paper.

1. puberty
2. menarche
3. spermarche
4. hormone
5. pituitary gland
6. adrenal glands
7. HPA axis
8. gonads
9. estradiol
10. testosterone
11. leptin
12. body image
13. anorexia nervosa
14. bulimia nervosa
15. growth spurt
16. primary sex characteristics
17. secondary sex characteristics
18. sexually transmitted infections (STIs)
19. child sexual abuse
20. adolescent egocentrism
21. personal fable
22. invincibility fable
23. imaginary audience
24. formal operational thought
25. hypothetical thought
26. deductive reasoning
27. inductive reasoning
28. dual-process model
29. intuitive thought
30. analytic thought
31. secondary education
32. middle school
33. digital divide
34. cyberbullying
35. high-stakes test

Answers

CHAPTER REVIEW

1. puberty; four years
2. menarche; $12^{1}/_{2}$ years
3. spermarche; (just under) 13
4. hypothalamus; pituitary gland; adrenal glands; HPA axis

5. GnRH (gonadotropin-releasing hormone); testes; ovaries; estradiol; testosterone
6. testosterone; estradiol; usually do; estradiol; testosterone; psychopathology; hormone
7. circadian rhythm; biorhythms; melatonin; little; girls
8. pituitary; phase delay; eveningness; males
9. 8; 14; precocious puberty: genes; monozygotic twins
10. body fat; earlier
11. leptin; females; males
12. malnutrition
13. secular trend; health; nutrition; has stopped
14. stress
15. accelerate
16. puberty; their fighting with their mother; an unrelated man living in the home
17. reproductive success
18. early

Early-maturing girls may be teased about their developing breasts. They tend to have older boyfriends, which may lead to drug and alcohol use; they have lower self-esteem, more depression, and poorer body image than their classmates do; they exercise less; and they are more likely to enter abusive relationships.

19. both early and late; Early; aggressive; lawbreaking; sexual activity; parenthood; Late
20. Girls: onset of breast growth, initial pubic hair, peak growth spurt, widening of the hips, first menstrual period, completion of pubic-hair growth, and final breast development

    Boys: growth of the testes, initial pubic hair, growth of the penis, first ejaculation of seminal fluid, facial hair, peak growth spurt, voice deepening, and completion of pubic-hair growth
21. GnRH
22. four years
23. **a.** is the answer. Late-maturing boys tend to be more anxious, depressed, and afraid of sex.
24. **a.** is the answer. Surprisingly, stress often results in an earlier onset of puberty.
25. estradiol
26. **b.** is the answer. Early-maturing girls tend to have lower self-esteem, more depression, and poorer body image than late-maturing girls.
27. do not; vending machines
28. body image; his or her body looks
29. eat erratically; diet pills; steroids
30. anorexia nervosa; body mass index; 18; 10
31. (a) refusal to maintain a body weight that is at least 85 percent of normal for age and height; (b) intense fear of weight gain; (c) disturbed body perception and denial of the problem; (d) absence of menstruation (in females)
32. bulimia nervosa; (a) bingeing and purging at least once a week for three months; (b) uncontrollable urges to overeat; (c) distorted perception of body size
33. eating together during childhood
34. **d.** is the answer. Many teenage girls, and some boys, suffer from anemia (iron deficiency).
35. growth; extremities; core
36. lungs; heart; decreases; increases; endurance

The fact that the more visible spurts of weight and height precede the less visible ones of the muscles and organs means that athletic training and weight lifting should match the young person's size of a year earlier.

37. lymphoid; less
38. primary sex characteristics
39. secondary sex characteristics

Males grow taller than females and their shoulders widen. Females take on more fat all over and become wider at the hips, and their breasts begin to develop. About 65 percent of boys experience some temporary breast enlargement. As the lungs and larynx grow, the adolescent's voice (especially in boys) becomes lower. Head and body hair become coarser and darker in both sexes.

40. biology; culture

    a. Teens have sexual experiences at younger ages.

    b. Most teenage mothers today have no husbands to help them.

    c. Raising a child has become more complex and expensive.

    d. Mothers of teenagers are often employed and therefore less available as caregivers.

    e. Sexually transmitted infections are more widespread and dangerous.
41. pregnancy; spontaneous abortion, high blood pressure, stillbirth, preterm birth, and a low-birthweight baby
42. sexually transmitted infections; biological defenses; treatment; chlamydia; human papillomavirus
43. child sexual abuse
44. 12; 15

45. **d.** is the answer.
46. different
47. fear; emotional impulses; before
48. age; experience
49. maturation
50. myelination; pruning; dopamine
51. 25
52. adolescent egocentrism
53. personal fable; invincibility fable
54. imaginary audience
55. formal operational; is not
56. determinants; conclusions

Three- to five-year-olds have no understanding of how to solve the problem. By age 7, children understand balancing the weights but don't know that distance from the center is also a factor. By age 10, they understand the concepts but are unable to coordinate them. By ages 13 or 14, they are able to solve the problem.

57. hypothetical
58. deductive; premise; logic; conclusions
59. deductive
60. hypothetical-deductive
61. dual-process; belief; intuitive thinking; analytic
62. quick; powerful; wrong
63. Possible answers follow.

Type of Thinking	Examples
Egocentrism	"Why do these catastrophes always happen to me and not to someone else?" (personal fable)
Hypothetical-Deductive	"I think there's a gremlin in my car and he's letting me know he's there." (thinking about possibilities that may not be real)
Intuitive Thought	"Last time this happened my car broke down. What am I going to do?" (experiential)
Analytic Thought	"I need to get my car to a mechanic as soon as possible." (logical thought)

64. **c.** is the answer. Although this statement is logically verifiable, preadolescents who lack formal operational thought cannot prove or disprove it.
65. **c.** is the answer. Monica now has the ability to use hypothetical-deductive reasoning.
66. **d.** is the answer. Hypothetical reasoning involves thinking about possibilities. a. is an example of the imaginary audience. b. is an example of the invincibility fable. c. is an example of adolescent egocentrism.
67. **b.** is the answer. The personal fable is the adolescent's belief that his or her feelings and thoughts are unique.
68. an imaginary audience.
69. inductive reasoning. This is reasoning that moves from the specific to reach a general conclusion.
70. **b.** is the answer. Solving mysteries is an example of deductive reasoning.
71. tertiary; secondary; middle
72. slows down

One reason for the decline is that students become less conscientious about their schoolwork. Another is that teachers and students are more disconnected from one another.

73. boys; girls; rich; poor; age
74. cyberbullying; self-mutilation
75. bullying; achievement; depression and eating disorders
76. analytic
77. high-stakes; dropouts
78. motivation; boredom; apprenticeships
79. small; clubs; athletics
80. **d.** is the answer.
81. **a.** is the answer. Middle school is a time when academic achievement slows down. Also, adolescents become more self-conscious socially because they are confronted by many new classmates.
82. **d.** is the answer.

PROGRESS TEST 1

Multiple-Choice Questions

1. **a.** is the answer. (p. 310)
2. **a.** is the answer. (p. 320)

   b. Girls gain more body fat than boys do.

   c. & d. The text does not indicate that these are different for boys and girls.
3. **a.** is the answer. (p. 320)
4. **c.** is the answer. This is because each menstrual period depletes some iron from the body. (p. 317)
5. **a.** is the answer. (pp. 310–311)

   b. This describes the gonads.

c. These include estradiol and testosterone.

d. This is the hypothalamus.

6. **d.** is the answer. (p. 320)
7. **b.** is the answer. (p. 310)
8. **d.** is the answer. (p. 311)
9. **b.** is the answer. (p. 314)
10. **a.** is the answer. (p. 318)

b. This is a healthy BMI.

c. & d. These BMIs are associated with being overweight.

11. **c.** is the answer. (p. 315)
12. **c.** is the answer. (p. 310)
13. **d.** is the answer. (pp. 310–311)
14. **a.** is the answer. (p. 324)

c. Brain maturation is asynchronous.

d. This may be true, but it doesn't explain why adolescents have always liked intensity and excitement.

15. **c.** is the answer. (p. 328)

a. Although moral reasoning becomes much deeper during adolescence, it is not limited to this stage of development.

b. & d. Concrete operational thought, which *is* logical, is the distinguishing feature of childhood thinking.

16. **a.** is the answer. (p. 328)

b. In Piaget's theory, this stage precedes formal operational thought.

c. & d. These are not stages in Piaget's theory.

17. **a.** is the answer. (pp. 327–328)

b. This concept refers to adolescents' tendency to imagine their own lives as unique, heroic, or even legendary.

c. This refers to adolescents' tendency to fantasize about how others will react to their appearance and behavior.

d. This is a concept in Freud's theory.

18. **d.** is the answer. These thought processes are manifestations of adolescents' tendency to see themselves as being much more central and important to the social scene than they really are. (pp. 326–328)
19. **c.** is the answer. (p. 326)
20. **d.** is the answer. (pp. 334–335)
21. **b.** is the answer. (p. 326)
22. **b.** is the answer. (p. 330)

a. Inductive reasoning moves from specific facts to a general conclusion.

c. By its very nature, intuitive thinking does not move logically either from a general conclusion to specific facts or from specific facts to a general conclusion.

d. Hypothetical reasoning involves thinking about possibilities rather than facts.

23. **c.** is the answer. (p. 330)
24. **b.** is the answer. (pp. 327–328)

a. The digital divide is the gap between those who have computer access and those who do not.

c. This refers to adolescents' tendency to fantasize about how others will react to their appearance and behavior.

d. Theory of mind refers to a person's theory about what other people are thinking.

25. **d.** is the answer. (p. 324)

a., b., & c. The hippocampus (a) and amygdala (b), which are both part of the limbic system (c), are important in quick emotional reactions.

True or False Items

1. F (p. 314)
2. T (p. 311)
3. F The first indicator of reproductive potential in males is ejaculation of seminal fluid containing sperm (spermarche). Menarche (the first menstrual period) is the first indication of reproductive potential in females. (p. 310)
4. T (p. 320)
5. T (p. 310)
6. F Hormonally and sexually, girls are ahead by only a few months. (p. 313)
7. F Boys also suffer from anemia, especially if they engage in physical labor or competitive sports. (p. 317)
8. T (p. 315)
9. T (p. 340)
10. T (p. 324)
11. T (p. 341)
12. T (p. 328)
13. T (p. 328)
14. F Deductive reasoning is a hallmark of formal operational thought. (p. 331)
15. T (p. 334)
16. T (p. 331)

PROGRESS TEST 2

Multiple-Choice Questions

1. **b.** is the answer. (p. 310)

2. **d.** is the answer. During adolescence, the lymphoid system *decreases* in size and the heart *doubles* in size. (p. 320)
3. **a.** is the answer. (p. 311)
   b. Testosterone increases markedly in boys.
   c. Testosterone is the best known of the androgens (the general category of male hormones).
   d. Menarche is the first menstrual period.
4. **b.** is the answer. (p. 317)
5. **b.** is the answer. (p. 320)
   a. The shoulders of males tend to widen during puberty.
   c. The torso typically lengthens during puberty.
   d. The eyes and nose *increase* in size during puberty.
6. **c.** is the answer. (p. 320)
   a. Although not a term used in the textbook, a gender-typed trait is one that is typical of one sex but not of the other.
   b. Primary sex characteristics are those involving the reproductive organs.
   d. This is not a term used by developmental psychologists.
7. **a.** is the answer. (pp. 310–311)
8. **d.** is the answer. (p. 321)
9. **a.** is the answer. (p. 323)
10. **c.** is the answer. (p. 314)
11. **c.** is the answer. (p. 310)
12. **b.** is the answer. Although the size of the heart increases during puberty, heart rate *decreases*. (p. 320)
13. **d.** is the answer. (p. 320)
14. **a.** is the answer. (pp. 327–328)
    b., c., & d. The invincibility fable leads some teens to believe that they are immune to the dangers of risky behaviors; it is not necessarily linked to depression, low self-esteem, or the likelihood that an individual will drop out of school.
15. **a.** is the answer. (p. 331)
    b. Deductive reasoning begins with a general premise and then draws logical conclusions from it.
    c. By its very nature, intuitive thinking does not move logically either from a general conclusion to specific facts or from specific facts to a general conclusion.
    d. Hypothetical reasoning involves thinking about possibilities rather than facts.
16. **b.** is the answer. (p. 334)
17. **b.** is the answer. (p. 326)
18. **b.** is the answer. (p. 328)
    a. This describes the invincibility fable.
    c. This describes the personal fable.
    d. This describes adolescent egocentrism in general.
19. **b.** is the answer. (p. 324)
    a. The prefrontal cortex is responsible for planning, analysis, and emotional regulation.
    c. & d. Dendrites and axons are parts of neurons.
20. **c.** is the answer. (p. 332)
21. **b.** is the answer. (p. 330)
22. **c.** is the answer. (p. 321)
23. **b.** is the answer. (p. 335)

Matching Items 1

1. b (p. 310)	**5.** f (p. 319)	**9.** l (p. 320)
2. d (p. 311)	**6.** i (p. 320)	**10.** g (p. 317)
3. k (p. 311)	**7.** a (p. 310)	**11.** c (p. 318)
4. e (p. 311)	**8.** j (p. 310)	**12.** h (p. 318)

Matching Items 2

1. b (pp. 327–328)	**5.** g (p. 330)	**9.** a (p. 326)
2. c (p. 328)	**6.** h (p. 331)	
3. i (p. 339)	**7.** f (p. 328)	
4. e (p. 330)	**8.** d (p. 331)	

KEY TERMS

1. **Puberty** is the period of rapid physical growth and sexual maturation that ends childhood and brings the young person to adult size, shape, and sexual potential. (p. 310)
2. **Menarche,** which refers to the first menstrual period, signals that the adolescent girl has begun ovulation. (p. 310)
3. **Spermarche**, which refers to the first ejaculation of sperm, signals sperm production in adolescent boys. (p. 310)
4. A **hormone** is an organic chemical substance produced by one body tissue that travels via the bloodstream to another to affect some physiological function. (p. 310)
5. The **pituitary gland** is a gland in the brain that responds to a biochemical signal from the hypothalamus by producing hormones that regulate growth and control other glands. (p. 310)
6. The **adrenal glands** are two glands, located above the kidneys, that secrete epinephrine and norepinephrine, hormones that prepare the body to deal with stress. (p. 310)

7. The **HPA (hypothalamus–pituitary–adrenal) axis** is the route followed by many hormones to trigger puberty and to regulate stress, growth, sleep, appetite, and sexual arousal. (p. 311)
8. The **gonads** are the paired sex glands in humans—the ovaries in females and the testes, or testicles, in males—that produce hormones and gametes. (p. 311)
9. **Estradiol** is a sex hormone that is secreted in much greater amounts by females than by males; considered the chief estrogen. (p. 311)
10. **Testosterone** is a sex hormone that is secreted much more by males than by females; considered the best-known androgen. (p. 311)
11. **Leptin** is a hormone that affects appetite and is believed to affect the onset of puberty. (p. 314)
12. **Body image** is a person's concept of his or her body's appearance. (p. 317)
13. **Anorexia nervosa** is an eating disorder characterized by self-starvation. (p. 318)
14. **Bulimia nervosa** is an eating disorder characterized by binge eating and purging. (p. 318)
15. The **growth spurt,** which is the relatively sudden and rapid physical growth of almost every part of the body, is one of the many observable signs of puberty. (p. 319)
16. During puberty, changes in the **primary sex characteristics** involve those sex organs that are directly involved in reproduction. (p. 320)
17. During puberty, changes in the **secondary sex characteristics** involve parts of the body that are not directly involved in reproduction but that signify sexual development. (p. 320)
18. **Sexually transmitted infections (STIs),** such as chlamydia, gonorrhea, genital herpes, and AIDS, are those that are spread by sexual contact. (p. 322)
19. **Child sexual abuse** is any erotic activity that arouses an adult and excites, shames, or confuses a child—whether or not the victim protests and whether or not physical contact is involved. (p. 323)
20. **Adolescent egocentrism** refers to the tendency of young adolescents to focus on themselves to the exclusion of others. (p. 326)
21. The **personal fable** refers to an adolescent's belief that his or her thoughts, feelings, or experiences are unique. (p. 327)
22. Adolescents who experience the **invincibility fable** feel that they are immune to the dangers of risky behaviors. (pp. 327–328)
23. Adolescents often create an **imaginary audience** for themselves, because they assume that others are as intensely interested in them as they themselves are. (p. 328)
24. In Piaget's theory, the last stage of cognitive development, which arises from a combination of maturation and experience, is called **formal operational thought.** A hallmark of formal operational thinking is more systematic logic and the ability to think about abstract ideas. (p. 328)
25. **Hypothetical thought** involves reasoning about propositions and possibilities that may not reflect reality. (p. 330)
26. **Deductive reasoning** is thinking that moves from the general to the specific, or from an abstract idea or premise to a logical conclusion; also called *top-down reasoning.* (p. 330)
27. **Inductive reasoning** is thinking that moves from one or more specific experiences or facts to a general conclusion; also called *bottom-up reasoning.* (p. 331)
28. The **dual-process model** is the idea that there are two thinking networks in the human brain, one for emotional thinking and one for analytical thinking. (p. 331)
29. **Intuitive thought** is that which arises from a hunch or emotion, often triggered by past experiences and cultural assumptions. (p. 332)
30. **Analytic thought** is logical thinking that arises from rational analysis and the systematic evaluation of consequences and possibilities. (p. 332)
31. **Secondary education** is education that follows primary education and precedes tertiary education, usually occurring from about age 12 to age 18. (p. 334)
32. **Middle school** refers to the years of school between elementary school and high school; usually begins with grade 5 or 6 and ends with grade 8. (p. 334)
33. The **digital divide** refers to the gap between people who have access to computers and those who do not. (p. 335)
34. **Cyberbullying** occurs when one person spreads insults or rumors about someone else via e-mail, texting, anonymous phone calls, and video embarrassment. (p. 337)
35. **High-stakes tests** are exams and other forms of evaluation that are critical in determining a person's success or failure. (p. 339)

10 chapter

ADOLESCENCE

Psychosocial Development

Chapter Overview

Chapter 10 focuses on the adolescent's psychosocial development. The first section explores the paths that lead to the formation of identity, which is required for the attainment of adult status and maturity. The next two sections examine the influences of family and friends on adolescent psychosocial development, including the development of romantic relationships and sexual activity. Depression, self-destruction, and suicide—the most perplexing problems of adolescence—are then explored. The special problems posed by adolescent lawbreaking are discussed, and suggestions for alleviating or treating these problems are given.

Although adolescence is, in many ways, a healthy time of life, the text also addresses a major health hazard that too often affects adolescence: the use of alcohol, tobacco, and other drugs. The chapter concludes with the message that with the help of family and friends, most adolescents make it through the teen years unscathed.

NOTE: Answer guidelines for all Chapter 10 questions begin on page 170.

Chapter Review

When you have finished reading the chapter, work through the material that follows to review it. Complete the sentences and answer the questions. In some cases, Study Tips explain how best to learn a difficult concept, while Think About It and Applications help you to know how well you understand the material. As you proceed, evaluate your performance for each section by consulting the answers beginning on page 170. Do not continue with the next section until you understand each answer. If you need to, review or reread the appropriate section in the textbook before continuing.

Identity (pp. 348–353)

1. The momentous changes that occur during the teen years challenge adolescents to find their own ________________ .

2. According to Erikson, the challenge of adolescence is ________________ ________________ ________________ ________________ .

3. The ultimate goal of adolescence is to establish a new identity that involves both rejection and acceptance of childhood values; this is called ________________ ________________ .

4. The young person who has few commitments to goals or values and is apathetic about defining his or her identity is experiencing ________________ ________________ .

5. The young person who prematurely accepts earlier roles and parental values without exploring alternatives or truly forging a unique identity is experiencing identity ________________ .

6. A time-out period during which a young person experiments with different identities, postponing important choices, is called an identity ________________ . An obvious institutional example of this in North America is attending ________________ .

7. Erikson described four aspects of identity: ________________ , ________________ , ________________ , and ________________ .

8. Today, a person's identification as either male or female is called ______________ ______________, which usually leads to a gender ______________ and a sexual ______________.

9. A person's sexual attraction to people of the same sex, other sex, or both sexes constitutes his or her ______________ ______________.

Sometimes the gender-identity crisis becomes the pathological condition called ______________ ______________ ______________.

10. Since Erikson's time, ______________ identity has become more important than ______________ identity. The more appropriate term has become ______________ ______________.

11. Vocational identity is rarely achieved before age ______________, in part because it takes years to acquire the needed skills.

12. Employment of 20 or more hours during adolescence is likely to weaken ______________ formation, strain ______________ relationships, lower ______________ achievement, and limit ______________ success.

STUDY TIP: To keep the differences among the identity statuses of role confusion, foreclosure, and moratorium straight, remember that role confusion is a state in which adolescents seem unfocused and unconcerned about their future. Foreclosure and moratorium represent different strategies for dealing with this state of confusion. You may find it helpful to think of how *foreclosure* is used in financial circumstances. Economic foreclosure occurs when someone who has borrowed money, typically to purchase a home, defaults on the loan. To *foreclose* is to deprive the borrower of the right to ownership. Similarly, adolescents who have foreclosed on their identities have deprived themselves of the healthy practice of thoughtfully questioning and trying out different possible identities before settling on one. In contrast, a moratorium is a time-out during which adolescents postpone their final identity, often by attending college or engaging in other socially acceptable activities that allow them to make a more mature decision.

APPLICATIONS:

13. From childhood, Sharon thought she wanted to follow in her mother's footsteps and be a homemaker. Now, at age 40 with a home and family, she admits to herself that what she really wanted to be was a medical researcher. Erik Erikson would probably say that Sharon
   a. adopted a negative identity when she was a child.
   b. experienced identity foreclosure at an early age.
   c. never progressed beyond the obvious role confusion she experienced as a child.
   d. took a moratorium from identity formation.

14. Jennifer has a well-defined religious identity. This is true because she
   a. often prays.
   b. worships regularly.
   c. reads scripture.
   d. does all of these things.

15. In 1998, 6-year-old Raisel and her parents emigrated from Mexico to the United States. Because her parents hold to the values and customs of their native land, Raisel is likely to
   a. have an easier time achieving her own unique identity.
   b. have a more difficult time forging her identity.
   c. stick with her parents' cultural identity.
   d. have a shorter span of time in which to forge her identity.

Relationships with Elders and Peers (pp. 353–360)

16. Adolescence is often characterized as a time of waning adult influence; this ______________ (is/is not) necessarily true. An important aspect of healthy development is supportive relationships with ______________ adults.

17. Parent–adolescent conflict peaks during ______________ ______________ and is particularly notable with ______________ (mothers/fathers) and their ______________ (sons/daughters). This conflict often involves ______________, which refers to repeated, petty arguments about daily habits.

18. By age 18, increased ______________ maturity and reduced ______________ bring some renewed appreciation for parents.

19. There ______________ (are/are not) cultural differences in parent–adolescent relationships. Some cultures value ______________ ______________ above all else and avoid conflict. Thus, the very idea of adolescent rebellion may be a ______________ construction of middle-class Westerners.

20. Four other elements of parent–teen relationships that have been heavily researched include ______________, ______________, ______________, and ______________.

21. In terms of family control, a powerful deterrent to drugs and risky sex is ______________ ______________. Too much interference, however, may contribute to adolescent ______________. Particularly harmful to teens are threats to withdraw love and support, or ______________ ______________.

22. Adolescents group themselves into clusters of close friends, called ______________, and larger groups, or ______________, who share common interests. These groups provide social ______________ and social ______________.

23. Social pressure to conform to peer activities is called ______________ ______________. This pressure is ______________ as often as it is ______________. Destructive peer support is called ______________ ______________.

24. Two helpful concepts in understanding the influence of peers are ______________, meaning that peers ______________ one another; and ______________, referring to the fact that peers encourage one another to do things that ______________________________.

25. Friends play a special role for adolescents whose parents are ______________. They are particularly important in protecting the adolescent's ______________, especially if the adolescent is of a(n) ______________ background.

APPLICATIONS:

26. Bill's parents insist on knowing his whereabouts and activities all times. Clearly, they are very good at ______________________________.

27. First-time parents Norma and Norman are worried that, during adolescence, their healthy parental influence will be undone as their children are encouraged by peers to become sexually promiscuous, drug-addicted, or delinquent. Their wise neighbor, who is a developmental psychologist, tells them that
   a. peers are constructive as often as they are destructive.
   b. research suggests that peers provide a negative influence in every major task of adolescence.
   c. only through authoritarian parenting can parents give children the skills they need to resist peer pressure.
   d. unless their children show early signs of learning difficulties or antisocial behavior, parental monitoring is unnecessary.

Sexuality (pp. 360–365)

Briefly outline the four-stage progression of heterosexual involvement.

28. Culture. ethnicity, gender, and socioeconomic status ______________ (affect/do not affect) the ______________ and ______________ of these stages, but the basic ______________ seems to be based on ______________ factors. In modern developed nations, each stage typically lasts several years.

29. For homosexual adolescents, added complications usually ______________ (slow down/speed up) romantic attachments.

30. Sexual experience among teens is influenced by many factors, including ______________, whether the adolescent is in a ______________ relationship, and

_______________ who monitor their behavior. Many parents _______________ (underestimate/overestimate) their adolescent's need for sexual information.

31. Religion is _______________ (more/less) of a factor in determining whether parents talk to their children about sex than _______________ and _______________.

32. Developmentalists agree that high schools _______________ (should/should not) teach sex education, and that sex also should be part of _______________-_______________ conversations.

33. Sex education _______________ (varies/does not vary) from nation to nation. The timing and content of sex education in the United States _______________ (varies/does not vary) by state and community.

State several characteristics of effective sex-education programs.

34. Sexual activity among adolescents _______________ (varies/does not vary) from nation to nation. The teen birth rate is _______________ (increasing/decreasing). At the same time, contraceptive use has _______________ (increased/decreased).

35. In the United States, the rate of teen abortions has (increased/decreased) in recent years.

THINK ABOUT IT: To help you understand the role of the peer group during adolescence, think about your own social experiences as a teenager. Did you hang out in loosely associated groups of girls and boys before gradually joining together? Did you double- or triple-date to avoid the awkwardness of being alone with someone you "liked"? Did you have a best friend of the same gender with whom you shared details of your sexual experiences in order to confirm that they were normal? _______________

APPLICATION:

36. Padma's parents are concerned because their 14-year-old daughter has formed an early romantic relationship with a boy. You tell them
   a. not to worry, because boys are more likely to say they have a girlfriend than vice versa.
   b. not to worry; healthy romances are a manifestation of good relationships with parents and peers.
   c. most romantic relationships last throughout high school.
   d. they should do everything they can to break up the relationship.

Sadness and Anger (pp. 368–373)

37. Adolescents who have one serious problem _______________ (often have/do not usually have) others.

38. The situation in which a person has two or more unrelated illnesses or disorders at the same time is _______________.

39. From late childhood through adolescence, people generally feel _______________ (more/less) competent, on average, each year in most areas of their lives.

40. Clinical depression _______________ (increases/decreases) at puberty, especially among _______________ (males/females). One explanation is that talking about and mentally replaying past experiences, which is called _______________, is more common among _______________ (males/females).

41. Thinking about committing suicide, called _______________ _______________, is _______________ (common/relatively rare) in mid-adolescence.

42. Adolescents are _______________ (more/less) likely to kill themselves than adults are.

43. When a town or school sentimentalizes the "tragic end" of a teen suicide, the publicity can trigger _______________ _______________.

44. Most suicide attempts in adolescence _______________ (do/do not) result in death. A deliberate act of self-destruction that does not result in death is called a _______________ .

45. List four factors that increase a teen's risk of suicide.

a. _______________

b. _______________

c. _______________

d. _______________

46. Around the world, cultural differences in the rates of suicidal ideation and completion _______________ (are/are not) apparent.

47. The rate of suicide is higher for adolescent _______________ (males/females). The rate of parasuicide is higher for _______________ (males/females).

48. Since 1990, rates of adolescent suicide have _______________ (risen/fallen), especially among those with more _______________ and _______________ .

49. Psychologists influenced by the _______________ perspective believe that adolescent rebellion and defiance are normal.

50. Lawbreakers who are under age _______________ are called _______________ _______________ . In terms of the frequency of arrests, _______________ (only a few/virtually all) adolescents break the law at least once before age 20.

Briefly describe data on gender and ethnic differences in adolescent arrests.

51. (A View from Science) Girls engage in _______________ (relational/physical) aggression as often as boys do.

52. Two clusters of factors predict who is likely to commit violent crimes: childhood factors are _______________-based and factors from adolescence are primarily _______________ .

List several of the childhood factors that correlate with delinquency.

53. Experts find it useful to distinguish _______________-_______________ offenders, whose criminal activity stops by age 21, from _______________-_______________-_______________ offenders, who become career criminals.

54. One innovative strategy for helping delinquents is _______________ _______________ _______________, in which violent youth are assigned to _______________ families trained to establish a relationship with this child and his or her teachers.

APPLICATIONS:

55. Carl is a typical 16-year-old adolescent who has no special problems. It is likely that Carl has

a. contemplated suicide.
b. engaged in some minor illegal act.
c. struggled with "who he is."
d. engaged in all of these behaviors.

56. Statistically, who of the following is most likely to commit suicide?

a. Elena, a female from South America
b. Yan, a male from the Eastern United States
c. James, a male from the Western United States
d. Alison, a female from western Europe

57. Coming home from work, Rashid hears a radio announcement warning parents to be alert for possible cluster suicide signs in their teenage children. What might have precipitated such an announcement?

a. government statistics that suicide is on the rise
b. the highly publicized suicide of a teen from a school in town
c. the recent crash of an airliner, killing all on board
d. any of these events

Drug Use and Abuse (pp. 373–378)

58. Most adolescents try _______________ drugs, some of which are legal and some of which are not.

59. Drug use generally increases from age _______________ to _______________ and then decreases. Middle school boys are particularly vulnerable to the use of _______________ drugs.

60. Overall, drug use among adolescents in the United States is _______________ (up/down) since 1976. Worldwide, _______________ (girls/boys) have higher rates of drug use than _______________ (girls/boys).

61. Few adolescents notice when they move past experimenting with drugs to harmful _______________ and then _______________, defined as needing the drug.

62. By impairing digestion, nutrition, and appetite, tobacco can limit adolescent _______________.

63. The drug most frequently abused among North American teenagers is _______________.

64. Alcohol impairs _______________ and _______________ by damaging the brain's _______________ and _______________ _______________.

65. The idea that each new generation forgets what the previous generation has learned is referred to as _______________ _______________.

APPLICATIONS:

66. Concluding her talk on adolescent alcohol use and brain damage, Maya notes that
    a. studies have shown only that alcohol use is correlated with damage to the prefrontal cortex.
    b. thus far, studies have shown only that alcohol use is correlated with damage to the hippocampus.
    c. animal research studies demonstrate that alcohol use results in slower thinking.
    d. alcohol use causes brain abnormalities only in teens who are genetically vulnerable.

67. Fifteen-year-old Norbert has a drinking problem. If he is typical of adolescents with one problem, it is likely that
    a. he also has several other problems.
    b. the problem is isolated and does not adversely affect other areas of development.
    c. the consequences are temporary and not severe.
    d. their earlier development during childhood was also problematic.

Progress Test 1

Multiple-Choice Questions

Circle your answers to the following questions and check them with the answers on page 171. If your answer is incorrect, read the explanation for why it is incorrect and then consult the appropriate pages of the text (in parentheses following the correct answer).

1. According to Erikson, the primary task of adolescence is that of establishing
    a. basic trust.
    b. an identity.
    c. intimacy.
    d. integrity.

2. According to developmentalists who study identity formation, foreclosure involves
    a. accepting an identity prematurely, without exploration.
    b. taking time off from school, work, and other commitments.
    c. opposing parental values.
    d. failing to commit oneself to a vocational goal.

3. A large group of adolescents who share common interests is a
    a. clique.
    b. peer group.
    c. crowd.
    d. cluster.

4. The main sources of social support for most young people who are establishing independence from their parents are
    a. older adolescents of the opposite sex.
    b. older siblings.
    c. teachers.
    d. peer groups.

5. For members of minority ethnic groups, identity achievement may be particularly complicated because
    a. their cultural ideal clashes with the Western emphasis on adolescent self-determination.
    b. peers, themselves torn by similar conflicts, can be very critical.
    c. parents and other relatives tend to emphasize ethnicity and expect teens to honor their roots.
    d. of all of these reasons.

6. In a crime-ridden neighborhood, parents can protect their adolescents by keeping close watch over activities, friends, and so on. This practice is called
   a. a moratorium.
   b. foreclosure.
   c. peer screening.
   d. parental monitoring.

7. Conflict between adolescent girls and their mothers is most likely to involve
   a. bickering over hair, neatness, and other daily habits.
   b. political, religious, and moral issues.
   c. peer relationships and friendships.
   d. relationships with boys.

8. Destructive peer support in which one adolescent shows another how to rebel against authority is called
   a. peer pressure.
   b. deviancy training.
   c. peer selection.
   d. peer facilitation.

9. In our society, obvious examples of institutionalized moratoria on identity formation are
   a. the Boy Scouts and the Girl Scouts.
   b. college and the military.
   c. marriage and divorce.
   d. bar mitzvahs and baptisms.

10. In a Disney movie, two high school students encourage each other to participate in the school musical. This type of peer influence is called
    a. peer pressure.
    b. deviancy training.
    c. selection.
    d. peer facilitation.

11. Jill, who has cut herself and engaged in other self-destructive acts, is receiving treatment for these acts of
    a. suicidal ideation.
    b. comorbidity.
    c. parasuicide.
    d. rumination.

12. Thirteen-year-old Adam, who never has doubted his faith, identifies himself as an orthodox member of a particular religious group. A developmentalist would probably say that Adam's religious identity is
    a. achieved.
    b. foreclosed.
    c. in moratorium.
    d. oppositional in nature.

13. The early predictors of life-course-persistent offenders include all of the following EXCEPT
    a. short attention span.
    b. hyperactivity.
    c. high intelligence.
    d. neurological impairment.

14. Regarding gender differences in self-destructive acts, the rate of parasuicide is ________ and the rate of suicide is __________ .
    a. higher in males; higher in females
    b. higher in females; higher in males
    c. the same in males and females; higher in males
    d. the same in males and females; higher in females

15. Conflict between parents and adolescents is
    a. most likely to involve fathers and their early-maturing offspring.
    b. more frequent in single-parent homes.
    c. more likely between daughters and their mothers.
    d. likely in all of these situations.

True or False Items

Write T (*true*) or F (*false*) on the line in front of each statement.

________ 1. Identity achievement is elusive for adolescents.

________ 2. Most adolescents have political views and educational values that are markedly different from those of their parents.

________ 3. Peer pressure is inherently destructive to the adolescent seeking an identity.

________ 4. For most adolescents, group socializing and dating precede the establishment of true intimacy with one member of the opposite sex.

________ 5. Worldwide, virtually every adolescent breaks the law at least once before age 20.

________ 6. Abstinence-only sex education has led to decreased rates of adolescent sex.

________ 7. Because of their tendency to ruminate, girls are more likely than boys to be clinically depressed.

________ 8. In finding themselves, teens try to find a consistent understanding of themselves.

________ 9. From ages 6 to 18, children feel more competent, on average, each year in most areas of their lives.

________ 10. Increased accessibility of guns is a factor in the increased rate of youth suicide in the United States.

Progress Test 2

Progress Test 2 should be completed during a final chapter review. Answer the following questions after you thoroughly understand the correct answers for the Chapter Review and Progress Test 1.

Multiple-Choice Questions

1. Which of the following is NOT one of the arenas of identity formation in Erik Erikson's theory?
   a. religious
   b. sexual
   c. political
   d. social

2. Which of the following is true of gender identity?
   a. It is a person's self-definition as male or female.
   b. It always leads to sexual orientation.
   c. It is a person's biological male/female characteristics.
   d. It is established at birth.

3. Rodesia repeatedly thinks and talks about past experiences to the extent that her doctor believes it is contributing to her depression. Rodesia's behavior is an example of
   a. comorbidity.
   b. deviancy training.
   c. parasuicide.
   d. rumination.

4. Ray endured severe child abuse, has difficulty controlling his emotions, and exhibits symptoms of autism. These factors would suggest that Ray is at high risk of
   a. becoming an adolescent-limited offender.
   b. becoming a life-course-persistent offender.
   c. developing an antisocial personality.
   d. foreclosing his identity prematurely.

5. Thinking about committing suicide is called
   a. cluster suicide.
   b. parasuicide.
   c. suicidal ideation.
   d. fratricide.

6. Which of the following was NOT noted in the text regarding peer relationships among gay and lesbian adolescents?
   a. Romantic attachments are usually slower to develop.
   b. In homophobic cultures, many gay teens try to conceal their homosexual feelings by becoming heterosexually involved.
   c. Many girls who will later identify themselves as lesbians are oblivious to these sexual urges as teens.
   d. Homosexual men report that they do not become aware of their interests until age 17.

7. The adolescent experiencing role confusion is typically
   a. very apathetic.
   b. experimenting with alternative identities without trying to settle on any one.
   c. willing to accept parental values wholesale, without exploring alternatives.
   d. one who rebels against all forms of authority.

8. Gender identity refers to a person's
   a. identification as being female or male.
   b. attraction toward a person of the same sex, the other sex, or both sexes.
   c. self-definition as a unique individual.
   d. self-definition in each of these areas.

9. Crime statistics show that during adolescence
   a. males and females are equally likely to be arrested.
   b. males are more likely than females to be arrested.
   c. females are more likely than males to be arrested.
   d. males commit more crimes than females but are less likely to be arrested.

10. Which of the following is the most common problem behavior among adolescents?
    a. pregnancy
    b. daily use of illegal drugs
    c. minor lawbreaking
    d. attempts at suicide

11. A time-out period during which a young person experiments with different identities, postponing important choices, is called
    a. foreclosure.
    b. a negative identity.
    c. identity diffusion.
    d. a moratorium.

12. Comorbidity is the situation in which
    a. one adolescent encourages another to participate in a dangerous activity.
    b. feelings of lethargy last two weeks or more.
    c. an overwhelming feeling of sadness disrupts a person's normal routine.
    d. two or more unrelated illnesses occur together at the same time.

13. Which of the following is NOT true regarding the rate of clinical depression among adolescents?
    a. At puberty the rate more than doubles.
    b. It affects a higher proportion of teenage boys than girls.
    c. Genetic vulnerability is a predictor of teenage depression.
    d. The adolescent's school setting is a factor.

14. Parent–teen conflict tends to center on issues related to
    a. politics and religion.
    b. education.
    c. vacations.
    d. daily details, such as musical tastes.

15. Suicidal ideation is
    a. not as common among high school students as it was in the past.
    b. more common among males than females.
    c. more common among females than males.
    d. more common among high-achieving students.

Matching Items

Match each term or concept with its corresponding description or definition.

Terms or Concepts

________ 1. identity achievement
________ 2. foreclosure
________ 3. clique
________ 4. role confusion
________ 5. moratorium
________ 6. peer selection
________ 7. peer pressure
________ 8. parental monitoring
________ 9. parasuicide
________ 10. cluster suicide

Descriptions or Definitions

a. premature identity formation
b. a group of suicides that occur in the same community, school, or time period
c. the adolescent has few commitments to goals or values
d. process by which adolescents choose their friends based on shared interests
e. self-destructive act that does not result in death
f. awareness of where children are and what they are doing
g. a time-out period during which adolescents experiment with alternative identities
h. the adolescent establishes his or her own goals and values
i. encouragement to conform with one's friends in behavior, dress, and attitude
j. a cluster of close friends

Key Terms

Using your own words, write a brief definition or explanation of each of the following terms on a separate piece of paper.

1. identity versus role confusion
2. identity
3. identity achievement
4. role confusion
5. foreclosure
6. moratorium
7. gender identity
8. sexual orientation
9. bickering
10. parental monitoring
11. clique
12. crowd
13. peer pressure
14. deviancy training
15. clinical depression
16. rumination
17. suicidal ideation
18. cluster suicide

19. parasuicide
20. juvenile delinquent
21. life-course-persistent offender
22. adolescent-limited offender
23. generational forgetting

Answers

CHAPTER REVIEW

1. identity
2. identity versus role confusion
3. identity achievement
4. role confusion (identity diffusion)
5. foreclosure
6. moratorium; college
7. religious; sex (gender); political (ethnic); vocation
8. gender identity; role; orientation
9. sexual orientation; sexual identity disorder
10. ethnic; political; identity politics
11. 25
12. identity; family; academic; career
13. **b.** is the answer. Apparently, Sharon never explored alternatives or truly forged a unique personal identity.
14. **d.** is the answer.
15. **b.** is the answer. Ethnic adolescents struggle with finding the right balance between transcending their background and becoming immersed in it.
16. is not; non-parent
17. early adolescence; mothers; daughters; bickering
18. emotional; egocentrism
19. are; family harmony; social
20. communication; support; connectedness; control
21. parental monitoring; depression; psychological control
22. cliques; crowds; control; support
23. peer pressure; constructive; destructive; deviancy training
24. selection; choose; facilitation; none of them would do alone
25. immigrants; self-esteem; Asian
26. parental monitoring
27. **a.** is the answer. Developmentalists recommend authoritative, rather than authoritarian, parenting. And, parental monitoring is important for all adolescents.

The progression begins with groups of same-sex friends. Next, a loose, public association of a girls' group and a boys' group forms. Then, a small, mixed-sex group forms from the more advanced members of the crowd. Finally, more intimate couples peel off.

28. affect; timing; manifestations; sequence; genetic
29. slow down
30. peers; romantic; parents; underestimate
31. less; gender; age
32. should; parent–child
33. varies; varies

The most effective sex-education programs (1) begin before high school, (2) include assignments that require parent–child communication, (3) focus on behavior (not just on conveying information), (4) provide medical referrals on request, and (5) last for years.

34. varies; decreasing; increased
35. decreased
36. **b.** is the answer. Girls are more likely to say they have a boyfriend than vice versa (a.). **c.** is not true; most teen romantic relationships last about a year. And, there's nothing to indicate that the daughter's boyfriend is a negative influence (d.). The relationship may actually be healthy for their daughter, so they shouldn't arbitrarily break it up.
37. often have
38. comorbidity
39. less
40. increases; females; rumination; females
41. suicidal ideation; common
42. less
43. cluster suicides
44. do not; parasuicide
45. **a.** the availability of guns
    b. lack of parental supervision
    c. use of alcohol and other drugs
    d. a culture that condones suicide
46. are
47. males; females
48. fallen; income; education
49. psychoanalytic
50. 18; juvenile delinquents; virtually all

Adolescent males are three times as likely to be arrested as females. Native Americans are arrested three times as often as African American youth, who are three times as likely to be arrested as European

Americans, who are three times as likely to be arrested as Asian Americans. However, self-reports find much smaller gender and ethnic differences.

51. relational

52. brain; contextual

Among the factors are short attention span, being the victim of severe child abuse, hyperactivity, inadequate emotional regulation, maternal cigarette smoking, slow language development, low intelligence, early and severe malnutrition, and autistic tendencies.

53. adolescent-limited; life-course-persistent

54. therapeutic foster care; foster

55. **d.** is the answer.

56. **c.** is the answer. Males are more likely to commit suicide, although parasuicide is more common among females. Suicide rates are higher in eastern Europe and Africa than in western Europe and South America, and in the western United States than in the eastern United States.

57. **b.** is the answer. Cluster suicides occur when the suicide of a local teen leads others to attempt suicide.

58. psychoactive

59. 10; 25; inhalant

60. down; boys; girls

61. abuse; addiction

62. growth

63. alcohol

64. memory; self-control; hippocampus; prefrontal cortex

65. generational forgetting

66. **c.** is the answer.

67. **a.** is the answer. Each health risk that an adolescent takes makes it more likely that he or she will take others.

PROGRESS TEST 1

Multiple-Choice Questions

1. **b.** is the answer. (p. 348)

a. According to Erikson, this is the crisis of infancy.

c. & d. In Erikson's theory, these crises occur later in life.

2. **a.** is the answer. (p. 348)

b. This describes an identity moratorium.

c. This describes an oppositional, negative identity.

d. This describes role confusion (identity diffusion).

3. **c.** is the answer. (p. 356)

4. **d.** is the answer. (p. 356)

5. **d.** is the answer. (pp. 352, 355)

6. **d.** is the answer. (p. 356)

a. A moratorium is a time-out during which adolescents experiment with different identities.

b. Foreclosure refers to the premature establishment of identity.

c. Peer screening is an aspect of parental monitoring, but it was not specifically discussed in the text.

7. **a.** is the answer. (p. 354)

8. **b.** is the answer. (p. 357)

9. **b.** is the answer. (p. 349)

10. **d.** is the answer. (p. 357)

11. **c.** is the answer. (p. 367)

12. **b.** is the answer. Foreclosed members of a religious group have, like Adam, never really doubted. (pp. 348, 349–350)

a. Because there is no evidence that Adam has asked the "hard questions" regarding his religious beliefs, a developmentalist would probably say that his religious identity is not achieved.

c. Adam clearly does have a religious identity.

d. There is no evidence that Adam's religious identity was formed in opposition to expectations.

13. **c.** is the answer. Life-course-persistent offenders tend to have low intelligence. (p. 371)

14. **b.** is the answer. (p. 368)

15. **c.** is the answer. (p. 354)

a. In fact, parent–child conflict is more likely to involve mothers and their daughters.

b. The text did not compare the rate of conflict in two-parent and single-parent homes.

True or False Items

1. T (p. 347)

2. F Parent–teen conflicts center on day-to-day details, not on politics or moral issues. (p. 354)

3. F The opposite is just as likely to be true. (p. 357)

4. T (p. 360)

5. T (p. 370)

6. F Researchers found no significant difference in rates of adolescent sex after abstinence-only sex education. (pp. 363–364)
7. T (p. 366)
8. T (p. 348)
9. F Just the opposite is true. (p. 366)
10. T (p. 368)

PROGRESS TEST 2

Multiple-Choice Questions

1. **d.** is the answer. (pp. 349–352)
2. **a.** is the answer. (p. 350)
3. **d.** is the answer. (p. 366)
4. **b.** is the answer. (p. 371)
5. **c.** is the answer. (p. 366)
6. **d.** is the answer. Homosexual men report that they become aware at age 11, but don't tell anyone until age 17. (p. 362)
7. **a.** is the answer. (p. 348)
   b. This describes an adolescent undergoing an identity moratorium.
   c. This describes identity foreclosure.
   d. This describes an adolescent who is adopting an oppositional, negative identity.
8. **a.** is the answer. (p. 350)
   b. This refers to sexual orientation.
   c. This refers to identity in general.
9. **b.** is the answer. (p. 370)
10. **c.** is the answer. (p. 370)
11. **d.** is the answer. (p. 349)
   a. Identity foreclosure occurs when the adolescent prematurely adopts an identity, without fully exploring alternatives.
   b. Adolescents who adopt an identity that is opposite to the one they are expected to develop have taken on a negative identity.
   c. Identity diffusion occurs when the adolescent is apathetic and has few commitments to goals or values.
12. **d.** is the answer. (p. 365)
13. **b.** is the answer. (p. 366)
14. **d.** is the answer. (p. 354)
   a., b., & c. In fact, on these issues parents and teenagers tend to show substantial *agreement.*
15. **c.** is the answer. (p. 366)

Matching Items

1. h (p. 348)	**5.** g (p. 349)	**9.** e (p. 367)
2. a (p. 348)	**6.** d (p. 357)	**10.** b (p. 367)
3. j (p. 350)	**7.** i (p. 357)	
4. c (p. 348)	**8.** f (p. 356)	

KEY TERMS

1. Erikson's term for the psychosocial crisis of adolescence, **identity versus role confusion,** refers to the adolescent's attempt to figure out "Who am I?" but is confused as to which of many possible roles to adopt. (p. 348)
2. **Identity** is a consistent definition of oneself in terms of roles, attitudes, beliefs, and aspirations. (p. 348)
3. In Erikson's theory, **identity achievement** occurs when adolescents attain their new identities by establishing their own goals and values and abandoning some of those set by their parents and culture and accepting others. (p. 348)
4. Adolescents who experience **role confusion,** according to Erikson, have few commitments to goals or values and are often apathetic about trying to find an identity; also called *identity diffusion.* (p. 348)
5. In **foreclosure,** according to Erikson, the adolescent forms an identity prematurely, accepting parents' or society's roles and values wholesale. (p. 348)
6. According to Erikson, in the process of finding a mature identity, many young people seem to declare an identity **moratorium,** a socially acceptable time-out during which they experiment with alternative identities without trying to settle on any one. (p. 349)
7. **Gender identity** is a person's self-identification of being female or male. (p. 350)
8. **Sexual orientation** refers to a person's sexual and romantic attraction toward a person of the other sex, the same sex, or both sexes. (p. 350)
9. **Bickering** refers to the repeated, petty arguing that typically occurs in early adolescence about common, daily life activities. (p. 354)
10. **Parental monitoring** is parental awareness about where their children are, what they are doing, and with whom. (p. 356)
11. A **clique** is a group of adolescents made up of close friends who are loyal to one another while excluding others. (p. 356)

12. A **crowd** is a larger group of adolescents who have something in common but who are not necessarily friends. (p. 356)
13. **Peer pressure** refers to the social pressure to conform with one's friends in behavior, dress, and attitude. It may be positive or negative in its effects. (p. 357)
14. **Deviancy training** is destructive peer pressure to rebel against authority or social norms. (p. 357)
15. **Clinical depression** describes the syndrome in which feelings of hopelessness, lethargy, and worthlessness last in a person for two weeks or longer. (p. 366)
16. **Rumination** is repeatedly thinking and talking about past experiences to the extent of contributing to depression. (p. 366)
17. **Suicidal ideation** refers to thinking about committing suicide, usually with some serious emotional and intellectual or cognitive overtones. (p. 366)
18. A **cluster suicide** refers to a series of suicides that are precipitated by one initial suicide and that occur in the same community, school, or time period. (p. 367)
19. **Parasuicide** is a deliberate act of self-destruction that does not result in death. (p. 367)
20. A **juvenile delinquent** is a person under 18 years of age who breaks the law. (p. 370)
21. **Life-course-persistent offenders** are adolescent lawbreakers who later become career criminals. (p. 371)
22. **Adolescent-limited offenders** are juvenile delinquents whose criminal activity stops by age 21. (p. 372)
23. **Generational forgetting** is the tendency of each new generation to forget what previous generations have learned. (p. 377)

11

chapter

EMERGING ADULTHOOD

Body, Mind, and Social World

Chapter Overview

In this chapter we encounter the developing person in the prime of life. During emerging adulthood overall health is good and fertility is high.

The chapter begins with a description of the growth, strength, and health of the individual during emerging adulthood, as well as changes in the efficiency of the body's systems. Sexual-reproductive health, a matter of great concern to young adults, is also discussed, with particular attention paid to trends in sexual responsiveness and sexually transmitted infections. Another risky behavior, drug user, is also explored. The section concludes with a discussion of how social norms can reduce the risk taking involved in drug use and abuse and violence and improve health habits in this age group.

During the course of adulthood, there are many shifts in cognitive development. The second section of the chapter describes how adult thinking differs from adolescent thinking. The experiences and challenges of adulthood result in a new, more practical and flexible thinking. This part of the chapter also examines the effect of the college experience on cognitive growth. Findings here indicate that years of education correlate with virtually every measure of cognition as thinking becomes progressively more flexible and tolerant.

The next section is concerned with personality development. During emerging adulthood, both positive and negative emotions are strong. The stresses of this period of life combine with genetic vulnerability in some individuals to trigger the development of mood disorders, anxiety disorders, or schizophrenia.

Next, the chapter discusses the two basic identity statuses of adulthood: ethnic identity and vocational identity. Ethnic identity is difficult to achieve for children of immigrants trying to reconcile their parents' background with their new social context. College education is an important stimulus for the development of vocational identity for many emerging adults. Because finding an identity now takes longer, intimacy needs have been interspersed with identity needs. The discussion of intimacy in adulthood focuses on the development of friendship, love, and marriage.

NOTE: Answer guidelines for all Chapter 11 questions begin on page 185.

Chapter Review

When you have finished reading the chapter, work through the material that follows to review it. Complete the sentences and answer the questions. As you proceed, evaluate your performance for each section by consulting the answers beginning on page 185. Do not continue with the next section until you understand each answer. If you need to, review or reread the appropriate section in the textbook before continuing.

1. The new stage called ________________ ________________ (also called ________________ ________________ or ________________), spans the years between 18 and 25 and is distinguished by later ________________ and ________________.

Cultural and National Differences (pp. 386–396)

2. Emerging adulthood ________________ (is/is not) a separate stage among all economic, ethnic, and national groups. Three macrosystems that contributed to this new stage of development are ________________, ________________, and ________________.

3. Girls usually reach their maximum height by age ________________, and boys by age ________________.

4. Growth in ________________ and increases in ________________ continue into the 20s.

5. For most adults, serious illness is not common until ________________ ________________. Advances in ________________, ________________, ________________, and ________________ ________________ make emerging adulthood the healthiest stage of development.

6. Every body system functions optimally at the beginning of ________________. This is true of the ________________, ________________, ________________, and ________________-________________ systems.

7. Many diagnostic tests, including ________________, ________________, and ________________ are not recommended until age 40 or 50.

8. Many of the body's functions serve to maintain ________________; that is, they keep physiological functioning in a state of balance. Many of these mechanisms are regulated by the ________________ gland via shifts in ________________ levels.

9. For body weight, there is a homeostatic ________________ ________________ that is affected by ________________, ________________, ________________, ________________, and ________________.

10. The older a person is, the ________________ (less time/longer) it takes for these adjustments to occur. This is one reason emerging adults are less likely to ________________ ________________ than older adults.

THINK ABOUT IT: Emerging adults seem inclined to risk their health and safety. To underscore this point, make a list of your own good and bad health habits. For each bad habit, explain the risks in persisting in the habit—for example, overeating may result in obesity, which increases the risk of many chronic illnesses. Then consider ways in which your culture supports and even promotes bad health habits. Finally, do the same for your good habits, such as regular exercise.

Briefly describe sexual activity and the health of the sexual-reproductive system in emerging adulthood.

11. Centuries ago, ________________ (large/small) families were essential for survival of the species. Advances in ________________ ________________ during the twentieth century contributed to the dramatic decrease in ________________ mortality and the resulting global population explosion.

12. Today, the birth rate is much ________________ (higher/lower) than in the past, and ________________ (higher/lower) than the ________________ rate.

13. Smaller families have children who are ________________, who have more ________________, and who live ________________ lives.

14. Most emerging adults today ________________ (condone/do not condone) premarital sex. Most sexually active adults have ________________ (one steady partner/multiple partners) at a time. This pattern of sexual activity is called ________________ ________________.

15. One consequence of sexual patterns among today's young adults is that the incidence of ________________ ________________ ________________ is higher today than ever before. ________________ (Men/Women/Both sexes) are transmitters, or ________________ of STIs.

16. Many emerging adults are attracted to recreational activities and occupations that include ________________, defined as

_______________. Other manifestations of the risk-taking impulse are competitive _______ _______, such as motocross.

17. Drug abuse is defined as using a drug in a manner that is _______________ _______________. When the absence of a drug in a person's system causes physiological or psychological craving, _______ _______ is apparent. When people who have been taking a drug for a long time suddenly stop, they are likely to exhibit _______ symptoms. Drug abuse is likely to be elicited by _______ itself or by the _______ _______.

18. The three leading causes of death from age 15 to 35 are _______, _______, and _______. Worldwide, young men are far more likely than women to die a _______ _______.

Briefly explain the social norms approach to reducing risky behavior.

THINK ABOUT IT: Many young adults are drawn to edgework—recreational and career activities that entail an element of risk and even danger. What activities do you engage in, or aspire to professionally, that could be characterized as edgework? Why are such activities often associated with emerging adulthood?

APPLICATIONS:

19. When we are hot, we perspire in order to give off body heat. This is an example of the way our body functions maintain
    a. diathesis.
    b. homeostasis.
    c. set point.
    d. dynamic systems.

20. Janine has decided to write her term paper on the brain's regulation of homeostatic processes. Her research should focus on the
    a. cortex.
    b. hippocampus.
    c. amygdala.
    d. pituitary.

21. Summarizing her presentation on sexual attitudes among emerging adults, Carla notes that most
    a. believe that physical relationships need not involve emotional connections.
    b. condone premarital sex.
    c. no longer believe that marriage is a desirable commitment.
    d. believe the primary purpose of sex is reproduction.

22. Elderly Mr. Wilson believes that young adults today have too many sexual partners. Fueling his belief is the fact that
    a. sexually transmitted infections were almost unknown in his day.
    b. half of all emerging adults in the United States have had at least one sexually transmitted infection.
    c. most sexually active adults have several partners at a time.
    d. all of these statements are true.

23. Michael is a college freshman who enjoys weekend "booze parties." He has just learned that a survey regarding drinking on campus found that most of his classmates avoid binge drinking. Michael is most likely to
    a. continue drinking on the weekends.
    b. follow this social norm.
    c. increase his drinking to prove he's not like everyone else.
    d. become more secretive about his drinking.

24. Responding to a question from a reporter, one of the authors of the CARDIA study notes that a key finding of the study was that
    a. the least fit participants were four times more likely to develop diabetes and high blood pressure.
    b. half of those who were obese as children became normal-weight young adults.
    c. young adults eat more fast food than those of other ages.
    d. people who weigh the least have shorter life expectancies.

Cognitive Maturity (pp. 396–404)

25. During emerging adulthood, ________________ thinking and ________________ thinking gradually become better aligned. In addition, young adults become capable of ________________, or thinking of things in relation to one another.

26. Thinking during emerging adulthood becomes ________________ (more/less) flexible and distinguished by the ability to combine ________________ thought and ________________ thought.

27. When the mere possibility of being negatively stereotyped arouses anxiety and disrupts cognition, ________________ ________________ has occurred.

28. Strong ________________ with one's group is healthier than ________________ (refusing to identify with the group) or ________________ (identifying with stereotypes about one's group).

29. (text and A View From Science) Stereotype threat affects people from ________________ (many groups/only certain ethnic groups and women). Research studies have shown that intellectual performance among students increases if they ________________ the concept that intelligence is plastic and can be changed.

30. Some researchers believe that some ________________ encourage flexible reasoning more than others. According to this view, ancient ________________ philosophy has led Europeans to use analytic ________________ ________________, whereas ________________ and ________________ have led Asians to seek ________________.

31. Compared with other adults, college graduates tend to be ________________ and ________________. In terms of health behaviors, college graduates smoke ________________ (more/less), eat ________________ (better/worse), exercise ________________ (more/less), and live ________________ (longer/shorter).

Briefly outline the year-by-year progression in how the thinking of college students becomes more flexible and tolerant.

32. William Perry found that the thinking of students over the course of their college careers progressed through ________________ levels of complexity.

33. Worldwide, the number of students who receive higher education ________________ (has increased/has not increased) since the first half of the twentieth century.

34. Collegiate populations have become ________________ (more/less) diverse in recent years. College majors also are changing, with fewer students concentrating on the ________________ ________________ and more on ________________ and the ________________.

THINK ABOUT IT: Many different kinds of problems arise in daily life. Based on your own experiences, or those of a typical college student, give an example of a problem that is likely to benefit from the cognitive flexibility and maturity that occurs during emerging adulthood.

APPLICATIONS:

35. Research suggests that a college sophomore or junior is most likely to have reached a phase in which he or she

- **a.** believes that there are clear and perfect truths to be discovered.
- **b.** questions personal and social values, and even the idea of truth itself.
- **c.** rejects opposing ideas in the interest of finding one right answer.
- **d.** accepts a simplistic either/or dualism.

36. (Table 11.3) In his scheme of cognitive and ethical development, Perry describes a position in which the college student says, "I see I'm going to have to make my own decisions in an uncertain world with no one to tell me I'm right." This position marks the culmination of a phase of
    a. either/or dualism.
    b. modified dualism.
    c. relativism.
    d. commitments in relativism.

37. Which of the following is an example of responding to a stereotype threat?
    a. Because Jessie's older sister teases her for not being as good as she is at math, Jessie protects her self-concept by devaluing math.
    b. Feeling angered that others may think him less capable because of his ethnicity, Liam becomes flustered when trying to solve a problem in front of the class.
    c. Dave writes a scathing criticism of an obviously racist comment made by a local politician.
    d. As an older adult, Kathy takes pride in displaying her quick wit and intelligence to others.

38. Who would be the most likely to agree with the statement, "College can be a powerful stimulus to cognitive growth"?
    a. Sternberg
    b. Piaget
    c. Erikson
    d. Perry

39. In concluding her presentation on "The College Student of Today," Coretta states that:
    a. "The number of students in higher education has increased significantly in virtually every country worldwide."
    b. "There are more low-income and ethnic-minority students in college today than ever before."
    c. "There are more women and minority instructors than ever before."
    d. all of these statements are true.

40. (A View from Science) Research demonstrates that stereotype threat can be reduced by
    a. creating educational environments among students who have gender in common.
    b. creating educational environments among students who have race in common.
    c. interventions that help students internalize the concept that intelligence can change.
    d. educational programs that sensitize male ethnic-majority students to the impact of gender and ethnic stereotypes on other students.

Personality Patterns (pp. 404–408)

41. Personality ________________ (is/is not) fixed by early adulthood. Psychological research on the personality traits of ________________ from ages 17 to 24 finds evidence of genetic ________________ and developmental ________________.

42. Average well-being ________________ (increases/decreases) in emerging adulthood. Two circumstances that reduce happiness are ________________ ________________ and ________________.

43. According to the ________________-________________ model, disorders such as schizophrenia are produced by the interaction of ________________ with ________________, or an underlying genetic vulnerability.

44. Before age 30, approximately ________________ percent of U.S. residents suffer from a mood disorder, such as ________________ ________________, which is defined as the loss of interest in nearly all activities lasting for ________________ (how long?) or more.

45. Another major problem is ________________ disorders, which are suffered by ________________ (what proportion) of young adults in the United States. These disorders include ________________-________________ ________________ ________________, ________________-________________ ________________, ________________ ________________, and ________________ ________________.

46. Anxiety disorders are affected by age and ________________ context. A common anxiety disorder that keeps some young adults away from college is ________________ ________________. In Japan, a new disorder called *hikikomori* is related to anxiety about the ________________ and ________________ pressures of high school and college.

47. Schizophrenia is experienced by about _______________ percent of all adults. This disorder is partly the result of _______________, and partly the result of vulnerabilities such as _______________ at birth, _______________ when the brain is developing, and extensive _______________ pressure. Symptoms of this disorder typically begin in _______________.

APPLICATIONS:

48. Professor Ryan begins class by asking, "Which disorder is a leading cause of impairment and premature death worldwide?" The correct answer is
- **a.** post-traumatic stress disorder.
- **b.** obsessive-compulsive disorder.
- **c.** schizophrenia.
- **d.** depression.

49. Twenty-three-year-old Yoko's anxiety about college has caused her to withdraw from most activities and stay in her room almost all the time. Yoko's problem would likely be diagnosed as
- **a.** depression.
- **b.** hikikomori.
- **c.** a phobia.
- **d.** obsessive-compulsive disorder.

50. Which of the following would be the WORST advice for a young adult entering the job market today?
- **a.** Seek education that fosters a variety of general abilities and human relations skills.
- **b.** Expect that educational requirements for work will shift every few years.
- **c.** To avoid diluting your skills, concentrate your education on preparing for one specific job.
- **d.** Be flexible and willing to adjust to the varied pacing and timing of today's jobs.

Identity and Intimacy (pp. 408–416)

51. Most developmentalists once believed that identity was usually achieved _______________ (before/after) adulthood. Today, they believe the identity crisis has been _______________ (shortened/lengthened).

52. Of the four identities, two that seem nearly impossible to achieve during adolescence are _______________ and _______________.

53. In the United States and Canada, about _______________ (what proportion?) of emerging adults are either children of immigrants or native-born adults of African, Asian, Indian, or Latino descent. Most of them _______________ (identify/do not identify) with specific ethnic groups.

54. Identity achievement _______________ (is/is not) particularly difficult for immigrants. Briefly explain why this is so. _______________
____

55. For many emerging adults, attending college is an important step toward achieving _______________ identity.

56. The correlation between college education and income is _______________ (weaker/stronger) today than in the past. This is because there are fewer _______________ jobs and more _______________-_______________ jobs.

57. In Erikson's theory, the identity crisis of adolescence is followed in emerging adulthood by the crisis of _______________ _______________ _______________.

58. As a buffer against stress, as trustworthy confidants, and reliable sources of support, _______________ are particularly important.

59. Traditionally, gender differences in friendship _______________ (were/were not) especially apparent during adulthood. In general, men's friendships were based on _______________ _______________ and _______________, whereas friendships between women tended to be more _______________ and _______________.

60. Cross-sex friendships are _______________ (more/less) common today than in the past.

61. Robert Sternberg has argued that love has three distinct components: _______________, _______________, and _______________.

62. Sternberg believes that the relative absence or presence of these components gives rise to _______________ (how many?) different forms of love.

63. Children ________________ (do/do not) add stress to a relationship but also make separation ________________ (more/less) likely.

64. When commitment is added to passion and intimacy, the result is ________________ love.

65. With time, ________________ tends to fade, ________________ may grow, and ________________ may develop.

66. The power of the social context helps to explain why few arranged marriages, which begin with ________________, end.

67. Sexual encounters without emotional commitment are called ________________. The desire for physical intimacy without emotional commitment may be stronger in ________________ (men/women), perhaps because of ________________ differences and ________________ beliefs.

68. Increasingly common among young adults in many countries is the living pattern called ________________, in which two unrelated adults live together in a committed romantic relationship.

69. Cohabitation ________________ (does/does not) seem to benefit the participants. Cohabitants tend to be ________________ (more/less) likely to end their relationship than married couples. Research also demonstrates that ________________ ________________ and ________________ ________________ are more common among cohabitants than among married couples.

70. Members of families have ________________ lives, meaning that experiences and needs of members at one stage are affected by those at other stages. Although emerging adults strive for independence, family support in the form of ________________ aid and gifts of time are important. Family dependence ________________ (varies/does not vary) between Western nations and developing nations.

THINK ABOUT IT: Do the characterizations of adult development offered by Erikson and other emerging adulthood theorists seem to apply to you at this particular time in your life? Why or why not?

APPLICATIONS:

71. Rwanda and Rodney have been dating for about a month. Their relationship is most likely characterized by
    a. strong feelings of commitment.
    b. consummate love.
    c. physical intimacy and feelings of closeness.
    d. all of these feelings.

72. I am 25 years old. It is most likely that I
    a. am married.
    b. am divorced.
    c. have never been married.
    d. am divorced and remarried.

73. If asked to explain the high failure rate of marriages between young adults, Erik Erikson would most likely say that
    a. achievement goals are often more important than intimacy in emerging adulthood.
    b. intimacy is difficult to establish until identity is formed.
    c. divorce has almost become an expected stage in development.
    d. today's cohort of young adults has higher expectations of marriage than did previous cohorts.

74. Arthur and Mabel have been married for 5 years. According to Sternberg, if their relationship is a satisfying one, which of the following best describes their relationship?
    a. They are strongly committed to each other.
    b. They are passionately in love.
    c. They are in the throes of establishing intimacy.
    d. They are beginning to wonder why the passion has left their relationship.

Progress Test 1

Multiple-Choice Questions

Circle your answers to the following questions and check them with the answers on page 187. If your answer is incorrect, read the explanation for why it is incorrect and then consult the appropriate pages of the text (in parentheses following the correct answer).

1. A difference between men and women during emerging adulthood is that men have
    a. a higher percentage of body fat.
    b. lower metabolism.
    c. proportionately more muscle.
    d. greater homeostasis.

2. The majority of young adults rate their own health as
   a. very good or excellent.
   b. average or fair.
   c. poor.
   d. worse than it was during adolescence.

3. The automatic adjustment of the body's systems to keep physiological functions in a state of equilibrium, even during heavy exertion, is called
   a. dynamic systems.
   b. homeostasis.
   c. stress.
   d. muscle capacity.

4. During emerging adulthood
   a. age signifies cognitive norms and abilities.
   b. age is a more imperfect guide to development than it was during childhood.
   c. social roles become more rigidly determined.
   d. cohort has little effect on behavior.

5. Compared with earlier generations, emerging adults today tend to
   a. marry later and prolong financial dependence on parents.
   b. marry later and be financially independent sooner.
   c. marry earlier and prolong financial dependence on parents.
   d. marry earlier and be financially independent sooner.

6. Which of the following is true of every body system?
   a. They all function optimally at the beginning of adulthood.
   b. They all begin to decline at the beginning of adulthood.
   c. They all undergo dramatic changes.
   d. They all begin to show the effects of early lifestyle choices.

7. Diagnostic tests such as mammograms and colonoscopy are not recommended until after age
   a. 25 or 30.
   b. 30 or 40.
   c. 40 or 50.
   d. 50 or 60.

8. Which of the following was NOT suggested as a reason for the high rate of drug use and abuse in emerging adulthood?
   a. Young adults overestimate how many of their peers use drugs.
   b. Young adults are trying to imitate their parents' behavior.
   c. Young adults may use drugs as a way of reducing anxiety.
   d. Young adults often fear social rejection.

9. Which of the following adjectives best describe(s) cognitive development during adulthood?
   a. multidirectional and dynamic
   b. linear
   c. steady
   d. tumultuous

10. Which of the following is true about college students today?
   a. More girls than boys attend college.
   b. They are more career oriented.
   c. They are more diverse.
   d. They have all of these characteristics.

11. According to Erik Erikson, the first basic task of adulthood is to establish
   a. a residence apart from parents.
   b. intimacy with others.
   c. generativity through work or parenthood.
   d. a career commitment.

12. The search for identity begins at puberty but it:
   a. takes longer to achieve than in the past.
   b. is usually achieved during adolescence.
   c. is harder for women to achieve than for men.
   d. is no longer a useful concept in developmental science.

13. Which of the following is true of emerging adults who are children of immigrants or native-born adults of African, Asian, Indian, or Latino descent?
   a. Their ethnic pride generally correlates with social adjustment.
   b. Their ethnic identity does not change throughout the life span.
   c. They easily reconcile their parents' background with their new social context.
   d. They tend to identify with very specific ethnic groups.

14. Of the four identities, which now seem almost impossible to achieve during adolescence?
   a. gender and political
   b. ethnic and vocational
   c. religious and ethnic
   d. gender and vocational

15. According to Erikson, the failure to achieve intimacy during emerging adulthood is most likely to result in
    a. generativity.
    b. stagnation.
    c. role diffusion.
    d. isolation.

16. Which of the following statements best characterizes today's job market?
    a. There are more unskilled jobs than in the past.
    b. There are more knowledge-based jobs than in the past.
    c. There are fewer jobs today than in the past.
    d. There are more jobs today than in the past.

17. According to Robert Sternberg, consummate love emerges
    a. as a direct response to passion.
    b. as a direct response to physical intimacy.
    c. when commitment is added to passion and intimacy.
    d. during the early years of parenthood.

True or False Items

Write T (*true*) or F (*false*) on the line in front of each statement.

_______ 1. The male body has a higher proportion of muscle than the female body.

_______ 2. Extreme sports such as motocross have existed since the 1950s.

_______ 3. Heavy drinking and illicit drug use increase during emerging adulthood.

_______ 4. The male/female ratio for violent deaths is about the same throughout the world.

_______ 5. Most sexually active young adults have several sexual partners at a time.

_______ 6. Colleges today do not help make students more mature, flexible thinkers.

_______ 7. Female and African American college students typically perform better when they attend schools where almost everyone is from their group.

_______ 8. (A View From Science) Students who internalize that intelligence is plastic are less likely to experience stereotype threat.

_______ 9. There is a positive correlation between college education and income.

_______ 10. According to Erikson, the emerging adult experiences a crisis of intimacy versus isolation after achieving identity.

_______ 11. According to Sternberg, early in a relationship, companionate love is at its highest.

_______ 12. Cross-sex friendships are rarer today than in the past.

_______ 13. Cohabitation solves all the problems that might arise after marriage.

Progress Test 2

Progress Test 2 should be completed during a final chapter review. Answer the following questions after you thoroughly understand the correct answers for the Chapter Review and Progress Test 1.

Multiple-Choice Questions

1. Serial monogamy refers to the practice among sexually active adults of
    a. having more than one partner at a time.
    b. having one steady partner at a time.
    c. engaging in premarital sex.
    d. engaging in extramarital sex.

2. During emerging adulthood, people follow patterns of development and behavior that vary by
    a. age.
    b. culture.
    c. cohort.
    d. all of these factors.

3. During emerging adulthood, many age differences in behavior and development
    a. result more from social factors than biological ones.
    b. result more from biological factors than social ones.
    c. are unpredictable.
    d. reflect developmental patterns that were established early in childhood.

4. The social norms approach refers to
    a. the particular settings of an individual's various homeostatic processes.
    b. an approach to prevention that increases young adults' awareness of social norms for risky behaviors.
    c. the technique for advancing flexible thinking in the young adult.
    d. the average age at which certain behaviors and events occur.

5. Relative to all other age groups, young adult males are at increased risk for virtually every kind of
   a. eating disorder.
   b. violence.
   c. acute disease.
   d. chronic disease.

6. Occupations or activities that require a degree of risk or danger are referred to as
   a. diathesis.
   b. edgework.
   c. homeostasis.
   d. addiction.

7. A classic study by Perry showed that the thinking of students in college progresses through how many levels of complexity?
   a. 6
   b. 9
   c. 12
   d. 15

8. The Western ideal of love is best described in Sternberg's theory as
   a. romantic.
   b. fatuous.
   c. companionate.
   d. consummate.

9. Traditionally, whereas men's friendships tended to be based on ________, friendships between women tended to be based on __________.
   a. shared confidences; shared interests
   b. cooperation; competition
   c. shared interests; shared confidences
   d. finding support for personal problems; discussion of practical issues

10. According to Robert Sternberg, the three dimensions of love are
    a. passion, intimacy, and consummate love.
    b. physical intimacy, emotional intimacy, and consummate love.
    c. passion, commitment, and consummate love.
    d. passion, intimacy, and commitment.

11. Research on cohabitation suggests that
    a. domestic violence is less likely to occur among cohabiting young adults.
    b. most merging adults in the United States, England, and northern Europe cohabit before age 25.
    c. adults who cohabit tend to be older and wealthier than married people.
    d. cohabitation leads to a stronger marriage.

12. Today, male–female relationships
    a. are more common than in the past.
    b. are not usually preludes to romance.
    c. can last a lifetime.
    d. have all of these characteristics.

13. The idea that psychopathology is the consequence of the interaction of a genetic vulnerability with challenging life events is expressed in the
    a. social norms approach.
    b. diathesis–stress model.
    c. homeostasis theory.
    d. social construction theory.

14. A loss of interest or pleasure in most activities that lasts for two weeks or more is likely to be diagnosed as
    a. social phobia.
    b. anxiety disorder.
    c. obsessive-compulsive disorder.
    d. major depression.

15. The disorder characterized by disorganized thoughts, delusions, and hallucinations is
    a. post-traumatic stress disorder
    b. anxiety disorder.
    c. schizophrenia.
    d. obsessive-compulsive disorder.

16. An arrangement in which two unrelated, unmarried adults live together in a romantic partnership is called
    a. cross-sex friendship.
    b. a passive-congenial pattern.
    c. cohabitation.
    d. affiliation.

17. Compared with adolescent thinking, adult thinking tends to
    a. be more flexible.
    b. be more practical.
    c. combine subjective and objective thinking.
    d. have all of these characteristics.

18. A hallmark of mature adult thought is
    a. dysregulated thinking.
    b. the reconciliation of both objective and subjective approaches to real-life problems.
    c. the adoption of purely logical thought.
    d. all of these abilities.

Matching Items

Match each definition or description with its corresponding term.

Terms

_______ 1. diathesis-stress
_______ 2. homeostasis
_______ 3. cohabitaton
_______ 4. set point
_______ 5. edgework
_______ 6. drug abuse
_______ 7. emerging adulthood
_______ 8. drug addiction
_______ 9. replacement rate
_______ 10. stereotype threat
_______ 11. extreme sports

Definitions or Descriptions

a. using a drug to the extent of impairing one's well-being
b. an occupation that requires a degree of risk
c. recreation that includes apparent risk of injury or death
d. view that disorders are caused by the interaction of a genetic vulnerability with stressful life events
e. a state of physiological equilibrium
f. arrangement in which two unrelated, unmarried adults live together in a committed romantic relationship
g. the period between the ages of 18 and 25
h. number of births per woman required to maintain a stable population
i. one's behavior is misused to confirm another person's prejudiced attitude
j. the body weight that a person's homeostatic processes strive to maintain
k. a condition in which the absence of a drug triggers withdrawal symptoms

Key Terms

Using your own words, write a brief definition or explanation of each of the following terms on a separate piece of paper.

1. emerging adulthood
2. homeostasis
3. replacement rate
4. edgework
5. extreme sports
6. drug abuse
7. drug addiction
8. social norms approach
9. stereotype threat
10. diathesis-stress model
11. cohabit

Answers

CHAPTER REVIEW

1. emerging adulthood; young adulthood; youth; marriage; parenthood
2. is; globalization; technology; medicine
3. 16; 18
4. muscle; fat
5. middle age; immunization; clean water; food distribution
6. adulthood; digestive; respiratory; circulatory; sexual-reproductive
7. PSA; mammograms; colonoscopy
8. homeostasis; pituitary; hormone
9. set point; genes; diet; age; hormones; exercise
10. longer; get sick, fatigued, or obese

The sexual-reproductive system is at its strongest during emerging adulthood. Young adults have a strong sex drive, infertility is rare, birth is easy, and orgasm is more frequent.

11. large; public health; infant
12. lower; lower; replacement
13. healthier; education; longer
14. condone; one steady partner; serial monogamy
15. sexually transmitted infections (STIs); Both sexes; vectors

16. edgework; occupations and recreational activities that entail a degree of risk or danger; extreme sports
17. harmful to the user's physical, cognitive, or psychosocial well-being; drug addiction; withdrawal; college; youth culture
18. accidents; homicides; suicides; violent death

The social norms approach uses survey responses to make emerging adults more aware of actual social norms for risky behaviors.

19. **b.** is the answer.

    a. Diathesis refers to genetic vulnerability.

    c. This refers to the weight that an individual's homeostatic processes strive to maintain.

    d. Dynamic systems refers to the fact that the body systems interact and each is affected by the others.
20. **d.** is the answer.
21. **b.** is the answer.

    a. & c. Most emerging adults believe that sexual activity should involve an emotional connection and that marriage is a desirable commitment.

    d. Most believe that the primary purpose of sex is to strengthen pair bonding.
22. **b.** is the answer.

    a. STIs have been part of life since the beginning of time.

    c. Most sexually active adults have one steady partner at a time.
23. b. is the answer.
24. a. is the answer.
25. logical; intuitive; relativizing
26. more; subjective; objective
27. stereotype threat
28. identification; disidentification; counter-identification
29. many groups; internalize
30. cultures; absolutist logic; Confucianism; Taoism; compromise
31. healthier; wealthier; less; better; more; longer

First-year students often believe that there are clear and perfect truths to be found. This phase is followed by a wholesale questioning of personal and social values. Finally, after considering opposite ideas, students become committed to certain values, at the same time realizing their opinions might change.

32. nine
33. has increased
34. more; liberal arts; business; professions
35. **b.** is the answer.

    a. First-year college students are more likely to believe this is so.

    c. & d. Over the course of their college careers, students become *less* likely to do either of these.
36. **c.** is the answer.
37. **b.** is the answer.
38. **d.** is the answer.
39. **d.** is the answer.
40. **c.** is the answer.
41. is not; twins; continuity; improvement
42. increases; single parenthood; living with one's parents
43. diathesis-stress; stress; diathesis
44. 15; major depression; two weeks
45. anxiety; one-fourth; post-traumatic stress disorder; obsessive-compulsive disorder; panic attacks; eating disorders
46. cultural; social phobia; social; academic
47. 1; genes; anoxia; malnutrition; social; adolescence
48. **d.** is the answer.
49. **b.** is the answer.
50. **c.** is the answer.

    a., b., & d. These would all be good pieces of advice for new workers today.
51. before; lengthened
52. ethnic; vocational
53. half; identify
54. is; Achieving identity is difficult for immigrants because it means reconciling their parents' background with their new social context.
55. vocational
56. stronger; unskilled; knowledge-based
57. intimacy versus isolation
58. friends
59. were; shared activities; interests; intimate; emotional
60. more
61. passion; intimacy; commitment
62. seven
63. do; less
64. consummate
65. passion; intimacy; commitment
66. commitment
67. hook-ups; men; hormonal; cultural

68. cohabitation
69. does not; more; domestic violence; excessive drinking
70. linked; financial; varies
71. **c.** is the answer.
    a. & b. These feelings emerge more gradually in relationships.
72. **c.** is the answer.
73. **b.** is the answer.
    a. In Erikson's theory, the crisis of intimacy *precedes* the need to be productive through work.
    c. & d. Although these items are true, Erikson's theory does not address these issues.
74. **a.** is the answer.

PROGRESS TEST 1

Multiple-Choice Questions

1. **c.** is the answer. (p. 386)
   a. This is true of women.
   b. This was not discussed but it is true of women.
   d. Men and women do not differ in this characteristic.
2. **a.** is the answer. (p. 387)
3. **b.** is the answer. (p. 388)
   a. This refers to the interaction of the body's systems and their effect on one another.
   c. Stress, which is not defined but is discussed in this chapter, refers to events or situations that tax the body's resources.
   d. This simply refers to a muscle's potential for work.
4. **b.** is the answer. (p. 383)
   c. & d. Just the opposite are true.
5. **a.** is the answer. (p. 386)
6. **a.** is the answer. (p. 387)
   d. These effects generally do not appear until later in life. Moreover, it is not until early adulthood that most individuals begin making such choices.
7. **c.** is the answer. (p. 387)
8. **b.** is the answer. In fact, just the opposite is true. Young adults may use drugs to express independence from their parents. (pp. 392, 395)
9. **a.** is the answer. (pp. 396–397)
   b. & c. Comparatively speaking, linear and steady are *more* descriptive of childhood and adolescent cognitive development.
10. **d.** is the answer. (p. 403)
11. **b.** is the answer. (p. 411)
12. **a.** is the answer. (p. 408)
    c. Identity formation is equally challenging for women and men.
13. **d.** is the answer. (p. 409)
14. **b.** is the answer. (p. 409)
15. **d.** is the answer. (p. 411)
    a. Generativity is a characteristic of the crisis following the intimacy crisis.
    b. Stagnation occurs when generativity needs are not met.
    c. Erikson's theory does not address this issue.
16. **b.** is the answer. (p. 410)
17. **c.** is the answer. (p. 413)
    d. Sternberg's theory is not concerned with the stages of parenthood.

True or False Items

1. T (p. 386)
2. F Extreme sports did not exist before emerging adulthood was identified in the 1990s. (p. 392)
3. T (p. 392)
4. F This ratio varies from country to country. (p. 394)
5. F Most sexually active adults have one steady partner at a time. (p. 391)
6. F Just the opposite is true. (p. 403)
7. T (p. 399)
8. T (p. 399)
9. T (p. 401)
10. T (p. 411)
11. F This comes only with time. (p. 412)
12. F Just the reverse is true. (p. 412)
13. F Cohabitation does *not* solve the problems of marriage. (p. 414)

PROGRESS TEST 2

Multiple-Choice Questions

1. **b.** is the answer. (p. 391)
2. **d.** is the answer. (p. 386)
3. **a.** is the answer. (p. 386)

4. **b.** is the answer. (p. 395)
5. **b.** is the answer. (p. 393)

   a. Eating disorders are more common in women than men.

   c. & d. Disease is relatively rare at this age.
6. **b.** is the answer. (p. 391)
7. **b.** is the answer. (p. 402)
8. **d.** is the answer. (p. 413)
9. **c.** is the answer. (p. 412)
10. **d.** is the answer. (p. 412)

    a., b., & c. According to Sternberg, consummate love emerges when commitment is added to passion and intimacy.
11. **b.** is the answer. (p. 414)

    a. Just the opposite is true.

    c. No such finding was reported in the text.

    d. Divorce is common among cohabiting adults.
12. **a.** is the answer. (p. 412)
13. **b.** is the answer. (p. 406)
14. **d.** is the answer. (p. 406)

    a. Social phobia is a fear of talking to people.

    b. Anxiety disorders include phobias and obsessive-compulsive disorder; the person does not necessarily lose interest in most activities.

    c. Obsessive-compulsive disorder is an anxiety disorder.
15. **c.** is the answer. (p. 407)

    a., b., & d. Post-traumatic stress disorder and obsessive-compulsive disorder are types of anxiety disorders. They do not involve disorganized thoughts, delusions, or hallucinations.
16. **c.** is the answer. (p. 414)
17. **d.** is the answer (p. 396)
18. **b.** is the answer. (pp. 396–397)

Matching Items

1. d (p. 406)	**5.** b (p. 391)	**9.** h (p. 389)
2. e (p. 388)	**6.** a (p. 392)	**10.** i (p. 398)
3. f (p. 414)	**7.** g (p. 385)	**11.** c (p. 392)
4. j (p. 388)	**8.** k (p. 392)	

KEY TERMS

1. Now thought of as a separate stage of development, **emerging adulthood** is the period between the ages of 18 and 25. (p. 385)
2. **Homeostasis** refers to the process by which body functions are automatically adjusted to keep our physiological functioning in a state of equilibrium. (p. 388)
3. The **replacement rate** is the number of births per woman required to maintain a stable population. (p. 389)
4. **Edgework** refers to recreational activities and jobs that entail some risk or danger. (p. 391)
5. **Extreme sports** are forms of recreation that include apparent risk of injury or death and are attractive and thrilling as a result. (p. 392)
6. **Drug abuse** is drug use to the extent of impairing the user's physical or psychological health. (p. 392)
7. **Drug addiction** is evident in a person when the absence of a drug in his or her body produces the drive to ingest more of the drug. (p. 392)
8. The **social norms approach** to reducing risky behaviors uses survey data regarding the prevalence of risky behaviors to make emerging adults more aware of social norms. (p. 395)
9. **Stereotype threat** is the possibility that one's behavior may be judged negatively to confirm another person's prejudiced attitude. (p. 398)
10. The **diathesis–stress model** is the view that mental disorders are caused by the interaction of a genetic vulnerability with stressful life events. (p. 406)
11. Increasingly common among young adults in all industrialized countries is the living pattern called **cohabitation**, in which two unrelated, unmarried adults live together in a committed romantic relationship. (p. 414)

12 chapter

ADULTHOOD

Body and Mind

Chapter Overview

This chapter deals with biosocial and cognitive development during the years from 25 to 65. The first section describes changes in appearance and in the functioning of the sense organs, noting the potential impact of these changes. This section also discusses the changes in the sexual-reproductive system that occur during middle adulthood. The next section discusses the health habits of adults, focusing on smoking, drinking, exercise, and gaining weight. The third section discusses the latest ways in which variations in health are measured to reflect quality of living as well as traditional measures of illness and death rates. This section concludes with an exploration of variations in health related to gender, income, and culture. The fourth section describes the changes that occur in the aging brain.

The way psychologists conceptualize intelligence has changed considerably in recent years. The contemporary view of intelligence emphasizes its multidimensional nature. Most experts now believe that there are several distinct intelligences rather than a single general entity.

The next section of the chapter focuses on the tendency of adults to select certain aspects of their lives to focus on as they age. In doing so, they optimize development in those areas and compensate for declines in others. Each person's cognitive development occurs in a unique context influenced by variations in genes, life experiences, and cohort effects. The section then discusses the cognitive expertise that often comes with experience, pointing out the ways in which expert thinking differs from that of the novice. Expert thinking is more specialized, flexible, and intuitive and is guided by more and better problem-solving strategies.

NOTE: Answer guidelines for all Chapter 12 questions begin on page 202.

Chapter Review

When you have finished reading the chapter, work through the material that follows to review it. Complete the sentences and answer the questions. As you proceed, evaluate your performance for each section by consulting the answers beginning on page 202. Do not continue with the next section until you understand each answer. If you need to, review or reread the appropriate section in the textbook before continuing.

The Aging Process (pp. 420–425)

1. The gradual physical decline that occurs with age is called ________________. The first visible changes are in the ________________, due in part to a decrease in the connective tissue ________________.

2. Some of the normal changes in appearance that occur during middle adulthood include ____.

3. During middle age, the lens of the eye gradually becomes ________________ ________________ and the cornea becomes ________________. This contributes to ________________, or difficulty seeing close objects. Difficulty seeing objects at a distance is called ________________.

4. The loss of hearing associated with senescence is called ________________. This often does not become apparent until about age ________________.

5. With age, sexual ________________ is slower and ________________ takes longer. In late

middle age, the ability to ________________ is virtually impossible for women and difficult for men.

6. In the United States, about ________________ percent of all couples are infertile. Male infertility may be the result of a low ________________ ________________. Female infertility may be the result of ________________ ________________ disease, but, as with men, may also be affected by ________________, ________________, ________________, and ________________.

7. The collective name for the various methods of medical intervention to restore fertility is ________________ ________________ ________________. The most common method is ________________ ________________, in which ________________ are surgically removed and fertilized in a laboratory.

8. At an average age of ________________, a woman reaches ________________, as ovulation and menstruation stop and the production of ________________, ________________, and ________________ drops considerably.

9. The psychological consequences of menopause are ________________ (variable/not variable).

10. Over the past 30 years, many women used ________________ ________________ ________________ to reduce post-menopausal symptoms.

11. Long-term use of HRT beyond menopause has been shown to increase the risk of ________________ ________________, ________________, and ________________ ________________, and has no proven effects on ________________.

12. Although some experts believe men undergo ________________, most believe that physiologically, men ________________ (do/do not) experience anything like menopause.

APPLICATIONS:

13. Josef has enjoyed playing football with friends during most of his adult life. He has just turned 45 and notices that he no longer tackles with the same force he had 10 years ago. This is probably because
    a. his reaction time has slowed.
    b. his muscles have weakened.
    c. he has more difficulty focusing on near objects.
    d. of all of these reasons.

14. Fifty-five-year-old Dewey is concerned because sexual stimulation seems to take longer and needs to be more direct than earlier in his life. As a friend, you should tell him
    a. "You should see a therapist. It is not normal."
    b. "See a doctor if your 'sexual prowess' doesn't improve soon. You may have some underlying physical problem."
    c. "Don't worry. This is normal for middle-aged men."
    d. "You're too old to have sex, so just give it up."

15. Female fertility may be affected by
    a. obesity.
    b. pelvic inflammatory disease.
    c. smoking.
    d. all of these factors.

16. Mark and Alexis have been trying for two years to have a baby. Before they decide to adopt, they are going to try one more thing—in vitro fertilization. Which of the following should they know about IVF?
    a. It is successful only about half the time.
    b. Birth defects are less likely with IVF.
    c. Low-birthweight twins or triplets are born in almost half of all IVF pregnancies.
    d. In some nations, couples may not undergo IVF if the man is over 40.

Poor Health Habits and Senescence (pp. 426–430)

17. Age-related declines are accelerated by a history of engaging in ________________ behavior or living in a community that is ________________.

18. Rates of drug abuse ________________ (increase/decrease) during adulthood, primarily because of ________________ and ________________.

19. In North America today, ________________ (fewer/more) people begin smoking than in the

past. Worldwide, rates of smoking are variable; almost ________________ the people in several European nations are smokers; in developing nations, rates of smoking are ________________ (decreasing/increasing). Variations among nations, cohorts, and the sexes are evidence that smoking is affected by ________________ ________________, ________________, and ________________.

20. Some studies find that adults who drink moderately may live longer, possibly because alcohol increases the blood's supply of ________________-________________ ________________, the "good" cholesterol, and reduces ________________-________________ ________________, the "bad" cholesterol.

List some of the health hazards of excessive alcohol use.

21. Overweight, defined as ________________ ________________, is present in ________________ (what percent?) of all adults in the United States. Obesity, defined as ________________, is a risk factor for every chronic disease, including ________________, ________________, and ________________.

22. Throughout much of the world, the rate of obesity is ________________ (increasing/decreasing). Rates of obesity within the United States ________________ (vary/do not vary) by geographical region.

23. Although body weight is partially determined by ________________, genes ________________ (can/cannot) account for the increase in obesity.

24. The typical U.S. family consumes a diet that is ________________-based, high in ________________, and low in ________________.

List some of the health benefits of regular physical activity.

25. Two factors that make it easier to exercise regularly are ________________ ________________.

THINK ABOUT IT: As emphasized in the text, lifestyle practices show a strong relationship to variations in health and susceptibility to disease. Are you practicing a healthy lifestyle? To find out, construct a personal chart of your good and bad health habits. For each bad habit, explain the risks involved if the habit is continued.

APPLICATION:

26. Jack, who is approaching adulthood, wants to know which health habits have the greatest influence on physical well-being. You point to
a. tobacco and alcohol use.
b. overeating.
c. exercise.
d. all of these habits.

Measuring Health (pp. 430–434)

27. Perhaps the most solid indicator of health of given age groups is the rate of ________________, or death. This rate is often ________________-adjusted to take into account the higher death rate among the very old. By this measure, the country with the lowest rate is ________________, and the country with the highest rate is ________________ ________________.

28. Another measure of health is ________________, defined as ________________ of all kinds.

29. To truly portray quality of life, we need to measure ________________, which refers to a person's inability to perform normal activities of daily life, and ________________, which refers to how healthy and energetic a person feels.

30. Worldwide, there are more old ______________ (women/men) than ______________ (women/men) because more ______________ (younger women and girls/younger men and boys) die. With the exception of ______________ disease in middle age, ______________ (women/men) are more likely to have every chronic disease. On average, women outlive men by ______________ (how many?) years.

31. Individuals who are relatively well-educated and financially secure tend to live ______________ (shorter/longer) lives and have ______________ (more/fewer) chronic illnesses or disabilities.

State several possible reasons for the relationship between socioeconomic status and health.

32. Because lung and breast cancer were once more common among the rich than the poor, these diseases were called ______________ ______________ ______________. Today in the U.S., ______________ (immigrants/native-born individuals) tend to have better health. The children and grandchildren of U.S. immigrants generally have more ______________, ______________, and ______________ ______________ than their elders. They also tend to have higher rates of ______________ and virtually every ______________.

APPLICATIONS:

33. Morbidity is to mortality as __________ is to __________.
    a. disease; death
    b. death; disease
    c. inability to perform normal daily activities; disease
    d. disease; subjective feeling of being healthy

34. Summarizing her report on gender differences in aging, Trisha notes that
    a. at every age, women are more likely than men to have nearly every chronic disease.
    b. at every age, men are more likely than women to have nearly every chronic disease.
    c. the number of years that women outlive men is decreasing.
    d. the number of years that women outlive men is increasing.

35. Kirk wants to move to the part of the world that has the lowest annual age-adjusted mortality. You tell him to buy a ticket to
    a. Germany.
    b. Canada.
    c. France.
    d. Japan.

36. Fifty-year-old Beth has a college degree and a good job and lives in the Midwest where there is little pollution. Compared with her sister, who dropped out of high school and is struggling to survive in an area where violence is common, Beth is most likely to
    a. live longer.
    b. have fewer chronic illnesses.
    c. have fewer disabilities.
    d. have all of these benefits.

Cognition in Adulthood (pp. 435–439)

37. With age, neurons in the brain fire more ______________ (slowly/rapidly). In addition, by middle adulthood there are fewer ______________ and ______________. These changes contribute to a slowing of ______________ ______________ and make ______________ more difficult.

38. Disrupted sleep ______________ (is/is not) characteristic of aging.

State several possible causes of dementia and brain loss that occur before old age.

39. Historically, psychologists have thought of intelligence as ______________ (a single entity/several distinct abilities).

40. A leading theoretician, ______________, argued that there is such a thing as general intelligence, which he called ______________.

41. For the first half of the twentieth century, psychologists were convinced that intelligence peaks during ________________ and then gradually declines. During the 1950s, Nancy Bayley found that when gifted individuals were retested as adults, their IQ scores ________________ (increased/decreased/remained unchanged) after age 20.

42. Follow-up research by Bayley demonstrated a general ________________ (increase/decrease) in intellectual functioning from childhood through young adulthood. This developmental trend was true on ________________, ________________, and ________________.

43. Bayley's study is an example of a ________________ (cross-sectional/longitudinal) research design. Earlier studies relied on ________________ (cross-sectional/longitudinal) research designs.

Briefly explain why cross-sectional research can sometimes yield a misleading picture of adult development.

44. Throughout the world, studies have shown a general trend toward ________________ (increasing/decreasing) average IQ over successive generations. This trend is called the ________________ ________________, and because of it, the ________________ of IQ tests have been raised several times.

45. Cite two reasons that longitudinal findings may be misleading.

a. ________________

b. ________________

46. One of the first researchers to recognize the problems of cross-sectional and longitudinal studies of intelligence was ________________.

47. Schaie developed a new research technique combining cross-sectional and longitudinal approaches, called ________________-________________ research.

Briefly explain this type of research design.

48. Using this design, Schaie found that on five ________________ ________________ ________________, most people improved throughout most of adulthood. The results of this research are known collectively as the ________________ ________________ ________________. Other researchers ________________ (have/have not) replicated these basic trends.

APPLICATIONS:

49. A contemporary developmental psychologist is most likely to disagree with the statement that
   a. many people show increases in intelligence during middle adulthood.
   b. for many behaviors, the responses of older adults are slower than those of younger adults.
   c. intelligence peaks during adolescence and declines thereafter.
   d. intelligence is multidimensional and multidirectional.

50. Regarding accuracy in measuring adult intellectual decline, cross-sectional research is to longitudinal research as ________ is to ________.
   a. underestimate; overestimate
   b. overestimate; underestimate
   c. accurate; inaccurate
   d. inaccurate; accurate

51. Dr. Hatfield wants to analyze the possible effects of retesting, cohort differences, and aging on adult changes in intelligence. Which research method should she use?
   a. cross-sectional
   b. longitudinal
   c. cross-sequential
   d. case study

52. A psychologist practicing during World War I would most likely be convinced that intelligence peaks during
   a. late childhood.
   b. adolescence.
   c. emerging adulthood.
   d. middle adulthood.

Components of Intelligence (pp. 439–442)

53. In the 1960s, researchers ________________ and ________________ differentiated two aspects of intelligence, which they called ________________ and ________________ intelligence.

54. As its name implies, ________________ intelligence is flexible reasoning used to draw inferences and understand relations between concepts. This type of intelligence is also made up of basic mental abilities, including ________________ ________________, ________________ ________________, ________________ ________________, and ________________ ________________.

55. The accumulation of facts, information, and knowledge that comes with education and experience is referred to as ________________ intelligence.

56. During adulthood, ________________ intelligence declines markedly, primarily because everything slows down with age. However, if a person's intelligence is simply measured by one ________________ score, this decline is temporarily disguised by a(n) ________________ (increase/decrease) in ________________ intelligence.

57. The theorist who has proposed that intelligence is composed of three fundamental aspects is ________________. The ________________ aspect consists of the mental processes that foster academic proficiency by making efficient learning, remembering, and thinking possible. This type of thinking is particularly valuable in ________________ ________________ and ________________.

58. The ________________ aspect enables the person to find a better match to their skills, values, or desires. It is most appreciated by ________________ ________________ (which age group?).

59. The ________________ aspect is particularly useful as people age and need to ________________________________.

60. In the Seattle Longitudinal Study, scores on tests of practical intelligence improved or remained steady well into ________________ ________________ (what age?).

61. The researcher who believes that there are eight distinct intelligences is ________________.

62. The value placed on different dimensions of intellectual ability ________________ (varies/does not vary) from culture to culture ________________ (and/but not) from one stage of life to another. Another factor is the ________________ context.

Study Tip: Historically, many standard tests of intelligence have been biased against older age cohorts. Based on skills that are more pertinent to and commonly practiced by younger persons, these tests typically underestimate the capabilities of older adults. As an exercise in the limitations of intelligence testing, think of a few "intelligence test" questions that would be biased in favor of persons in your age group. These questions may include vocabulary, expressions, and other examples of crystallized intelligence, or they may assess memory, speed of thinking, and other aspects of fluid intelligence that might differentiate one age group from another.

APPLICATIONS:

63. Sharetta knows more about her field of specialization now at age 45 than she did at age 35. This increase is most likely due to
    a. an increase in crystallized intelligence.
    b. an increase in fluid intelligence.
    c. increases in both fluid and crystallized intelligence.
    d. a cohort difference.

64. When Merle retired from teaching, he had great difficulty adjusting to the changes in his lifestyle. Robert Sternberg would probably say that Merle was somewhat lacking in which aspect of his intelligence?
    a. analytic
    b. creative
    c. practical
    d. plasticity

65. Compared with her 20-year-old daughter, 40-year-old Lynda is likely to perform better on measures of what type of intelligence?
    a. fluid
    b. practical
    c. analytic
    d. none of these types of intelligence

66. Who would be most likely to agree with the statement, "There are multiple intelligences, each of which is influenced by the individual's age and culture"?
   a. Schaie
   b. Gardner
   c. Spearman
   d. Perlmutter

Selective Gains and Losses (pp. 443–451)

67. Researchers such as Paul and Margaret Baltes have found that people devise alternative strategies to compensate for age-related declines in ability. They call this ________________ ________________ ________________ ________________.

68. Some developmentalists believe that as we age, we develop specialized competencies, or ________________, in activities that are important to us. In other words, each person becomes a ________________ ________________.

69. There are several differences between experts and novices. First, novices tend to rely more on ________________ (formal/informal) procedures and rules to guide them, whereas experts rely more on their ________________ ________________ and the immediate ________________ to guide them. This makes the actions of experts more ________________ and less ________________.

70. Second, many elements of expert performance become ________________, almost instinctive, which enables experts to process information more quickly and efficiently.

71. A third difference is that experts have more and better ________________ for accomplishing a particular task.

72. A final difference is that experts are more ________________.

73. In developing their abilities, experts point to the importance of ________________, usually at least ________________ (how long?) before their full potential is achieved. This highlights the importance of ________________ in the development of expertise.

74. Research studies indicate that the benefits of expertise are quite ________________ (general/specific) and that practice and specialization ________________ (can/cannot) always overcome the effects of age.

75. (A View from Science) The theorist who has outlined six stages in the development of faith is ________________.

76. (A View from Science) In the space below, identify and briefly describe each stage in the development of faith.

   Stage 1: ________________________________

   Stage 2: ________________________________

   Stage 3: ________________________________

   Stage 4: ________________________________

   Stage 5: ________________________________

   Stage 6: ________________________________

77. (A View from Science) Although Fowler's stage theory of faith ________________ (is/is not) totally accepted, the idea that religion plays an important role in human development ________________ (is/is not).

78. Compared with novice chess players, chess experts most likely ________________________________

Think About It: Expert thinking is more specialized, flexible, and intuitive, and is guided by more and better problem-solving strategies. In addition, many elements of expert performance are automatic. Think about your own areas of expertise. What aspects of your performance in these areas fit these characteristics of expertise?

____

Progress Test 1

Multiple-Choice Questions

Circle your answers to the following questions and check them with the answers beginning on page 204. If your answer is incorrect, read the explanation for why it is incorrect and then consult the appropriate pages of the text (in parentheses following the correct answer).

1. During the years from 25 to 65, the average adult
   a. becomes proportionally slimmer.
   b. gains about 5 pounds per year.
   c. gains about 1 pound per year.
   d. is more likely to have pockets of fat settle on various parts of the body.

2. Senescence refers to
   a. the average age at which menopause begins.
   b. the average age at which andropause begins.
   c. age-related physical decline.
   d. premature dementia.

3. Regarding age-related changes in vision, most older adults are
   a. nearsighted.
   b. farsighted.
   c. nearsighted and farsighted.
   d. neither nearsighted or farsighted.

4. As we age
   a. neurons fire more slowly.
   b. the size of the brain is reduced.
   c. there are fewer synapses.
   d. each of these events occurs.

5. At midlife, individuals who ________________ tend to live longer and have fewer chronic illnesses or disabilities.
   a. are relatively well educated
   b. are financially secure
   c. live in a nonviolent neighborhood
   d. are or do all of these things

6. The term that refers to diseases of all kinds is
   a. mortality.
   b. morbidity.
   c. disability.
   d. vitality.

7. On average, women reach menopause at age
   a. 39.
   b. 42.
   c. 46.
   d. 51.

8. Among older adults, the need for regular sleep
   a. is diminished.
   b. increases.
   c. is about the same as it was during early adulthood.
   d. varies widely from individual to individual.

9. Mortality is usually expressed as
   a. the number of deaths each year per 1,000 individuals in a particular population.
   b. the total number of deaths per year in a given population.
   c. the average age of death among the members of a given population.
   d. the percentage of people of a given age who are still living.

10. The most common method of treatment for infertile couples is
    a. assisted reproductive technology.
    b. in vivo fertilization.
    c. in vitro fertilization.
    d. surrogate parenting.

11. Most of the evidence for an age-related decline in intelligence came from
    a. cross-sectional research.
    b. longitudinal research.
    c. cross-sequential research.
    d. random sampling.

12. The major flaw in cross-sectional research is the virtual impossibility of
    a. selecting people who are similar in every aspect except age.
    b. tracking all people over a number of years.
    c. finding volunteers with high IQs.
    d. testing intelligence.

13. Because of the limitations of other research methods, K. Warner Schaie developed a new research design based on
    a. observer-participant methods.
    b. in-depth questionnaires.
    c. personal interviews.
    d. both cross-sectional and longitudinal methods.

14. Why don't traditional intelligence tests reveal age-related cognitive declines during adulthood?
    a. They measure only fluid intelligence.
    b. They measure only crystallized intelligence.
    c. They separate verbal and nonverbal IQ scores, obscuring these declines.
    d. They yield a single IQ score, allowing adulthood increases in crystallized intelligence to mask these declines.

15. Which of the following is most likely to *decrease* with age?
    a. vocabulary
    b. accumulated facts
    c. working memory
    d. practical intelligence

16. The basic mental abilities that go into learning and understanding any subject have been classified as
    a. crystallized intelligence.
    b. plastic intelligence.
    c. fluid intelligence.
    d. rote memory.

17. Some psychologists contend that intelligence consists of fluid intelligence, which _______ during adulthood, and crystallized intelligence, which _________ .
    a. remains stable; declines
    b. declines; remains stable
    c. increases; declines
    d. declines; increases

18. Charles Spearman argued for the existence of a single general intelligence factor, which he referred to as
    a. *g*.
    b. practical intelligence.
    c. analytic intelligence.
    d. creative intelligence.

19. The Flynn effect refers to
    a. the trend toward increasing average IQ.
    b. age-related declines in fluid intelligence.
    c. ethnic differences in average IQ scores.
    d. the impact of practice on expertise.

20. The shift from conscious, deliberate processing of information to a more unconscious, effortless performance requires
    a. automatic responding.
    b. subliminal execution.
    c. plasticity.
    d. encoding.

21. Concerning expertise, which of the following is true?
    a. In performing tasks, experts tend to be more set in their ways, preferring to use strategies that have worked in the past.
    b. The reasoning of experts is usually more formal, disciplined, and stereotypic than that of the novice.
    c. In performing tasks, experts tend to be more flexible and to enjoy experimentation more than novices do.
    d. Experts often have difficulty adjusting to situations that are exceptions to the rule.

22. In general, as people age they specialize in activities that are personally meaningful. In other words, each person
    a. develops fluid intelligence.
    b. develops crystallized intelligence.
    c. develops analytic intelligence.
    d. becomes a selective expert.

23. Which of the following describes the results of Nancy Bayley's follow-up study of members of the Berkeley study?
    a. Most people reached a plateau in intellectual functioning at age 21.
    b. The typical person at age 36 improved on 2 of 10 subtests of adult intelligence scales: picture completion and arithmetic.
    c. The typical person at age 36 was still improving on the most important subtests of the intelligence scale.
    d. No conclusions could be reached because the sample was not representative.

24. Which of the following is NOT one of the general conclusions of research about intellectual changes during adulthood?
    a. In general, most intellectual abilities increase or remain stable throughout early and middle adulthood until late adulthood.
    b. Cohort differences have a powerful influence on intellectual differences in adulthood.
    c. Intellectual functioning is affected by educational background.
    d. Intelligence becomes less specialized with increasing age.

25. The psychologist who has proposed that intelligence is composed of analytic, creative, and practical aspects is
    a. Charles Spearman.
    b. Howard Gardner.
    c. Robert Sternberg.
    d. K. Warner Schaie.

True or False Items

Write T (*true*) or F (*false*) on the line in front of each statement.

_______ 1. Europe is the world leader of the obesity and diabetes epidemics.

_______ 2. Approximately half of all adults in the United States are obese.

_______ 3. Moderate users of alcohol are more likely than teetotalers to have heart attacks.

_______ 4. Those who exercise regularly have lower rates of serious illness than do sedentary people.

_______ 5. Rates of drug abuse increase over adulthood.

_______ 6. During middle adulthood, sexual responses slow down.

_______ 7. Senescence refers specifically to the psychological changes that accompany menopause.

_______ 8. Despite popular reference to it, there is no "male menopause."

_______ 9. The cost of treating disease in the United States is the highest in the world.

_______ 10. Age impairs the ability to multitask.

_______ 11. To date, cross-sectional research has shown a gradual increase in intellectual ability.

_______ 12. Longitudinal research usually shows that intelligence in most abilities increases throughout early and middle adulthood.

_______ 13. By age 60, most people decline in even the most basic cognitive abilities.

_______ 14. IQ scores have shown a steady upward drift over most of the twentieth century.

_______ 15. Historically, most psychologists have considered intelligence to be comprised of several distinct abilities.

_______ 16. Today, most researchers studying cognitive abilities believe that intelligence is multidimensional.

_______ 17. Compared with novices, experts tend to be more intuitive and less stereotyped in their work performance.

Progress Test 2

Progress Test 2 should be completed during a final chapter review. Answer the following questions after you thoroughly understand the correct answers for the Chapter Review and Progress Test 1.

Multiple-Choice Questions

1. The first visible age-related changes are seen in the
   a. hair.
   b. muscles.
   c. teeth.
   d. skin.

2. Problems that correlate with loss of brain cells in adulthood include
   a. drug abuse.
   b. excessive stress.
   c. poor circulation.
   d. all of these problems.

3. Infertility among U.S. couples is due in large part to
   a. problems with the male's reproductive organs.
   b. blockage of the woman's fallopian tubes.
   c. a low sperm count.
   d. postponing childbearing until they are well past their peak reproductive years.

4. Menopause is caused by a sharp decrease in the production of
   a. sex hormones.
   b. neurons.
   c. synapses.
   d. all of these elements.

5. To be a true index of health, morbidity rates must be refined in terms of which of the following health measure(s)?
   a. mortality rate
   b. disability and mortality rates
   c. vitality
   d. disability and vitality

6. The term *male menopause* was probably coined to refer to
   a. the sudden dip in testosterone that sometimes occurs in men who have been sexually inactive.
   b. age-related declines in fertility among men.
   c. men suffering from erectile dysfunction.
   d. age-related declines in testosterone levels in middle-aged men.

7. Which of the following is NOT true regarding hormone replacement therapy (HRT)?
   a. Long-term use (10 years or more) increases the risk of heart disease, stroke, and breast cancer.
   b. HRT reduces hot flashes and decreases osteoporosis.
   c. HRT has no proven effects on dementia.
   d. For most women, the benefits of HRT outweigh the risks.

8. Which of the following was NOT cited as a possible reason for the high incidence of being overweight among children and adults?
   a. genes
   b. eating high-calorie foods
   c. culture
   d. glandular problems

9. Which of the following is NOT true regarding alcohol consumption?
   a. Alcohol decreases the blood's supply of high-density lipoprotein.
   b. Alcohol abuse is implicated in 60 diseases.
   c. Heavy drinking increases the risk of violent death.
   d. Alcohol abuse damages the liver.

10. Adults need to eat less and move more because
   a. metabolism increases by one-third between 20 and 50.
   b. fruits and vegetables increase LDL.
   c. metabolism decreases by one-third between 20 and 50.
   d. exercise has a minimal effect on health after age 40.

11. Which of the following is true of sexual expressiveness in adulthood?
   a. Menopause impairs a woman's sexual relationship.
   b. Men's frequency of ejaculation increases until approximately age 55.
   c. Signs of arousal in a woman are as obvious as they were at age 20.
   d. The levels of sex hormones gradually diminish and responses slow down.

12. A BMI over 30
   a. is less harmful among people of African American, Latino, or Asian American ethnicity.
   b. is less harmful among European Americans.
   c. is less harmful to women than men.
   d. is always harmful.

13. The debate over the status of adult intelligence focuses on the question of its inevitable decline and on
   a. pharmacological deterrents to that decline.
   b. the accompanying decline in moral reasoning.
   c. its possible continuing growth.
   d. the validity of longitudinal versus personal-observation research.

14. The accumulation of facts that comes about with education and experience has been classified as
   a. crystallized intelligence.
   b. plastic intelligence.
   c. fluid intelligence.
   d. rote memory.

15. According to the text, the current view of intelligence recognizes all of the following characteristics *except*
   a. multidirectionality.
   b. plasticity.
   c. interindividual variation.
   d. *g*.

16. Thinking that is more intuitive, flexible, specialized, and automatic is characteristic of
   a. fluid intelligence.
   b. crystallized intelligence.
   c. expertise.
   d. plasticity.

17. The __________ nature of intelligence was attested to by Howard Gardner, who proposed the existence of nine different intelligences.
   a. multidirectional
   b. multidimensional
   c. plastic
   d. practical

18. Marion Perlmutter's research study of the skills required for successful waitressing discovered that
   a. experience had little impact on work performance.
   b. expertise required 10 years or more to attain.
   c. younger women outperformed their older counterparts in every area.
   d. age did not make a significant difference in performance.

19. At the present stage of research in adult cognition, which of the following statements has the most research support?
   a. Intellectual abilities inevitably decline from adolescence onward.
   b. Each person's cognitive development occurs in a unique context influenced by variations in genes, life experiences, and cohort effects.
   c. Some 90 percent of adults tested in cross-sectional studies show no decline in intellectual abilities until age 40.
   d. Intelligence becomes crystallized for most adults between ages 32 and 41.

20. Research on expertise indicates that during adulthood, intelligence
    a. increases in most primary mental abilities.
    b. increases in specific areas of interest to the person.
    c. increases only in those areas associated with the individual's career.
    d. shows a uniform decline in all areas.

21. Research indicates that during adulthood declines occur in
    a. crystallized intelligence.
    b. fluid intelligence.
    c. both crystallized and fluid intelligence.
    d. neither crystallized nor fluid intelligence.

22. Fluid intelligence is based on all of the following *except*
    a. working memory.
    b. abstract analysis.
    c. inductive reasoning.
    d. general knowledge.

23. In recent years, researchers are more likely than before to consider intelligence as
    a. a single entity.
    b. primarily determined by heredity.
    c. entirely the product of learning.
    d. made up of several abilities.

24. Which of the following is a drawback of longitudinal studies of intelligence?
    a. They are especially prone to the distortion of cohort effects.
    b. People who are retested may show improved performance as a result of practice.
    c. The biases of the experimenter are more likely to distort the results than is true of other research methods.
    d. All of these are drawbacks.

25. To a developmentalist, an *expert* is a person who
    a. is extraordinarily gifted at a particular task.
    b. is significantly better at a task than people who have not put time and effort into performing that task.
    c. scores at the 90th percentile or better on a test of achievement.
    d. is none of the above.

26. One reason for the variety in patterns in adult intelligence is that during adulthood
    a. intelligence is fairly stable in some areas.
    b. intelligence increases in some areas.
    c. intelligence decreases in some areas.
    d. people develop specialized competencies in activities that are personally meaningful.

Matching Items

Match each definition or description with its corresponding term.

Terms

________ 1. mortality
________ 2. morbidity
________ 3. vitality
________ 4. menopause
________ 5. andropause
________ 6. ART
________ 7. HRT
________ 8. fluid intelligence
________ 9. disability
________ 10. crystallized intelligence
________ 11. analytic intelligence
________ 12. selective optimization with compensation
________ 13. general intelligence
________ 14. creative intelligence
________ 15. practical intelligence
________ 16. Seattle Longitudinal Study
________ 17. selective expert
________ 18. Flynn effect

Definitions or Descriptions

a. disease of all kinds
b. collective term for infertility treatments
c. often prescribed to treat the symptoms of menopause
d. the accumulation of facts, information, and knowledge
e. all the mental abilities that foster academic proficiency
f. death; as a measure of health, it usually refers to the number of deaths each year per thousand individuals
g. the cessation of ovulation and menstruation
h. more important to quality of life than any other measure of health
i. male menopause
j. the inability to perform normal activities
k. intellectual skills used in everyday problem solving
l. Spearman's idea that intelligence is one basic trait, underlying all cognitive abilities
m. first study of adult intelligence that used a cross-sequential research design
n. flexible reasoning used to draw inferences
o. the capacity for flexible and innovative thinking
p. the tendency of adults to optimize certain aspects of their lives in order to offset declines in other areas
q. trend toward increasing average IQ
r. someone who is more skilled than the average person about personally meaningful activities

Key Terms

Using your own words, write a brief definition or explanation of each of the following terms on a separate piece of paper.

1. senescence
2. presbycusis
3. in vitro fertilization (IVF)
4. menopause
5. hormone replacement therapy (HRT)
6. andropause
7. mortality
8. morbidity
9. disability
10. vitality
11. general intelligence (*g*)
12. Seattle Longitudinal Study
13. fluid intelligence
14. crystallized intelligence
15. selective optimization with compensation
16. selective expert

Answers

CHAPTER REVIEW

1. senescence; skin; collagen
2. hair turns gray and thins; skin becomes thinner, less flexible, and more wrinkled; middle-age spread occurs; pockets of fat settle on the upper arms, buttocks, abdomen, and chin; back muscles, connecting tissues, and bones lose density, causing some individuals to become shorter
3. less elastic; flatter; farsightedness; nearsightedness
4. presbycusis; 60
5. responsiveness; orgasm; reproduce
6. 15; sperm count; pelvic inflammatory; smoking; extreme dieting; obesity
7. assisted reproductive technology; in vitro fertilization; ova
8. 51; menopause; estrogen; progesterone; testosterone
9. variable
10. hormone replacement therapy (HRT)
11. heart disease; stroke; breast cancer; dementia
12. andropause; do not
13. **d.** is the answer.
14. **c.** is the answer.
15. **d.** is the answer.
16. **c.** is the answer.
17. self-destructive; unhealthy
18. decrease; maturity; marriage
19. fewer; half; increasing; social norms; laws; advertising
20. high-density lipoprotein (HDL); low-density lipoprotein (LDL)

Heavy drinking is implicated in 60 diseases, including damage to the liver and cancer of the stomach, throat, and breast; contributes to osteoporosis; decreases fertility; and increases the risk of violent death.

21. a BMI above 25; 66 percent; a BMI of 30 or more; heart disease; diabetes
22. increasing; vary
23. genetics; cannot
24. meat; fat; fiber

Exercise reduces blood pressure; strengthens the heart and lungs; and makes depression, osteoporosis, heart disease, arthritis, and even some cancers less likely.

25. supportive friendships and communities that offer bike paths and other safe places to exercise
26. **d.** is the answer.
27. mortality; age; Japan; Sierra Leone
28. morbidity; illnesses
29. disability; vitality
30. women; men; younger men and boys; heart; women; five
31. longer; fewer

Education may teach healthy habits. Education may also lead to a higher income, better health care, and a home away from high pollution and violence.

32. diseases of affluence; immigrants; education; income; English fluency; obesity; disease
33. **a.** is the answer.

    b. This answer would be correct if the statement was "Mortality is to morbidity."

    c. This answer would be correct if the statement was "Disability is to morbidity."

    d. This answer would be correct if the statement was "Morbidity is to vitality."
34. **a.** is the answer.
35. **d.** is the answer.
36. **d.** is the answer. People who are relatively well-educated, financially secure, and live in an area with low pollution and little or no violence tend to receive all of these benefits.
37. slowly; neurons; synapses; reaction time; multitasking
38. is

A younger person who develops dementia may have inherited a dominant gene for Alzheimer disease; may have Down syndrome or another serious genetic condition; may have suffered major brain damage through trauma or may have had a massive stroke. Lifestyle factors, such as drug abuse, excessive stress, poor circulation, and viruses, also affect brain loss.

39. a single entity
40. Charles Spearman; *g*
41. adolescence; increased
42. increase; vocabulary; comprehension; information
43. longitudinal; cross-sectional

Cross-sectional research may be misleading because each cohort has its own unique history of life experiences and because in each generation, academic intelligence increases as a result of improved education.

44. increasing, Flynn effect; norms

45. a. People who are retested several times may improve their performance simply as a result of practice.
b. People who drop out of lengthy longitudinal studies may have lower IQ scores.

46. K. Warner Schaie

47. cross-sequential

In this approach, each time the original sample is retested, a new group is added and tested at each age interval.

48. primary mental abilities; Seattle Longitudinal Study; have

49. c. is the answer.

50. b. is the answer.

c. & d. Both cross-sectional and longitudinal research are potentially misleading.

51. c. is the answer.

a. & b. Schaie developed the cross-sequential research method to overcome the drawbacks of the cross-sectional and longitudinal methods, which were susceptible to cohort and retesting effects, respectively.

d. A case study focuses on a single subject and therefore could provide no information on cohort effects.

52. a. is the answer.

53. Raymond Cattell; John Horn; fluid; crystallized

54. fluid; inductive reasoning; abstract analysis; reaction speed; working memory

55. crystallized

56. fluid; IQ; increase; crystallized

57. Robert Sternberg; analytic; high school; college

58. creative; emerging adults

59. practical; manage their daily lives

60. late adulthood

61. Howard Gardner

62. varies; and; social

63. a. is the answer.

b. & c. According to the research, fluid intelligence declines markedly during adulthood.

d. Cohort effects refer to generational differences in life experiences.

64. b. is the answer. Creative intelligence enables the person to accommodate successfully to changes in the environment, such as those accompanying retirement.

a. This aspect of intelligence consists of mental processes that foster efficient learning, remembering, and thinking.

c. This aspect of intelligence concerns the extent to which intellectual functions are applied to situations that are familiar or novel in a person's history.

d. Plasticity refers to the flexible nature of intelligence; it is not an aspect of Sternberg's theory.

65. b. is the answer.

66. b. is the answer.

a. Schaie developed the cross-sequential research method.

c. Spearman proposed that there is a single entity, which he called general intelligence.

d. Perlmutter conducted research studies on expertise.

67. selective optimization with compensation

68. expertise; selective expert

69. formal; past experiences; context; intuitive; stereotypic

70. automatic

71. strategies

72. flexible (or creative)

73. practice; 10 years; motivation

74. specific; cannot

75. James Fowler

76. Intuitive-projective faith is magical, illogical, filled with fantasy, and typical of children ages 3 to 7.

Mythic-literal faith, which is typical of middle childhood, is characterized by taking the myths and stories of religion literally.

Synthetic-conventional faith is a nonintellectual acceptance of cultural or religious values in the context of interpersonal relationships.

Individual-reflective faith is characterized by intellectual detachment from the values of culture and the approval of significant others.

Conjunctive faith incorporates both powerful unconscious ideas and rational, conscious values.

Universalizing faith is characterized by a powerful vision of universal compassion, justice, and love that leads people to put their own personal welfare aside in an effort to serve these values.

77. is not; is

78. are quite flexible in their play, relying on their years of practice and accumulated experience.

PROGRESS TEST 1

Multiple-Choice Questions

1. **d.** is the answer. (p. 420)
   b. & c. Weight gain varies substantially from person to person.
2. **c.** is the answer. (p. 420)
3. **c.** is the answer. (p. 421)
4. **d.** is the answer. (p. 435)
5. **d.** is the answer. (p. 432)
6. **b.** is the answer. (p. 430)
   a. This is the overall death rate.
   c. This refers to a person's inability to perform normal activities of daily living.
   d. This refers to how physically, intellectually, and socially healthy an individual feels.
7. **d.** is the answer. (p. 424)
8. **b.** is the answer. (p. 435)
9. **a.** is the answer. (p. 430)
10. **c.** is the answer. (p. 423)
11. **a.** is the answer. (p. 437)
    b. Although results from this type of research may also be misleading, longitudinal studies often demonstrate age-related *increases* in intelligence.
    c. Cross-sequential research is the technique devised by K. Warner Schaie that combines the strengths of the cross-sectional and longitudinal methods.
    d. Random sampling refers to the selection of participants for a research study.
12. **a.** is the answer. (p. 437)
    b. This is a problem in longitudinal research.
    c. & d. Neither of these is particularly troublesome in cross-sectional research.
13. **d.** is the answer. (p. 438)
    a., b., & c. Cross-sequential research as described in this chapter is based on *objective* intelligence testing.
14. **d.** is the answer. (p. 441)
    a. & b. Traditional IQ tests measure both fluid and crystallized intelligence.
15. **c.** is the answer. (p. 440)
    a., b., & d. These often increase with age.
16. **c.** is the answer. (p. 440)
    a. Crystallized intelligence is the accumulation of facts and knowledge that comes with education and experience.
    b. Although intelligence is characterized by plasticity, "plastic intelligence" is not discussed as a specific type of intelligence.
    d. Rote memory is memory that is based on the conscious repetition of to-be-remembered information.
17. **d.** is the answer. (p. 440)
18. **a.** is the answer. (p. 436)
    b. Practical intelligence refers to the intellectual skills used in everyday problem solving and is identified in Sternberg's theory.
    c. & d. These are two other aspects of intelligence identified in Sternberg's theory.
19. **a.** is the answer. (p. 436)
20. **a.** is the answer. (p. 445)
    b. This was not discussed in the chapter.
    c. Plasticity refers to the flexible nature of intelligence.
    d. Encoding refers to the placing of information into memory.
21. **c.** is the answer. (p. 447)
    a., b., & d. These are more typical of *novices* than experts.
22. **d.** is the answer. (p. 444)
    a. & b. Women and men do not differ in their tendencies toward emotion- or problem-focused coping.
23. **c.** is the answer. (p. 437)
    b. The text does not indicate that they improved on those tests.
    d. No such criticism was made of Bayley's study.
24. **d.** is the answer. In fact, intelligence often becomes *more specialized* with age. (p. 444)
25. **c.** is the answer. (p. 441)
    a. Charles Spearman proposed the existence of an underlying general intelligence, which he called *g*.
    b. Howard Gardner proposed that intelligence consists of eight autonomous abilities.
    d. K. Warner Schaie was one of the first researchers to recognize the potentially distorting cohort effects on cross-sectional research.

True or False Items

1. F The United States is the world leader of the obesity and diabetes epidemics. (p. 428)
2. F Approximately two of every three are overweight, and 33 percent are obese. (p. 428)
3. F Moderate use of alcohol is associated with reduced risk of heart attacks. (p. 427)

4. T (p. 429)
5. F Rates actually decrease. (p. 426)
6. T (p. 422)
7. F Senescence is the gradual physical decline that occurs with age. (p. 420)
8. T (p. 425)
9. T (p. 429)
10. T (p. 435)
11. F Intellectual functioning as measured by IQ tests is powerfully influenced by school achievement. (p. 437)
12. T (p. 437)
13. F Many adults show intellectual improvement over most of adulthood, with no decline, even by age 60. (p. 439)
14. T (p. 437)
15. F Historically, psychologists have conceived of intelligence as a single entity. (p. 436)
16. T (p. 439)
17. T (p. 444)

PROGRESS TEST 2

Multiple-Choice Questions

1. **d.** is the answer. (p. 420)
2. **d.** is the answer. (p. 436)
3. **d.** is the answer. (p. 422)
4. **a.** is the answer. (p. 424)
5. **d.** is the answer. (pp. 430–431)
6. **a.** is the answer. (p. 425)

   b. Most men continue to produce sperm throughout adulthood and are, therefore, theoretically fertile indefinitely.

   c. This disorder was not discussed.

   d. For men, there is no sudden drop in hormone levels during middle adulthood.
7. **d.** is the answer. (p. 424)
8. **d.** is the answer. (pp. 427–428)
9. **a.** is the answer. Alcohol increases the blood's supply of HDL, which is one possible reason that adults who drink in moderation may live longer than "teetotalers." (p. 427)
10. **c.** is the answer. (p. 428)
11. **d.** is the answer. (pp. 422, 424)
12. **d.** is the answer. (p. 428)
13. **c.** is the answer. (pp. 438–439)
14. **a.** is the answer. (p. 440)

    b. Although intelligence is characterized by plasticity, "plastic intelligence" is not discussed as a specific type of intelligence.

    c. Fluid intelligence consists of the basic abilities that go into the understanding of any subject.

    d. Rote memory is based on the conscious repetition of to-be-remembered information.
15. **d.** is the answer. This is Charles Spearman's term for his idea of a general intelligence, in which intelligence is a single entity. (p. 436)

    a. Multidirectionality simply means that abilities follow different trajectories with age, as explained throughout the chapter.

    b. Plasticity simply refers to the ability to change.

    c. Interindividual variation is a way of saying that each person is unique.
16. **c.** is the answer. (pp. 444–447)
17. **b.** is the answer. (p. 442)

    a., c., & d. Gardner dealt with the multidimensionality of intelligence, not its direction, plasticity, or practicality.
18. **a.** is the answer. (p. 450)

    b. Expertise at waiting on tables took far less than 10 years to attain.

    c. & d. Older women outperformed younger women in the number of customers served.
19. **b.** is the answer. (p. 438–439)

    a. There is agreement that intelligence does *not* peak during adolescence.

    c. Cross-sectional research usually provides evidence of *declining* ability throughout adulthood.

    d. Crystallized intelligence refers to the accumulation of knowledge with experience; intelligence does not "crystallize" at any specific age.
20. **b.** is the answer. (p. 444)
21. **b.** is the answer. (p. 441)

    a., c., & d. Crystallized intelligence typically *increases* during adulthood.
22. **d.** is the answer. This is an aspect of crystallized intelligence. (p. 440)
23. **d.** is the answer. (pp. 439–442)

    a. Contemporary researchers emphasize the different aspects of intelligence.

    b. & c. Contemporary researchers see intelligence as the product of both heredity and learning.
24. **b.** is the answer. (p. 438)

    a. This is a drawback of cross-sectional research.

c. Longitudinal studies are no more sensitive to experimenter bias than other research methods.

25. **b.** is the answer. (p. 444)

26. **d.** is the answer. (p. 444)

Matching Items

1. f (p. 430)	**7.** c (p. 424)	**13.** l (p. 436)
2. a (p. 430)	**8.** n (p. 440)	**14.** o (p. 441)
3. h (p. 430)	**9.** j (p. 431)	**15.** k (p. 441)
4. g (p. 424)	**10.** d (p. 440)	**16.** m (p. 438)
5. i (p. 425)	**11.** e (p. 441)	**17.** r (p. 444)
6. b (p. 423)	**12.** p (p. 443)	**18.** q (p. 437)

KEY TERMS

1. **Senescence** refers to the gradual physical decline that accompanies aging. (p. 420)
2. **Presbycusis** is the loss of hearing associated with aging. (p. 421)
3. **In vitro fertilization (IVF)** is a fertility treatment in which egg cells are surgically removed from a woman and fertilized in the laboratory. (p. 423)
4. At **menopause,** which usually occurs around age 51, ovulation and menstruation stop and the production of the hormones estrogen, progesterone, and testosterone drops. (p. 424)
5. **Hormone replacement therapy (HRT)** is intended to help relieve menopausal symptoms, especially in women who experience an abrupt drop in hormone level because their ovaries are surgically removed. (p. 424)
6. **Andropause**, or male menopause, refers to age-related changes in sexual desire, muscle mass, and other physical changes that accompany decreases in testosterone levels. (p. 425)
7. **Mortality** means death. As a measure of health, it usually refers to the number of deaths each year per thousand members of a given population. (p. 430)
8. **Morbidity** means disease. As a measure of health, it refers to the rate of diseases of all kinds in a given population, which can be sudden and severe (acute) or extend over a long time period (chronic). (p. 430)
9. **Disability** refers to a person's inability to perform normal activities of daily life. (p. 430)
10. **Vitality** refers to how healthy and energetic—physically, intellectually, and socially—an individual actually feels. (p. 431)
11. **General intelligence (*g*)** is the idea that intelligence is one basic trait, underlying all cognitive abilities, according to Spearman. (p. 436)
12. The **Seattle Longitudinal Study** was the first study of adult intelligence that used a cross-sequential research design. (p. 438)
13. **Fluid intelligence** is made up of those basic mental abilities—inductive reasoning, abstract thinking, short-term memory, speed of thinking, and the like—required for understanding any subject matter. (p. 440)
14. **Crystallized intelligence** is the accumulation of facts, information, and knowledge that comes with education and experience within a particular culture. (p. 440)
15. **Selective optimization with compensation** describes the tendency of adults to select certain aspects of their lives to focus on, and optimize, in order to compensate for declines in other areas. (p. 443)
16. A **selective expert** is someone who is notably more skilled and knowledgeable than the average person about whichever activities are personally meaningful. (p. 444)

13 chapter

ADULTHOOD

Psychosocial Development

Chapter Overview

Chapter 13 is concerned with adulthood, which was commonly believed to be a time of crisis and transition. Today, researchers realize the fluidity of age boundaries and that good and bad events may occur at any age. The chapter begins by examining the concept of stages during adulthood, then identifies five basic clusters of personality traits that remain fairly stable throughout adulthood. One personality trend that does occur during middle age, as gender roles become less rigid, is the tendency of both sexes to take on characteristics typically reserved for the opposite sex.

The second section explores changes in relationships with friends and relatives and in the marital relationship in adulthood. It also depicts the effects of divorce and remarriage on family interaction.

The next section examines the importance of generativity during adulthood. As many women and men begin to balance their work lives with parenthood, caring for parents, and other concerns, the motivation for many adults shifts from extrinsic rewards to intrinsic ones.

The final section of the chapter discusses coping with stress. Adults experience many stressors and use a number of different coping strategies as they seek to meet their intimacy and generativity needs. These stressors may negatively affect their health.

NOTE: Answer guidelines for all Chapter 13 questions begin on page 215.

Chapter Review

When you have finished reading the chapter, work through the material that follows to review it. Complete the sentences and answer the questions. As you proceed, evaluate your performance for each section by consulting the answers beginning on page 215. Do not continue with the next section until you understand each answer. If you need to, review or reread the appropriate section in the textbook before continuing.

Ages and Stages (pp. 456–464)

1. In Erikson's theory, the identity crisis of adolescence is followed in early adulthood by the crisis of _______________ _______________ _______________, later by the crisis of _______________ _______________ _______________, and finally by the crisis of _______________ _______________ _______________.

2. The theorist who described five stages of development, not necessarily linked to chronological age, is _______________. In order, these stages are _______________, _______________, _______________ _______________, _______________, _______________, _______________ _______________, and _______________. In his later years, he suggested a sixth level, _______________. Together, these stages form a _______________ of _______________.

3. Today, most social scientists regard adult lives as more _______________ than stage models suggest.

4. Although most developmentalists _______________ (take/do not take) a strict stage view of adulthood, they do recognize that development is influenced by the _______________ _______________, which is defined as _______________.

5. The social clock is affected by cultural and _______________ norms. A powerful influence on the social clock is _______________ _______________. The lower a person's SES, the _______________ (younger/older) the age at which he or she is expected to leave school, begin work, marry, have children, and so forth.

6. The social clock is ________________ (more/less) restrictive now that age boundaries ________________ (have/have not) been relaxed.

7. The notion of a midlife crisis ________________ (is/is not) accepted by most developmentalists as an inevitable event during middle age.

8. The major source of developmental continuity and identity during adulthood is the stability of ________________.

9. List and briefly describe the Big Five personality factors.

   a. ________________________________
   ____

   b. ________________________________
   ____

   c. ________________________________
   ____

   d. ________________________________
   ____

   e. ________________________________
   ____

10. The stability of personality results in large part from the fact that beginning in early adulthood most people have settled into an ________________ ________________.

11. Although personality certainly begins with ________________ and is manifested in the decisions that form the person's lifestyle, it may shift if the ________________ shifts.

12. Of the Big Five traits, ________________ and ________________ tend to increase slightly with age, while ________________, ________________, and ________________ tend to decrease.

13. (A View from Science) Some social scientists believe that a sixth trait, known as ________________ on others, is significant in ________________ cultures.

14. During middle age, gender roles ________________ (loosen/become more rigid). Some researchers even believe that there is a ________________ ________________ of personality traits.

THINK ABOUT IT: Although the stability of personality is a subject of considerable debate, most developmentalists agree that personality tends to remain stable unless there is a sudden, critical break—such as an unexpected tragedy or an unexpected windfall—in the continuity of the individual's life situation. Think about your own life and that of other family members. Have you experienced any major events? Can you say that you or someone in your family have changed significantly? Permanently or temporarily?

APPLICATIONS:

15. For her class presentation, Christine plans to discuss the Big Five personality traits. Which of the following is NOT a trait that Christine will discuss?
   a. extroversion
   b. openness
   c. independence
   d. agreeableness

16. It was once assumed that, for biological reasons, I will inevitably experience a midlife crisis. I am
   a. a middle-aged man.
   b. a middle-aged woman.
   c. either a middle-aged man or a middle-aged woman.
   d. neither a middle-aged man nor a middle-aged woman.

17. All his life, Bill has been a worrier, often suffering from bouts of anxiety and depression. Which personality cluster best describes these traits?
   a. neuroticism
   b. extroversion
   c. openness
   d. conscientiousness

18. Jan and her sister Sue have experienced similar frequent changes in careers, residences, and spouses. Jan has found these upheavals much less stressful than Sue and so is probably characterized by which of the following personality traits?
   a. agreeableness
   b. conscientiousness
   c. openness
   d. extroversion

Intimacy (pp. 464–473)

19. The group of people with whom we form relationships that guide us through life constitutes our ________________ ________________.

20. The most crucial members of the social convoy tend to be ________________.

21. Some closeness between parents and children is ________________. In North America, Europe, and Australia, older adults cherish their ________________. In China and some other nations, where ________________ is a desirable trait, intergenerational living is not considered a burden.

22. The belief that family members should care for and support one another is called ________________ .

23. Someone who becomes accepted as part of a family to which he or she is unrelated is called ________________ ________________ .

24. Generally, married people are ________________, ________________, and ________________ than never-married ones.

25. The time in parents' lives when grown children leave the family home is called the ________________ ________________ .

26. Older couples have less ________________-________________ stress, fewer ________________, higher ________________, and more time together than younger couples.

27. Research findings on marital success and satisfaction generally ________________ (apply/do not apply) to homosexual partners.

28. In the United States, nearly one out of every ________________ marriages ends in divorce. In fact, over the past two decades, every nation has seen ________________ (fewer/more) marriages and ________________ (fewer/more divorces. Divorce is most likely to occur within ________________ (how many?) years of marriage.

29. Divorce reduces ________________, severs ________________, and weakens ________________ ________________ .

Divorce following a long-term marriage is typically ________________ (more/less) difficult than divorce early in a marriage.

30. Second marriages end in divorce ________________ (more/less) often than first marriages.

APPLICATIONS:

31. Ben and Nancy have been married for 10 years. Although they are very happy, Nancy worries that with time this happiness will decrease. Research would suggest that Nancy's fear
    a. may or may not be reasonable, depending on whether she and her husband are experiencing a midlife crisis.
    b. is reasonable, because marital discord is most common in couples who have been married 10 years or more.
    c. is unfounded, because after the first 8 years or so, the longer a couple has been married, the happier they tend to be.
    d. is probably a sign of neuroticism.

32. Concluding her presentation on culture and personality, Jaya notes that a sixth personality dimension, known as dependence on others, is significant in
    a. Western Europe.
    b. Africa.
    c. Scandinavia.
    d. Asia.

Generativity (pp. 473–485)

33. According to Erikson, after intimacy comes ________________ versus ________________ .

Besides being creative, adults tend to satisfy their need to be generative through ________________ and ________________ .

34. Because of their role in maintaining the links between the generations, mature adults become the ________________ . In the past, this role was filled most often by ________________ (women/men); with today's smaller families, however, gender equity in this role ________________ (is/is not) more apparent.

35. For most adults, the chief form of generativity involves caring for ________________ . Most parents ________________ (do/do not) manage to cope with the demands of raising children.

36. Proportionately, about ________________ of all North American adults will become stepparents, adoptive parents, or foster parents at some point in their lives.

37. Many adopted or foster children ________________ (do/do not) remain attached to their birth parents. These attachments may become problematic if the birth parents were ________________ . A worse situation is if the children don't form any ________________ at all.

38. In stepfamilies, the adults' ________________ and the nature of the marriage determine whether the family will survive.

39. Because they are legally connected to their children for life, ________________ (adoptive/step/foster) parents have an advantage in establishing bonds with their children.

40. Middle-aged people are sometimes called the ________________ generation because they feel pressured to fulfill the needs of both younger and older generations. Care for elderly parents tends to tilt toward the ________________ (husband's/wife's) parents. Caregiving is determined not only by need but also by ________________ and ________________.

41. Unemployment is associated with higher rates of ________________ ________________, ________________, ________________, and many other social problems.

42. Buying fancy cars and other things for the purpose of showing off to others is called ________________ ________________.

43. Over the past 50 years, average income has ________________ (increased/decreased) in the United States. At the same time, happiness has ________________ (increased/decreased/remained unchanged).

44. The idea that people's satisfaction is determined by how they compare with others in their group is called ________________ ________________.

45. As people age, the ________________ (intrinsic/extrinsic) rewards associated with working tend to become more important than the ________________ (intrinsic/extrinsic) rewards.

46. The nature of economies in advanced nations has shifted from being based on ________________ to ________________ and ________________ economies.

47. Increasing diversity in the workplace has created a need for more experienced workers, called ________________, to help train new employees.

48. Job change ________________ (is/is not) common after emerging adulthood. Between 25 and 42 years of age, the average worker in the U.S. today has ________________ (how many?) different employers.

49. State three reasons that changing jobs is more difficult for older workers.

a. ________________

b. ________________

c. ________________

50. Today, shift work is increasingly ________________ (common/rare) in the workplace. This more flexible arrangement of work schedules is called ________________.

51. One solution to potential conflict between work and family roles is ________________.

STUDY TIP: To facilitate your understanding of psychosocial development at a later time during your adult life, project yourself into the future and imagine that you are preparing to attend your 25th high school reunion. How will your life story have been shaped by the social clock that was ticking during your adult years? If you are an older student, simply speculate about a later reunion.

APPLICATIONS:

52. Manuel is 50 years old. Although he is financially independent, he continues to work. Which of the following was NOT mentioned as a way that work helps meet his generativity needs?
    a. It helps Manuel with his need to accumulate personal wealth.
    b. It helps him express creative energy.
    c. It helps him support the health of his family.
    d. It helps him contribute to the community.

53. Compared with when they were younger, middle-aged Sarah is likely to become more ________, while middle-aged Donald becomes more ________.
    a. introverted; extroverted
    b. assertive; emotionally expressive
    c. disappointed with life; satisfied with life
    d. extroverted; introverted

54. Forty-five-year-old Elena has been working for the telephone company for 20 years. Because of technological advances, she has been laid off. According to the text, this job loss is devastating to her because:
    a. she can't work the long hours new jobs require.
    b. she doesn't have the knowledge needed to perform available jobs.
    c. she wants to spend time with her grandchildren and all new jobs are 9 A.M. to 5 P.M.
    d. her husband planned on retiring as long as she was still bringing in a paycheck.

55. Jack doesn't plan to retire as long as his job continues to be satisfying and boosts his self-esteem. Jack is clearly motivated by
   a. extrinsic rewards of work.
   b. intrinsic rewards of work.
   c. familism.
   d. generativity.

Coping With Stress (pp. 485–489)

56. The total burden of stress and disease that an individual must cope with is called ________________ ________________ . Research has shown that the accumulated ________________ of many stressors is pivotal; too great a buildup of stress has the potential to cause a ________________ or ________________ breakdown.

57. The capacity of the body's organs to cope with stress is called ________________ ________________. During emergencies, ________________ ________________ is activated to help the body meet the challenge.

58. In ________________-________________ coping, people try to cope with stress by tackling the problem directly. In ________________-________________ coping, people cope with stress by trying to change their emotions. Generally speaking, ________________ (younger/older) adults are more likely to be emotion-focused and ________________ (younger/older) adults to be more problem-focused. Women may be more ________________-focused than men, as their bodies produce the hormone ________________ that triggers ________________-________________-________________ behaviors.

APPLICATIONS:

59. Cathy's life is stress-filled because she is unemployed, a single parent, and the primary caregiver for her ailing mother. A developmentalist would say Cathy
   a. has a high allostatic load.
   b. needs more problem-focused coping.
   c. needs more emotion-focused coping.
   d. has a low allostatic load.

60. Compared with his sister, Melvin is more likely to respond to stress
   a. in a problem-focused manner.
   b. in an emotion-focused manner.
   c. in a tend-and-befriend manner.
   d. with lower arousal of his sympathetic nervous system.

61. After a painful phone call with her unhappy mother, your college roommate confides her fear that she will not be able to handle the burdens of children, career, and caring for her aging parents. Your response is that
   a. she's right to worry, because women who juggle these roles simultaneously almost always feel unfairly overburdened.
   b. her mother's unhappiness is a warning sign that she herself may be genetically prone toward developing a midlife crisis.
   c. Both a. and b. are true.
   d. If these roles are important to her, if her relationships are satisfying, and if the time demands are not overwhelming, filling these roles is likely to be a source of satisfaction.

Progress Test 1

Multiple-Choice Questions

Circle your answers to the following questions and check them with the answers beginning on page 216. If your answer is incorrect, read the explanation for why it is incorrect and then consult the appropriate pages of the text (in parentheses following the correct answer).

1. Which of the following best describes development during adulthood?
   a. rigidity
   b. fluidity
   c. dependence
   d. disability

2. The Big Five personality factors are
   a. emotional stability, openness, introversion, sociability, locus of control.
   b. neuroticism, extroversion, openness, emotional stability, sensitivity.
   c. extroversion, agreeableness, conscientiousness, neuroticism, openness.
   d. neuroticism, gregariousness, extroversion, impulsiveness, openness.

3. Concerning the prevalence of midlife crises, which of the following statements has the *greatest* empirical support?
   a. Virtually all men, and most women, experience a midlife crisis.
   b. Virtually all men, and about 50 percent of women, experience a midlife crisis.
   c. Women are more likely to experience a midlife crisis than are men.
   d. Few contemporary developmentalists believe that the midlife crisis is a common experience.

4. Shifts in personality during adulthood often reflect
   a. increased agreeableness, conscientiousness, and generativity.
   b. rebellion against earlier life choices.
   c. the tightening of gender roles.
   d. all of these events.

5. During middle age, gender roles tend to
   a. become more distinct.
   b. reflect patterns established during early adulthood.
   c. converge.
   d. be unpredictable.

6. Regarding the concept of the "sandwich generation," most developmentalists agree that
   a. middle-aged adults often are burdened by being pressed on one side by adult children and on the other by aging parents.
   b. women are more likely than men to feel "sandwiched."
   c. men are more likely than women to feel "sandwiched."
   d. this concept is largely a myth.

7. In the United States and other Western countries, the lower a person's socioeconomic status
   a. the younger the age at which the social clock is "set" for many life events.
   b. the older the age at which the social clock is "set" for many life events.
   c. the more variable are the settings for the social clock.
   d. the less likely it is that divorce will occur.

8. In families, one member tends to function as the __________, celebrating family achievements, keeping the family together, and staying in touch with distant relatives.
   a. sandwich generation
   b. nuclear bond
   c. intergenerational gatekeeper
   d. kinkeeper

9. According to Erikson, the failure to achieve intimacy during early adulthood is most likely to result in
   a. generativity.
   b. stagnation.
   c. role diffusion.
   d. isolation.

10. The theorist who described a hierarchy of needs occurring in five stages of adult development is
    a. Erikson.
    b. Maslow.
    c. Freud.
    d. Neugarten.

11. Erikson theorized that if generativity is not attained, the adult is most likely to experience
    a. lack of advancement in his or her career.
    b. infertility or childlessness.
    c. feelings of emptiness and stagnation.
    d. feelings of profound aloneness or isolation.

12. Concerning the degree of stability of personality traits, which of the following statements has the greatest research support?
    a. There is little evidence that personality traits remain stable during adulthood.
    b. In women, but less so in men, there is notable continuity in many personality characteristics.
    c. In men, but less so in women, there is notable continuity in many personality characteristics.
    d. In both men and women, there is notable continuity in many personality characteristics.

13. People who exhibit the personality dimension of __________ tend to be outgoing, active, and assertive.
    a. extroversion
    b. agreeableness
    c. conscientiousness
    d. neuroticism

14. The strategy often used by older adults for dealing with stressors is
    a. problem-focused coping.
    b. emotion-focused coping.
    c. fight-or-flight.
    d. recovery reserve.

15. Which of the following personality traits was NOT identified in the text as either increasing or decreasing slightly during adulthood?
    a. neuroticism
    b. introversion
    c. openness
    d. conscientiousness

16. A single parent with two children would benefit from a job in which the employer allows for
    a. familism.
    b. flextime.
    c. mentoring.
    d. extrinsic rewards.

True or False Items

Write T (*true*) or F (*false*) on the line in front of each statement.

_______ 1. By middle adulthood, most people have reached Maslow's stage of self-actualization.
_______ 2. At least 75 percent of American men experience a significant midlife crisis between ages 38 and 43.
_______ 3. The Big Five personality traits remain quite stable throughout adulthood.
_______ 4. Younger adults tend to be more emotion-focused when responding to stress.
_______ 5. Intergenerational living is more acceptable in China than in the United States.
_______ 6. A prime influence on the cultural clock-setting is socioeconomic status.
_______ 7. Children do not necessarily improve marital satisfaction.
_______ 8. Adults marry earlier in life than previous generations did.
_______ 9. Adoptive parents, being legally connected to their children for life, have an advantage over foster parents in bonding with their children.
_______ 10. There is no evidence that the stability of personality traits is influenced by heredity.

Progress Test 2

Progress Test 2 should be completed during a final chapter review. Answer the following questions after you thoroughly understand the correct answers for the Chapter Review and Progress Test 1.

Multiple-Choice Questions

1. An individual's social convoy is most likely to be made up of
    a. older relatives.
    b. younger relatives.
    c. people who are supportive.
    d. members of the same generation.

2. Which of the following would be a good example of an ecological niche?
    a. an extrovert marries an introvert
    b. a conscientious person cohabits with someone who is disorganized
    c. a sculptor marries a canvas artist
    d. a workaholic marries a homebody

3. The prime effect of the social clock is to make an individual aware of
    a. his or her socioeconomic status.
    b. the diversity of psychosocial paths during early adulthood.
    c. the means of fulfilling affiliation and achievement needs.
    d. the "right" or "best" time for assuming adult roles.

4. Allostatic load refers to
    a. the combined burden of stress and disease that an individual must cope with.
    b. the idea that family members share all aspects of each other's lives.
    c. the idea that family members should support one another.
    d. the difficulty stepparents sometimes have in forming strong bonds with stepchildren.

5. Whether a person ranks high or low in each of the Big Five personality factors is determined by
    a. heredity.
    b. temperament.
    c. his or her lifestyle.
    d. the interaction of genes, culture, and early experiences.

6. Regarding the strength of the contemporary family bond, most developmentalists believe that
    a. family links are considerably weaker in the typical contemporary American family than in earlier decades.
    b. family links are considerably weaker in the typical contemporary American family than in other cultures.
    c. both a. and b. are true.
    d. despite the fact that families do not usually live together, family links are not weaker today.

7. Your brother, who became a stepparent when he married, complains that he can't seem to develop a strong bond with his 9-year-old stepchild. You tell him
   a. strong bonds between parent and child are particularly hard to create once a child is old enough to have formed attachments to other caregivers.
   b. the child is simply immature emotionally and will, with time, warm up considerably.
   c. most stepparents find that they eventually develop a deeper, more satisfying relationship with stepchildren than they had ever imagined.
   d. he should encourage the child to think of him as the child's biological father.

8. Which of the following statements explains why couples in long-term marriages are particularly likely to report an increase in marital satisfaction?
   a. Marital satisfaction is closely tied to financial security, which tends to improve throughout adulthood.
   b. The successful launching of children is a source of great pride and happiness.
   c. Old arguments are settled.
   d. All of these statements are correct.

9. Which of the following are typically the most supportive members of a person's social convoy?
   a. parents
   b. children
   c. coworkers
   d. friends

10. Which of the following is NOT true concerning divorce and remarriage during adulthood?
    a. Divorce is most likely to occur within the first five years of a wedding.
    b. Women with children are less likely to remarry.
    c. Remarriages break up more often than first marriages.
    d. Remarried people report higher average levels of happiness than people in first marriages.

11. Jan has been so much a part of her best friend's life that she effectively has been "adopted" by her family. In other words, Jan has become
    a. a kinkeeper.
    b. fictive kin.
    c. part of the sandwich generation.
    d. part of the social convoy.

12. Which of the following personality traits tends to remain quite stable throughout adulthood?
    a. agreeableness
    b. neuroticism
    c. openness
    d. all of these traits

13. (A View from Science) Which of the following is NOT true regarding personality traits?
    a. Research has shown that dependence on others is common in Asian cultures.
    b. The Big Five differ slightly by state in the United States.
    c. National events have a significant effect on personality.
    d. People tend to choose a spouse, neighbors, and employment that match their inclinations.

14. The belief that family members should care for each other, sacrificing personal freedom and success to do so, is called:
    a. familism.
    b. kinkeeping.
    c. empty nest syndrome.
    d. gender convergence.

15. Even decades after divorce, which of these factors still tend(s) to be lower for divorced adults than for nondivorced adults?
    a. income
    b. family welfare
    c. self-esteem
    d. All of these are lower.

16. Virginia's husband has been promoted at his job but it requires that they move to another state. Because she very much enjoys her job, she asks her employer if she could be allowed to
    a. arrange flextime.
    b. mentor.
    c. telecommute.
    d. change ecological niches.

Matching Items

Match each definition or description with its corresponding term or concept.

Terms of Concepts

_______ 1. kinkeepers
_______ 2. sandwich generation
_______ 3. extroversion
_______ 4. agreeableness
_______ 5. conscientiousness
_______ 6. neuroticism
_______ 7. social convoy
_______ 8. ecological niche
_______ 9. familism
_______ 10. openness
_______ 11. organ reserve

Definitions or Descriptions

a. tendency to be outgoing
b. tendency to be imaginative
c. tendency to be organized
d. those who focus more on the family
e. tendency to be helpful
f. those pressured by the needs of the older and younger generations
g. tendency to be moody
h. the belief that family members should remain close and supportive of one another
i. a chosen lifestyle and context
j. "a protective layer of social relations"
k. capacity of the body to cope with unusual stress

Key Terms

Using your own words, write a brief definition or explanation of each of the following terms on a separate piece of paper.

1. social clock
2. midlife crisis
3. ecological niche
4. gender convergence
5. social convoy
6. familism
7. fictive kin
8. empty nest
9. kinkeeper
10. sandwich generation
11. relative deprivation
12. extrinsic rewards of work
13. intrinsic rewards of work
14. mentor
15. flextime
16. telecommuting
17. stressor
18. allostatic load
19. organ reserve
20. problem-focused coping
21. emotion-focused coping

Answers

CHAPTER REVIEW

1. intimacy versus isolation; generativity versus stagnation; integrity versus despair
2. Abraham Maslow; physiological; safety; love and belonging; success and esteem; self-actualization; self-transcendence; hierarchy; needs
3. fluid
4. do not take; social clock; a timetable for behaviors set by social norms
5. historical; socioeconomic status; younger
6. less; have
7. is not
8. personality
9. **a.** openness: imaginative, curious
   b. conscientiousness: organized, conforming
   c. extroversion: outgoing, assertive
   d. agreeableness: kind, helpful
   e. neuroticism: anxious, moody
10. ecological niche
11. genes; circumstances
12. agreeableness; conscientiousness; extroversion; openness; neuroticism
13. dependence; Asian
14. loosen; gender convergence
15. **c.** is the answer.
16. **c.** is the answer. Researchers have found no evidence that a midlife crisis is inevitable in middle adulthood.
17. **a.** is the answer.
    b. This is the tendency to be outgoing.

c. This is the tendency to be imaginative and curious.
d. This is the tendency to be organized, deliberate, and conforming.

18. **c.** is the answer. Openness to new experiences might make these life experiences less threatening.
19. social convoy
20. friends
21. cultural; independence; dependence
22. familism
23. fictive kin
24. happier; healthier; richer
25. empty nest
26. child-rearing; arguments; incomes
27. apply
28. two; fewer; more; five
29. income; friendships; family ties; more
30. more
31. **c.** is the answer.
    a. Marital satisfaction can be an important buffer against midlife stress.
    d. There is no reason to believe Nancy's concern is abnormal, or neurotic.
32. **d.** is the answer.
33. generativity; stagnation; caregiving; employment
34. kinkeepers; women; is
35. children; do
36. one-third
37. do; abusive; attachments
38. temperament
39. adoptive
40. sandwich; wife's; personality; familism
41. child abuse; alcoholism; depression
42. conspicuous consumption
43. increased; remained unchanged
44. relative deprivation
45. intrinsic; extrinsic
46. industry; information; service
47. mentors
48. is; five
49. **a.** Older workers may never have learned the skills required for a new job.
    b. Older workers are paid more and have more respect in the previous job.
    c. Older workers find relocation more difficult.
50. common; flextime
51. telecommuting
52. **a.** is the answer.
53. **b.** is the answer. This is an example of the convergence of gender roles during middle adulthood.
    a. & d. Extroversion is a relatively stable personality trait. Moreover, there is no gender difference in the developmental trajectory of this trait.
    c. There is no gender difference in life satisfaction at any age.
54. **b.** is the answer.
55. **b.** is the answer.
56. allostatic load; interaction; physical; emotional
57. organ reserve; recovery reserve
58. problem-focused; emotion-focused; older; younger; emotion; oxytocin; tend-and-befriend
59. **a.** is the answer.
60. **a.** is the answer.
    b., c., & d. Each of these is more typical of women.
61. **d.** is the answer.

PROGRESS TEST 1

Multiple-Choice Questions

1. **b.** is the answer. (p. 456)
2. **c.** is the answer. (p. 460)
3. **d.** is the answer. (p. 459)
   a. & b. Recent studies have shown that the prevalence of the midlife crisis has been greatly exaggerated.
   c. The text does not suggest a gender difference in terms of the midlife crisis.
4. **a.** is the answer. (p. 461)
   b. This answer reflects the notion of a midlife crisis—a much rarer event than is popularly believed.
   c. Gender roles tend to loosen in middle adulthood.
5. **c.** is the answer. (p. 463)
   a. Gender roles become *less* distinct during middle adulthood.
   b. Gender roles often are most distinct during early adulthood, after which they tend to loosen.
   d. Although there *is* diversity from individual to individual, gender-role shifts during middle adulthood are nevertheless predictable.
6. **d.** is the answer. (p. 477)
   b. & c. Women are no more likely than men to feel burdened by the younger and older generations.
7. **a.** is the answer. (p. 458)
   d. Low SES is actually a risk factor for divorce.
8. **d.** is the answer. (p. 474)
   a. This was a term used to describe adult women and men who are pressured by the needs of both the younger and older generations.
   b. & c. These terms are not used in the text.

9. **d.** is the answer. (p. 456)

   a. Generativity is a characteristic of the crisis following the intimacy crisis.

   b. Stagnation occurs when generativity needs are not met.

   c. Erikson's theory does not address this issue.

10. **b.** is the answer. (p. 457)
11. **c.** is the answer. (p. 456)

    a. Lack of career advancement may prevent generativity.

    b. Erikson's theory does not address these issues.

    d. Such feelings are related to the need for intimacy rather than generativity.

12. **d.** is the answer. (p. 461)
13. **a.** is the answer. (p. 460)

    b. This is the tendency to be kind and helpful.

    c. This is the tendency to be organized, deliberate, and conforming.

    d. This is the tendency to be anxious, moody, and self-punishing.

14. **b.** is the answer. (p. 487)

    a. Problem-focused coping is often used by younger adults.

    c. Fight-or-flight is a problem-focused coping response.

    d. Recovery reserve refers to the body's homeostatic responses to stressors.

15. **b.** is the answer. (p. 461)
16. **b.** is the answer. (p. 484)

    a. Familism refers to the belief that family members should sacrifice for one another.

    c. mentoring involves an experienced person assisting an inexperienced one.

    d. Flextime would be an intrinsic reward.

True or False Items

1. F Some adults never achieve self-actualization. (p. 457)
2. F Studies have found that crises at midlife are not inevitable. (p. 459)
3. T (p. 461)
4. F Younger adults are more problem-focused. (p. 487)
5. T (p. 466)
6. T (p. 458)
7. T (p. 469)
8. F Just the opposite is true. (p. 468)
9. T (p. 475)
10. F The stability of personality is at least partly attributable to heredity. (p. 459)

PROGRESS TEST 2

Multiple-Choice Questions

1. **c.** is the answer. (p. 464)
2. **c.** is the answer. (p. 460)
3. **d.** is the answer. (p. 457)
4. **a.** is the answer. (p. 486)

   b. This refers to linked lives.

   c. This is familism.

5. **d.** is the answer. (pp. 460–461)
6. **d.** is the answer. (p. 465)
7. **a.** is the answer. (p. 475)

   b. Many stepchildren remain fiercely loyal to the absent parent.

   c. Most stepparents actually have unrealistically high expectations of the relationship they will establish with their stepchildren.

   d. Doing so would only confuse the child and, quite possibly, cause resentment and further alienation.

8. **d.** is the answer. (p. 469)
9. **d.** is the answer. (p. 464)
10. **d.** is the answer. (pp. 472–473)
11. **b.** is the answer. (p. 467)
12. **d.** is the answer. (p. 461)
13. **c.** is the answer. (p. 462)
14. **a.** is the answer. (p. 466)
15. **d.** is the answer. (p. 471)
16. **c.** is the answer. (p. 484)

    a. Being in a different state, she wouldn't normally spend time in the main office.

    b. mentoring involves an experienced person assisting an inexperienced one.

    d. Ecological niche has to do with lifestyle and social context.

Matching Items

1. d (p. 474)	**6.** g (p. 460)	**11.** k (p. 487)
2. f (p. 477)	**7.** j (p. 464)	
3. a (p. 460)	**8.** i (p. 460)	
4. e (p. 460)	**9.** h (p. 466)	
5. c (p. 460)	**10.** b (p. 460)	

KEY TERMS

1. The **social clock** represents the culturally set timetable that establishes when various events and behaviors in life are appropriate and called for. (p. 457)
2. A once-popular myth, the **midlife crisis** is a period of unusual anxiety, radical self-reexamination, and sudden transformation that is widely associated with middle age but has more to do with developmental history than with chronological age. (p. 459)
3. **Ecological niche** refers to the lifestyle and social context adults settle into that are compatible with their individual personality needs and interests. (p. 460)
4. **Gender convergence** is the tendency of the sexes to become more similar as women and men move through middle age. (p. 463)
5. A **social convoy** is a group of people who guide, encourage, and socialize individuals as they move through life. (p. 464)
6. **Familism** is the idea that family members should support one another because family unity is more important than individual freedom and success. (p. 466)
7. **Fictive kin** refers to a person who becomes accepted as part of a family to which he or she has no blood relation. (p. 467)
8. The **empty nest** refers to the time in the lives of parents when their grown children have left the home to pursue their own lives. (p. 469)
9. The **kinkeepers** are caregivers who celebrate family achievements, gather the family together, and keep in touch with family members who have moved away. (p. 474)
10. Middle-aged adults were once commonly referred to as the **sandwich generation** because of the false belief that they are often squeezed by the needs of the younger and older generations. (p. 477)
11. **Relative deprivation** is the idea that people's satisfaction is determined by comparing themselves to others in their group. (p. 479)
12. The **extrinsic rewards of work** include salary, health insurance, pension, and other tangible benefits. (p. 480)
13. The **intrinsic rewards of work** include job satisfaction, self-esteem, and other intangible benefits. (p. 480)
14. A **mentor** is a skilled and knowledgeable person who advises or guides an inexperienced person. (p. 482)
15. **Flextime** refers to a work schedule that is flexible so that workers can balance their personal and employment responsibilities. (p. 484)
16. **Telecommuting** is working at home and using electronic means of keeping in touch with the office. (p. 484)
17. **Stressors** are situations, events, experiences, or other stimuli that cause a person to feel stressed. (p. 485)
18. **Allostatic load** refers to the total burden of stress and illness that a person must cope with. (p. 486)
19. **Organ reserve** is the capacity of the body's organs to allow the body to cope with unusual stress. (p. 487)
20. Often used by younger adults, **problem-focused coping** occurs when a person attempts to change a stressor in order to reduce its impact. (p. 487)
21. Often used by older adults, **emotion-focused coping** occurs when a person changes how they feel about a stressor rather than attempting to change the stressor directly. (p. 487)

LATE ADULTHOOD

Body and Mind

14 chapter

Chapter Overview

Chapter 14 covers biosocial development during late adulthood, discussing the myths and reality of this final stage of the life span. In a society such as ours, which glorifies youth, there is a tendency to exaggerate the physical decline brought on by aging. In fact, the changes that occur during the later years are largely a continuation of those that began earlier in adulthood, and the vast majority of the elderly consider themselves to be in good health.

Nonetheless, the aging process is characterized by an increased incidence of impaired vision and hearing, and by declines in the major body systems. These are all changes to which the individual must adjust. In addition, the incidence of life-threatening diseases becomes more common with every decade.

Next, the chapter describes the changes in cognitive functioning associated with late adulthood, beginning with the usual changes associated with the information-processing system. These include the declines in older adults' control processes, including their retrieval strategies.

The main reason for reduced cognitive functioning during late adulthood is dementia. This pathological loss of intellectual ability can be caused by a variety of diseases and circumstances; risk factors, treatment, and prognosis differ accordingly.

The chapter concludes by making it clear that cognitive changes during late adulthood are by no means restricted to declines in intellectual functioning. For many individuals, late adulthood is a time of great aesthetic, creative, philosophical, and spiritual growth.

NOTE: Answer guidelines for all Chapter 14 questions begin on page 229.

Chapter Review

When you have finished reading the chapter, work through the material that follows to review it. Complete the sentences and answer the questions. As you proceed, evaluate your performance for each section by consulting the answers beginning on page 229. Do not continue with the next section until you understand each answer. If you need to, review or reread the appropriate section in the textbook before continuing.

Ageism (pp. 497–504)

1. Social scientists who study aging are called ________________ . The prejudice that people tend to feel about older people is called ________________ .
2. Sometimes, younger adults automatically lapse into ________________ when they talk to older adults.

Describe this form of speech.

3. Anxiety that others hold prejudiced beliefs about them, or ________________ ________________ , can also be debilitating for the elderly.
4. Older adults who are healthy, financially secure, and integrated into the lives of their families and communities are classified as ________________-________________ . These people make up the ________________ (smallest/largest) number of older adults in the United States.
5. Older adults who suffer physical, mental, or social deficits are classified as ________________-________________ . The ________________-________________ are dependent on others for almost everything;

they are ________________ (the majority/a small minority) of those over age 65. Age ________________ (is/is not) an accurate predictor of dependency. For this reason, some gerontologists prefer to use the terms ________________ aging, ________________ aging, and ________________ aging.

6. In the past, when populations were sorted according to age, the resulting picture was a ________________ ________________, with the youngest and ________________ (smallest/largest) group at the bottom and the oldest and ________________ (smallest/largest) group at the top.

List three reasons for this picture.

a. ____

____

b. ____

____

c. ____

____

7. Today, because of ________________ (fewer/more) births and increased ________________, the shape of the population is becoming closer to a(n) ________________.

8. The shape of the population pyramid ________________ (varies/is the same) throughout the world.

9. The ratio of self-sufficient, productive adults to dependent children and elderly adults is called the ________________ ________________. Because of the declining ________________ rate and the small size of the cohort just entering ________________ ________________, this ratio is ________________ (better/worse) than it has ever been. As people live longer, the ratio will ________________.

10. Approximately ________________ percent of the elderly live in nursing homes.

11. Most older adults remain self-sufficient today because the time any person spends ill or disabled by a serious condition has been reduced; that is, there is a(n) ________________ ________________ ________________. This trend is due to improved ________________, ________________, and ________________ ________________.

12. Older men are more likely to suffer problems with the sense of ________________ than older women are.

13. After age 65, only about ________________ percent of adults can see well without glasses. Fortunately, ________________ is available for every sensory loss. Passive acceptance of sensory loss, such as not wearing hearing aids, ________________ (increases/decreases) morbidity.

THINK ABOUT IT: Consider your probable appearance, behavior, and traits when you reach late adulthood. Which of your current behaviors will be similar and which ones will be different when you are 75? In what ways will you look like you do now and in what ways will your appearance be different? What do you think your eyesight, hearing, and physical strength will be like at age 75?

APPLICATIONS:

14. Which of the following is most likely to be a result of ageism?
   a. the participation of the elderly in community activities
   b. laws requiring workers to retire by a certain age
   c. an increase in multigenerational families
   d. greater interest in the study of gerontology

15. Loretta majored in psychology at the local university. Because she wanted to serve her community, she applied to a local agency to study the effects of aging on the elderly. Loretta is a
   a. developmental psychologist.
   b. behaviorist.
   c. gerontologist.
   d. demographer.

16. An 85-year-old man enjoys good health and actively participates in family and community activities. This person is best described as being
   a. ageist.
   b. young-old.
   c. old-old.
   d. a gerontologist.

Health and Sickness (pp. 504–512)

17. In discussing the aging process, or ________________, gerontologists distinguish between the irreversible changes that occur with

time, called ________________

________________ , and ________________

________________ , which refers to changes caused by poor ________________

________________ , ________________ vulnerability, and other influences. This latter category of age-related changes ________________ (is/is not) inevitable with the passage of time. The distinction between these categories of age-related changes ______________ (is/is not) clear-cut.

18. The risk factors for cardiovascular disease include

________________ , ________________ ,

________________ ________________ ,

________________ ________________

________________ , lack of ________________ ,

and ________________ ________________ .

This disease is considered ________________ aging because not everyone develops it. Even so, there is a ________________ aging component in that the major risk factors for the disease are more common with ________________ .

19. As people age, they need ________________ (more/fewer) daily calories because bodies become ________________ (more/less) efficient at digesting food and using its nutrients.

20. Among health habits, both ________________ and ________________ may be even more important in later life than earlier. Regular exercise is a proven way to compress

________________ .

21. A key factor in how people age is how well they respond with ________________

________________ ________________

________________ , choosing activities they can do well as their adjustment to aging.

22. Falls become more of a hazard for the elderly, partly because of fragile bones, or

________________ .

23. Drinking no more than ________________ glasses of wine or beer a day benefits the heart and may postpone dementia.

24. The oldest age to which members of a species can live, called the ________________

________________ ________________ , which in humans is approximately ________________ years, is quite different from ________________

________________ ________________

________________ , which is defined as

____

________________________________ .

25. In the United States today, average life expectancy at birth is about ________________ for men and ________________ for women.

26. In ancient times, average life expectancy was only about ________________ years, due to the fact that ________________________________ .

In 1900, in developed nations, the average life expectancy was about age ________________ .

This increase was due largely to

________________ , ________________ ,

________________ , ________________

________________ , and ________________

________________ .

27. A person who has lived 100 years or more is called a ________________ . Although the size of this group is ________________ (increasing/decreasing/stable), ________________ (few/most) scientists believe that efforts to stop aging, or ________________ , can succeed.

28. (Thinking Like a Scientist) One promising strategy for slowing the aging process, which involves reducing food consumption, is

________________ ________________ .

STUDY TIP: Many people's perceptions of aging are inaccurate and reflect ageist stereotypes of biosocial development in late adulthood. These stereotypes stem from our preoccupation with physical decline that is more the result of disease than it is of aging per se. Think of two elderly adults (relatives, friends, or even public personalities), one who is healthy and vigorous and one who has suffered major physical, mental, or social losses. Write a few sentences describing each person's health, personality, and lifestyle. Also indicate the extent to which each person fits, or does not fit, the usual stereotypes of the older adult.

APPLICATIONS:

29. With regard to nutrition, most elderly should probably be advised to
    a. take large doses of vitamins and, especially, antioxidants.
    b. eat foods that are high in calories.
    c. consume a varied and healthy diet.
    d. eat large meals but eat less often.

30. In concluding her presentation on human longevity, Katrina states that
    a. current average life expectancy is about twice what it was at the turn of the century.
    b. current maximum life span is about twice what it was at the turn of the century.
    c. both average life expectancy and maximum life span have increased since the turn of the century.
    d. although maximum life span has not increased, average life expectancy has, because infants are less likely to die.

Thinking in Late Adulthood (pp. 512–525)

31. Although new ________________ and ________________ grow in the brain during adulthood, one universal change is a ________________ in brain processes. This can be traced to reduced production of ________________, including ________________, ________________, ________________, and ________________. Some experts believe that speed is the basis for ________________, or general intelligence.

32. One cognitive change that everyone experiences is that with age, we think more ________________. In addition, the brain ________________ as it ages, including in the ________________, which is crucial for memory, and the ________________ ________________, which is necessary for planning and coordinating thoughts. Even so, older adults use ________________ (fewer/more) parts of the brain when thinking than younger adults.

33. For stimuli to become information that is perceived, they must be ________________.

34. Reduced sensory input ________________ (impairs/does not necessarily impair) cognition. Most experts believe that reduced sensory input among the elderly is a problem in the ________________ (brain/senses/brain and the senses).

35. Once information is perceived, it must be placed in ________________. With age, memory for vocabulary (________________ ________________) tends to be good, while memory for events (________________ ________________) declines. A common memory error is ________________ ________________, not remembering who or what was the source of a specific piece of information.

36. Working memory has two interrelated functions: to temporarily ________________ information and then to ________________ it. These functions ________________ (are reduced/are not reduced) with aging.

37. Older adults are particularly likely to experience difficulty in multitasking, because it requires screening out ________________ and inhibiting ________________ ________________.

38. The idea that memory should be measured in everyday tasks and circumstances, not as laboratory tests assess it, is called ________________ ________________.

39. Retrieval strategies and other methods for regulating the flow of information are called ________________ ________________. These processes usually depend on the brain's ________________ ________________, which tends to ________________ with age.

40. Older adults are more likely to rely on prior ________________, general ________________, ________________, and ________________ ________________ ________________. This is called a ________________-________________ decision-making strategy and involves using ________________ (inductive/deductive) reasoning.

41. During late adulthood, ________________ is a better predictor of cognition than

______________. In addition, cognitive ability can be improved with ______________.

42. The overall slowdown of cognitive abilities that often occurs in the days or months before death is called ______________ ______________.

STUDY TIP: To enhance your understanding of the very different learning styles of different age groups, imagine that you are going to be visited by a 10-year-old and an 80-year-old who don't' know each other. What kind of game or other activity would you suggest that would accommodate the intellectual ability of both guests?

APPLICATIONS:

43. Although 75-year-old Sharonda remembers a relative once telling her that her ancestors were royalty in their native country, she can't recall which relative it was. Like many older adults, Sharonda is evidently displaying signs of
  a. multi-infarct dementia.
  b. Alzheimer disease.
  c. subcortical dementia.
  d. source amnesia.

44. Because of deficits in sensory input, older people may tend to
  a. forget the names of people and places.
  b. be distracted by irrelevant stimuli.
  c. miss details in a dimly lit room.
  d. reminisce at length about the past.

45. At the present stage of research into cognitive development during late adulthood, which of the following statements has the greatest support?
  a. There is uniform decline in all stages of memory during late adulthood.
  b. Long-term memory shows the greatest decline with age.
  c. Working memory shows the greatest decline with age.
  d. The decline in memory may be the result of the failure to use effective input and retrieval strategies.

46. Although pathological loss of intellectual ability in elderly people is often referred to as ______________, a more precise term for this loss is ______________, which literally means ______________.
Not everyone with memory loss has this problem; not remembering names or places as well as they once did represents ______________ ______________.

47. The most common form of dementia is ______________ ______________.
This disorder is characterized by abnormalities that form in the ______________ ______________, called ______________ and ______________, which destroy normal brain functioning.

48. Plaques are formed from a protein called ______________-______________; tangles are twisted masses of threads made of a protein called ______________ within the neurons. Plaques and tangles proliferate especially in the ______________ of the brain.

49. When Alzheimer disease (AD) appears in middle adulthood, the person either has ______________-______________ or has inherited one of three genes: ______________, ______________, or ______________. However, this is quite ______________ (common/rare), and the disease usually progresses ______________ (less/more) quickly, reaching the last phase within ______________ years.

50. Most cases of AD begin at age ______________ or so. Many genes have some impact, including ______________ and ______________.

51. The beginning stages of Alzheimer disease are marked by ______________ that is ______________ (more/less) than the normal age-related slowness. The affected person is likely to become ______________ in his or her own neighborhood. Changes in ______________ are also likely.

52. Every year, symptoms worsen. Eventually, memory loss becomes dangerous and ______________ because the person can no longer manage ______________ ______________ ______________. People in the final stage require ______________-______________ ______________. Finally, people no longer______________ and do not respond with any action or emotion at all. In general, death comes ______________ (how many years?) after the first signs appear.

53. The second major type of dementia is ________ ________. This condition occurs because a temporary obstruction of the ________ ________, called a(n) ________, prevents a sufficient supply of blood from reaching the brain. This causes destruction of brain tissue, commonly called a(n) ________.

54. Unlike the person with Alzheimer disease, the person with VaD shows a ________ and ________ loss of intellectual functioning.

55. Another category of dementias, called ________ ________ dementia, originates in brain areas that regulate emotion and social behavior (the ________ and the ________ ________).

56. A common dementia that produces muscle tremors or rigidity results from ________ ________. This disease is related to the degeneration of neurons that produce the neurotransmitter ________.

57. In a related form of dementia, round deposits of protein are found throughout the brain. The main symptom of this dementia, called ________ ________ dementia, is loss of ________.

58. The incidence of dementia can be cut in half through regular ________. The other major preventive measure is to avoid the ________ that cause dementia.

59. The first step in treating dementia is to ________. The next step is to get a proper ________.

60. Oftentimes, the elderly are thought to be suffering from brain disease when, in fact, their symptoms are a sign of ________ dementia caused by some other factor.

61. The causes of reversible dementia include ________ ________.
Symptoms of dementia can result from drug ________ that occurs when a person is taking several different medications.

APPLICATIONS:

62. Because she has trouble screening out distractions and inhibiting irrelevant thoughts, 70-year-old Lena is likely to
   a. have suffered a mini-stroke.
   b. be at increased risk of developing dementia.
   c. experience typical age-related declines in her working memory.
   d. have some type of reversible dementia.

63. A patient has the following symptoms: blurred vision, slurred speech, and mental confusion. The patient is probably suffering from
   a. Alzheimer disease.
   b. vascular dementia.
   c. Huntington's disease.
   d. Parkinson's disease.

64. Lately, Wayne's father, who is 73, harps on the fact that he forgets small things such as where he put the house keys. He also has trouble eating and sleeping. The family doctor diagnoses Wayne's father as
   a. being in the early stages of Alzheimer disease.
   b. being in the later stages of Alzheimer disease.
   c. suffering from senile dementia.
   d. possibly suffering from depression.

65. Leland's parents are in their 70s, and he wants to do something to ensure that their cognitive abilities remain sharp for years to come. As a friend, what would you encourage Leland to suggest that his parents do?
   a. They should take long walks several times a week.
   b. They should spend time reading and doing crossword puzzles.
   c. They should go to a neurologist for regular checkups.
   d. They should take long walks often and spend time reading and doing crossword puzzles.

66. According to Erik Erikson, older adults are more interested in ________ ________ than younger adults and, as the "social witnesses" to life, are more aware of the ________ of the generations.

67. According to Abraham Maslow, older adults are more likely to achieve ________.

68. Many people become more appreciative of ________ and ________ ________ as they get older.

69. Many people also become more _______________ and _______________ than when they were younger.

70. One form of this attempt to put life into perspective is called the _______________ _______________, in which the older person connects his or her own life with the future.

71. One of the most positive attributes commonly associated with older people is _______________, which one summary defines as "an expert knowledge system dealing with the _______________ and _______________ of life.

APPLICATIONS:

72. Abner believes that his grandfather's tendency to reminisce
   a. represents an unhealthy preoccupation with the self and the past.
   b. is an underlying cause of age segregation.
   c. is a necessary and healthy process.
   d. is a result of a heightened aesthetic sense.

73. Sixty-five-year-old Andrea is becoming more reflective and philosophical as she grows older. A developmental psychologist would probably say that Andrea
   a. had unhappy experiences as a younger adult.
   b. is demonstrating a normal, age-related tendency.
   c. will probably become introverted and reclusive as she gets older.
   d. feels that her life has been a failure.

Progress Test 1

Multiple-Choice Questions

Circle your answers to the following questions and check them with the answers on page 230. If your answer is incorrect, read the explanation for why it is incorrect and then consult the appropriate pages of the text (in parentheses following the correct answer).

1. Ageism is
   a. the study of aging and the aged.
   b. prejudice or discrimination against older people.
   c. the genetic disease that causes children to age prematurely.
   d. the view of aging that the body and its parts deteriorate with use.

2. The U.S. population pyramid is becoming a square because of
   a. increasing birth rates and life spans.
   b. decreasing birth rates and life spans.
   c. decreasing birth rates and increasing life spans.
   d. rapid population growth.

3. Primary aging refers to the
   a. changes that are caused by illness.
   b. changes that can be reversed or prevented.
   c. irreversible changes that occur with time.
   d. changes that are caused by poor health habits.

4. Gerontology is the
   a. medical specialty devoted to aging.
   b. study of secondary aging.
   c. multidisciplinary study of old age.
   d. study of optimal aging.

5. Although cognition gradually declines in late adulthood, this decline can be slowed or halted by health and
   a. control processes.
   b. medical intervention.
   c. drugs.
   d. training.

6. The two basic functions of working memory are
   a. storage that enables conscious use and processing of information.
   b. temporary storage and processing of sensory stimuli.
   c. automatic memories and retrieval of learned memories.
   d. permanent storage and retrieval of information.

7. Strategies to retain and retrieve information are part of which basic component of information processing?
   a. sensory register
   b. working memory
   c. control processes
   d. explicit memory

8. The plaques and tangles that accompany Alzheimer disease usually begin in the
   a. temporal lobe.
   b. frontal lobe.
   c. hippocampus.
   d. cerebral cortex.

9. Factors that may explain some declines in cognitive functioning include
   a. problems with sensory input.
   b. disparaging self-perceptions of cognitive abilities.
   c. difficulty with traditional methods of measuring cognitive functioning.
   d. all of these things.

10. When using working memory, older adults have particular difficulty
    a. performing several tasks at once.
    b. picking up faint sounds.
    c. processing blurry images.
    d. recalling the meaning of rarely used vocabulary.

11. A common cause of reversible dementia is
    a. a temporary obstruction of the blood vessels.
    b. genetic mutation.
    c. overmedication.
    d. depression.

12. Dementia refers to
    a. pathological loss of intellectual functioning.
    b. the increasing forgetfulness that sometimes accompanies the aging process.
    c. abnormal behavior associated with mental illness and with advanced stages of alcoholism.
    d. a genetic disorder that doesn't become overtly manifested until late adulthood.

13. Alzheimer disease is characterized by
    a. a proliferation of plaques and tangles in the cerebral cortex.
    b. a destruction of brain tissue as a result of strokes.
    c. rigidity and tremor of the muscles.
    d. an excess of fluid pressing on the brain.

14. Medication has been associated with symptoms of dementia in the elderly for all of the following reasons *except*
    a. standard drug dosages are often too strong for the elderly.
    b. the elderly tend to become psychologically dependent upon drugs.
    c. drugs sometimes have the side effect of slowing mental processes.
    d. the intermixing of drugs can sometimes have detrimental effects on cognitive functioning.

15. The primary purpose of the life review is to
    a. enhance one's spirituality.
    b. produce an autobiography.
    c. give advice to younger generations.
    d. put one's life into perspective.

True or False Items

Write T (*true*) or F (*false*) on the line in front of each statement.

_______ 1. The dependency ratio is higher than it has ever been.

_______ 2. Because of demographic changes, the majority of America's elderly population is now predominantly old-old rather than young-old.

_______ 3. Gerontologists focus on distinguishing aging in terms of the quality of aging, that is, in terms of young-old versus old-old.

_______ 4. Although average life expectancy is increasing, maximum life span has remained unchanged.

_______ 5. The importance of lifestyle factors in contributing to longevity is underscored by studies of the long-lived.

_______ 6. As long as their vision and hearing remain unimpaired, older adults are no less efficient than younger adults at inputting information.

_______ 7. Reduced sensory input impairs cognition by increasing the power of interference.

_______ 8. In studies of problem solving in real-life contexts, the scores of older adults were better than those of younger adults.

_______ 9. Dementia refers to pathological loss of brain functioning caused by brain damage or disease.

_______ 10. Alzheimer disease is partly genetic.

_______ 11. Late adulthood is often associated with a narrowing of interests and an exclusive focus on the self.

_______ 12. According to Maslow, self-actualization is actually more likely to be reached during late adulthood.

Progress Test 2

Progress Test 2 should be completed during a final chapter review. Answer the following questions after you thoroughly understand the correct answers for the Chapter Review and Progress Test 1.

Multiple-Choice Questions

1. An important demographic change in America is that

a. ageism is beginning to diminish.
b. population growth has virtually ceased.
c. the median age is falling.
d. the number of older people in the population is increasing.

2. Heart disease is

a. caused by aging.
b. a genetic disease.
c. an example of secondary aging.
d. all of these things.

3. As a result of the ________ birth rate, the population dependency ratio in most industrialized countries is ________ than it has ever been.

a. increasing; higher
b. increasing; lower
c. decreasing; higher
d. decreasing; lower

4. In ancient times, the average life expectancy was only about 20 years primarily because

a. so many babies died.
b. there were few effective treatments for serious illnesses.
c. accidents and warfare took scores of lives in most parts of the world.
d. people did not understand the importance of a healthy diet to longevity.

5. In humans, average life expectancy varies according to all of the following *except*

a. historical factors.
b. ethnic factors.
c. cultural factors.
d. socioeconomic factors.

6. Research suggests that aging results in

a. increased sensitivity of sensory memory.
b. a significant decrease in the sensitivity of the sensory system that cannot usually be compensated for.
c. declines in memory for events.
d. no noticeable changes in sensory memory.

7. Which of the following most accurately characterizes age-related changes in working memory?

a. The ability to screen out distractions and inhibit irrelevant thoughts declines.
b. Storage capacity declines while processing efficiency remains stable.
c. Storage capacity remains stable while processing efficiency declines.
d. Both storage capacity and processing efficiency remain stable.

8. In general, with increasing age the control processes used to remember new information

a. become more efficient.
b. become more complex.
c. become more intertwined.
d. become simpler and less efficient.

9. Regarding the role of genes in Alzheimer disease, which of the following is NOT true?

a. Most cases of AD begin at age 75 or so.
b. Some people inherit a gene that increases their risk of developing the disease.
c. The disease in middle age progresses slowly.
d. In people with AD, the plaques and tangles proliferate, especially in the hippocampus.

10. Dementia

a. is more likely to occur among the aged.
b. has no relationship to age.
c. cannot occur before the age of 60.
d. is an inevitable occurrence during late adulthood.

11. The most common form of dementia is

a. Alzheimer disease.
b. multi-infarct dementia.
c. Parkinson's disease.
d. alcoholism and depression.

12. Organic causes of dementia include all of the following *except*

a. Parkinson's disease.
b. multiple sclerosis.
c. Huntington's disease.
d. leukemia.

13. The psychological illness most likely to be misdiagnosed as dementia is

a. schizophrenia.
b. anxiety.
c. personality disorder.
d. depression.

14. On balance, it can be concluded that positive cognitive development during late adulthood
    a. occurs only for a small minority of individuals.
    b. leads to thought processes that are more appropriate to the final stage of life.
    c. makes older adults far less pragmatic than younger adults.
    d. is impossible in view of increasing deficits in cognitive functioning.

15. A key factor underlying the older adult's cognitive developments in the realms of aesthetics, philosophy, and spiritualism may be
    a. the realization that one's life is drawing to a close.
    b. the despair associated with a sense of isolation from the community.
    c. the need to leave one's mark on history.
    d. a growing indifference to the outside world.

Matching Items

Match each term or concept with its corresponding description or definition.

Terms or Concepts

________ 1. young-old
________ 2. old-old
________ 3. compression of morbidity
________ 4. primary aging
________ 5. secondary aging
________ 6. working memory
________ 7. control processes
________ 8. dementia
________ 9. Alzheimer disease
________ 10. Parkinson's disease
________ 11. source amnesia
________ 12. life review
________ 13. frontal lobe dementias

Descriptions or Definitions

a. the universal changes that occur as we grow older
b. limiting the time a person is ill
c. the majority of the elderly
d. the minority of the elderly
e. age-related changes that are caused by health habits, genes, and other conditions
f. the inability to remember the origins of a specific piece of information
g. temporarily stores information for conscious processing
h. strategies for retaining and retrieving information
i. severely impaired thinking, memory, or problem-solving ability
j. caused by a degeneration of neurons that produce dopamine
k. putting one's life into perspective
l. characterized by plaques and tangles in the cerebral cortex
m. brain disorders that do not directly involve thinking and memory

Key Terms

Using your own words, write a brief definition or explanation of each of the following terms on a separate piece of paper.

1. ageism
2. elderspeak
3. young-old
4. old-old
5. oldest-old
6. population pyramid
7. dependency ratio
8. compression of morbidity
9. primary aging
10. secondary aging
11. cardiovascular disease
12. maximum life span
13. average life expectancy
14. centenarian
15. calorie restriction
16. ecological validity
17. control processes
18. dementia
19. Alzheimer disease
20. vascular dementia (VaD)
21. frontal lobe dementia
22. self-actualization
23. life review

Answers

CHAPTER REVIEW

1. gerontologists; ageism
2. elderspeak

Like baby talk, elderspeak uses simple and short sentences, exaggerated emphasis, slower talk, higher pitch, and repetition.

3. stereotype threat
4. young-old; largest
5. old-old; oldest-old; a small minority; is not; optimal; usual
6. population pyramid; largest; smallest

   a. Each generation of young adults gave birth to more than enough children to replace themselves.

   b. About half of all children died before age 5.

   c. Those who lived to be middle-aged rarely survived diseases like cancer or heart attacks.
7. fewer; survival; square
8. varies
9. dependency ratio; birth; late adulthood; better; reverse (from 2:1 to 1:2)
10. 4
11. compression of morbidity; lifestyle; medicine; technological aids
12. hearing
13. 10; technology; increases
14. **b.** is the answer.
15. **c.** is the answer.

    a. Although Loretta is probably a developmental psychologist, that category is too broad to be correct.

    b. Behaviorism describes her approach to studying, not what she is studying.

    d. Demographics is the study of populations.
16. **b.** is the answer.

    a. An ageist is a person who is prejudiced against the elderly.

    c. People who are "old-old" have social, physical, and mental problems that hamper their successful aging.

    d. A gerontologist is a person who studies aging.
17. senescence; primary aging; secondary aging; health habits; genetic; is not; is not
18. diabetes; smoking; abdominal fat; high blood pressure; exercise; high cholesterol; secondary; primary; age
19. fewer; less
20. diet; exercise; morbidity
21. selective optimization with compensation
22. osteoporosis
23. one or two
24. maximum life span; 122; average life expectancy; the number of years the average newborn in a population group is likely to live
25. 75; 81
26. 20; so many babies died; 50; sanitation, immunization, antibiotics; medical care; safe water
27. centenarian; increasing; few; anti-aging
28. calorie restriction
29. **c.** is the answer.

    a. Large doses of vitamins can be harmful.

    b. Older adults need fewer calories to maintain body weight.

    d. This is an unhealthy dietary regimen.
30. **d.** is the answer.

    a. Current average life expectancy is 28 years more than it was at the turn of the century.

    b. & c. Maximum life span has not changed since the turn of the century.
31. neurons; dendrites; slowdown; neurotransmitters; glutamate; acetylcholine; serotonin; dopamine, *g*
32. slowly; shrinks; hypothalamus; prefrontal cortex; more
33. detected
34. impairs; brain and the senses
35. storage (memory); semantic memory; episodic memory; source amnesia
36. store; process
37. distractions; irrelevant thoughts
38. ecological validity
39. control processes; prefrontal cortex; shrink
40. knowledge; principles; familiarity; rules of thumb; top-down; deductive
41. health; age; training
42. terminal decline
43. **d.** is the answer.

    a., b., & c. Sharonda's inability to recall the source of this information is a common form of forgetfulness among older adults; it is not necessarily a sign of dementia.
44. **c.** is the answer.

    a. & d. Sensory refers to noticing sensory events rather than memory.

    b. Age-related deficits in sensory input are most likely for ambiguous or weak stimuli.

45. **d.** is the answer.

    a. Some aspects of information processing, such as long-term memory, show less decline with age than others, such as working memory.

    b. & c. The text does not indicate that one particular subcomponent of memory shows the greatest decline.

46. senility; dementia; severely impaired judgment, memory, or problem-solving ability; mild cognitive impairment
47. Alzheimer disease (AD); cerebral cortex; plaques; tangles
48. beta-amyloid; tau; hippocampus
49. trisomy-21 (Down syndrome); APP; presenilin 1; presenilin 2; rare; more; three to five
50. 75; SORL1; ApoE4
51. forgetfulness; more; disoriented; personality
52. debilitating; basic daily needs; full-time care; talk; 10 to 15
53. vascular dementia (multi-infarct dementia); blood vessels; infarct; stroke (or ministroke [TIA})
54. sporadic; progressive
55. frontal lobe dementia; amygdala; frontal lobes
56. Parkinson's disease; dopamine
57. Lewy body; inhibition
58. exercise; pathogens
59. care for the overall health of the person; diagnosis
60. reversible
61. inadequate nutrition, dehydration, brain tumors, physical illness, and overmedication; polypharmacy
62. **c.** is the answer.

    a., b., & d. Lena's symptoms are not indicative of any type of dementia.

63. **b.** is the answer.
64. **d.** is the answer.

    a., b., & c. The symptoms Wayne's father is experiencing are those of depression, which is often misdiagnosed as dementia in the elderly.

65. **d.** is the answer. While c. might be something they should do, the most important things are for them to get exercise and maintain activities that promote cognitive stimulation.
66. arts, children, and the whole of human experience; interdependence
67. self-actualization
68. nature; aesthetic experiences
69. reflective; philosophical
70. life review
71. wisdom; conduct; understanding
72. **c.** is the answer.

    d. This would lead to a greater appreciation of nature and art, but not necessarily to a tendency to reminisce.

73. **b.** is the answer.

PROGRESS TEST 1

Multiple-Choice Questions

1. **b.** is the answer. (p. 497)

    a. This is gerontology.

    c. This is progeria.

    d. This theory is not discussed.

2. **c.** is the answer. (pp. 500–501)
3. **c.** is the answer. (p. 504)

    a., b., & d. These are examples of secondary aging.

4. **a.** is the answer. (p. 497)
5. **d.** is the answer. (p. 516)
6. **a.** is the answer. (p. 514)

    b. These are the functions of sensory memory.

    c. This refers to long-term memory's processing.

    d. This is the function of long-term memory.

7. **c.** is the answer. (p. 516)
8. **c.** is the answer. (p. 518)
9. **d.** is the answer. (pp. 498, 514–515)
10. **a.** is the answer. (pp. 515)

    b. & c. These may be true, but they involve sensory memory rather than working memory.

    d. Memory for vocabulary, which generally is very good throughout adulthood, involves long-term memory.

11. **c.** is the answer. (p. 522)
12. **a.** is the answer. (p. 517)
13. **a.** is the answer. (p. 518)

    b. This describes multi-infarct dementia.

    c. This describes Parkinson's disease.

    d. This was not given in the text as a cause of dementia.

14. **b.** is the answer. (pp. 521–522)
15. **d.** is the answer. (p. 524)

True or False Items

1. F The ratio is lower than it has ever been, with fewer people who are dependent on others for care. (p. 501)
2. F Although our population is aging, the terms *old-old* and *young-old* refer to degree of physical and social well-being, not to age. (p. 499)
3. T (pp. 499–500)
4. T (p. 508)
5. T (p. 510)
6. F The slowing of perceptual processes and decreases in attention associated with aging are also likely to affect efficiency of input. (p. 514)
7. T (p. 514)
8. T (p. 515)
9. T (p. 517)
10. T (p. 518)
11. F Interests often broaden during late adulthood, and there is by no means exclusive focus on the self. (pp. 523–524)
12. T (p. 523)

PROGRESS TEST 2

Multiple-Choice Questions

1. **d.** is the answer. (pp. 500–501)

   a. Ageism is prejudice, not a demographic change.

   b. Although birth rates have fallen, population growth has not ceased.

   c. Actually, with the "squaring of the pyramid," the median age is rising.
2. **c.** is the answer. (p. 504)

   a. & b. Over time, the interaction of accumulating risk factors with age-related weakening of the heart and relevant genetic weaknesses makes the elderly increasingly vulnerable to heart disease.
3. **d.** is the answer. (p. 501)
4. **a.** is the answer. (p. 508)

   b. Serious illnesses are more likely among older adults.

   c. & d. Although both of these may be true, neither is the primary reason for an average life expectancy of only 20 years.
5. **b.** is the answer. (p. 508)
6. **c.** is the answer. (p. 514)
7. **a.** is the answer. (p. 515)
8. **d.** is the answer. (p. 516)
9. **c.** is the answer. Just the opposite is true. (p. 518)
10. **a.** is the answer. Although age is not the key factor, it is true that dementia is more likely to occur in older adults. (p. 517)
11. **a.** is the answer. (p. 518)

    b. MID is responsible for about 15 percent of all dementia.

    c. & d. Compared to Alzheimer disease, which accounts for about 70 percent of all dementia, these account for a much lower percentage.
12. **d.** is the answer. (pp. 519–520)
13. **d.** is the answer. (p. 521)

    a. & c. These psychological illnesses are less common in the elderly than in younger adults, and less common than depression among the elderly.

    b. This disorder was not discussed in association with dementia.
14. **b.** is the answer. (pp. 523–524)

    a. & d. Positive cognitive development is typical of older adults.

    c. Pragmatism is one characteristic of wisdom, an attribute commonly associated with older people.
15. **a.** is the answer. (p. 524)

    b. & c. Although these may be true of some older adults, they are not necessarily a key factor in cognitive development during late adulthood.

    d. In fact, older adults are typically more concerned with the whole of human experience.

Matching Items

1. c (p. 499)	**6.** g (p. 514)	**11.** f (p. 514)
2. d (p. 499)	**7.** h (p. 516)	**12.** k (p. 524)
3. b (p. 502)	**8.** i (p. 517)	**13.** m (p. 519)
4. a (p. 504)	**9.** l (p. 518)	
5. e (p. 504)	**10.** j (p. 519)	

KEY TERMS

1. **Ageism** is prejudice against older people. (p. 497)
2. **Elderspeak** is a condescending way of speaking to older adults that resembles baby talk, using simple sentences, a slower rate, higher pitch, and repetition. (p. 498)
3. Most of America's elderly can be classified as **young-old,** meaning that they are healthy and vigorous, relatively well-off financially, well integrated into the lives of their families and communities, and politically active. (p. 499)

4. Older people who are classified as **old-old** are those who suffer severe physical, mental, or social problems in later life. (p. 499)
5. Elderly adults who are classified as **oldest-old** are dependent on others for almost everything. (p. 499)
6. The **population pyramid** graphically represents the entire population as a series of stacked bars in which each bar represents a different age cohort, with the youngest cohort at the bottom. (p. 500)
7. The **dependency ratio** is the ratio of self-sufficient, productive adults to children and elderly adults in a given population. (p. 501)
8. Researchers who are interested in improving the health of the elderly focus on a **compression of morbidity,** that is, a limiting of the time any person spends ill or infirm. (p. 502)
9. **Primary aging** refers to the universal and irreversible physical changes that occur as people get older. (p. 504)
10. **Secondary aging** refers to changes that are more common as people age but are caused by health habits, genes, and other influences that vary from person to person. (p. 504)
11. **Cardiovascular disease (CVD)** refers collectively to the various diseases that affect the heart and the circulatory system. (p. 504)
12. The **maximum life span** is the maximum number of years that a particular species is genetically programmed to live. For humans, the maximum life span is approximately 122 years. (p. 508)
13. **Average life expectancy** is the number of years the average newborn in a particular population is likely to live. (p. 508)
14. A **centenarian** is a person who is 100 years of age or older. (p. 510)
15. **Calorie restriction** is the practice of limiting dietary energy intake while still consuming sufficient vitamins, minerals, and other important nutrients in an effort to slow down aging. (p. 511)
16. **Ecological validity** is the idea that memory should be measured via everyday tasks, rather than in laboratory tests. (p. 515)
17. **Control processes** include memory and retrieval strategies, selective attention, and rules or strategies for problem solving. (p. 516)
18. **Dementia** is severely impaired judgment, memory, or problem-solving ability that is irreversible and caused by organic brain damage or disease. (p. 517)
19. **Alzheimer disease (AD),** a progressive disorder that is the most common form of dementia, is characterized by plaques and tangles in the cerebral cortex that destroy normal brain functioning. (p. 518)
20. **Vascular dementia (VaD),** which accounts for about 15 percent of all dementia, occurs because an infarct, or temporary obstruction of the blood vessels (often called a stroke), prevents a sufficient supply of blood from reaching an area of the brain. It is characterized by sporadic and progressive loss of brain functioning; also called *multi-infarct dementia (MID)*. (p. 519)
21. **Frontal lobe dementia** is a form of dementia characterized by personality changes caused by damage to the frontal lobe of the brain; also called *frontotemporal lobar degeneration*. (p. 519)
22. Characterized by aesthetic and spiritual understanding, **self-actualization** is the final stage in Maslow's hierarchy of needs. (p. 523)
23. In the **life review,** an older person attempts to put his or her life into perspective by recalling and recounting various aspects of life to members of the younger generations. (p. 524)

15 chapter

LATE ADULTHOOD

Psychosocial Development

Chapter Overview

There is great variation in development after age 65. Certain psychosocial changes are common during this stage of the life span—retirement, the death of a spouse, and failing health—yet people respond to these experiences in vastly different ways.

Individual experiences may help to explain the fact that theories of psychosocial aging, discussed in the first section of the chapter, are often diametrically opposed. The second section of the chapter focuses on the challenges to generativity that accompany late adulthood, such as finding new sources of achievement once derived from work. In the third section, the importance of marriage, friends, neighbors, and family in providing social support is discussed, as are the different experiences of married and single older adults. The final section focuses on the frail elderly—the minority of older adults, often poor and/or ill, who require extensive care.

NOTE: Answer guidelines for all Chapter 15 questions begin on page 241.

Chapter Review

When you have finished reading the chapter, work through the material that follows to review it. Complete the sentences and answer the questions. As you proceed, evaluate your performance for each section by consulting the answers beginning on page 241. Do not continue with the next section until you understand each answer. If you need to, review or reread the appropriate section in the textbook before continuing.

Theories of Late Adulthood (pp. 530–537)

1. Theories of psychosocial development in late adulthood include ________________ ________________ theories and ________________ theories.

2. Theories that emphasize the active part that individuals play in their own psychosocial development are ________________ theories.

3. The most comprehensive theory is that of ________________, who called life's final crisis ________________ versus ________________.

4. According to ________________ theory, people experience the changes of late adulthood in much the same way they did earlier in life. Thus, the so-called ________________ personality traits are maintained throughout old age.

5. Some people cope with aging through ________________ ________________ ________________ ________________, which is the idea that individuals set their own ________________, assess their own ________________, and then figure out how to accomplish what they want to achieve despite the ________________ and ________________ of later life.

6. The general personality shift known as the ________________ ________________ refers to the tendency of elderly people to perceive, prefer, and remember positive experiences more than negative ones.

7. With age, the gap between what people hope for themselves (the ________________ ________________) and how they actually perceive themselves (the ________________ ________________) becomes ________________ (smaller/larger).

8. Theorists who emphasize ________________ maintain that ________________ forces and ________________ influences limit individual ________________ and direct life at every stage. One form of this theory focuses on ________________ ________________, reflecting how industrialized nations segregate the oldest generation.

9. According to ________________ theory, in old age the individual and society mutually withdraw from each other. This theory is ________________ (controversial among/almost universally accepted by) gerontologists.

10. The opposite idea is expressed in ________________ theory, which holds that older adults remain socially active. According to this theory, if older adults do disengage, they do so ________________ (willingly/unwillingly).

11. Two other categories of stratification that are especially important in late adulthood are ________________ and ________________.
Another stratification theory, which draws attention to the values underlying the gender divisions promoted by society, is ________________ theory. According to this theory, ________________ policies and ________________ values make later life particularly burdensome for women.

12. Some theorists believe that stratification theory may distort reality. They point out that elderly ________________ (non-White/White) women are often nurtured and respected by their families. Similarly, grown children tend to be more nurturing toward their ________________ (mothers/fathers). Because women tend lifelong to be ________________ and ________________, they are better able than men to derive satisfaction from these roles.

STUDY TIP: Stratification theories maintain that social forces are particularly powerful during late adulthood, when a person's ability to function depends largely on the person's place in society. To focus your study of this important point, create "stratification profiles" of two hypothetical elderly adults, one who is functioning optimally, and one who is not.

APPLICATIONS:

13. Professor Martin states that "membership in certain groups can place the elderly at risk for a number of dangers." Professor Martin evidently is an advocate of which theory of psychosocial development?
   a. self theories
   b. stratification
   c. continuity
   d. Erikson's theory

14. Jack, who is 73, looks back on his life with a sense of pride and contentment; Eleanor feels unhappy with her life and that it is "too late to start over." In Erikson's terminology, Jack is experiencing ________________, while Eleanor is experiencing ________________.
   a. generativity; stagnation
   b. identity; emptiness
   c. integrity; despair
   d. completion; termination

Activities in Late Adulthood (pp. 537–544)

15. Recent research has found that employment has a positive ________________ and ________________ impact on both men and women.

16. It was once believed that people were happiest working and that retirement led to ________________ and ________________. The paradox is that today, people are retiring ________________ (earlier/later). One problem with retirement is that people do not ________________ adequately.

17. Generativity, social connections, and some of the other benefits of working are provided by ________________. Additionally, there is a strong link between volunteering and good ________________ and less ________________.
Older, retired people are ________________ (more/less) likely to volunteer than are middle-aged, employed people.

Identify four reasons for the lack of volunteering among the elderly.

18. Rather than moving, many elderly people prefer to ________________ ________________ ________________ by remaining in the neighborhoods in which they raised their children. By doing so, they create ________________ ________________ retirement communities.

19. Many of the elderly use the time they once spent earning a living to pursue ________________ interests. The eagerness of the elderly to pursue educational interests is exemplified by the rapid growth of ________________, a program in which older people take short courses on college campuses while students are on vacation.

20. Although attendance at religious services is ________________ (more/less) likely among older adults, religious faith ________________ (increases/remains stable/decreases) as people age. Religious involvement correlates with ________________ and ________________ health.

Identify three reasons for the connection between religion and well-being.

21. By many measures, the elderly are more ________________ active than any other age group. Compared to younger people, the elderly are more likely to ____.

The idea that the political concerns of the elderly clash with those of the young ________________ (is/is not) confirmed by the data.

22. The major U.S. organization advocating for the elderly is ________________.

STUDY TIP: Many older adults stay busy by maintaining their homes and yards, reflecting the desire to age in place. One result of this is that many of the elderly live by themselves. What are some of the advantages of aging in place? What are some of the disadvantages?

APPLICATIONS:

23. When they retire, most older adults
    a. immediately feel more satisfied with their new way of life.
    b. engage in a variety of social activities.
    c. have serious, long-term difficulties adjusting to retirement.
    d. disengage from other roles and activities as well.

24. The one most likely to agree with the statement, "Older adults have an obligation to help others and serve the community," is
    a. a middle-aged adult.
    b. an older woman.
    c. an older man.
    d. an older adult.

Friends and Relatives (pp. 544–553)

25. The phrase ________________ ________________ highlights the fact that the life course is traveled in the company of others.

26. Elderly Americans who are married tend to be ________________, ________________, and ________________ than unmarried people their age.

27. Studies indicate that homosexuals ________________ (do/do not) benefit from having an intimate partner who is committed to their well-being lifelong.

28. Long-term relationships are characterized by an ________________ of the partners, mutual ________________, and ________________ ________________.

29. If both spouses are employed, it ________________ (is/is not) best for them to retire together.

30. The average married woman experiences about ________________ (how many?) years of widowhood.

31. The death of a mate usually means not only the loss of a close friend and lover but also a reduction in ________________, ________________, social ________________, and ________________.

32. In general, living without a spouse is somewhat easier for ________________ (widows/widowers).

Explain why it is somewhat easier for this spouse to live without the other spouse..

33. Elderly widowers are more likely to be physically ill and ________________ ________________. They are ________________ (more/less) likely to remarry than are widows. This is because widowers tend to be ________________ than widows and also because the ________________ ________________ is in their favor.

34. Because more people are living longer, more older people are part of ________________ families than at any time in history. Sometimes, this takes the form of a ________________ family, in which there are more ________________ than in the past but with only a few members in each generation.

35. The idea that adult children are obligated to care for their aging parents is called ________________ ________________. This idea ________________ (is/is not) found in every culture.

36. While intergenerational relationships are clearly important to both generations, they also are likely to include ________________ and ________________. The ________________–________________ relationship is an example of this.

37. Today, when one generation needs help, assistance typically flows from the ________________ (younger/older) generation to their ________________ (parents/children) instead of vice versa.

38. By age 65, ________________ (what percent?) of all people are grandparents.

39. Grandparent–grandchild relationships take one of four forms: ________________, ________________, ________________, or ________________ parents. In the past, grandparents adopted a ________________ role.

40. Most contemporary grandparents seek the ________________ role as they strive for the love and respect of their grandchildren while maintaining their own ________________.

41. Grandparents who take over the work of raising their children's children are referred to as ________________ ________________. This role is more common when parents are ________________ ________________.

42. Grandparents are most likely to provide surrogate care for infants who are ________________-________________ or school-age boys who are ________________, for example. If the relationship is the result of a legal decision that the children were maltreated, it becomes ________________ ________________.

43. Grandparents who are responsible for full-time care for grandchildren have more ________________, ________________, and ________________ problems than other elders do.

44. (A View From Science) The idea that the more time grandparents spend with their grandchildren the better ________________ (is/is not) supported by research. For this reason, social workers prefer grandparents for ________________ care.

45. Approximately ________________ percent of adults over age 65 in the United States have never married. This ________________ (is/is not) the most married cohort in history. Those who have never married tend to be ________________ (quite content/lonely and unsupported).

46. Having a partner and children ________________ (is necessary/is not necessary) for happiness in old age.

47. In buffering against stress, having at least one close ________________ is crucial.

48. Successful aging requires that people keep themselves from becoming ________________ ________________.

STUDY TIP: In terms of physical and emotional adjustment, women generally have an easier time coping with the loss of a spouse than do men. Make a list of reasons that this is so.

APPLICATION:

49. Of the following older adults, who is most likely to be involved in a large network of intimate friendships?
    - a. William, a 65-year-old who never married
    - b. Darrel, a 60-year-old widower
    - c. Florence, a 63-year-old widow
    - d. Kay, a 66-year-old married woman

The Frail Elderly (pp. 553–560)

50. Elderly people who are physically infirm, very ill, or cognitively impaired are called the ________________ ________________.

51. The crucial sign of frailty is an inability to perform the ________________________________, which comprise five tasks: ________________, ________________, ________________, ________________, and ________________________________.

52. Actions that require some intellectual competence and forethought are classified as ________________________________. These include such things as ________________________________.

53. The frail elderly are particularly vulnerable to ________________ ________________. Most cases of elder maltreatment ________________ (involve/do not involve) family members.

54. Many older Americans and their relatives feel that ________________ ________________ should be avoided at all costs. An intermediate form of care is ________________ ________________, which provides some privacy and independence, along with some ________________ supervision.

APPLICATIONS:

55. Claudine is the primary caregiver for her elderly parents. The amount of stress she feels in this role depends above all on
    - a. how frail her parents are.
    - b. her subjective interpretation of the support she receives from others.
    - c. her relationship to her parents prior to their becoming frail.
    - d. her overall financial situation.

56. Wilma's elderly mother needs help in taking care of the instrumental activities of daily life. Such activities would include which of the following?
    - a. bathing
    - b. eating
    - c. paying bills
    - d. all of these activities

Progress Test 1

Multiple-Choice Questions

Circle your answers to the following questions and check them with the answers on page 242. If your answer is incorrect, read the explanation for why it is incorrect and then consult the appropriate pages of the text (in parentheses following the correct answer).

1. According to disengagement theory, during late adulthood people tend to
    - a. become less role-centered and more passive.
    - b. have regrets about how they have lived their lives.
    - c. become involved in a range of new activities.
    - d. exaggerate lifelong personality traits.

2. The intermediate form of elder care that provides some of the privacy and independence of living at home, along with some medical supervision, is
    - a. Elderhostel.
    - b. a naturally occurring retirement community.
    - c. respite care.
    - d. assisted living.

3. Elderhostel is
    - a. a special type of nursing home in which the patients are given control over their activities.
    - b. a theory of psychosocial development advocating that the elderly can help each other.
    - c. an agency that allows older people of the opposite sex to live together unencumbered by marriage vows.
    - d. a program in which older people take short courses on college campuses while students are on vacation.

4. An advocate for feminist theory would point out that
- **a.** because men usually had higher-paying jobs, it was women who quit their jobs to take care of infirm relatives.
- **b.** social pressures have often led to diminished old age among women.
- **c.** lifelong stratification may lead to poverty, frailty, and dependence in women.
- **d.** all of these statements are true.

5. Which of the following would be included as an activity of daily life (ADL)?
- **a.** eating
- **b.** bathing
- **c.** toileting
- **d.** All of these are ADLs.

6. Because women tend to be caregivers, as older adults they are
- **a.** more likely than men to be depressed.
- **b.** more likely than men to be lonely.
- **c.** more likely than men to be depressed and lonely.
- **d.** less likely than men to be lonely or depressed.

7. The idea that individuals set their own goals, assess their abilities, and figure out how to accomplish what they want to achieve during late adulthood is referred to as
- **a.** disengagement.
- **b.** selective optimization with compensation.
- **c.** continuity.
- **d.** age stratification.

8. After retirement, the elderly are likely to
- **a.** pursue educational interests.
- **b.** become politically involved.
- **c.** do volunteer work because they feel a particular commitment to their communities.
- **d.** do any of these activities.

9. Which of the following theories does NOT belong with the others?
- **a.** disengagement theory
- **b.** feminist theory
- **c.** activity theory
- **d.** continuity theory

10. Research indicates that the primary perpetrators of elder abuse are
- **a.** professional caregivers.
- **b.** mean-spirited strangers.
- **c.** extended family members.
- **d.** middle-aged children.

11. On average, older widows
- **a.** live about 4 to 10 years after their husband dies.
- **b.** almost always seek another husband.
- **c.** find it more difficult than widowers to live without a spouse.
- **d.** experience all of these things.

12. In general, during late adulthood the *fewest* problems are experienced by individuals who
- **a.** are married.
- **b.** have always been single.
- **c.** have long been divorced.
- **d.** are widowed.

13. Which of the following is true of adjustment to the death of a spouse?
- **a.** It is easier for men in all respects.
- **b.** It is initially easier for men, but over the long term it is easier for women.
- **c.** It is emotionally easier for women but financially easier for men.
- **d.** It is determined primarily by individual personality traits, and therefore shows very few sex differences.

14. An advocate of which of the following theories would be most likely to agree with the statement, "Because of their more passive style of interaction, older people are less likely to be chosen for new roles"?
- **a.** disengagement
- **b.** continuity
- **c.** self
- **d.** positivity

15. Which of the following most accurately expresses the most recent view of developmentalists regarding stratification by age?
- **a.** Aging makes a person's social sphere increasingly narrow.
- **b.** Disengagement is always the result of ageism.
- **c.** Most older adults become more selective in their social contacts.
- **d.** Older adults need even more social activity to be happy than they did earlier in life.

True or False Items

Write T (*true*) or F (*false*) on the line in front of each statement.

________ **1.** Preschool girls are more likely to live with grandparents than rebellious school-age boys are.

_______ 2. As one of the most disruptive experiences in the life span, losing a spouse tends to have similar effects on men and women.
_______ 3. Continuity theory stresses how people adjust to aging and circumstances.
_______ 4. Religious faith increases with age.
_______ 5. Older adults do not understand the social concerns of younger age groups.
_______ 6. Most developmentalists support the central premise of disengagement theory.
_______ 7. In the United States, the rate of volunteering decreases with age.
_______ 8. Most older people suffer significantly from a lack of close friendships.
_______ 9. Nearly one in two older adults makes a long-distance move after retirement.
_______ 10. Financial and emotional assistance typically flows from the younger generation to the older generation.

Progress Test 2

Progress Test 2 should be completed during a final chapter review. Answer the following questions after you thoroughly understand the correct answers for the Chapter Review and Progress Test 1.

Multiple-Choice Questions

1. Critics of disengagement theory point out that
   a. older people want to substitute new involvements for the roles they lose with retirement.
   b. disengagement usually is not voluntary on the part of the individual.
   c. disengagement often leads to greater life satisfaction for older adults.
   d. disengagement is more common at earlier stages in the life cycle.

2. A beanpole family is one that consists of
   a. fewer generations with fewer members than in the past.
   b. fewer generations with more members than in the past.
   c. more generations than in the past but with only a few members in each generation.
   d. more generations with more members than in the past.

3. According to continuity theory, during late adulthood people
   a. become less role-centered.
   b. become more passive.
   c. become involved in a range of new activities.
   d. cope with challenges in much the same way they did earlier in life.

4. Developmentalists who believe that stratification theory unfairly stigmatizes women and minority groups point out that
   a. African Americans often outlive European Americans.
   b. elderly women are less likely than men to be lonely and depressed.
   c. multigenerational families and churches often nurture Hispanic Americans.
   d. all of the above are true.

5. Following retirement, most elderly people
   a. relocate to sunny climate.
   b. spend less time on housework and unnecessary chores.
   c. prefer to age in place.
   d. move in with their children.

6. When elderly Mr. Flanagan reflects on his life, he remembers mostly good times and experiences. This selectivity in thinking is called
   a. the positivity effect.
   b. respite care.
   c. aging in place.
   d. disengagement.

7. The major U.S. organization advocating for the elderly is
   a. Elderhostel.
   b. AARP.
   c. Foster Grandparents.
   d. Service Corps of Retired Executives.

8. Critics of stratification theory point out that
   a. old European females are lonelier than old men.
   b. grown children tend to be more nurturing toward their aging mothers.
   c. women are less able than men to cope with the role of caregiver.
   d. men benefit from close relationships with others of their sex.

9. Which of the following would NOT be included as an instrumental activity of daily life?
   a. grocery shopping
   b. paying bills
   c. making phone calls
   d. taking a walk

10. One of the most important factors contributing to life satisfaction for older adults appears to be

a. contact with friends.
b. contact with younger family members.
c. the number of new experiences to which they are exposed.
d. continuity in the daily routine.

11. Beyonce's mother wishes to age in place. This means that she

a. plans to continue working as long as possible.
b. wishes to remain in her home even after her health begins to decline.
c. plans to move back to her childhood home.
d. will do each of these things.

12. In general, the longer a couple has been married, the more likely they are to

a. be happier with each other.
b. have frequent, minor disagreements.
c. feel the relationship is not equitable.
d. do all of these things.

13. Which of the following is NOT true regarding long-term partnerships?

a. Married elders tend to be healthier than those who never married.
b. Absolute levels of conflict and emotional intensity drop over time.
c. Relationships generally change for the better in late adulthood.
d. Relationships improve in late adulthood, unless one spouse becomes seriously ill.

14. Relationships between parents and adult children are affected by many factors. For example

a. sons feel stronger affection; daughters feel stronger obligation.
b. assistance always depends on the older adult.
c. love is influenced by the interactions remembered from childhood.
d. frequency of contact is related to affection, not geographical proximity.

15. According to Erikson, achieving integrity during late adulthood above all involves

a. the ability to perceive one's own life as worthwhile.
b. being open to new influences and experiences.
c. treating other people with respect.
d. developing a consistent and yet varied daily routine.

Matching Items

Match each definition or description with its corresponding term or concept.

Terms or Concepts

________ **1.** disengagement theory
________ **2.** self theories
________ **3.** continuity theory
________ **4.** positivity effect
________ **5.** activity theory
________ **6.** stratification theories
________ **7.** activities of daily life (ADLs)
________ **8.** instrumental activities of daily life (IADLs)
________ **9.** aging in place
________ **10.** Elderhostel

Definitions or Descriptions

a. theories such as Erik Erikson's that emphasize self-actualization
b. an educational program for the elderly
c. eating, bathing, toileting, dressing, and transferring from a bed to a chair
d. remaining in the same home and community, even when health fails
e. theory that people become less role-centered as they age
f. actions that require intellectual competence and forethought
g. tendency for elderly people to perceive, prefer, and remember positive experiences
h. theories such as feminist theory and critical race theory that focus on the limitations on life choices created by social forces
i. theory that elderly people become socially withdrawn only involuntarily
j. theory that each person copes with late adulthood in the same way he or she did earlier in life

Key Terms

Using your own words, write a brief definition or explanation of each of the following terms on a separate piece of paper.

1. self theories
2. integrity versus despair
3. continuity theory
4. positivity effect
5. stratification theories
6. disengagement theory
7. activity theory
8. aging in place
9. naturally occurring retirement community
10. AARP
11. filial responsibility
12. frail elderly
13. activities of daily life (ADLs)
14. instrumental activities of daily life (IADLs)
15. assisted living

Answers

CHAPTER REVIEW

1. self; stratification
2. self
3. Erik Erikson; integrity; despair
4. continuity; Big Five
5. selective optimization with compensation; goals; abilities; limitations; declines
6. positivity effect
7. ideal self; real self; smaller
8. stratification; social; cultural; choice; age stratification
9. disengagement; controversial among
10. activity; unwillingly
11. gender; ethnicity; feminist; social; cultural
12. non-White; mothers; caregivers; kinkeepers
13. **b.** is the answer. "Groups" are the social "strata" that is the focus of this theory.

    a., c., & d. These theories emphasize the efforts of the individual to reach his or her full potential (self theories, including Erikson's) by interpreting experiences in the face of ever-changing social contexts (continuity theory [c.]).
14. **c.** is the answer.

    a. This is not the crisis of late adulthood in Erikson's theory.

    b. & d. These are not crises in Erikson's theory.
15. physical; psychological
16. illness; death; earlier; plan
17. volunteering; health; depression; less

Ageism may discourage volunteering. Institutions lack good strategies for training and attracting older volunteers. Older adults may be too focused on their own concerns to volunteer. Some forms of volunteering, such as babysitting and caregiving, are not reflected in statistics.

18. age in place; naturally occurring
19. educational; Elderhostel
20. less; increases; physical; emotional

Faith encourages a healthy lifestyle. Religious attendance fosters social relationships. Faith also seems to reduce stress.

21. politically; vote in elections, write letters to their elected representatives, and identify with a political party; is not
22. AARP (formerly the American Association of Retired Persons)
23. **b.** is the answer.

    a. Although the text does not say this specifically, the discussion of the many activities engaged in by elderly people suggests a strong level of satisfaction.

    d. There is much evidence that conflicts with disengagement theory.
24. **d.** is the answer.

    a. Middle-aged adults tend to be more focused on individual and family needs.

    b. & c. The text does not suggest that there is a gender difference in older adults' sense of obligation to serve others.
25. social convoy
26. healthier; wealthier; happier
27. do

One reason may be traced to the effects of their children, who were a prime source of conflict when they were younger but are now a source of pleasure. Another is that all the shared contextual factors tend to change both partners in similar ways, bringing them closer together in memories and values.

28. interdependence; respect; sexual intimacy
29. is
30. 4 to 10
31. status; income; activities; identity
32. widows

One reason is that with time many older widows come to enjoy their independence. For companionship and social support, widows usually rely on women friends or grown children, and they typically expand their social network after their husband's death.

33. socially isolated; more; lonelier; sex ratio
34. multigenerational; beanpole; generations
35. filial responsibility; is
36. tension; conflict; mother–daughter
37. older; children
38. 85
39. remote; involved; companionate; surrogate: remote
40. companionate; independence (autonomy)
41. surrogate parents; poor, young, ill, drug- or alcohol-addicted
42. drug-affected; rebellious; kinship care
43. illness; depression; marital
44. is not; kinship
45. 4; is; quite content
46. is not necessary
47. confidant
48. socially isolated
49. **c.** is the answer.

    a. & b. At every age, women have larger social circles and more intimate relationships with their friends than men.

    d. Widows tend to be more involved in friendship networks than married women.
50. frail elderly
51. activities of daily life (ADLs); eating; bathing; toileting; dressing; transferring from a bed to a chair
52. instrumental activities of daily life (IADLs); shopping, paying bills, driving a car, taking medications, and keeping appointments
53. elder abuse; involve
54. nursing homes; assisted living; medical
55. **b.** is the answer.
56. **c.** is the answer.

    a. & b. These are examples of "activities of daily life."

PROGRESS TEST 1

Multiple-Choice Questions

1. **a.** is the answer. (p. 534)

    b. This answer depicts a person struggling with Erikson's crisis of integrity versus despair.

    c. This answer describes activity theory.

    d. Disengagement theory does not address this issue.
2. **d.** is the answer. (p. 559)
3. **d.** is the answer. (p. 541)
4. **d.** is the answer. (pp. 534–535)
5. **d.** is the answer. (p. 554)
6. **d.** is the answer. (pp. 546–547)
7. **b.** is the answer. (p. 532)

    a. This is the idea that the elderly withdraw from society as they get older.

    c. This is the idea that older adults behave as they have behaved in earlier periods of life.

    d. According to this theory, the oldest generation is segregated from the rest of society.
8. **d.** is the answer. Contrary to earlier views that retirement was not a happy time, researchers now know that the elderly are generally happy and productive, spending their time in various activities. (pp. 539–541)
9. **d.** is the answer. Each of the other theories can be categorized as a stratification theory. (p. 532)
10. **d.** is the answer. (p. 557)
11. **a.** is the answer. (p. 546)

    b. & c. In fact, just the opposite is true.
12. **a.** is the answer. (p. 544)
13. **c.** is the answer. (pp. 546–547)
14. **a.** is the answer. (p. 534)

    b. Continuity theory, a type of self theory, maintains that older adults cope with aging in much the same ways as when they were younger.

    c. Self theories in general emphasize the quest for self-fulfillment.

    d. This effect is an aspect of self theory.
15. **c.** is the answer. (pp. 533–534)

    a. This is the central idea behind disengagement theory.

    b. & d. These ideas are expressions of activity theory.

True or False Items

1. F Grandparents are more likely to become surrogate parents to rebellious boys. (p. 550)

2. F Women tend to be more prepared and have more friends to sympathize with them. Men find it hard to turn to others for help. (pp. 546–547)
3. T (p. 532)
4. T (p. 541)
5. F In fact, older adults are willing to vote against the interests of their own group if a greater good is at stake. (p. 543)
6. F In fact, disengagement theory has *few* serious defenders. (p. 534)
7. T (p. 539)
8. F Most older adults have at least one close friend. (p. 552)
9. F A minority of older adults moves to another state. (p. 540)
10. F Aid flows in the opposite direction. (p. 549)

PROGRESS TEST 2

Multiple-Choice Questions

1. **a.** is the answer. (p. 534)
   b. If disengagement were *not* voluntary, this would not be a choice of the elderly.
   c. & d. Neither of these answers is true, nor a criticism of disengagement theory.
2. **c.** is the answer. (p. 547)
3. **d.** is the answer. (p. 532)
   a. & b. These answers describe disengagement theory.
   c. This answer pertains to activity theory.
4. **d.** is the answer. (p. 536)
5. **c.** is the answer. (p. 540)
6. **a.** is the answer. (p. 532)
7. **b.** is the answer. (p. 543)
   a. Elderhostel is an educational program for older adults.
   c. & d. These service organizations affect a much smaller percentage of the elderly.
8. **b.** is the answer. (p. 536)
9. **d.** is the answer. (p. 554)
10. **a.** is the answer. (p. 552)
    b., c., & d. The importance of these factors varies from one older adult to another.
11. **b.** is the answer. (p. 540)
12. **a.** is the answer. (pp. 544–546)
    b. & c. The longer a couple has been married, the *less* likely they are to have frequent disagreements or feel that the relationship is not equitable.
13. **d.** is the answer. Generally, older spouses accept each other's frailties and tend to each other's needs with feelings of affection. (pp. 544–546)
14. **c.** is the answer. (p. 549)
15. **a.** is the answer. (p. 530)

Matching Items

1. e (p. 534)	**5.** i (p. 534)	**8.** f (p. 554)
2. a (p. 530)	**6.** h (p. 533)	**9.** d (p. 540)
3. j (p. 532)	**7.** c (p. 554)	**10.** b (p. 541)
4. g (p. 532)		

KEY TERMS

1. **Self theories,** such as Erik Erikson's theory, focus on the core self, or the search to maintain one's integrity and identity. (p. 530)
2. The final stage of development, according to Erik Erikson, is **integrity versus despair,** in which older adults seek to integrate their unique experiences with their vision of community. (p. 530)
3. According to the **continuity theory** of aging, each person copes with late adulthood in much the same way that he or she coped with earlier periods of life. (p. 532)
4. The **positivity effect** is the tendency for elderly people to perceive, prefer, and remember positive experiences and images more than negative ones. (p. 532)
5. **Stratification theories** emphasize that social forces limit individual choices and affect the ability to function. (p. 533)
6. According to **disengagement theory,** aging results in role relinquishment, social withdrawal, and passivity. (p. 534)
7. **Activity theory** is the view that older people remain active in a variety of social spheres and become withdrawn only unwillingly. (p. 534)
8. Many elderly people prefer to **age in place** by remaining in the same home and community, adjusting but not leaving when their health declines. (p. 540)
9. **Naturally occurring retirement communities (NORC)** are neighborhoods or apartment complexes created by elders who moved to the location as younger adults and never left. (p. 541)

10. **AARP** (formerly the American Association of Retired Persons) is the major organization representing elderly adults in the United States. (p. 543)
11. **Filial responsibility** is the idea that adult children are obligated to care for their aging parents. (p. 548)
12. The **frail elderly** are the minority of adults over age 65 who are physically infirm, very ill, or cognitively impaired. (p. 553)
13. In determining frailty, gerontologists often refer to the **activities of daily life (ADLs),** which comprise five tasks: eating, bathing, toileting, dressing, and transferring from a bed to a chair. (p. 554)
14. The **instrumental activities of daily life (IADLs)** are actions that are important to independent living and require some intellectual competence and forethought, such as shopping for food, paying bills, and taking medication. (p. 554)
15. **Assisted living** is an intermediate form of elder care that provides some of the privacy and independence of living at home, along with some medical supervision. (p. 559)

epilogue

Death and Dying

Epilogue Overview

Death marks the close of the life span—a close individuals must come to terms with, both for themselves and for their loved ones. Indeed, an understanding and acceptance of death is crucial if life is to be lived to the fullest.

The first section focuses on how dying is viewed throughout the life span and in different cultures and religions. The next section discusses hospice and other forms of palliative care designed to help the terminally ill patient to die "a good death."

Although the concept of an unvarying sequence of stages among the dying is not universally accepted, the pioneering work of Elisabeth Kübler-Ross was instrumental in revealing the emotional gamut of terminally ill patients and the importance of honest communication.

The final section deals with changing expressions of bereavement and how people can be aided in the process of recovery.

NOTE: Answer guidelines for all Epilogue questions begin on page 251.

Epilogue Review

When you have finished reading the Epilogue, work through the material that follows to review it. Complete the sentences and answer the questions. As you proceed, evaluate your performance for each section by consulting the answers beginning on page 251. Do not continue with the next section until you understand each answer. If you need to, review or reread the appropriate section in the textbook before continuing.

Introduction (pp. 565–566)

1. The study of death and dying is ______________. Customs and rituals related to dying, death, and bereavement function to bring ______________ in death, ______________ of dying, and then ______________ of life through bereavement.

STUDY TIP: Today, death occurs at a later age, takes longer, and more often occurs in hospitals. Focus your study of death and dying by listing the various reasons why these changes have occurred.

APPLICATION:

2. Dr. Aziz, who specializes in the study of death, would most likely describe himself as a(n)
   a. palliative care specialist.
   b. thanatologist.
   c. geriatric specialist.
   d. euthanist.

Death and Hope (pp. 566–574)

3. (Table EP.1) Briefly describe five changes in death over the past 100 years.

   a. ______________
   b. ______________
   c. ______________
   d. ______________
   e. ______________

4. Children as young as ________ have some understanding of death. Dying children often fear that death means ________ ________. For this reason, telling children that the deceased person is sleeping or in heaven ________ (is/is not) helpful.

5. Adolescents and emerging adults die in ________, ________, and ________, partly because they may ________ death.

6. A major shift in attitudes about death occurs when adults become responsible for ________ and ________. From age 25 to 60, terminally ill adults worry about ________.

7. Attitudes about death are often ________, as revealed by the classic moral puzzle called the ________ ________.

8. According to ________ ________ theory, people adopt cultural values and moral principles in order to cope with their own fear of death.

9. During late adulthood, anxiety about death ________ (increases/decreases). Many developmentalists view acceptance of one's own mortality during late adulthood as a sign of ________ ________.

10. Belief in life after death is directly related to people's estimate of ________ ________. For this reason, the aged tend to be ________ (more/less) religious than the young.

11. Some people who survive a serious illness report having had a ________-________ ________ in which they left their bodies. These experiences often include ________ elements.

THINK ABOUT IT: The specific meanings attached to death vary from individual to individual. List three regrets you would have if you should die immediately. Compare your regrets with those you might report were your death to occur at a much older age.

Dying and Acceptance (pp. 574–582)

12. A *good death* is one that is ________, ________, and ________ and that occurs in ________ surroundings, surrounded by ________ and ________.

13. A major factor in our understanding of the psychological needs of the dying was the pioneering work of ________.

14. Kübler-Ross's research led her to propose that the dying go through ________ (how many?) emotional stages. In order, the stages of dying are ________, ________, ________, ________, and ________.

15. Another set of stages of dying is based on ________ hierarchy of needs, which are ________ needs, ________, and ________, ________, and ________.

16. Other researchers typically ________ (have/have not) found the same five stages of dying occurring in sequence.

17. Most dying people ________ (want/do not want) to talk honestly with medical and religious professionals.

18. The institution called the ________ provides care to terminally ill patients.

State two principles of hospice care.

19. Medical care that is designed not to treat an illness but to relieve pain and suffering is called ________ ________.

20. The least tolerable physical symptom of fatal illness is ________. Physicians once worried about causing ________ if pain

relievers such as ______________ were given too freely. Pain medication for dying patients may have the ______________ ______________ of reducing pain while ______________ ______________.

21. Today, death is defined as a cessation of ______________ ______________.

22. All competent individuals have the legal right to control decisions related to life-prolonging treatments, including ______________ ______________, in which a seriously ill person is allowed to die naturally, and ______________ ______________, in which someone intentionally acts to terminate the life of a suffering person. Usually, if a patient prefers to die naturally, the order ______________ is placed on that person's hospital chart.

23. Active euthanasia is ______________ (legal/illegal) in most parts of the world. When a doctor provides the means for someone to end his or her own life, it is referred to as ______________-______________ ______________.

24. In the United States, the state of ______________ has allowed physician-assisted suicide since 1994 but under very strict guidelines. Many critics note that legalizing euthanasia or physician-assisted-suicide will create a ______________ ______________ in which societies begin hastening death. Since that time, concerns that physician-assisted suicide might be used more often with the old and the poor ______________ (have/have not) been proven to be well-founded.

25. One way of increasing personal choice about death is to leave instructions regarding end-of-life care, called a(n) ______________ ______________. Also, some people make a ______________ ______________ to indicate what medical intervention they want if they become incapable of expressing those wishes. To avoid complications, each person should also designate a ______________ ______________ ______________, someone who can make decisions for them if needed. Proxies ______________ (do/do not) guarantee a problem-free death. One problem is that ______________ members may disagree with the proxy; another is that proxy directives may be ______________ by hospital staff.

STUDY TIP: To underscore the ways in which Western culture "denies" death, list five ways in which you do so yourself—for example, by avoiding funerals you do not have to attend.

APPLICATIONS:

26. The terminally ill patient who is convinced his laboratory tests must be wrong is probably in which of Kübler-Ross's stages?
    a. denial
    b. anger
    c. depression
    d. bargaining

27. Dr. Welby writes the orders DNR (do not resuscitate) on her patient's chart. Evidently, the patient has requested
    a. a living will.
    b. passive euthanasia.
    c. active euthanasia.
    d. an assisted suicide.

28. Armand has directed his lawyer to prepare a document specifying that he does not what to be kept alive by artificial means. His lawyer is creating
    a. a health care proxy.
    b. grief work.
    c. a double effect.
    d. a living will.

29. The doctor who injects a terminally ill patient with a lethal drug is practicing
    a. passive euthanasia.
    b. active euthanasia.
    c. an assisted suicide.
    d. an act that became legal in most countries in 1993.

Bereavement (pp. 582–588)

30. The sense of loss following a death is called ______________. The powerful sorrow that the individual feels at the death of another is called ______________.

31. The ceremonies and behaviors that comprise the public response to a death are called ________________. These ceremonies are designed by a ________________ or ________________ to channel ________________ toward ________________ of life.

32. A crucial factor in mourning is people's search for ________________ in death. The normal reaction at first is intense, with a strong desire to assess ________________. Emotions gradually ease as the person engages in ________________ ________________.

33. In recent times, mourning has become more ________________, less ________________, and less ________________.

34. As rituals diminish, problems such as ________________ ________________ may become more common. This is a situation in which a bereaved person is ________________ ________________.

35. Modern life also increases the incidence of ________________ ________________, in which the bereaved are ________________.

36. Another problem is ________________ ________________, in which circumstances such as ________________ and ________________ result in police investigations and press reports that interfere with the grief process.

37. List two steps that others can follow to help a bereaved person.

a. ________________

b. ________________

APPLICATIONS:

38. Following 30-year-old Ramón's unexpected and violent death, which of the following individuals is most likely to experience disenfranchised grief?
   a. Kent, his unmarried partner
   b. Janet, the younger sister with whom he has not been in touch for years
   c. his father, who divorced Kent's mother two years earlier
   d. his biological mother, who put Kent up for adoption when he was a baby

39. Which of the following statements would probably be the most helpful to a grieving person?
   a. "Why don't you get out more and get back into the swing of things?"
   b. "You're tough; bear up!"
   c. "If you need someone to talk to, call me any time."
   d. "It must have been his or her time to die."

40. Dr. Robins is about to counsel her first terminally ill patient and his family. Research suggests that her most helpful strategy would be to
   a. keep most of the facts from the patient and his family in order not to upset them.
   b. be truthful to the patient but not his family.
   c. be truthful to the family only, and swear them to secrecy.
   d. honestly inform both the patient and his family.

Progress Test 1

Circle your answers to the following questions and check them with the answers beginning on page 252. If your answer is incorrect, read the explanation for why it is incorrect and then consult the appropriate pages of the text (in parentheses following the correct answer).

Multiple-Choice Questions

1. Passive euthanasia is most accurately described as
   a. care designed to relieve pain and suffering.
   b. a situation in which treatment relieves pain while at the same time hastens death.
   c. a situation in which a person is allowed to die naturally.
   d. a situation in which someone takes action to bring about another person's death.

2. Children as young as ________ (what age?) have some understanding of death.
   a. 4
   b. 7
   c. 2
   d. 9

3. Kübler-Ross's stages of dying are, in order
   a. anger, denial, bargaining, depression, acceptance.
   b. depression, anger, denial, bargaining, acceptance.
   c. denial, anger, bargaining, depression, acceptance.
   d. bargaining, denial, anger, acceptance, depression.

4. Most adults hope that they will die

a. with little pain.
b. peacefully.
c. swiftly.
d. in all of these ways.

5. *Hospice* is best defined as

a. a document that indicates what kind of medical intervention a terminally ill person wants.
b. mercifully allowing a person to die by not doing something that might extend life.
c. an alternative to hospital care for the terminally ill.
d. providing a person with the means to end his or her life.

6. Palliative care refers to

a. heroic measures to save a life.
b. conservative medical care to treat an illness.
c. efforts to relieve pain and suffering.
d. allowing a terminally ill patient to die naturally.

7. Adolescents and emerging adults are more likely than other age groups to die in suicides, accidents, and homicides in part because they

a. are easily influenced by others.
b. romanticize death.
c. have poor relationships with their parents.
d. cannot establish an identity.

8. Which of the following is a normal response in the bereavement process?

a. experiencing powerful emotions
b. culturally diverse emotions
c. a lengthy period of grief
d. All of these are normal responses.

9. A double effect in medicine refers to a situation in which

a. the effects of one drug on a patient interact with those of another drug.
b. medication relieves pain and has a secondary effect of hastening death.
c. family members disagree with a terminally ill patient's proxy.
d. medical personnel ignore the wishes of a terminally ill patient and his or her proxy.

10. Near-death experiences

a. often include angels and other religious elements.
b. occur more often following serious injuries than serious illnesses.
c. occur in most people who come close to dying.
d. are characterized by each of these things.

True or False Items

Write T (*true*) or F (*false*) on the line in front of each statement.

_______ **1.** (Table EP.2) Hospice care is affordable to all who need it.
_______ **2.** Subsequent research has confirmed the accuracy of Kübler-Ross's findings regarding the five stages of dying.
_______ **3.** Studies have found that doctors spend less time with patients who are known to be dying.
_______ **4.** Following the death of a loved one, the bereaved often feel sadness at first, then resume their normal activities.
_______ **5.** To help a bereaved person, one should ignore the person's depression.
_______ **6.** Researchers agree that the hospice is beneficial to the dying person and his or her family.
_______ **7.** Physician-assisted suicide is legal almost everywhere in the world.
_______ **8.** Hospices administer pain-killing medication but do not make use of artificial life-support systems.
_______ **9.** In the long run, the bereavement process may have a beneficial effect on the individual.
_______ **10.** Fear of death increases in late adulthood.

Progress Test 2

Progress Test 2 should be completed during a final review of the Epilogue. Answer the following questions after you thoroughly understand the correct answers for the Epilogue Review and Progress Test 1.

Multiple-Choice Questions

1. Kübler-Ross's primary contribution was to
   a. open the first hospice, thus initiating the hospice movement.
   b. show how the emotions of the dying occur in a series of clear-cut stages.
   c. bring attention to the psychological needs of dying people.
   d. show the correlation between people's conceptualization of death and their developmental stage.

2. In recent times, mourning has become all of the following *except*
   a. more private.
   b. less emotional.
   c. more likely to lead to social isolation.
   d. more religious.

3. (Table EP.2) Which of the following is NOT a limitation of hospices?
   a. To receive hospice care the patient must be terminally ill, with death anticipated within six months.
   b. Hospice care can be very expensive.
   c. Patients and caregivers must accept death.
   d. The dying typically do not receive skilled medical care.

4. A health care proxy is most accurately described as a(n)
   a document that indicates what medical intervention an individual wants if he or she becomes incapable of expressing those wishes.
   b. person chosen by another person to make medical decisions if the second person becomes unable to do so.
   c. situation in which, at a patient's request, someone else ends his or her life.
   d. indication on a patient's chart not to use heroic, life-saving measures.

5. As a result of ongoing police investigations, the bereaved members of a murder victim's family may be at increased risk of experiencing
   a. absent grief.
   b. disenfranchised grief.
   c. incomplete grief.
   d. a good death.

6. Research reveals that Kübler-Ross's stages of dying
   a. occur in sequence in virtually all terminally ill patients.
   b. do not occur in hospice residents.
   c. are typical only in Western cultures.
   d. make feelings about death seem much more predictable and universal than they actually are.

7. Living wills are an attempt to
   a. make sure that passive euthanasia will not be used in individual cases.
   b. specify the extent of medical treatment desired in the event of terminal illness.
   c. specify conditions for the use of active euthanasia.
   d. ensure that death will occur at home rather than in a hospital.

8. Funerals in many ________________ denominations include food, drink, music, and dancing.
   a. Buddhist
   b. Muslim
   c. Christian
   d. Jewish

9. Ritual is to emotion as
   a. grief is to mourning.
   b. mourning is to grief.
   c. affirmation is to loss.
   d. loss is to affirmation.

10. Healing after the death of a loved one is most difficult when
    a. the death is a long, protracted one.
    b. the bereaved is not allowed to mourn in the way he or she wishes.
    c. a period of grief has already elapsed.
    d. no other mourners are present.

Matching Items

Match each term or concept with its corresponding description or definition.

Terms or Concepts

_______ 1. DNR
_______ 2. hospice
_______ 3. living will
_______ 4. passive euthanasia
_______ 5. double effect
_______ 6. physician-assisted suicide
_______ 7. palliative care
_______ 8. grief
_______ 9. bereavement
_______ 10. advance directive

Definitions or Descriptions

a. hospice treatment that relieves suffering and safeguards dignity
b. an alternative to hospital care for the terminally ill
c. hospital chart order to allow a terminally ill patient to die naturally
d. a document expressing a person's wishes for treatment should he or she become terminally ill and incapable of making such decisions
e. providing the means for a terminally ill patient to end his or her life
f. an individual's response to the loss of a loved one
g. the sense of loss following a death
h. allowing a seriously ill person to die naturally by withholding medical intervention
i. situation in which a pain-relieving drug also hastens the death of a terminally ill patient
j. legal document detailing an individual's end-of-life instructions

Key Terms

Using your own words, write a brief definition or explanation of each of the following terms on a separate piece of paper.

1. thanatology
2. terror management theory (TMT)
3. near-death experience
4. good death
5. hospice
6. palliative care
7. double effect
8. passive euthanasia
9. DNR (do not resuscitate)
10. active euthanasia
11. physician-assisted suicide
12. slippery slope
13. advance directive
14. living will
15. health care proxy
16. bereavement
17. grief
18. mourning
19. absent grief
20. disenfranchised grief
21. incomplete grief

Answers

EPILOGUE REVIEW

1. thanatology; hope; acceptance; reaffirmation
2. **b.** is the answer.

   a. Palliative care is care aimed at relieving the suffering of a dying person.

   c. Such a person would study elderly people, but not necessarily those who are dying.

   d. There is no such term.
3. **a.** Death occurs at a later age.

   b. Death takes longer.

   c. Death more often occurs in hospitals.

   d. The major causes of death have also shifted, from infectious diseases to chronic illnesses such as cardiovascular disease and cancer.

   e. Today's young adults recognize cultural and religious diversity, and so they question earlier generations' beliefs about life after death, and such.

4. 2; being abandoned by the people they love; is not
5. suicides; accidents; homicides; romanticize
6. work; family; leaving something undone or leaving family members alone
7. irrational; trolley car dilemma
8. terror management
9. decreases; mental health
10. how likely they are to die soon; more
11. near-death experience; religious
12. quick; painless; peaceful; familiar; friends; family
13. Elisabeth Kübler-Ross
14. five; denial; anger; bargaining; depression; acceptance
15. Maslow's; physiological; safety; love; acceptance; respect; self-actualization
16. have not
17. want
18. hospice

    Each patient's autonomy and decisions are respected. Family members and friends are counseled before the death, shown how to provide care, and helped after the death.
19. palliative care
20. pain; addiction; morphine; double effect; speeding up death
21. brain waves
22. passive euthanasia; active euthanasia; DNR (do not resuscitate)
23. illegal; physician-assisted suicide
24. Oregon; slippery slope; have not
25. advance directive; living will; health care proxy; do not; family; ignored
26. **a.** is the answer.
27. **b.** is the answer.

    a. A living will is a document expressing how a person wishes to be cared for should he or she become incapable of expressing those wishes.

    c. This is when a person intentionally acts to end another's life.

    d. In this situation, a person provides the means for another to take his or her own life.
28. **d.** is the answer.

    a. A health care proxy is a person chosen to make decisions for a person unable to do so.

    b. Grief work is the experience and expression of strong emotions on the death of a loved one.

    c. In the double effect, pain is eased but death is hastened.
29. **b.** is the answer.
30. bereavement; grief
31. mourning; culture; religion; grief; reaffirmation
32. meaning; blame; grief work
33. private; emotional; religious
34. absent grief; not expected or allowed to go through a mourning period
35. disenfranchised grief; not allowed to mourn publicly because of cultural customs or social restrictions
36. incomplete grief; suicides; murders
37. **a.** Be aware that powerful, complicated, and unexpected emotions are likely.

    b. A friend should listen and sympathize, never implying that the person is too grief-stricken or not grief-stricken enough.
38. **a.** is the answer.

    b., c., & d. Because each of these individuals is biologically related to Ramón, none is likely to be excluded from mourning his death.
39. **c.** is the answer.

    a., b., & d. These statements discourage the bereaved person from mourning.
40. **d.** is the answer.

PROGRESS TEST 1

Multiple-Choice Questions

1. **c.** is the answer. (p. 578)

    a. This describes palliative care.

    b. This is the double effect that sometimes occurs with morphine and other opiate drugs.

    d. This is active euthanasia.
2. **c.** is the answer. (p. 567)
3. **c.** is the answer. (p. 575)
4. **d.** is the answer. (p. 574)
5. **c.** is the answer. (p. 575)

    a. This is a living will.

    b. & d. These are forms of euthanasia.
6. **c.** is the answer. (p. 576)
7. **b.** is the answer. (p. 568)
8. **d.** is the answer. (pp. 584–586)

9. **b.** is the answer. (p. 576)
10. **a.** is the answer. (p. 573)

    b. & c. Near-death experiences, which occur in some people who are dying, are no more likely to occur following a serious injury than an illness.

True or False Items

1. F Hospice care is too expensive for most. (p. 577)
2. F Later research has not confirmed Kübler-Ross's findings that the emotions of an individual faced with death occur in orderly stages. (p. 575)
3. T (p. 574)
4. T (p. 586)
5. F A friend should listen, sympathize, and not ignore the mourner's pain. (p. 587)
6. F Hospices have significant benefits, but some people are critical of them in part because they deny hope to the dying and because they are expensive. (pp. 576, 577)
7. F These practices are *illegal* throughout most of the world. (p. 579)
8. T (pp. 575–576)
9. T (p. 578)
10. F Just the opposite is true. (p. 570)

PROGRESS TEST 2

Multiple-Choice Questions

1. **c.** is the answer. (p. 575)
2. **d.** is the answer. In recent times, mourning has become less religious than formerly. (p. 584)
3. **d.** is the answer. Hospices generally *do* provide patients with skilled medical care. (p. 577)
4. **b.** is the answer. (p. 580)

    a. This is a living will.

    c. This is active euthanasia.

    d. This refers to DNR.
5. **c.** is the answer. (p. 585)

    a. Absent grief occurs when people cut themselves off from the community and customs of grief and mourning.

    b. Disenfranchised grief occurs when bereaved people are not permitted to mourn publicly.

    d. A good death is one that is swift and painless and that occurs in the company of loved ones.
6. **d.** is the answer. (p. 575)

    b. & c. There is no evidence that hospice residents experience different emotional stages than others who are dying or that these stages are a product of Western culture.
7. **b.** is the answer. (p. 580)
8. **c.** is the answer. (p. 571)
9. **b.** is the answer. Mourning refers to the ceremonies and rituals that a religion or culture prescribes for bereaved people, and grief refers to an individual's emotional response to bereavement. (pp. 582, 583)
10. **b.** is the answer. (p. 585)

    a. & c. In such situations, death is expected and generally easier to bear.

    d. This issue was not discussed.

Matching Items

1. c (p. 578)	**5.** i (p. 576)	**9.** g (p. 582)
2. b (p. 575)	**6.** e (p. 578)	**10.** j (p. 580)
3. d (p. 580)	**7.** a (p. 576)	
4. h (p. 578)	**8.** f (p. 582)	

KEY TERMS

1. **Thanatology** is the study of death and dying. (p. 565)
2. According to **terror management theory (TMT),** people adopt cultural values and moral principles in order to cope with their fear of death. (p. 570)
3. A **near-death experience** is an episode in which a person comes close to dying but survives and reports having left his or her body and having moved toward a bright white light while feeling peacefulness and joy. (p. 573)
4. A **good death** is one that is peaceful, quick, and painless and that occurs at the end of a long life, in the company of family and friends, and in familiar surroundings. (p. 574)
5. A **hospice** is an institution or program in which terminally ill patients receive palliative care. (p. 574)
6. **Palliative care,** such as that provided in a hospice, is care that relieves suffering while safeguarding the person's dignity. (p. 576)
7. A **double effect** is a situation in which medication has the intended effect of relieving a dying person's pain and the secondary effect of hastening death. (p. 576)
8. **Passive euthanasia** involves allowing a seriously ill person to die naturally by withholding medical interventions. (p. 578)

9. **DNR (do not resuscitate)** is a written order from a physician that no attempt should be made to revive a dying patient if he or she suffers cardiac or respiratory arrest. (p. 578)
10. **Active euthanasia** involves a person taking action to end another person's life in order to relieve suffering. (p. 578)
11. A **physician-assisted suicide** is one in which a doctor provides the means for a person to end his or her life. (p. 578)
12. A **slippery slope** is an argument that a given action will start a chain of events that will end in an undesirable outcome. (p. 580)
13. An **advance directive** is a legal document containing instructions for end-of-life medical care. (p. 580)
14. A **living will** is a document that specifies what kinds of medical intervention a person wants if he or she becomes incapable of expressing those wishes. (p. 580)
15. A **health care proxy** is a person chosen to make medical decisions for someone else if the second person becomes unable to do so. (p. 580)
16. **Bereavement** is the sense of loss people feel following a death. (p. 582)
17. **Grief** refers to the powerful sorrow a person feels at the death of another. (p. 582)
18. **Mourning** refers to the ceremonies and rituals that a religion or culture prescribes for bereaved people. (p. 583)
19. **Absent grief** occurs when people cut themselves off from the community and customs of grief and mourning. (p. 585)
20. **Disenfranchised grief** occurs when bereaved people are not permitted to mourn publicly. (p. 585)
21. **Incomplete grief** occurs when circumstances, such as a criminal investigation, interfere with grieving. (p. 585)

More on Research Methods

B
appendix

Appendix B Overview

The first section describes two ways of gathering information about development: library research and using the Internet. The second section discusses the various ways in which developmentalists ensure that their studies are valid.

NOTE: Answer guidelines for all Appendix B questions begin on page 393.

Appendix B Review

When you have finished reading Appendix B, work through the material that follows to review it. Complete the sentences and answer the questions. As you proceed, evaluate your performance for each section by consulting the answers beginning on page 393. Do not continue with the next section until you understand each answer. If you need to, review or reread the appropriate section in the textbook before continuing.

Make It Personal (p. B-1)

1. Before asking questions as part of a research assignment, remember that observing ________________ ________________ comes first.
2. Before interviewing someone, you should ________________ the person of your purpose and assure him or her of ________________.
3. Research studies that may be published require that you inform the college's ________________ ________________ ________________.

Read the Research (pp. B-1–B-3)

4. Four journals that cover development in all three domains are ________________, ________________, ________________, and ________________.
5. The best journals are ________________-________________, which means that scientists other than an article's authors decide if it is worthy of publication.
6. Two good handbooks in development are ________________, and ________________.
7. Two advantages of using the Internet to learn about development are
   a. ________________
   b. ________________
8. Two disadvantages of using the Internet are
   a. ________________
   b. ________________
9. To help you select appropriate information, use general topic lists, called ________________, and ________________ ________________, which give you all the sites that use a particular word or words.

Additional Terms and Concepts (pp. B-3–B-5)

10. To make statements about people in general, called a ________________, scientists study a group of research ________________, called a ________________.
11. When a sample is typical of the group under study—in gender, ethnic background, and other

important variables—the sample is called a(n) ________________ ________________.

12. Ideally, a group of research participants constitute a ________________ ________________, which means that everyone in the population is equally likely to be selected. To avoid ________________ ________________, some samples are ________________, and trace development of some particular characteristic in an entire cluster.

13. In a ________________ study, researchers begin with a group of participants that already share a particular characteristic and then look "backward" to discover other characteristics of the group.

14. Every researcher begins by formulating a ________________.

15. When the person carrying out research is unaware of the purpose of the research, that person is said to be ________________ to the hypothesized outcome.

16. Researchers use ________________ ________________ to define variables in terms of specific, observable behavior that can be measured precisely.

17. Journal articles that summarize past research are called ________________.

18. A study that combines the findings of many studies to present an overall conclusion is a ________________.

19. Researchers often report quantitative analyses that measure ________________ ________________, which indicates whether or not a particular result could have occurred by chance.

20. The statistic that indicates how much of an impact the independent variable had on the dependent variable is ________________ ________________.

Progress Test

Circle your answers to the following questions and check them with the answers on page 394. If your answer is incorrect, read the explanation for why it is incorrect and then consult the appropriate pages of the text (in parentheses following the correct answer).

1. A journal article that summarizes past research is
   a. *Psycscan: Developmental Psychology.*
   b. *Child Development Abstracts and Bibliography.*
   c. *Developmental Psychology.*
   d. a review article.

2. Which of the following is *not* one of the journals that publish research on all three domains of development ?
   a. *The Developmentalist*
   b. *Developmental Psychology*
   c. *Human Development*
   d. *Child Development*

3. Which of the following is a disadvantage of conducing Internet research?
   a. You can spend hours sifting through information that turns out to be useless.
   b. Anybody can put anything on the Internet.
   c. There is no evaluation of bias on Internet sites.
   d. Each of the above is a disadvantage of Internet research.

4. To say that the study of development is a science means that developmentalists
   a. use many methods to make their research more objective and more valid.
   b. take steps to ensure that a few extreme cases do not distort the overall statistical picture.
   c. recognize the importance of establishing operational definitions.
   d. do all of these things.

5. The entire group of people about whom a scientist wants to learn is called the
   a. reference group.
   b. sample.
   c. representative sample.
   d. population.

6. A researcher's conclusions after conducting a study are not valid because a few extreme cases distorted the results. In designing this study, the researcher evidently failed to pay attention to the importance of
   a. sample size.
   b. "blindness."
   c. representativeness.
   d. all of these factors.

7. Rachel made a study of students' opinions about different psychology professors. She took great care to survey equal numbers of male and female students, students who received high grades and students who received low grades, and members of various minorities. Clearly, Rachel wished to ensure that data were obtained from a
   a. population.
   b. "blind" sample.
   c. representative sample.
   d. comparison group.

8. A person who gathers data in a state of "blindness" is one who
   a. is unaware of the purpose of the research.
   b. is allowing his or her personal beliefs to influence the results.
   c. has failed to establish operational definitions for the variables under investigation.
   d. is basing the study on an unrepresentative sample of the population.

9. Which of the following is an example of a good operational definition of a dependent variable?
   a. walking
   b. aggression
   c. 30 minutes of daily exercise
   d. taking steps without support

10. The technique of combining the results of many studies to come to an overall conclusion is
    a. meta-analysis.
    b. effect size.
    c. a prospective study.
    d. a retrospective study.

11. For a psychologist's generalizations to be valid, the sample must be representative of the population under study. The results must also be
    a. statistically significant.
    b. derived from participants who are all the same age.
    c. large enough.
    d. none of these things.

12. The particular individuals who are studied in a specific research project are called the
    a. independent variables.
    b. dependent variables.
    c. participants.
    d. population.

13. A research study that begins with participants who share a certain characteristic and then "looks backward" is a
    a. prospective study.
    b. retrospective study.
    c. meta-analysis.
    d. representative sample.

14 A research study that begins with participants who share a certain characteristic and then "looks forward" is a
    a. prospective study.
    b. retrospective study.
    c. meta-analysis.
    d. representative sample.

15. Summarizing the results of his research study, Professor Schulman notes that "the effect size was zero." By this she means that the:
    a. independent variable had no impact on the dependent variable.
    b. independent variable had a large impact on the dependent variable.
    c. dependent variable had no impact on the independent variable.
    d. dependent variable had a large impact on the independent variable

Key Terms

Using your own words, write a brief definition or explanation of each of the following terms on a separate piece of paper.

1. population
2. participants
3. sample
4. representative sample
5. blind
6. operational definition
7. meta-analysis
8. effect size

Answers

APPENDIX B REVIEW

1. ethical standards
2. inform; confidentiality
3. Institutional Review Board (IRB)
4. *Developmental Psychology; Child Development; Developmental Review; Human Development*
5. peer-reviewed
6. *Handbook of Child Psychology; Handbook of Aging*
7. **a.** Virtually everything you might want to know is on the Internet.

   b. The Internet is quick and easy to use, any time of the day or night.
8. **a.** There is so much information available on the Internet that it is easy to waste time.

   b. Anybody can put anything on the Internet.
9. directories; search engines
10. population; participants; sample
11. representative sample
12. random sample, selection bias; prospective
13. retrospective
14. hypothesis
15. blind
16. operational definitions
17. reviews
18. meta-analysis
19. statistical significance
20. effect size

PROGRESS TEST

1. **d.** is the answer. (p. B-4)
2. **a.** is the answer. (p. B-1)
3. **d.** is the answer. (p. B-2)
4. **d.** is the answer. (pp. B-3–B-5)
5. **d.** is the answer. (p. B-3)
6. **a.** is the answer. (p. B-3)

   b. "Blindness" has no relevance here.

   c. Although it is true that a distorted sample is unrepresentative, the issue concerns the small number of extreme cases—a dead giveaway to sample size.
7. **c.** is the answer. Rachel has gone to great lengths to make sure that her student sample is typical of the entire population of students who takes psychology courses. (p. B-3)
8. **a.** is the answer. (p. B-4)
9. **d.** is the answer. (p. B-4)

   a., b., & c. Each of these definitions is too ambiguous to qualify as an operational definition.
10. **a.** is the answer. (p. B-4)
11. **a.** is the answer. (p. B-4)
12. **c.** is the answer. (p. B-3)

    a. These are the factors that a researcher manipulates in an experiment.

    b. These are the outcomes that a researcher measures in an experiment.

    d. It is almost always impossible to include every member of a population in an experiment.
13. **b.** is the answer. (p.4)
14. **a.** is the answer. (p. 4)
15. **a.** is the answer. (p. 4)

    b. In this case, the effect size would be a number close to 1.0.

    c. & d. Independent variables impact dependent variables, and not vice versa.

KEY TERMS

1. The **population** is the entire group of individuals who are of particular concern in a scientific study. (p. B-3)
2. **Participants** are the people who are studied in a research project. (p. B-3)
3. A **sample** is a subset of individuals who are drawn from a specific population. (p. B-3)
4. A **representative sample** is a group of research subjects who accurately reflect key characteristics of the population being studied. (p. B-3)
5. **Blind** is the situation in which data gatherers and sometimes their research participants are deliberately kept unaware of the purpose of the study in order to avoid unintentionally biasing the results. (p. B-4)
6. An **operational definition** is a precise description of a behavior or variable being studied so that another person will know whether it occurred, and how it is measured. (p. B-4)
7. **Meta-analysis** is a research technique in which the results of many studies are combined to produce one overall result (p. B-4)
8. **Effect size** is a statistical measure of how much impact an independent variable had on a dependent variable in a research study. (p. B-4)